Real, Recent, or Replica

CARIBBEAN ARCHAEOLOGY AND ETHNOHISTORY

L. Antonio Curet, Series Editor

Real, Recent, or Replica

Precolumbian Caribbean Heritage as Art, Commodity, and Inspiration

Edited by Joanna Ostapkowicz and Jonathan A. Hanna

Foreword by Peter E. Siegel

Epilogue by L. Antonio Curet

The University of Alabama Press
Tuscaloosa

The University of Alabama Press
Tuscaloosa, Alabama 35487-0380
uapress.ua.edu

Typeface: Minion Pro

Cover image: Stone sculpture from the Dominican Republic or Puerto Rico;
copyright Pitt Rivers Museum, 1917.53.288; photo by Joanna Ostapkowicz
Cover design: David Nees

Cataloging-in-Publication data is available from the Library of Congress.
ISBN: 978-0-8173-2087-4
E-ISBN: 978-0-8173-9345-8

Contents

Foreword

PETER E. SIEGEL

THIS IMPORTANT BOOK addresses difficult and overlapping issues in Caribbean archaeology. Difficult in that the contributors consider seemingly irreconcilable problems, which crosscut archaeology, ethics, law, heritage, and economics. From the dawn of humanity, humans have invested considerable creative energy in fabricating items that have been admired and desired by others. I would venture to speculate that from the earliest stages in the formation of human cognition, humans have been interested in—and to varying degrees, consumed by—aesthetics, the past, and our place in the cosmic order of the universe (Finlayson 2019; Laughlin and d'Aquile 1974; Lewis-Williams and Pearce 2005; Pearson 2002; Renfrew and Zubrow 1994). How do these aspects unique to human thought relate to the topics in the following pages? Our species, and perhaps its immediate evolutionary ancestors, has engaged in a variety of ways to express and sometimes celebrate creative urges, our historical and mythical past, social and economic bonds across communities, and understanding of the universe and our relationship to it. Physical representations of these expressions are those aspects of the archaeological record sought by looters, collectors, museums, antiquities dealers, art galleries, and, yes, archaeologists. There may be close alliances between looters and some antiquities dealers and perhaps less-than-highly publicized alliances between some antiquities dealers and museums. Results are the same: objects from humanity's past frequently are removed from their original contexts and placed into display cases of museums or private individuals with little to no information about provenience. By stripping them of context, these objects then enter the realm of objets d'art or fetishized pieces with little to no understanding of, or concern with, why they were made and for what purposes.

Here are some difficult questions: is it ethically irresponsible to display aesthetically appealing objects with little to no provenience information if they provide inspiration to modern artists in their craft or instill appreciation by viewers for creative output of past or otherwise different cultures? Is it acceptable for archaeologists to work with private collectors of antiquities and study their collections when attempting to build models of past human behavior?

For many of today's archaeologists, piece-plotting of artifacts or precision to the centimeter in *x-y-z* coordinates is the ideal for context. Making inferences into past human behavior from acontextual finds can at best be only general. Of course, degree of locational precision varies. Past generations of archaeologists often recorded very general contextual information during excavations: 12-in layers within 10 ft × 10 ft blocks, quadrant of site, or sometimes even only by site. As some contributors to this volume observed, museum accessions may list artifacts simply by island name.

Another form of artifact retrieval is by private individuals who make personal collections. These people, referred to as "collectors," often keep records of find locations. Artifacts deemed "collectable" are generally those that are visually expressive or technologically sophisticated, including finely made projectile points, decorated pottery, exquisitely crafted ground-stone implements, and anthropo/zoomorphic items fabricated from a variety of materials. Archaeologists think of these classes of artifacts as culturally and temporally diagnostic, analogous to index fossils for paleontologists. Crucial for these collections to be of use for archaeologists is some minimal degree of locational information, like specific farm fields or tracts of land that can be plotted on maps. Again, the more precise the records the better. One early example of systematically using collectors' data comes from the American midcontinent in the lower Illinois Valley (Farnsworth 1973). Mapping temporally distinctive artifacts and collections by regional collector territories enabled Kenneth Farnsworth to reconstruct shifting settlement and land-use patterns through the Middle Woodland period in his survey universe. In this example, archaeologists and private artifact collectors were able to coexist and cooperate. The degree of reliable documentation maintained by artifact collectors will determine the confidence we place in regional and perhaps intrasite behavioral reconstructions using those data.

Caribbean archaeologists have also worked with collectors or amateur archaeologists, perhaps not as systematically or as explicitly in reporting their methods as Farnsworth. Examples include Ripley Bullen's work on Grenada (Bullen 1964); extensive surveys by Ricardo Alegría, Jesse Walter Fewkes, Froelich Rainey, and Irving Rouse on Puerto Rico (Alegría 1983; Fewkes 1907; Rainey 1940; Rouse 1952a, 1952b); M. R. Harrington's work on Cuba (Harrington 1921); collections made by James Lee on Jamaica (Allsworth-Jones 2008); Theodoor de Booy's and Gudmund Hatt's surveys of the Virgin Islands (De Booy 1919; Hatt 1924); and Fewkes's (1922) Caribbean-wide survey. Large collections of Caribbean artifacts were made under the auspices of the private Heye Foundation in the early twentieth century. George Gustav Heye, a wealthy New York engineer and banker, established the Museum of the American Indian in which he curated and displayed enormous collections of archaeological and ethnographic Native American artifacts and documentation. These collections were transferred to the Smithsonian Institution in 1989 and formed the basis of the National Museum of the American Indian.

There are distinctions between artifact collectors and looters. Following Farnsworth, artifact collectors keep records of find locations (with variable degrees of precision, just as with professionally trained archaeologists) and looters do not. Artifact collectors maintain and keep their collections intact; looters trade or sell artifacts and the integrity of collections is irrelevant. In my opinion, professional archaeologists who treat collectors with disdain and ignore those collections do a disservice to the archaeological record and handicap their own archaeological interpretations. Collectors are not going to cease their activities just because archaeologists tell them to do so. Alternatively, archaeologists who engage productively with collectors (and many collectors work as groups in amateur archaeological societies) may and frequently do impart improved collecting standards. One example comes from my work on Puerto Rico. Following our excavations in Maisabel, amateur archaeologists under the direction of Daniel Silva from the Sociedad de Investigaciones Arqueológicas e Históricas Sebuco in Vega Baja excavated a trench in the area we identified to be a cemetery. They recovered and mapped 10 human burials. The map was sufficiently detailed so that I was able to link the trench to our excavation grid coordinates, thereby integrating their findings with the overall project (Siegel 1992:243, Figures 2.13, 5.30).

The conduct of archaeology should be an ongoing process of sound science coupled with public engagement and education, and outreach to the full range of interest groups including collectors, the interested general public, developers, and government officials and policy makers. Ultimately, consistent efforts by archaeologists and heritage managers to educate the multiple publics or interest groups will promote declining levels of heritage destruction in general and looting specifically.

Given the competing interests by groups ranging from looters to archaeologists, encouraging the production, exchange, and display of replicas should be a good thing; the archaeological record does not suffer. However, as several contributors to this volume suggest, archaeological interpretations may be flawed at best, if not downright wrong when replicas or fakes are thought to be artifacts fabricated by people from precolumbian times.

The replication of objects, behaviors, processes, and systems has a long history in experimental archaeology (Ascher 1961; Coles 1973, 1979; David and Kramer 2001; Mathieu 2002; Saraydar 2008; Schiffer 2009; Semenov 1964).

Object replication, relevant for the topic of this book, has been divided between visual and functional replicas (Mathieu 2002:2–3). In the production of visual replicas, there is little to no concern in using materials or technologies consistent with the artifacts being replicated. However, visual replicas that are treated as antiquities enter the realm of archaeological fakes.

Functional replicas typically are manufactured using identical raw materials to the objects being replicated and are crucial to the success of experimental studies in archaeology (Andrefsky 1998; Odell 2000, 2001; Saraydar 2008). For example, lithic use-wear analysis requires replication and use of stone tools to experimentally produce damage patterns similar to those documented on archaeological tools. Projectile points and other tool forms produced by especially accomplished flint knappers may be indistinguishable from archaeological specimens, and if incorporated into archaeological collections may result in flawed interpretations of past human behavior or reconstructions of culture history.

If flint knappers conduct replication studies in undeveloped areas of landscapes, lithic scatters and perhaps more intensively occupied "sites" may be created, potentially further confounding future interpretations of settlement patterns. It is important that knapping sessions take place on ground cloths or tarps so that debitage and other products of stone-tool production are collected and removed to avoid the creation of lithic scatters. If experiments require the inclusion of naturally occurring elements like sand or silt particles in the soils to be in contact with lithic debris or finished stone tools, then the ground surface should be carefully cleaned of such debris following the experiments. If studies require experimentally produced artifacts to be in long-term contact with or buried in sediments, then GPS coordinates demarcating the study areas should be filed with local or regional authorities charged with managing archaeological or heritage resources. Ideally, finished forms are inscribed with diamond styli to distinguish replicas from archaeological artifacts. Precautions regarding stone-tool studies apply equally to the full range of experiments in the service of archaeology, including those addressing pottery, shell, wood, bone, coral, and features, among others.

Objects that are manufactured to qualify as archaeological artifacts are called fakes (Feder 2017). Fakes are often produced for sale to unwitting individuals and museums. In some cases, museums have exemplified the problem by displaying known fakes with explanations: "This figure is labeled in our records as 'pre-Columbian' but is probably a fake made in Mexico less than 100 years ago. In the 19th century, museums across the world began fervently collecting ancient artifacts from Mexico. The supply was limited, so entrepreneurial artisans began selling forgeries to unknowing collectors. Some of these fakes made their way into museum collections and, if the forgery was excellent, the object's true origin may remain a secret" (Cat. No. 2010.001.0427JJ, San Diego Museum of Man).

It is important that museums like San Diego's Museum of Man recognize the very real problems surrounding the purchasing of antiquities and the production of fakes to satisfy market demands. One option of course is for museums to deaccession fakes once they are identified. However, by highlighting and displaying fakes for what they are ultimately helps to improve our abilities as well as to educate others in distinguishing real antiquities from replicas, one of the topics of this book.

Looting and the production of fakes represent two pathways to potentially seriously flawed interpretations of the past. Looting destroys archaeological sites and contextual associations of artifacts. Removing artifacts from sites and sites from landscapes—all in the absence of documentation—results in skewed interpretations of past human behavior at both intrasite and regional scales. Expertly produced fakes potentially add bogus information to archaeological datasets, especially if the fakes are accompanied by fabricated find locations (Feder 2017).

This book adds to the growing body of literature addressing the increasing pressures on the preservation and interpretations of heritage resources in the Caribbean. As discussed in the following pages, the production of replicas and fakes has a long history in the region. Passing off such objects as archaeological artifacts should, but unfortunately too often does not, trigger considerations of heritage preservation (or heritage fabrication), archaeological ethics, and legal ramifications. In the face of very real economic and social pressures confronting legislators and policy planners of Caribbean island nations, heritage considerations generally are low in priority lists of problems to address. As several contributors to this volume and I have emphasized, fundamental steps to protecting and considering heritage in the face of global and local pressures may come through the systematic inclusion of sound heritage instruction in educational programs at all levels of school curricula from primary through higher education (Siegel 2011; Siegel et al. 2013). It is through such programs, from which newly elected young legislators have graduated, that the passage *and enforcement* of heritage legislation may result. Otherwise, individual island nations or blocks of nations with common interests (e.g., the Organisation of Eastern Caribbean States) are liable to relinquish their past in exchange for short-term profits.

Preface

JOANNA OSTAPKOWICZ AND JONATHAN A. HANNA

IN 2016, TOURISTS vacationing in Grenada thought they had discovered a new form of prehistoric art in the stone sculptures lining their hotel's corridors. Through a convoluted series of emails and events, the coeditors of this volume (and many contributors) began a conversation that, ultimately, led to the volume before you. Initially, our chief interest was in the sculptures—not how old they were, nor where they came from, per se, but who on the island had made them. These were not only clear fakes—or neo-artifacts ("new," rather than ancient, artifacts)—but the modern artists were astonishingly prolific. Hundreds of these figures cluttered the hallways, gardens, gazebo, and dining areas of the hotel, even on the bathroom sinks. The details of this phenomenon, which traces its roots to a well-intentioned replica-making workshop, are further described in chapter 5 herein.

Our initial email correspondence quickly broadened to similar occurrences of Amerindian-style or "neo-Amerindian" artwork throughout the wider Caribbean. In April 2018, the coeditors organized a session for the 83rd Society for American Archaeology conference in Washington, DC, where early versions of many of the chapters were presented. Some who participated then were unable to contribute to the present volume, due to the usual restrictions of time and prior commitments, but on the whole, the conversation that began in those emails and continued at and after the SAA conference has now been further developed here. Efforts were subsequently made to involve an even greater range of regional commentary, and colleagues—including José R. Oliver and Roberto Valcárcel Rojas and company—contributed excellent overviews of critical regions (see page xviii for the core areas of the volume's focus). Nonetheless, as the first book of its kind about Caribbean fakes and forgeries—and the related cultural heritage issues (looting, unprovenienced artifacts, black markets, etc.)—we can only skim the surface. Equally, we can only introduce some of the issues surrounding the legitimate emergence of an Amerindian-*inspired* art and the varied directions (from personal self-representation to nationalist agendas) this takes. Our focus in this compilation is restricted to modern (largely twentieth century) reinterpretations of precolumbian art in a variety of media (stone, wood, bone, plastic, resin, paper, etc.)—a largely unexplored subject that continues to have a significant impact on our understanding of the past. The issues addressed here represent an important first step in what we hope will become a continued discussion on these issues in the Caribbean.

It must be kept in mind that not all islands of the Caribbean have artists working on art inspired by the indigenous past, nor do they (knowingly or not) contribute to black markets that support the sale of forgeries. These aspects, for example, are more overt in the Greater, rather than Lesser, Antilles (with the exception of the examples featured in this volume); even in the Greater Antilles, the scale is variable (e.g., forgeries are not such a dominant issue in Puerto Rico or Cuba—and hardly anything is known regarding Haiti's current situation on this subject [but see Doucet 2015 for a rare insight into efforts to place indigenous cultural patrimony on the national agenda]—in contrast to the significant scale of production in the Dominican Republic). For this reason, among others, we were unable to secure contributing case studies from islands such as, for example, Trinidad and Tobago, Haiti, or the Virgin Islands—though this is not to say that looting and potentially small-scale artistic production do not occur in these areas. The same is true for much of the Lesser Antilles excluded here.

There are many other threats to cultural heritage that are intertwined with looting and the antiquities market (e.g., Fitzpatrick 2010). Destruction of sites due to natural disasters, sea level rise, and developments are aspects that affect the entire region; it is anticipated that by 2100 (i.e., within the next 80 years), much of the Caribbean's material heritage will be destroyed by increasingly catastrophic storms and rising seas (e.g., Erlandson 2008; Siegel et al. 2013). As the region's protective dunes and beaches erode, innumerable cultural objects from the past will emerge. Without adequate protection and monitoring programs, each instance presents a potentially incalculable loss to the region's cultural patrimony and the world's knowledge of the Caribbean's past.

A NOTE ON TERMINOLOGY

The volume uses the term "precolumbian" throughout, though alternative spellings and phrasings have been retained when in original quotes. We recognize the problems of drawing a chronological line at Columbus's "Discovery," but the term "prehistoric" is not much better (given the pejorative assumption that people without writing had no history), nor is "indigenous" (which is also used for modern native peoples), although both appear herein on occasion. The European contact period marks the beginning of a fairly rapid turnover of the entire Western Hemisphere—in this sense, "precolumbian" conveys a lot of information quickly. The term "neo-Taíno" art is also used here as it was first defined by Herrera Fritot (1946; Herrera Fritot and Youmans 1946:13; see also Vega 1987)—referring specifically to art inspired by indigenous iconography of the Greater Antilles but embracing the modern in an open, completely transparent way—whether in style (e.g., contemporary graphic arts, such as Puerto Rico's limited edition cartels or posters) or in concept (imagery in the service of self/national identity). The terms "neo-Amerindian" or "neo-artwork" can also be defined in this way and are mostly used interchangeably here. As Oliver (chapter 3) notes, some may find these terms objectionable; absolutely no disrespect is meant—this is simply to distinguish modern reinterpretations of indigenous iconography from ancient material culture. In a similar vein, "neo-artifact" is used to refer to "new-artifacts," specifically made to appear as ancient objects—essentially, fakes and forgeries. The term "new-artifacts," among others, is further defined in the volume's introduction. American spelling has been the default setting, except when quoting directly from international sources (e.g., artifact versus artefact, the latter correct in the United Kingdom).

ACKNOWLEDGMENTS

The foundation of this volume is the inherited artistry of the Caribbean region—both its ancient roots and its modern reinventions. The legacy Caribbean collections held at the national and international museums and the artifacts that continue to emerge through permitted (legal) excavations are the backbone to the progress made in understanding the rich artistic heritage of the region. To the many museums and cultural institutions who have safeguarded this heritage and enthusiastically engaged with the issues raised in this volume—from allowing access to their collections to being open about the dubious pieces relegated to the "dark corners" of their storage areas— we owe a collective debt of gratitude. To the pioneers—René Herrera Fritot, Emile de Boyrie Moya, Fernando Morban Laucer, Luis A. Chanlatte Baik, and Irving Rouse, among others—we are grateful for the challenging path that they have set in breaking new ground on a controversial subject. And to the artists who have taken inspiration from the "old masters," reinventing ancient styles in completely innovative and (critically) open ways—Ivan Gundrum, Daniel Silva, and the many exceptional Puerto Rican, Dominican, Grenadian, and wider Caribbean artists; theirs is an art form that deserves greater recognition for its skill, vision, and deep resonance with place and identity.

Recent, Real, or Replica

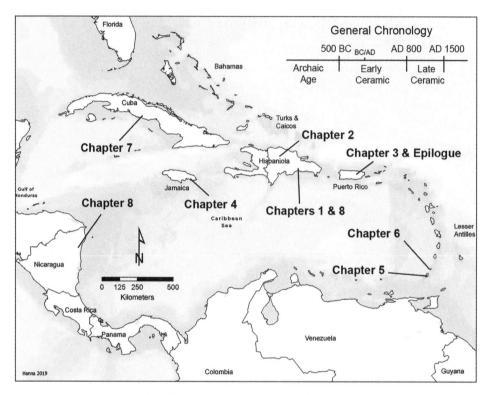

General chronology of prehistoric insular Caribbean and map of Caribbean basin with countries demarked by chapter. (Courtesy Jonathan A. Hanna; base map courtesy Environmental Systems Research Institute [ESRI])

Introduction

Precolumbian Caribbean Heritage in Flux,
the Old and the Not So Old

Joanna Ostapkowicz and Jonathan A. Hanna

Fakes show us what our fantasies of the originals were and how
far they were off the mark.
—Pasztory 2002:159

There is a rich literature on the archaeology of the Caribbean region (e.g.,
Keegan and Hofman 2017; Keegan et al. 2013; Rouse 1992; Wilson 2007; and
see Keegan 2017 for annotated bibliography) and a growing focus on heritage issues (e.g., Ariese-Vandemeulebroucke 2018; Cummins et al. 2013; Hofman and Haviser 2015; Siegel and Righter 2011), but much less on the looting
of sites, or indeed the misrepresentation of archaeological heritage through
fakes and forgeries. Only a few have written on the subject of forgeries publicly (e.g., Herrera Fritot 1942; Morban Laucer 1989), so perhaps it should
not be surprising that the literature on this subject is very thin on the ground.
But the Caribbean has some rather sobering examples to offer the growing
literature on forgery arts in the Americas—and the escalation of forgeries in
the last few decades has been unprecedented; it is high time this lacuna was
addressed. These aspects are discussed in the chapters of this volume to raise
awareness of the significant increase in heritage destruction in the Caribbean
specifically as well as the ethical dilemmas of reconstructing the past through
unprovenienced collections and replicas. According to some, archaeology itself has a lot to answer for when it comes to the looting situation: the birth of
the field was linked with amateur "excavations" by practitioners who would be
considered little more than looters by today's standards.[1] Archaeologists have
in the past paid for finds, creating a market that incentivized communities of
looters and forgers (e.g., Hollowell-Zimmer 2003:50). Museums were (and re-

main to varying degrees) part of the same equation: "the bulk of [museum] archaeological acquisitions have a checkered history. If we took all the looted artifacts out of our museums, most would be very empty indeed. Worried about funding and appearances, museums end up hiding behind honorable-sounding in-house ethical policies, yet are still unwilling to educate the public and openly address issues of how materials came to occupy exhibits and space in their institutions" (Hollowell-Zimmer 2003:48).

The volume's title, *Real, Recent, or Replica*, is intended to be broad and provocative (Table I.1). Each of these terms can be defined (as we have in the table), often having moral, ethical, and value-laden connotations, but they are also surprisingly changeable depending on the context. "Real" implies "authenticity," which is itself an elusive concept (e.g., see Geurds, chapter 9 in this volume). Can a precolumbian forgery be "authentic" if an artist introduces their distinctive style into traditional iconography, creating a unique, recognizable oeuvre? The result is certainly "real" in the tangible, tactile sense— even aesthetic (see Sandis 2016)—but given that it is conceived specifically to deceive as a "genuine" artifact, some would argue that it cannot be upheld as anything other than a fraudulent enterprise. Further, is the appropriation of an "authentic" indigenous iconography acceptable when both past and present Caribbean situations rather encompass a cultural mosaic (e.g., Wilson 1993), and so would be better served through a nuanced reflection of this multiheritage? What the market deems as more desirable, based on the whims of collectors and aesthetic trends, is in many ways still linked to colonialism and imperialism—and the search for that ever-elusive "curio" for the cabinet.

Another issue: is a heavily reconstructed artifact still "real"? Some ceramic reconstructions in museum displays are built on just a few genuine fragments; some forgers use genuine ceramic fragments to create complete vessels for a more lucrative sale—at what point does over-restoration aimed at creating a complete object create a forgery instead? "Gilding the lily," as Kelker and Bruhns (2010:19) identify overly enthusiastic restoration, introduces all manner of errors and exaggerations through modern reinterpretations of an object that is then used to inform on past lifeways. These are global issues that all archaeologists, at some point, must contend with. In Greece, for example, such forgeries have become so pervasive that scholars continue to debate issues of Bronze Age Minoan ritual practices based entirely on known fakes, "heavily restored" objects, and others of questionable provenience (German 2012). As this volume shows, the Caribbean is not far behind. We must be mindful of discussions and interpretations of Amerindian imagery, belief systems, and other cultural elements that rely on unprovenienced objects and collections. As will be discussed, neo-Amerindian artworks and replicas may not necessarily be the problem themselves—they are often masterfully done and hold great economic potential for artists in the developing world. Rather,

TABLE I.1. SOME TERMS USED IN THIS VOLUME

	With Provenience	Without Provenience
Real	Precolumbian artifacts	Looted antiquities
Recent	Over-restored artifacts; Neo-Amerindian artworks	Fakes and forgeries (neo-artifacts)
	Replicas	

Note: These illustrate the overlap between categories, depending on the object's provenience status (originating context). Broadly speaking, an object without provenience is either fake or looted. However, artifacts in historic/legacy collections (including those in many museums) occupy a unique yet highly ambiguous space between all categories; those without provenience are not necessarily looted or illegally acquired, nor are they necessarily composed of entirely real, precolumbian artifacts, since they may contain intentional forgeries, intentional replicas, and replicas without provenience that became de facto forgeries.

the problem is the acceptance and legitimacy granted by authorities in various fields who present these creations as authentic relics of the past—from dealers and auction houses to researchers and curatorial staff. It is not the object, but rather our engagement and interpretation of it that raises ethical issues (e.g., see Swogger, chapter 6 in this volume).

Indeed, what of the position of replicas within a "real" museum setting? Some argue that replicas (specifically those created without intention to deceive) are in many ways better than the originals in certain contexts, particularly for hands-on interaction, or those of imperialist institutions: What is "authentic'" about exhibiting the Elgin Marbles in the British Museum, so far from Greece, their "authentic" home (Sandis 2016:258)? What is the intellectual value of an object excised from its provenience? For Caribbean visitors to London or New York, or the diaspora communities living in those cities, seeing a Caribbean artifact in the British Museum or Metropolitan Museum of Art may instill a sense of pride at seeing their cultural patrimony displayed amid the masterpieces of the world; for others, who have never seen such objects (apart from images in books or replicas) on their native island, this is an increasingly problematic issue (e.g., Brown 2019; Poupeye 2019a, 2019b). These are some of the myriad issues when dealing with such loaded concepts, which can only be partially introduced in this volume.

A distinction is often made between historic/legacy collections and those acquired subsequent to the heritage protection laws in source countries, or UNESCO (1970, 1972)[2] and UNIDROIT (1995)[3] conventions. The conventions are used as benchmarks by international ethical committees—whether by museums (in acquisition policies), universities (in teaching students how to engage with "antiquities"), or by publishers (in declining to publish studies on unprovenienced artifacts). This in no way diminishes the issues legacy collections raise, such as calls for repatriation of cultural patrimony, or the fact that some were the product of antiquarian "excavations" (what is viewed today as "looting") before archaeology emerged as a field. This was well before the "New Archaeology" of the 1960s built its foundations on the scientific method for excavations and, subsequently, post-processualism provided a critical self-consciousness and stronger awareness of the issues raised by colonialism. Indeed, the fact that collections are historic does not shield them from the need to engage with the ways they were acquired.

THE "REAL": AUTHENTICITY AND THE CREATIVE PROCESS

- *real* (adj.)—not imitation or artificial; genuine; true or actual.[4]

In our context, the term "real" encompasses the work of ancient Caribbean cultures as well as current ones—at least those that create art as a cultural asset, in the service of self-identity or nationhood, not as forgeries.[5] It refers to material excavated from an undisturbed archaeological context, museum collections scrutinized against established history, provenience (origin), provenance (a record of ownership),[6] and "sympathetic" intervention (i.e., reconstruction). These archaeological and early historic materials are the building blocks of our interpretations of the past. They are also inspiration for contemporary reinterpretations of heritage, fueled by a sense of connection to place.

There has long been a focus on the artistic achievements of the precolumbian Caribbean, but much less visibility is given to the new directions this old art inspires. There are varied ways in which people creatively engage with the past and varied purposes behind this engagement. Here we distinguish between contemporary productions created to mimic ancient styles in order to manufacture an "antiquity" for deception and profit (fakes; see discussion for "recent" further on) and cultural heritage used as inspiration for new artistic directions clearly and fully credited to those who produce it (neo-Amerindian art). This is particularly apparent in Puerto Rico, where artisans inspired by indigenous iconography are recognized for their artistic achievements, and there is a history of supporting this vein of nationalist art through such cultural centers as the Instituto de Cultura Puertorriqueña (established 1955) (see Oliver, chapter 3 in this volume). Here, artists get technical instruction

Figure I.1. Poster by R. Ortiz for an exhibit of Luis Leal's work at the Museo Universidad de Puerto Rico in 1968, featuring both Saladoid- and Chican Ostioniod–style replica ceramics. Leal (1920–1990) had worked with Ivan Gundrum in the Dominican Republic in 1955 as part of Cooperativa de Industrias Artesanales (COINDARTE) and was later the founder and director of the ceramic workshops at the Institute of Puerto Rican Culture (Marichal Lugo 1998:432; Miranda 1998:320). (Photo courtesy Joanna Ostapkowicz)

and links to promoters of fairs and exhibitions. What they produce are not simply replicas or copies of famous archaeological pieces (indeed, in the shops of Viejo San Juan, it is Dominican imports that largely cater to this form of "tourist art"). Rather, they reintegrate indigenous design elements in completely novel directions, whether for graphic posters advertising local cultural events (Figure I.1) or as both physical and conceptual inspiration, such as Jaime Suárez's modernist ceramic "totem" sculpture, taking pride of place in San Juan's Quincentennial Plaza (Fullana Acosta 2016; see Figure 1.12). Critically, the traditional designs integrated into modern artworks are recognized not only for "the artistic quality of the designs, but [as] an affirmation of the cultural heritage of Puerto Ricans" (El Museo del Barrio 1981).

While Cuba and the Dominican Republic had a strong and inspirational launch with an initiative dubbed "neo-Taíno" art during the mid-twentieth century (Herrera Fritot 1946; Herrera Fritot and Youmans 1946:13), where artists such as Ivan Gundrum were recognized for raising the profile of indigenous-inspired art (Figure I.2), it lost momentum in the late 1960s/early 1970s, and artists attempting to use indigenous designs now struggle to find a mainstream commercial outlet for their work beyond tourist sales. For the Dominican Republic in particular, this may have been due to the Paredones scandal, in which an art form initially masquerading as precolumbian was later rebranded as a new form of "folk art" (see Ostapkowicz, chapter 1 this volume). Several affluent Dominicans had purchased large collections of the Paredones sculptures, believing they were safeguarding these "genuine" precolumbian pieces for the nation (Boyrie Moya MS, II:6; Peabody Rouse Archives ANTAR.042255), and the subsequent revelations may have soured the idea of indigenous-inspired artworks for some. Indeed, the Dominican Cooperativa de Industrias Artesanales (COINDARTE), established in the 1950s, and which supported the work of Gundrum and others, went into decline in the late 1960s, failing to retain established craftspeople, which in turn led to diminishing quality and output (Valera Castillo and Peralta Montero 2012:172;

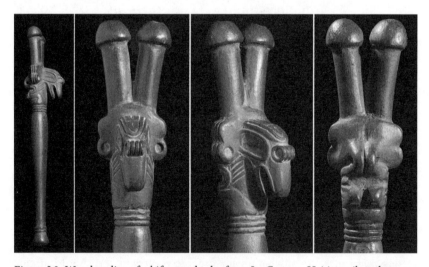

Figure I.2. Wood replica of a bifurcated tube from La Gonave, Haiti, attributed to the workshop of Ivan Gundrum (for a comparable example in a Cuban collection, see Gutiérrez Calvache 2017:Figure 5). The original tube was part of the Louis Maximilien private collection (ca. 1940s), and now is part of a private collection in Paris. L: 24 cm. (Courtesy National Museum of the American Indian, 0241863.000; photo: Joanna Ostapkowicz)

Vega 1987). The underdeveloped tourism industry also limited the market for these crafts (Vega 1987).

While a handful of further initiatives were made in the following decades (e.g., ALFADOM in the 1980s—see Valera Castillo and Peralta Montero 2012: 172), few attained long-term success. Bernardo Vega's *Arte NeoTaíno* (1987) was to serve as visual reference specifically with the aim of improving the nascent creativity of indigenous-inspired art. Today, the Dominican Republic, and indeed many of the islands of the Caribbean (e.g., see Hanna, chapter 5 in this volume), struggle to find the needed institutional and financial support for their artists. While recognizing the huge potential of this sector to the tourist industry, on which so many of the islands depend,[7] Valera Castillo and Peralta Montero (2012:167) note that many of the problems are a result of a lack of a clearly defined state policy on artisanal production and protection. Foreign imports have saturated the market, creating "unfair competition" for Dominican artisans; with little financial incentive to work in the sector, there is significant unemployment among artisans in areas that are already economically hard hit. The lack of development opportunities and supportive policies hinders artisanal advancement (Valera Castillo and Peralta Montero 2012:167). For example, the excellent volume *Artesanía Dominicana: Un arte popular* features the work of several artisans working in the "Neo-Taíno" style (e.g., de la Cruz and Durán Núñez 2012:75; see also Enrique Méndez 2011). However, without an infrastructure to showcase this work, ideally through an arts initiative endorsed by the government, and without being clearly labeled as modern reinterpretations, these creations, if convincingly styled in the "classic Taíno" aesthetic, may easily be misconstrued as precolumbian once they leave the country (and indeed, even within the Dominican Republic itself). Once out of the artist's hands, the anonymity of such work—unsigned and largely replicating an "ancient" aesthetic—means that the artists themselves remain unrecognized and the history of the object, as a contemporary creation, is entirely lost.

One can argue that it is indeed the lack of infrastructure on many islands that hinders, rather than encourages, engagement with local artistic legacies. The 2013 UNESCO Creative Economy Report, *Widening Local Development Pathways*, recognized that "there remains an institutional and commercial bias against indigenous creative content in the home market, discouraging creative entrepreneurship, investment and market development. This is compounded by uncompetitive package and branding, weak marketing and poor distribution. The island economies thus have large and widening trade imbalances in creative goods, services and intellectual property" (Ikhlef 2014:20). At the same time, the Kingston Outcome Document "recognized the importance of promoting cultural identity for advancing sustainable development and calls for a people-centered approach to poverty eradication" (Ikhlef

2014:20). Further, the Summit of the Community of Latin American and Caribbean States (CELAC) of 2014 enacted a declaration on *Culture as a Promoter of Human Development*, whereby they stressed "the contribution of culture to eradicating poverty, reducing social inequalities, increasing job opportunities and reducing social exclusion rates, as part of the process towards the promotion of more equitable societies" (CELAC 2014:5). If, indeed, such aims are realized, perhaps the days of anonymous artists creating forgeries to earn a living—as explored below under "recent"—are numbered. Then again, some would argue this industry will never disappear as long as demand from collectors continues to drive the market.

THE "RECENT": FORGERIES AS AGENT PROVOCATEURS

• *Recent* (adj.)—having happened, begun or been done not long ago; belonging to a past period comparatively close to the present.

While the "real" neo-Taíno artwork already mentioned is also "recent," we turn now to the modern neo-artifacts made to deceive, specifically those targeted at the antiquarian and collectors markets, that is, fakes and forgeries. Hillel Schwartz (1966) argues that fakes and forgeries act as agent provocateurs, challenging and undermining our obsession with the authentic. Forgeries are not new to the Caribbean, with the earliest documentation going back to the late nineteenth century (Pinart 1890), but the escalation seen since the mid-twentieth century indicates a worrying trend. From the estimated 25,000 forged Paredones neo-artifacts (1940s–1960s, see Ostapkowicz, chapter 1 in this volume), to the increasingly sophisticated neo-artifacts available through auction houses and internet sales hosted in the United States and Europe, the scale of Caribbean forgeries on the market and in private collections is now "truly hallucinatory" (Delpuech 2016:47; for a wider international context, see Mackenzie et al., 2019, and Tremain and Yates 2019). These range from coarse tourist art to subtle forgeries inspired by illustrations in museum catalogs. Indeed, forgers—or at least those who commission them—have had access to catalogs of photographed artifacts from the turn of the twentieth century onward (e.g., Fewkes 1907), with the Kerchache (1994) and Brecht et al. (1997) exhibit catalogs featuring professional glossy photographs. Sellen (2014:160), writing about Mesoamerican forgeries, notes that in some instances even pieces identified as forgeries in the mid-twentieth century still remain in museum displays, featured as the genuine article—the same can be said for a handful of Caribbean pieces, though identifying Caribbean forgeries in collections is in its infancy (many more are likely to come to light with further work). Such neo-artifacts, if perpetuated as genuine for the sake of "saving face," do serious damage to our understanding of the past;

they inform more on midcentury aesthetic trends than precolumbian reality. As pointed out by Jones and colleagues (1990:11–13), forgeries "provide unrivalled evidence of the values and perceptions of those who made them, and of those for whom they were made . . . [they are], before all else, a response to demand, an ever changing portrait of human desires."

Recent here also refers to a less recognized distortion of the past: the reliance on restoration to complete a damaged object or the combining of disparate objects into one. The most desired artifact is a complete one, whether on display in a museum or in a private collection; the countless thousands of broken sherds in museum collections provide little sense to museum visitors of how objects would have originally appeared, unless they are reconstructed. These restorations range from the innocuous—such as minor work on the forearms of the exceptional ceramic figure of Deminan Caracaracol (a Taíno mythological hero) in the collections of the Smithsonian's National Museum of the American Indian (NMAI) (Figure I.3)—to more interpretive reconstructions (for example, the infill on the face and upper ridge of the wood reliquary in the NMAI collections; Figure I.4). The cemí/belt in the collections of Rome's Pigorini Museum provides a rather different case: in the early sixteenth century two separate cotton artifacts—a belt and figurine (which may actually be a headdress)—were nailed down to a wooden base for display purposes (Ostapkowicz et al. 2017a); this reconstruction was aesthetically so convincing that it influenced interpretations well into the 1990s (Roe 1994). As Jones and colleagues (1990:14) note, restoration is "a process that provides the same kind of evidence for the history of taste as fakes themselves. The history of restoration is indeed inextricably linked with that of fakes." This is all the more apparent when one considers the restorations performed by looters, aimed to increase the value of their finds (e.g., see Figure 5.3)

Figure I.3. W. C. Orchard reconstructing the missing arms of the ceramic figure of Deminan Caracaracol, ca. 1916. (Courtesy National Museum of the American Indian, Catalog No. L00400)

Figure I.4. Two views of reconstructive infill (outlined in white) on the La Gonave carving, acquired during an expedition to Haiti funded by George Gustav Heye in 1934. The damage was considerable, and the reconstruction may have been done, in part, to consolidate the damaged areas. *Guaiacum* sp., cal AD 1294–1400 (95.4%, OxA-19169). (Courtesy National Museum of the American Indian, 198807.000; photo: Joanna Ostapkowicz)

THE "REPLICA"

- *Replica* (noun)—an exact copy or model of something; a duplicate.

During the Renaissance, artists would use plaster casts of Greco-Roman statues to learn the styles and techniques of ancient masters. Museums later embraced the trade to fill voids in their collections, and since at least the late nineteenth century, such copies have included Caribbean replicas. These have been widely distributed: the Smithsonian's National Museum of Natural History has shared its casts with national and international venues, from Yale's Peabody Museum of Natural History and the British Museum (e.g., the cast

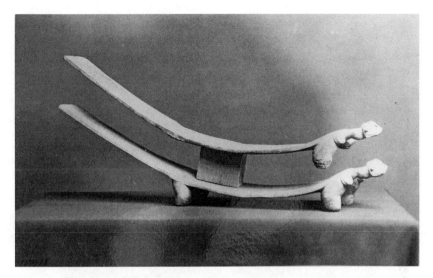

Figure I.5. Photograph titled *U.S. National Museum, casts for exchange . . .* , featuring the original "Gabb" duho, provenienced to the Turks and Caicos Islands (NMNH A30052), and its cast. The damaged sections of the original (*top*) have been infilled in the cast (*bottom*). (British Museum Archives, 2116/794; photo: Joanna Ostapkowicz)

of a duho from the Turks and Caicos) (Figure I.5) to the Världskultur Museerna (Museum of World Cultures), Gothenburg, Sweden (e.g., trigoliths and stone collars), among others. In 1939, plaster casts of the three Jamaican Carpenter's Mountain sculptures were presented by the British Museum to the Institute of Jamaica and have since featured in numerous displays on the island—a situation that is not without its political undercurrents, given that it has not been possible to facilitate the return of the originals, exported to London in the eighteenth century, even on loan, despite their renown as inalienable cultural patrimony and as frequent points of reference for artistic expression and national identity (Ostapkowicz 2015:54). Cuba was at the forefront of creating replicas for museum displays and study, specifically to safeguard original artifacts from damage (Valcárcel Rojas et al., chapter 7 in this volume). In Guadeloupe, a masterpiece of shell carving, the original still in private hands, has been replicated by a local artist for the Musée Edgar Clerc; it serves to document the artistic heritage of the island for wider audiences (Figure I.6). Another two replicas—one in the Smithsonian's National Museum of the American Indian and one in the Museo Montané in Havana, Cuba (Gutiérrez Calvache 2017:Figure 5)—depict an exceptional bifurcated snuff tube found in a cave on La Gonave, Haiti (see Figure I.2); this master-

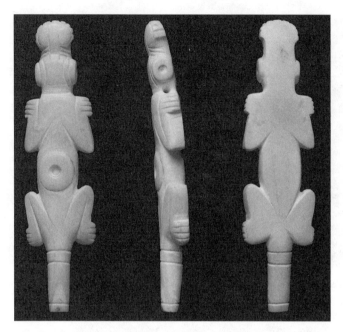

Figure I.6. Shell replica in the form of a caiman. The original was found on Marie Galante and is in a private collection. L: 16 cm; W: 4 cm; D: 1.5 cm. (Musée Edgar Clerc, Guadeloupe, SL. 84.12. Photo courtesy Joanna Ostapkowicz)

piece has remained in private hands since the 1930s and would be completely unknown to researchers were it not for such well-made replicas. In Trinidad, artists from the Santa Rosa community were commissioned to create hand-carved replicas of the wooden artifacts recovered from Pitch Lake, specifically for handling collections and displays of the National Museum and Art Gallery of Trinidad and Tobago (Ostapkowicz et al. 2017b). Replicas need not always be material objects: as part of the *Pre-Hispanic Caribbean Sculptural Arts in Wood* project (2007–2010), digital technology enabled the 3D imaging of selected Caribbean wood sculptures, enabling viewers to virtually handle and examine the artifacts in detail (Ostapkowicz 2009).

But replicas raise their own ethical issues: in Grenada, a workshop was held in 2000 with the specific incentive to stop looting at the Pearls site by shifting the focus to the manufacture of replicas, which instead spurred the proliferation of forgeries—many of which ended up in the local museums (Hanna, chapter 5 this volume). And replicas of a large trigolith recovered in Carriacou were produced for two local museums, but its varied use and display has raised several ethical questions (Swogger, chapter 6 this volume).

Outside of museums, replicas of precolumbian Caribbean pieces are frequently made for the tourist market. These include fine artisan pieces, such as Vieques "condor pendants"—inspired by the archaeology of La Sorcé (Figure I.7)—and handmade ceramics, such as those by the Guillén brothers, which take inspiration from known precolumbian artifacts (Figure I.8). Such work has even traveled on exhibit—for example, the *Cemies en Valencia* exhibit in July 2017, featuring 22 Guillén reproductions, all identified as such in the displays and accompanying literature. These creations are not entirely straightforward copies of known artifacts; rather, they are an artistic engagement with the traditions that inspired the originals, showcasing the suitability of these designs and forms to modern entrepreneurial ventures. This is in the same vein as Gundrum's work (see Valcárcel Rojas et al., chapter 7 in this volume), also based on reinterpreting indigenous designs from originals.

Most replicas are built to withstand handling and closer inspection—specifically to engage touch. And it is exactly the tactile aspect that brings people into more direct contact with the past, enabling a greater appreciation of indigenous aesthetics, ingenuity, and abilities. Whether in a museum or commercial setting, replicas connect the visitor with a patrimony that otherwise remains behind glass, in storage, or held in distant locations. London's Victoria and Albert Museum, for example, has had its Cast Court since 1873—an enormous space dedicated to replicas of masterpieces from around the world, including a 5-meter-high cast of Michelangelo's David. The British Museum has displayed only a small fraction of the 500 casts of Maya stelae taken by Alfred Maudsley in the 1880s, but these are of significant value given that many of the original monuments were later looted, destroyed, or

Figure I.7. Resin replica of Vieques "condor" ornament (H: 4.5 cm). (Photo courtesy Joanna Ostapkowicz)

Figure I.8. Wood cemí (H: 32 cm) and ceramic replica (*right,* 11 cm) in the collections of the Museum of Anthropology and Ethnography, University of Turin, Italy. The replica was made by the Guillén brothers. (Courtesy Museum of Anthropology and Ethnography, Turin; photo: Joanna Ostapkowicz)

damaged by weathering. Work is currently underway to create 3D scans of the collection, with the aim of making it available online (Jarvis 2017). Replicas therefore have great potential in making cultural patrimony more widely accessible, not least for the Caribbean.

"AN OPEN SECRET," BUT STILL LARGELY A SECRET

The situation of looting and forgeries in the Caribbean is not dissimilar from that of the wider circum-Caribbean region and beyond. However, unlike Mexico and Peru, where the issues have been discussed for over a century (e.g., see summaries in Boone 1982; Coggins 1969; Walsh 2005; and overviews in Bruhns and Kelker 2010; Kelker and Bruhns 2010; and Tremain and Yates 2019), the Caribbean situation remains—in the words of Irving Rouse some eight decades ago—"an open secret" (Rouse 1942:44), known to any who chose to look, but not widely discussed or written about. Unsurprisingly, the subject is largely taboo: no collector or museum wants to know that their prized artifact is a forgery, and financial considerations and those of status and reputation largely censure wider discussion. But more concerningly, as Jones and colleagues (1990:16) point out, forgeries, "loosen our hold on reality, deform and falsify our understanding of the past," and as such, many think that they are best glossed over and forgotten, banished to the dark corners of museum storage or destroyed (see Jones et al. 1990 for an alternative view). But that is only if they are exposed as forgeries—if not, then they may retain the spotlight and accolades, a secret known only to those who created them. Forgeries are thus a Pandora's box of illusions, entangled with issues of authenticity. Unopened (undisclosed), they suggest an illusionary past; opened, they generate ever-increasing problems and ethical dilemmas that span social and class boundaries, institutional and private interests, touching on our perceptions of what is authentic and valued (e.g., Schwartz 1996).

A brief look at the issues in the wider circum-Caribbean region provides some context to our discussions. The origins of "collecting" in the New World could be placed at the Columbian Exchange—certainly this provoked the rise of "curiosity cabinets" throughout Europe, and efforts to catalog the world. Yet, the Spanish contact period is an arbitrary boundary, dividing only ancient and modern forms of collecting. Humans naturally find meaning in certain objects over others, and those that are more exotic or rare tend to be considered more valuable—these are not tendencies that arose after Columbus. Indeed, this is often a premise for labeling ancient artifacts as "prestige" or "elite" goods in archaeological contexts (e.g., Dark 1995:126). Exotic goods are a means of social signaling, or communicating some rare or esoteric knowledge of the beholder. They command respect and privileged status. These, too, are not tendencies that arose after Columbus. It should not be surprising, then, that shortcuts to such prestige (forgeries) are quite common as well.

In Mexico, forgeries emerged after the War of Independence (1810–1821), when the country opened to foreign investment, and Mexican museums (and later international museums) were heavily reinvesting in their collections (Kelker and Bruhns 2010:15, 34; Walsh 2005:3). There is evidence to suggest dubious pieces were entering private collections in the 1820s (see Walsh 2005:3, 4). By 1861, Edward B. Tylor (in Walsh 2005:2), would note with some shock the presence of "a number of sham antiquities, the manufacture of which is a regular thing in Mexico, as it is in Italy" on shelves at the National Museum of Mexico, something confirmed a few years later by Desiré Charnay: "As for the long rows of so-called 'ancient vases' [displayed at Mexico's National Museum], there is not one that is not imitation," (in Walsh 2005:3). They were noted in international collections shortly thereafter: "these monsters strut about in the beautiful glass cases of our museums in Europe" (Eugene Boban in Walsh 2005:4). So little was known at this point of the basics of Mesoamerican material culture, based on well-provenienced artifacts, that precolumbian art "connoisseurship" developed in a vacuum, based on few facts and overwhelmed with the variety of neo-artifacts being produced in major metropolises (Walsh 2005:17). This, in turn, led to the acquisition of a variety of artifacts that favored certain styles over others, many appealing to Western notions of non-Western art (Pasztory 2002:159–165; Walsh 2005:17; and see Geurds, chapter 9 in this volume). Some eventually entered museum collections, and despite a long pedigree of display, glossy catalog entries, and learned treaties, have since been exposed as forgeries (e.g., Sax et al. 2008; Tremain 2017).

A similar history can be established for precolumbian Caribbean forgeries. While the timing (if the still-limited information on Caribbean forgeries is anything to go by) suggests that the Caribbean scenario was some decades behind mainland developments, and far smaller in scale, it had caught up by the late twentieth century in terms of the sophistication of techniques and artistic (re)interpretations. The idea of selling fakes to elite foreigners is perhaps a natural inclination—and one early reference on the manufacture of "fake" pieces by campesinos specifically for interested antiquarians emerges out of Puerto Rico in the 1890s (Pinart 1890:6; see Ostapkowicz, chapter 1 this volume). Irving Rouse (1942:44), referring to 1930s Cuba, similarly notes that the country folk, "have not been slow in realizing that it is easier to meet the demand for Indian artifacts by making fraudulent objects than by digging specimens out of the ground." Villagers in Barrio Mulas were creating forgeries, so that "every [local] collection . . . has its share of falsifications" (Rouse 1942:44). Several exposés on forged Cuban collections emerge from the writings of Herrera Fritot (1942) and Royo (1948) (see Valcárcel Rojas et al., chapter 7 this volume). The scale of some of these private collections is quite astonishing: the Pinar del Rio collection of Augusto Fornaguera consisted of some 5,000 artifacts, only 72 of which were deemed authentic by a team from Cuba's National Board of Archaeology and Ethnology (Royo 1948:101) (Figure I.9). In the Dominican Republic, Emile de Boyrie Moya, among other major collectors, had significant holdings of Paredones carvings (see Figure 8.2), but once the Paredones forgery industry was exposed in the media, such collections were dispersed, hidden, or destroyed (see Ostapkowicz, chapter 1 in this volume). By the late 1980s, Morban Laucer (1989) wrote a seminal paper on the status of forgeries and looting in the Dominican Republic, highlighting the irreversible damage done by both. The scale has certainly not diminished since his warnings, with the industry getting more covert and sophisticated at its higher end and pieces continuing to enter museum collections.

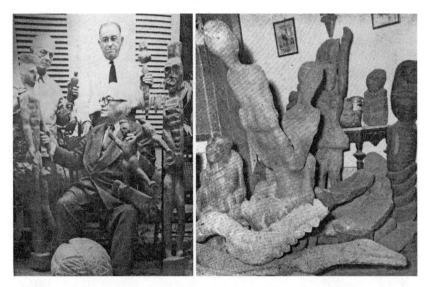

Figure I.9. Augusto Fornaguera's collection of Cuban folk art. (From Fernando Royo, *La colección Fornagueara. Revista de Arqueología y Etnología*, Aña III, época II [6–7]:99–101).

THE ROLE OF MUSEUMS AND THEIR COLLECTIONS: POTENTIALS, PITFALLS, AND THE ETHICS OF ENGAGEMENT

As Walsh (2005:2) notes, "We should maintain and document our museum collections to better educate our eyes, to strengthen and improve our expertise, and to fill in the blanks in our knowledge, thereby enlarging our often fragmented view of the worlds we study." There are many different kinds of museums, and the differences in orientation and mission has huge effects on how a museum collection formed. The way a large natural history museum or art museum acquired its collection may differ greatly from that of a small town museum or interpretation center at a specific archaeological site, whether this be the Caribbean, United States, or Europe. However, we generally understand that "museums collect, they preserve and study what they collect, and they share both the collections and the knowledge derived therefrom for the instruction and self-enlightenment of an audience" (Whiting 1983:2). Thus, all museum collections hold rich potential for engagement, not only with past cultures but, critically, with present ones. Their collections are a nonrenewable resource and, properly conserved, they are the nation's legacy from one generation to the next.

Of course, museums are not without their problems; many are still viewed as active signifiers of political, economic, and cultural power—colonial institutions that display imperial holdings (whether in Europe or the United States)—though this is slowly shifting to a more ethical approach to issues of worldwide cultural patrimony (e.g., Boone 1993; van Broekhoven et al. 2010). The background to this for the Caribbean specifically is insightfully summarized by Cummins (2006:47–48):

> [There has been] decades of indifference and disrespect towards cultural patrimony in the Caribbean region as a direct consequence, largely subconscious, of the history of conquest, colonization and colonialism. . . . These patterns of destruction and power have so structured the history of [the Caribbean Commonwealth] that it has been difficult to arouse either pride or respect for their culture and heritage as a legitimate basis upon which to build new national and regional identities. . . . Caribbean governments have historically displayed an official, almost benign neglect for the acknowledged cultural heritage. . . . Effective legislation for the protection of cultural property has been a relative rarity in some countries, leaving the region's cultural heritage, particularly trafficable objects, open to the depredations of modern-day pirates. More significantly, this vulnerability has led to the transfer of important collections, specimens, and artefacts to the galleries and storerooms of foreign universities and museums and into the hands of private collectors.

Indeed, in his survey of Caribbean institutions, Whiting (1983:13) indicated that one of the main concerns raised by the heritage sector was the lack of control over the excavation of known archaeological sites and the export of archaeological materials—even after the UNESCO Convention of 1970. Over thirty-five years on, Whiting's report is as relevant as the day it was written. Archaeological resources continue to disappear off island, most into private hands rather than public institutions tasked with the responsibility of safeguarding their cultural patrimony. And, although less common, some professional archaeologists continue to remove artifacts and samples without explicit permission from local governing bodies, taking advantage of lax or nonexistent regulations (see Byer, Appendix, in this volume) and shirking ethical responsibilities to encourage local heritage development. Thankfully, such behavior is increasingly less frequent, and movements to "decolonize" archaeology (e.g., Curet 2011; Douglass et al. 2019; Haber 2016) are "waking" many to such responsibilities.

Add to this the fact that museums in general suffer from issues relating to the historic management (and mismanagement) of collections—from the state of their inventory information to the histories (and authenticity) of their acquisitions, all of which combine to create a minefield for the unwary. Museums variously contain material that was at one time considered important to collect (e.g., during field excavations) as well as collections acquired purely by chance (e.g., donated acquisitions). Donations of entire private collections by wealthy benefactors may hold a handful of pieces that fit institutional collection remits, and hundreds that do not—all of which might come with limited documentation supplied by auction houses or dealers. In some instances, museums might be seen as facilitating the legitimization of questionable collections, whether knowingly or not, through, for example, the loan of a private collection for a particular exhibit, or featuring it as a promised donation.

There are also the issues of how politics—and financial pressure—influence museum acquisitions; some museums/curators are unwilling to say no to a donor who is also a heavy supporter of the institution, even if they know the pieces they have collected are poor on provenience or are outright forgeries (e.g., see discussion in Kelker and Bruhns 2010:51–58). This was an issue in the past, and it is even more of an issue now. Small institutions, without curatorial expertise, might unknowingly acquire dubious pieces; large institutions are not immune, even with experts in post. Further, the quality of database and archival information is largely a product of museum histories—from the time (or lack of it) invested in cataloging and filing archival information, to the impact of natural disasters and wars (e.g., both World War I and II gutted many museums throughout the United Kingdom and Europe, not to mention other areas of combat such as northern Africa, Russia, and the Pacific). Wading through the often tortuously labyrinthine histories in efforts to trace documentation for artifacts is sometimes a trial for even the most dedicated researchers.

Collectors are, of course, not the only source of museum collections; since the nineteenth century, archaeologists have also filled museums, sometimes to the bursting point, with material from their excavations. The expectation is that archaeological material is rich in detailed information, down to the level (i.e., the exact location and depth, usually within 10 cm), but this is often not the case for various reasons, including in-field and post-field (e.g., museum) documentation and data-sharing protocols.[8] The history of archaeology as a discipline, just like the history of museums, has a role to play—as do the varied approaches of professionals over the years. Few archaeologists before 1960 were meticulous in their record keeping; for example, Herbert Krieger's (1889–1970) Caribbean collection at the National Museum of Natural History has the bare minimum of information. He also never fully published his results for his Caribbean "excavations" while going so far as to ban other scholars such as Irving Rouse and Julian Granberry from consulting "his" material, despite its deposit in a national institution (e.g., Rouse 1939; for Krieger's excavation methods, see, for example, Davis and Oldfield 2003:1). What may appear today as a cowboy approach to archaeology was not altogether unusual then; even the field techniques of well-respected archaeologists such as Jesse Walter Fewkes (1850–1930) and Theodoor de Booy (1882–1919) were questioned by contemporaries: geologist John Bullbrook (1882–1967), who excavated several Trinidad sites with them in 1913 and 1915, noted that "neither of their excavations was carried out with anything approaching the scientific exactitude demanded today, and they left the study of Trinidad archaeology almost entirely unadvanced" (Bullbrook 1960:7). Conversely, Gudman Hatt's 1922–1923 excavation and documentation techniques in the US Virgin Islands are regarded as highly advanced for the time (Figueredo 1974:2; Toftgaard 2017), as were John Bullbrook's in Trinidad (PMNH Rouse Archives).

Further linked to this are issues of responsibility—then, as now—to the originating island nations. Cummins (2006:48) notes: "Decades after the excavation of archaeological artefacts, the issues of ownership, censorship, and the control of cultural property that has been removed from its country of origin during the course of research projects continue to form the core of the problem. Efforts to repatriate collections to the region have not been wholly successful. On the other hand, it might have been expected that, with regard to the ownership of artefacts by the country of origin, the sharing and communication of information regarding finds and the careful handling of the documentary evidence that accompanies the collections, the actions of the researchers would ultimately be guided by the professional and ethical standards that apply in their own countries. Unfortunately, this has not always been the case."

Fieldwork techniques aside, it was not unusual for early archaeologists to purchase material during fieldwork, or through collectors—particularly given that the expansion of institutional collections was paramount, and there was considerable competition for acquisitions. Indeed, a large portion of the Caribbean collections amassed for the Smithsonian by Fewkes were purchased during reconnaissance trips. Fewkes largely focused on established (mostly private) collections, traveling specifically to meet with collectors and negotiate for the purchase of either individual specimens or whole collections. He kept detailed notes on private collections in his diaries, illustrating pieces in his clear pencil drawings (Ostapkowicz 1998). It is likely that his interest in these older collections may have spurred a return to known supply sources (i.e., archaeological sites), if not the workshop of a local artisan. Many established collections were, essentially, just older finds, likely acquired via campesinos, whether as chance finds made in the course of agricultural work or guano mining—or specifically sourced to cater to the market demand. A return to these historical collections, therefore, presents many challenges, raising both methodological and ethical issues. In almost all cases, intensive background research of documented museum collections is needed to assess their chronological positioning.

But "museum salvage" (Levine and Martínez de Luna 2013)—essentially efforts to restore, recover, and reinstate information for artifacts, and do so in an ethically responsible way—is possible; it just takes time. This, according to some, is a new frontier for research (e.g., Childs 2003:204; and see Curet, Epilogue to this volume). Indeed, according to the Society for American Archaeology's (SAA) Principles of Archaeological Ethics (adopted 1996), archaeologists should "encourage . . . responsible use of collections, records, and reports in their research as one means of preserving the in situ archaeological record" (SAA 1996: Principle No. 7). There is a need, as Barker (2003:80) notes, for "systematic, collections-based research, [with an] emphasis on the research value and utility of extant collections, and careful consideration of the strengths and weaknesses of the collections curated in museums and repositories as subjects of substantive, relevant research." As Whiting (1983:2) notes, specifically with reference to holdings of Caribbean materials: "most collections, unregistered and understudied, have far less interpretive value than those that are catalogued and well researched. Without scholarly research, thoughtful study and documentation, the interpretive, educational function of the museum is shallow, offering little towards the understanding of, and appreciation for, the collective heritage."

But while the study of historic archaeological collections in public institutions may be acceptable (with the caveats stated above)—what of the situation in engaging the private sector collectors? The ethics of dealing with private collections is an important consideration for both archaeologists and museologists. Both are tasked with the responsibility of engaging with, and providing information to, the public, and both have clear guidelines on how to deal with private collectors. In the past, these may have been more lax, but with the escalation of "the destructive effects of commercial involvement," ethical codes of practice have been developed to keep the profession separate from the market (Brodie and Gill 2003:39). Professional organizations now have very clear codes of conduct that their membership must comply with—for the members of the International Association for Caribbean Archaeology (IACA) the code of ethics requires that they "support and comply with the terms of the UNESCO convention . . . [1970] on prohibition and prevention of the illicit export and import, transfer of ownership or 'destruction' through unscientific investigations or looting or faking, of archaeological and other cultural property" (the clear reference to forgeries suggests that IACA has been aware of this as a regional problem). The Society for American Archaeology's (SAA's) Principles of Archaeological Ethics notes that the SAA (emphasis added) long recognized that the buying and selling of objects out of archaeological context is contributing to the destruction of the archaeological record on the American continents and around the world. The commercialization of archaeological objects—their use as commodities to be exploited for personal enjoyment and profit—results in the destruction of archaeological sites and of contextual information that is essential to understanding the archaeological record. Archaeologists should therefore carefully weigh the benefits to scholarship of a project against the costs of potentially enhancing the commercial value of archaeological objects. *Whenever possible they should discourage, and should themselves avoid, activities that enhance the commercial value of archaeological objects, especially objects that are not curated in public institutions, or readily available for scientific study, public interpretation, and display.*

Much the same language is included in the Codes of Conduct for the Register of Professional Archaeologists (RPA 2019), Chartered Institute for Archaeologists (CIfA 2019), and a recent pledge by radiocarbon labs around the world (Hajdas et al. 2019). This clearly discourages, for example, authenticating an object for an auction house or dealer—given the clear expectation that it will be sold; or working on a private collection and publishing the results, which in turn raises the profile of the material and increases its commercial value (e.g., Brodie and Gill 2003:39; see, for example, discussion in Pitblado 2014:389–390). As Brodie and Gill (2003:39) note, "the effect that professional archaeologists may exert on the market goes beyond direct authentication or identification, as the study and publication of unprovenienced material will in itself provide a provenance of sorts, an academic pedigree. Once material is accepted into the validated corpus, its academic significance might translate into monetary value and provide a spur for further looting to find similar objects."

In short, engaging with private collections is an ethical minefield. It can support the private circulation of materials, with little public benefit, and it encourages the commodification of heritage. Yet there are private museum collections in the Caribbean, some with a long history of making their collections available for research (e.g., Altos de Chavón Regional Museum of Archaeology; La Romana and Sala de Arte Pre-Hispánico, Santo Domingo; Centro Cultural Eduardo León Jimenes, Santiago)—how do these institutions, straddling two seemingly opposing realms, fit into the equation? In many instances, such institutions were born out of efforts to safeguard cultural heritage for the benefit of local communities, particularly preventing its export beyond island shores. Privately funded, the Dominican museums listed above often have higher standards of collections management than their government counterparts—their collections, which are cataloged (with copies lodged with the government as per cultural patrimony regulations—see Alvarez et al., chapter 2 in this volume), are held in secure, climate-controlled storage and appear frequently in publications on the prehistoric art and archaeology of the region. These holdings were amassed by collectors with a deep interest in the prehistory of the region, and documentation is, as a result, better than the norm. The use of "collector" in these contexts is more akin to "avocational archaeologist"; indeed, there is a spectrum of "collecting," ranging from the profit-motivated kind to benign salvagers and diligent record-keepers/avocational archaeologists. The latter are separated by a thin line with professional archaeologists themselves. Further, given laws on some islands (e.g., Dominican Republic), which clearly articulate that cultural patrimony belongs to the nation, these institutions are often viewed as custodians rather than owners—a situation that is also common across the Mesoamerican region (Joyce 2019:12).[9] Such situations make us reexamine the lines often drawn between institutions and private collectors (Joyce 2019:12). As pointed out by Pitblado (2014), wholesale alienation of the collecting public is itself a violation of the SAA's Principles (though see Goebel 2015 for a dimmer view). Pitblado posits that responsible collectors can and have advanced archaeology when collaborating with archaeologists, and that this involvement has its own ethical imperative.

It is worthwhile to also briefly explore the code of ethics from the museum side, particularly given the very real issues faced by some on the ground in the Caribbean (see Alverez et al., chapter 2 in this volume). Most museums are established for public benefit, and many undertake artifact identifications for members of the public. Strict conduct guidelines often govern this engagement. In the United Kingdom, for example, the code of ethics for the Museums Association stipulates that staff are to "undertake identifications to the highest scholarly standards and provide as many significant facts about an item as possible" (Museums Association 2008:3:17), but they are to "encourage public appreciation of the cultural rather than financial value of items [by] refus[ing] to put a financial value on items" (2008:3:18). Further, they should:

- "Reject . . . any item if there is any suspicion that, since 1970, it may have been stolen, illegally excavated or removed from a monument, site or wreck contrary to local law or otherwise acquired in or exported from its country of origin . . . in violation of that country's laws or any national and international treaties, unless the museum is able to obtain permission from authorities with the requisite jurisdiction in the country of origin" (2008:5:10).
- "Report any suspicion of criminal activity to the police. Report any

other suspicions of illicit trade to other museums collecting in the same area and to organisations that aim to curtail the illicit trade" (2008:5:14).

- "Avoid appearing to promote or tolerate the sale of any material without adequate ownership history through inappropriate or compromising associations with vendors, dealers or auction houses" (2008:5:15).
- "Decline to offer expertise on, or otherwise assist the current possessor of any item that may have been illicitly obtained, unless it is to assist law enforcement or to support other organisations in countering illicit activities" (2008:5:16; see also Brodie et al. 2000).

There is also strict guidance on the display of unprovenienced material: the International Council of Museums (ICOM 2017:4:5) advises that "museums should avoid displaying or otherwise using material of questionable origin or lacking provenance. They should be aware that such displays or usage can be seen to condone and contribute to the illicit trade in cultural property."

The above guidelines clearly state that, for both archaeologists and museologists, one of the key issues when dealing with private collections of unprovenienced artifacts is transparency—in expectations, conduct, and aims. Researchers need to explicitly engage with the ethical issues of studying such material. Publishing images of private precolumbian collections to complement reports or books (including exhibit catalogs) is a case in point. Often, all that is listed in the name of the collector and site (if known), with little or no mention of the histories or problematic nature of such collections, nor an acknowledgment of the fact that highlighting them in such public ways increases their "value," and not simply as a scholarly resource. This material remains in private hands, and if research can verify "authenticity," there are no safeguards in place to protect the collection from eventually being sold on for profit, and disappearing entirely. While there are conventions for regulating cultural heritage and laws specifically addressing the export/import of illicit materials, these are rarely enforced (Seigel and Righter 2010; see Yates, chapter 10 in this volume; Byer, Appendix, in this volume). Both archaeologists and museum professionals should therefore be aware that we are, in many ways, on the front lines of these issues: we often come into direct contact with people who own archaeological material, and our involvement should be in line with the guidelines of the institutions and professional associations of which we are members.

But what of forgeries? Should archaeologists and museum professionals assist in identifying these? At the very least, there are grounds to argue that this should be undertaken as a matter of priority for public collections. As

Kelker and Bruhns (2010:13–14) point out: "Today the flood of forgeries, noted as early as the late nineteenth century . . . , has become a tidal wave. Exhibition after exhibition, catalog and catalog, showy picture-book after showy picture-book all promulgate the most egregious forgeries as if they were genuine testimonials to something other than the cupidity of the art market and its customers. There are many museums whose prized collection of Precolumbian art is well over half Postcolumbian—to put it nicely." While this may be true of collections of Peruvian and Mesoamerican artifacts in major US institutions, it may be a stretch to say this for Caribbean materials at present—though some of the self-published catalogs of private collections are another matter. The public's assumption is that such collections were vetted prior to their debut in publications; a further assumed reassurance is that publicly accountable institutions are scrupulous in establishing, through due diligence, the history and authenticity of a profiled piece. For forgeries, however, this simply establishes a history on trust—a pedigree for the neo-artifact that is then perpetuated until debunked. These pieces are then sometimes used in university courses—whether archaeology or art history, and despite the best practice approach of not using artifacts without provenience (not least without vetting)—to educate the next generation of scholars on style and function. Simply put, such pieces cause chaos for research, "because undetected fakes in museum collections invariably distort our carefully constructed models of the ancient past" (Sellen 2014:151). Even established academics, who should have experience in handling artifacts and have a good sense of their stylistic range, sometimes suspend disbelief; occasionally, even obvious forgeries are included in academic treatises. If forgeries can fool even a trained eye, then an unquestioning approach to museum collections is a danger that can easily undermine scholarship by building a foundation that completely skews understanding of the past. Conversely, identifying such creations accurately, and exploring them more appropriately as replicas or modern artworks, establishes a more nuanced (and positive) engagement. One step toward this has recently been taken by the Centro León, Santiago, which has begun classifying relevant collections as "20th century" in their records—it can only be hoped that more institutions in the Dominican Republic, and other Caribbean and indeed international nations, begin to explore this issue with similar openness.

ORGANIZATION OF THE VOLUME

Many of the issues raised here are difficult ones, for which we do not always have definitive answers. The authors of this volume address many of these same issues from different perspectives, all with the aim of casting a new light within a circum-Caribbean context. In these efforts, the authors illuminate new understandings and strategies for both combating the global antiquities trade and encouraging sustainable economic impacts for those who make a living creating reinterpretations of the past, for the present. The volume begins in the Greater Antilles and follows several case studies from island to island, from Cuba down to Grenada, ending with connections to parallel issues in Central America and an overview of the legal landscape of the English- and Spanish-speaking Antilles.

We open, in chapter 1, with the most notorious incident thus far known from the region—the Paredones scandal in the Dominican Republic, which succeeded in defrauding the art world and the archaeological community for over two decades (from circa 1946 to 1968). Joanna Ostapkowicz outlines the history and eventual public exposure of the affair and explores aspects of the thriving neo-artifact industry of the Dominican Republic since the event. The chapter discusses the vested interests of the various players involved—from the economic hardship that drove campesino artists to create an "indigenous" art (later exposed and rebranded as "folk art") to the entrenched reactions of the collectors and, indeed, some archaeologists, who refused to accept the growing evidence that these creations were forged, including the confessions from the forgers themselves. The scandal was remarkable on a number of levels, most notably the sheer scale of forgeries (beyond 25,000 by some estimates; the majority sold openly on the market as antiquities) and the fact that the forgers used their experience working with archaeologists to their advantage: by planting neo-artifacts via tunnels they cleverly kept the overlaying stratigraphy intact, giving the impression of undisturbed contexts. But what is equally remarkable is that without the media scrutiny of this event, it would have simply disappeared from record, known only to the handful of people involved—with the neo-artifacts continuing to saturate the collections of both local and international museums. What it spurred, at least in the immediate aftermath of the event, was a scrutiny of collections and collecting practices, and by the time the Museo del Hombre Dominicano opened in 1973, Paredones material were relegated to the museum storerooms rather than displays, even as folk art. It eroded, for a time, any interest in collecting Amerindian material for all but the most dedicated collectors and undermined government incentives to support artistic movements inspired by precolumbian art, driving some initiatives further underground. But far from disappearing, the art of forgery has escalated over the last five decades and is now thriving in the Dominican Republic; indeed, judging by style, the majority of neo-artifacts circulating on US and European markets come from this country (Figure I.10).

In chapter 2, Arlene Alvarez, Corinne L. Hofman, and Mariana C. Françozo explore some of the legal background and aftermath of the Paredones in-

Figure I.10. Neo-artifact in the display window of a Paris antique shop, June 2008. (Photo courtesy Joanna Ostapkowicz)

cident. The early adoption of heritage laws in the Dominican Republic (beginning from the mid-nineteenth century onward) was laudable, but ultimately ineffective, and remains so even in the twenty-first century. It is clear from the early efforts that a serious situation had emerged regarding the looting of sites; attempts to further curb the destruction and raise public awareness of cultural heritage issues emerged in the 1960s and 1970s, with new laws and the creation of both public and private museums (the latter being quite prominent in the country). One major failing is the fact that there are no adequate systems of management and no efficient systems of record-keeping or curation, ultimately undermining efforts to safeguard national heritage. Alvarez and colleagues argue that this lack of capacity for managing records and collections in the Dominican Republic is the result of colonial mismanagement and the export of many important documents from the colony, effectively outsourcing these much-needed skills to the metropole. Key issues—then and now—include the lack of government policy and economic support and limited professional training in collection management. Thus, the system was inadequately prepared for the burgeoning forgery industry that erupted in the mid-twentieth century. Solutions to the situation are difficult to implement, particularly in a country that has no curricula dedicated to archaeology or museology that can train the very individuals who are needed to effect change (see also Cummins 2006:48). Alverez and colleagues, however, argue that it is the country's museums that can play a critical role in guiding educational policy—and thus changing attitudes toward the country's heritage. This can be established not only by informing museum audiences about archaeological site conservation and the local antiquity trade but by establishing a museum policy that discourages the purchases of unprovenienced materials. Critically, engagement needs to be particularly active with communities living in close proximity to heritage-rich sites.

In chapter 3, José Oliver explores a very different situation in neighboring Puerto Rico, where reverence for the island's past effectively curtails most forms of looting. The symbols of the Taíno have become the symbols of national pride, complete with subtle resistance to colonialism. As Oliver notes, items from Puerto Rico's cultural marketplace are not fakes—they are authentic material reproductions imbued with meaning. Thus, there is no need to destroy ancient sites in search of authentic artifacts. Oliver traces the history of Puerto Rico's Taíno identity to, especially, the importation of binary racial categories from the United States in the early twentieth century, which ultimately increased the desirability of an alternative precolonial ethnic category. This identity was further cemented by Puerto Rico's Instituto de Cultura Puertorriqueña (ICP) adopting a "three root model" of Puertoriqueñidad (with Spanish, African, and Indian contributions). Oliver's chapter provides critical background to Curet's Epilogue, which, like Oliver, offers personal perspectives of how each author has traversed, as both scientist and Puerto Rican national, the many challenges of their island's newfound cultural identity. Despite the specific historical circumstances that have created Puerto Rico's situation, many islands (least not Dominica, St. Vincent, and Trinidad) have long-neglected Amerindian roots that might be profitably engaged for similar forms of national pride. Even where an island's ancient pasts seem foreign and irrelevant to the majority of its population, the landscape itself is testament to the relationship. In Grenada, for instance, people take pride knowing their "naval string" (umbilical cord) was buried on Grenadian soil. Yet Amerindians once buried their birth cords in the same places—these are shared cultural landscapes, separated only by time.

Lesley-Gail Atkinson Swaby's contribution (chapter 4) provides an overview of the legal background of cultural heritage in Jamaica. The failure to implement and enforce legislation is evident in her numerous examples of unchecked looting and destruction of well-known heritage sites while government officials did, and continue to do, nothing. This, of course, is not unique to Jamaica—this is a wider issue that stems from a lack of heritage education throughout the region. As Cummins (2006:48) points out, this compounds, "the lack of awareness, appreciation, and even basic knowledge of what constitutes cultural property. . . . Few export controls exist for cultural heritage but where they do, the ignorance of officials regarding what constitutes valuable cultural property and their inability to identify material that is culturally unique to the region renders this form of control ineffectual." Interestingly, like the Dominican Republic (chapters 1 and 2) and Grenada (chapter 5), Jamaica has a curious preponderance of stone sculpture forgeries. Atkinson Swaby highlights the refusal of collectors to accept this designation; it inspires, instead, a tenacious determination to find any authority to validate their claims. But this predicament does little for the contemporary artists who actually create these works and who gain little recognition for taking Amerindian-inspired iconography in new directions. The perception that collectors desire an ancient Amerindian iconography over potential local folk art remains untested, as no stone sculptors have come forward to challenge this assumption. Jamaica's artistic heritage is world renowned and appreciated; sculpture artists would do well to break from chicanery and promote their creations as local art.

Grenada's sculptural arts (chapter 5) are at a similar crossroads. Ever since the airport at Pearls was constructed, the nearby Amerindian site has been continuously looted by locals, collectors, and tourists alike. Jonathan Hanna's discussion explores the looter-collector-archaeologist continuum in Grenada, from the seemingly endless looting at the Pearls site to various attempts at replica-making by archaeologists, and onward to the ways in which the past is perceived and reinvented by the citizens of this small, developing nation. Ultimately, we are left with the conclusion that neo-Amerindian art has the potential to equate or even surpass the value of its ancient equivalents. With so many artists producing fake Amerindian sculptures, perhaps it is only a matter of time before Grenada's folk art achieves the nationalistic authenticity that propels Puerto Rico's cultural market.

John Swogger (chapter 6) focuses on an object from Grenada's sister-island of Carriacou on display at the Grenada National Museum in St. George's. In a case of mistaken identity, Swogger examines how a replica at the museum was inadvertently transformed into a fake when put on display without the word "replica" on the label. The discussion of ethical considerations that follow should provide much inspiration to those at the intersection of archaeology, museology, creative reconstruction, and public outreach (something which, Swogger argues, we should strive to integrate). He concludes with a vision for Grenada specifically (but applicable anywhere), arguing that archaeologists have a critical role to play in helping developing countries celebrate and draw attention to their heritage. This is starkly different from the neoliberal gentrification pursued by Grenada's government, supported by several loans from the International Monetary Fund (IMF), since the 1990s. How can local artists compete against cheap trinkets in a globalizing economy?

The creative backdrop of Swogger's chapter (and others) presents a middle ground—a "third way"—between the otherwise binary categories of real and fake, genuine and reproduction. Many archaeologists and art historians hold the uncompromising perspective that replicas must be exact copies of originals—anything less is mere kitsch. Yet this perfectionism reinforces and maintains the monetary value of ancient objects because even the highest-fidelity replica can never be as "valuable" as the original. Surely this is counterproductive. Such thinking also minimizes the potential for new, reimagined creations inspired by Amerindian iconography. The possibilities for such art go far beyond that of ancient looted objects—indeed, in a perfect world, they could stall the black market entirely. .

But accurate replicas also hold great educational potential—far beyond that of the ancient artifact behind a glass barrier. In this sense, Roberto Valcárcel Rojas and colleagues (chapter 7), describe the highly proactive replica industry in Cuba. During the pre-Revolutionary years, competition among Cuba's collectors was reminiscent of the nineteenth-century "dinosaur wars" in the United States—complete with sabotage and intrigue. This social environment saw not only prolific forgeries but—intriguingly—a robust replica industry, with museums across the island endeavoring to amass large replica collections—a process that was later supported and continued by the revolutionary government. As such, museums across Cuba now contain high-quality replicas of important artifacts and artifact-types from all over the island—not just ceramics and stone tools, but also beads, shell and bone adornments, wood carvings, skeletal assemblages, and even life-sized petroglyphs. At such a nationwide scale, one can see the great potential for replicas in both public and formal education as well as accessible reference collections for local and international researchers.

In chapter 8, Joanna Ostapkowicz and Roger Colten offer a rare perspective on the late Irving Rouse, the father of modern Caribbean archaeology. Rouse's wise circumspection is clear in his correspondence with those asking his expert opinion on unprovenienced objects—suspicious of anything he had never seen and handled but cautious to definitively label all but the crudest of fakes. Rouse was initially hesitant to offer opinions on authenticity to those outside the archaeological discipline, but his curatorial role in the Peabody Museum of Natural History meant that public inquiries were entirely within his remit of responsibility. As his confidence grew, so too his hesitation decreased, particularly following the Paredones affair. Rouse believed that fakes, as items specifically created to deceive, were dangerous to both collectors and archaeologists alike, but he also admitted a positive position to which contemporary artistic movements might eventually aspire ("[folk art] may some day become as valuable as aboriginal art"[10]). Yet he maintained that some of the Paredones "artifacts" might be genuine, even after the forgers came clean—as did many other archaeologists at the time. It may be that Rouse was deceived by the intact stratigraphy and the precolumbian ceramics scattered among modern sculptures, or he thought the similarities between Paredones and some of the Puerto Rican artifacts he had previously studied from a private collection (Rouse 1961) set a precedent. Regardless, Rouse applied the same caution to "blatant fakes" as he did to those he was unsure about, and reading his correspondence on the subject is an instructive lesson in the history of Caribbean forgeries.

In chapter 9, Alexander Geurds explores the notion of authenticity and its effects on the antiquities market in the wider region. In particular, Geurds highlights how the paramount importance of age as a means of determining authenticity excludes—by definition—replicas or contemporary reinterpretations, no matter how well made or well known. He explores the background to the New World antiquities market and the common origins of private and museum collections in the nineteenth century. Although focused more on Central America (with an eye to the Caribbean) and the state's role in manufacturing authenticity, Geurds also describes the impact of archaeology on the thriving local pottery industry in Nicaragua, particularly the impact of a classic text by Samuel Lothrop in fueling innovation and new Amerindian-inspired designs. This, among other examples in this volume, underscores the significant influence that archaeology and archaeologists can have on new art movements (whether community level or nationalist, replicas or forgeries), however unintentional.

In chapter 10, Donna Yates offers a shift in focus toward the core driver of the black market economy. By equating antiquities collecting with other "white-collar crimes," Yates argues offenders have the resources (both wealth and power) to avoid legal penalties. In response, academics need to ignore private (i.e., looted) collections and expose those in the discipline who fail to do so. Supporting the inclusion of private archaeological collections in an academic publication has ethical ramifications for the field; it is not the message we want to be sending to the next generation of Caribbean scholars. And while we push for stronger legal structures, voice concerns over art museums acquiring unprovenienced materials, "out" the "big players" (e.g., auction houses, major antiquities dealers, etc.) for dealing in looted artifacts, and advocate for more public awareness, we must avoid engagement with collections of unprovenienced material that remain in private hands. Without the necessary means of authenticating (and thus, adding value to) looted material, "investment" collectors lose that which antiquities offer them—money, influence, and prestige. When you force them to hide a recently acquired ancient polychrome vessel from a visitor's view, you make them think twice about paying for another.

Amanda Byer's Appendix provides a much-needed overview of the various legal structures surrounding cultural heritage protection in the English- and Spanish-speaking Caribbean, in line with the focus of the volume. As archaeologists know too well, the regional legal systems are idiosyncratic and subjective, such that no two islands are the same. This makes broad, archipelagic research across multiple jurisdictions difficult to conduct. And while most islands have some semblance of cultural resource legislation, few enforce these laws, partly in fear of scaring off foreign investors. As Donna Yates points out (chapter 10), "a well-written and well-intentioned antiquities protection law is meaningless if it is neither implementable nor enforceable, and if the protection of heritage is not a government priority." In this vein, Byer calls on all heritage advocates (officials, archaeologists, NGOs) to encourage communities to become stewards of their local heritage and enforce the protections themselves, as a grassroots effort. This is the only way governments will pay attention. Archaeologists and museum professionals have a crucial role to play in this regard, for when we fail to engage the communities we work near, we sow the seeds for many problems down the line.

CONCLUDING THOUGHTS

This volume spans diverse issues related to what we have broadly termed the "real, recent, and replica" in Caribbean material culture studies. It deals with difficult subject matter: from the continued looting of archaeological sites in the region, to the seismic increase of forgeries, to the imbalanced power and economic relations between the producers of neo-Amerindian art and those who consume it. It highlights the continued desire for the authentic precolumbian artifact, no matter the cost. These issues are still often glossed over once a coveted piece finds pride of place on a collector's mantel or a museum display. While acquisition policies have changed for many museums in the last few decades, with a critical eye cast on the acceptance of unprovenienced material, there are still some art museums and galleries that occasionally turn a blind eye and accept new, unprovenienced collections to fill their vitrines with tax-deductible donations, or launder pieces as loans. In contrast, some institutions in the Caribbean feel forced to accept looted and (knowingly or not) forged material in order to "save" the island's cultural patrimony from leaving their shores. Neither of these situations would be viable if heritage laws had the necessary "bite." If anything, a growing scrutiny of these issues will increasingly make the situation untenable—particularly for those who profit from the illicit traffic of cultural patrimony. It is our hope that this volume contributes to making that a reality.

NOTES

1. In archaeology, the term *looting* specifies digging or collecting artifacts without the use of any scientific methods (e.g., recording contextual information), usually for onward sale on the antiquities market or for incorporation into personal collections. Among other things (e.g., issues of ethics/morality), the lack of provenience information makes looted material largely meaningless to archaeologists. However, the terms *looted* and *unprovenienced* are not entirely interchangeable, as not all unprovenienced material was looted, as described below.

2. UNESCO Convention on the Means of Prohibiting and Preventing the Illicit Import, Export, and Transfer of Ownership of Cultural Property (1970) and UNESCO World Heritage Convention (1972).

3. UNIDROIT Convention on Stolen or Illegally Exported Cultural Objects.

4. All terms are defined using the Oxford English Dictionary.

5. There is a huge literature on the "reality" of nationalistic art, as well as the use of indigenous art in the interpretation of histories—and the levels of "truth" versus myth in these interpretations (e.g., Kohl et al. 2014).

6. Note: In British English, "provenance" is used to refer to place of origin (e.g., archaeological context) as well as collection history, even in the archaeological literature; similarly, some US scholars use "provenience" in all usages. Nonetheless, we see the usefulness of differentiating the two words and definitions in this volume, as recently proposed by American archaeologists (e.g., Hirst 2018).

7. Valera Castillo and Peralta Montero (2012:167), estimate that over 90% of handmade art in the Dominican Republic is made for tourist consumption, with clear implications for generating important revenue for the national economy.

8. It is not unusual for archaeological collections to get detached from their provenience in museum collections; even with the best intentions, pieces lose labels or labels are misplaced, their long histories in storage sometimes working against them. Large collections of similar objects (e.g., ceramic lugs) are often cataloged in groups, hundreds of artifacts accessioned under one inventory number; rarely are individual pieces in such large accessions individually inscribed, unless volunteers or students working on specific projects dedicate time to this.

9. "Important cultural institutions have been developed by private individuals or groups of citizens who have in their possession collections that might at first glance be viewed as simply commodified products of a market. Such nongovernmental mu-

seums build on the existence of forms of private custody of cultural properties uniformly designated as national patrimony in these countries. Such groups and individuals bring capital otherwise unavailable from government to projects that might otherwise never have happened. Under the laws in place throughout the region . . . these museums serve only as custodians, not owners, of archaeological objects" (Joyce 2019:12).

10. Rouse, June 19, 1984, Rouse Archives, PMNH.

1

Caribbean Indigenous Art
Past, Present, Future

The View from the Greater Antilles

Joanna Ostapkowicz

In the collections of the National Museum of the American Indian (NMAI) is a coiled snake sculpture from Maracayo, Puerto Rico, that has been featured in publications as a prehistoric carving (Brecht et al. 1997:Figure 98), but which recent study has identified as relatively modern, most probably dating to cal AD 1810–1926 (69.3%, OxA-19120) (Ostapkowicz et al. 2012:2246) (Figure 1.1). The museum's archival information only confirms that the piece was purchased in 1926. Acquisitions through purchase were common at the time, given the spending power of George Gustav Heye, the preeminent collector of Native American arts in the early twentieth century and then owner/director of the Heye Foundation's Museum of the American Indian (MAI, the founding collection of the NMAI in 1989). The carving's placement within the MAI's archaeological holdings clearly identified it as prehistoric, one of many Caribbean artifacts in the expanding Heye collections (e.g., Curet and Galban 2019). Given this history, it is clear that several things converged to secure its status as an ancient Antillean carving, hence its inclusion among precolumbian pieces in the Museo del Barrio's *Taíno: Pre-Columbian Art and Culture from the Caribbean* exhibit (Brecht et al. 1997). Yet it is a highly unusual carving, clearly taking advantage of the natural twists in a vine (*Clusia* sp.) and quite atypical of the stylized conventions seen in much of the "classic Taíno" art of the Greater Antilles. For these and other reasons, I had previously considered it a postcolonial piece (Ostapkowicz 1998:131), something subsequently confirmed by the radiocarbon date; indeed, the end of its greatest probability range (cal AD 1810–1926) is the year the piece was purchased. In our paper (Ostapkowicz et al. 2012:2246), we suggested that it could be a *jíbaro*/campesino carving, or perhaps a piece made specifically for the emerging late nineteenth-, early twentieth-century tourist and antiquarian markets in Puerto Rico.

The carving's original intention (as folk art or forgery) remains unknown; however, its recent display in the del Barrio exhibit cemented its reading as a precolumbian artifact. As such, the radiocarbon results were a surprise to many, and the carving remains a good introduction to the interests of various sectors for creating, and then perpetuating, a desired authenticity—that of an ancient indigenous, rather than contemporary, art form (something encountered repeatedly in the various histories briefly explored in this chapter, and throughout the book). It also exposes a misapprehension: the expectation that the Caribbean region, unlike neighboring South and Central America, with their long history of forgeries (Bruhns and Kelker 2010; Kelker and Bruhns 2010), is somehow immune to such disreputable practice. Many (whether archaeologists, collectors, dealers, or museums) still hide behind the belief that Caribbean cultures are much less known than the cultures of Mexico and Peru (whose precolonial artworks are the most commonly faked in the Americas) and the deceptive practice cannot fake what it does not know—but this is an illusion. Indeed, the art world has fully embraced the artistic heritage of the ancient Caribbean, particularly the dramatic sculptural forms of the "Taíno." Blockbuster exhibits in Paris and New York, the epicenters of the "tribal art" worlds, have secured its position as one of the most desirable and coveted art forms of the precolumbian Americas. And rarity drives demand: old collections rarely come onto the market, meaning that the coveted art has to be found through other means: whether the looting of a site or the skills of a forger. Many sites in the Caribbean have been plundered for their artifacts, which are essentially viewed as portable, saleable commodities despite the national and international laws—some over a century old—for the protection

Figure 1.1. Snake carving, Maracayo, Puerto Rico, *Clusia* sp., cal AD 1810–1926 (69.3% probability; OxA-19120); L: 55 cm; W: 50 cm; H: 18 cm (max). (Courtesy National Museum of the American Indian, Smithsonian Institution, Washington, DC 145110.000; photo: Joanna Ostapkowicz)

of the cultural heritage of island nations (e.g., Alvarez et al., chapter 2 in this volume; Byers, Appendix, in this volume; Siegel and Righter 2011). Further, this practice is not just a result of the Columbus quincentenary interest; antiquarian interest in the past, and later archaeology as a field, emerged in the Caribbean in the late 1800s (Curet 2011), and it is likely that this created opportunities early on for some to profit from an illicit trade, as looters or as forgers. Indeed, Puerto Rico has the dubious honor of being the source of the earliest currently known Caribbean forgeries: the Piedras de Padre Nazario carvings (Figure 1.2). Originally numbering some 800 pieces, the Nazario carvings were first documented in the 1880s, but were denounced as largely dubious shortly thereafter (e.g., Fewkes 1907; Pinart 1890:6r; see discussion in Rodríguez Ramos 2019; Schiappacasse 1994:349–350); they remain controversial to this day.[1] Alphonse Pinart, who first wrote about them in 1890, thought them "bizarre," and noted that "for some time, the country people, seeing the interest the intelligent but naïve priest had in these forms, began to manufacture them. Today, many of these pieces that are brought by the locals are fake" (Pinart 1890:6r). But Puerto Rico is far from isolated in this regard—what is becoming clear is that no island is immune: from the Bahamas (Figure 1.3) to Jamaica (Atkinson Swaby, chapter 4 in this volume); Cuba (Valcárcel Rojas et al., chapter 7 in this volume); and the Lesser Antilles (Hanna, chapter 5 in this volume)—and most especially the island of Hispaniola (Dominican Republic/Haiti) (Alvarez et al., chapter 2 in this volume), the Caribbean's core of illicit traffic, and the source of many of the examples in this chapter.

Figure 1.2. Three views of a "Padre Nazario" stone featuring an as-yet undeciphered "script," attributed variously to either Phoenician, Sumerian, Quechuan, or Libyco-Berber (e.g., Fell 1987). Guayanilla, Puerto Rico, ca. 1880. H: 13 cm; W: 12 cm; D: 5 cm. (Copyright 2020 President and Fellows of Harvard College, Peabody Museum of Archaeology and Ethnology, 19-21-30/C9057; photo: Joanna Ostapkowicz)

Figure 1.3. Twentieth-century Hispaniolan "neo-artifacts" imported into the Bahamas and Turks and Caicos Islands. *Top row*: three carvings in the collections of the National Museum of the Bahamas (AMMC), roughly to scale (*largest, upper right*: H: 12 cm); their associated label reads: "found in 1986 . . . in a shop on Grand Turk." *Middle row*: selection of stone Taíno "zemis" in the collections of the Albert Lowe Museum, Green Turtle Cay, Abaco. The carving on the far right appears to be carved from a weathered brick (H: 12 cm). *Bottom row*: selection of carvings from the Turks and Caicos National Museum (TCNM), Grand Turk (*carving on right*: H: 19 cm). (Courtesy National Museum of the Bahamas [AMMC], the TCNM, and the Albert Lowe Museum; photos: Joanna Ostapkowicz)

This chapter explores a variety of forgeries, starting with the Los Paredones scandal, which affects directly what archaeologists hold most dear: provenience and the excavation of sites. Many in the archaeological community are under the impression that forgery and its sister specter, looting, are mainly museum issues, given that museums acquire pieces via collectors; archaeologists are above the ethnical quagmire of dealing with unprovenienced collections. But as the Paredones case makes clear, archaeologists are a contributing factor to the issue simply by the work that they do (e.g., Santos 1983:258). Their excavations and explorations directly contribute to people's interest in the past, and the ramifications of this interest may not be to their liking (e.g., Brodie and Gill 2003:38–40; see also Hanna, chapter 5 in this volume; Swogger, chapter 6 this volume). For example, the "excavation experience" was promoted by some Dominican entrepreneurs in the 1980s, who "invited tourists on an attractive 'tour' of a cave in Macao, [Dominican Republic], where they would be allowed to dig and take home all the archaeological material they obtained" (Abreu Collado in Morban Laucer 1989:56). Indeed, the impact of forgeries and looting extends far beyond just museums—that impact is a much more complex phenomenon with many contributing factors. The following sections chart the escalation of the problem from the mid-twentieth century, though as noted above with the Padre Nazario material, Caribbean forgeries may have a deeper history than currently recognized.

LOS PAREDONES: FORGED ANTIQUITIES, CONTEMPORARY ART (1940s–1960s)

These people have been born and raised on Taíno cemeteries. They
have obtained their means of subsistence from these cemeteries
where they excavated tombs and found bones. Their art is a result of
all these circumstances.

—Ugarte 1969g:182

In 1948,[2] some residents from La Caleta, just north of Santo Domingo, brought to the National Museum several sculptures, purportedly indigenous artifacts found in the Los Paredones caves. So unusual was the carving style that they were initially considered forgeries, or perhaps folk art (Boyrie Moya 1952: 181); it would later emerge that both classifications were true. While these initial finds were dismissed, similar carvings began to appear in number, to the extent that Santo Domingo University's Instituto Dominicano Investigaciones Antropológica organized excavations to "verify the authenticity" of the carvings (Boyrie Moya 1952:181). The first official excavation got underway on January 6, 1950, led by Emile de Boyrie Moya and assisted by Luis Chanlatte Baik, with a large contingency of local volunteers, some of whom had fortuitously "found" the first artifacts that came to define the "Paredones culture" (Figure 1.4)—most notable among them, Ramón María Mosquea ("Benyí") (Boyrie Moya 1952:182; Morban Laucer 1968). The excavators recovered a number of carvings between 30 and 70 cm in depth, noting that "neither skeletal remains nor ceramics have appeared in the levels corresponding to these pieces and only on the surface were Taíno pieces found" (Boyrie Moya

Figure 1.4. Morban Laucer excavating at the site of Los Paredones, aided by local volunteers, as featured in Morban Laucer (1968) *Los Paredones: Un santuario prehistórico*. (Courtesy Instituto Dominicano de Investigaciones Antropológicas, Universidad Autonóma de Santo Domingo)

Figure 1.5. Image featured in Boyrie Moya's 1952 publication on Los Paredones, depicting "Grupo de piezas antropomorfas y de cuentas de collares, talladas en material travertinico por los indigenas que habitaron en las Cuevas de los Paredones." Note particularly the presence of the anthropomorphic figurines in typical Paredones "folk" style. The second piece from the left is 9.9 cm high (Boyrie Moya 1952:186, Plate 4). (Rouse Archive, ANT.ARC.00121. Courtesy Peabody Museum of Natural History, New Haven, Connecticut)

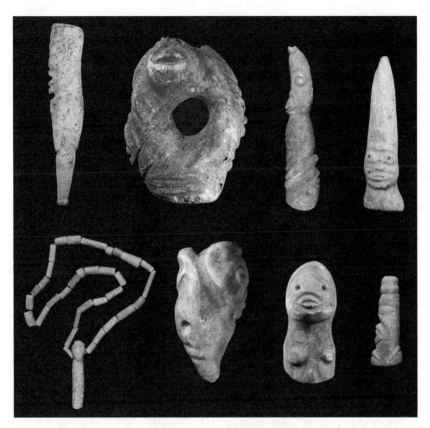

Figure 1.6. Selection of Los Paredones carvings. *Top row, left to right*: anthropomorphic carving, originally displayed as part of a large panel in Boyrie Moya's collection (see Figure 1.7, *left*), Museo del Hombre Dominicano (MHD), H: 38.5 cm; multifaced carving, MHD, H: 31 cm; multifigure carving, Altos de Chavon Museum (AdCh); H: 30.5 cm; conical shaped head, MHD: H: 27.5 cm. *Bottom row, left to right*: necklace, AdCh: L: 46 cm, with pendant: L: 9.8 cm; multihead carving, MHD, H: 23 cm; anthropomorphic carving, AdCh, H; 19 cm; head carving, AdCh: H: 12 cm. All artifacts are unaccessioned. (Courtesy Museo del Hombre Dominicano [MHD] and Altos de Chavon Museum [AdCh], Dominican Republic; photos: Joanna Ostapkowicz)

1952:183; see also B. Fernández 1969:209). The carvings were described as "primitive" and crude, featuring multiple anthropomorphic figures carved on the cylindrical surfaces of the speleothems with a flattened base to hold them upright (Boyrie Moya 1952:182–183) (Figures 1.5 and 1.6). Boyrie Moya (1952:183) suggested that all the carvings had a ceremonial, symbolic, or ornamental purpose and presented his initial interpretations at the 1952 Congreso Histórico Municipal Interamericano. While most attendees, including such luminaries as René Herrera Fritot (the Cuban archaeologist who had excavated the neighboring La Caleta site in 1945 and had written one of the first exposés on forgeries in 1942—see Valcárcel Rojas et al., chapter 7 herein), kept their opinions about this "new culture" to themselves—or at least out of print (Mañón Arredondo 1969:148),[3] Professor Alfonso Ortega Martínez opined that the stylistic aspects of the carvings suggested the work of "escaped African slaves" (i.e., historic, rather than ancient, artworks) (Pérez Guerra 1999:238). Boyrie Moya's 1952 paper was published in the proceedings of the congress—the first academic investigation of the Paredones carvings, and a milestone on many levels, serving to bring the phenomenon to wider scholarly and public attention.

Subsequent excavations in 1956 and 1963 revealed an ever-increasing trove of large-scale "finds," some nearly a meter in height, in forms that some called "strange" (Narganes 2016; Vega 2015:50), while others praised them for their "formidable expression, astonishing in its modernity and vital force" (Veloz Maggiolo 1968b:78). By the 1960s, a proliferation of Paredones sculptures was on the market, circulating widely among collectors—estimates ranged from a conservative 4,000 carvings (Morban Laucer 1968:4) to well over 25,000 (Ugarte 1969a:111). The scale was extraordinary (Ugarte 1969b:163), and the media with growing alarm blamed the "mining" of these "archaeological" pieces on national institutions that clearly had failed in their responsibility to conserve national patrimony (Priego 1967:50). But in an ironic twist, it turns out that in this instance the collector's initiatives were entwined with the push to safeguard this particular national heritage: Boyrie Moya, who himself acquired a large personal collection of Paredones materials (see Ostapkowicz and Colten, chapter 8 herein and Figure 8.2), noted that one of the main incentives of involving collectors in the acquisition of "looted" Paredones sculptures was "above all to prevent archaeological material from stopping in the hands of 'tourists' and leaving the country fraudulently. [As] a lesser evil, when IDIA [Instituto Dominicano Investigaciones Antropológica] and the Museum lacked official funding to be able to acquire [the carvings]—they allowed and even recommended their acquisition by national collectors of recognized commitment to the protection of our cultural heritage" (Boyrie Moya MS, II:5–6; see also García Arévalo 1968:66). Several major collectors were thus encouraged to acquire Paredones carvings, which were held "in trust," with some inventoried and open to study (Boyrie Moya MS, II:6).

But these efforts did not stop pieces being exported out of the country. Paredones carvings appeared in New York galleries, with interested buyers contacting museums to authenticate potential purchases; experts such as Junius Bird and Irving Rouse advised.[4] Indeed, Rouse and his colleague José M. Cruxent flew to Santo Domingo in 1967 to assess the situation, to take samples for radiocarbon dates from the purported sites, and to define what some were already calling the "sensational appearance of an unprecedented Caribbean culture" (Veloz Maggiolo 1968b:78; see Ostapkowicz and Colten, chapter 8 herein). Their reluctance to be drawn into the subject without due investigation caused some consternation amid the growing excitement, suggesting that their lack of opinion aimed "fundamentally to hinder a new vision of Caribbean cultures" (Veloz Maggiolo 1968b:78). Several prominent Dominican archaeologists had no such hesitations, particularly given the precedent set 16 years earlier by Boyrie Moya's publication on the site, and his anticipated work with Rouse and Cruxent on the subject (see Ostapkowicz and Colten, chapter 8 herein): in 1968, Fernando Morban Laucer's *Los Paredones: Un Santuario Prehistorico* and Veloz Maggiolo's (1968a) *Interpretación Socio-Cultural del Arte de Los Paredones (La Caleta)*, were published by the Universidad Autonóma de Santo Domingo. Morban Laucer cautiously noted that despite the passage of nearly two decades since the first excavations, "little has been achieved [to clarify Paredones] . . . while the looting has been progressive and devastating." He further noted that the "symbolism is something as little deciphered as the culture itself." Veloz Maggiolo (1968b), however, argued for these sculptures to be the work of sedentary pre-Taíno fisher/hunters, based on the absence of ceramics and a single radiocarbon date of 1680 ± 100 BP (cal AD 127–581, 95.4%; Y-1850, Yale Radiocarbon Lab) obtained from a hearth in an occupation layer in one of the Paredones caves.[5] Veloz Maggiolo (1968b:78–85) considered the "Paredones Cultural complex" to have overtones of totemism, given the frequent depiction of animals and "transformative" iconography, as well as a focus on fecundity.

But there was a growing unease: in 1966, large quantities of Paredones carvings were emerging daily, some even featuring Greek- and Egyptian-inspired designs, others depicting unusual iconography, from "Indians in military-style caps" to children in diapers (Ugarte 1969c:101, 102). In December 1968, just after Francisco Henriquez Vazquez, Morban Laucer, and Veloz Maggiolo published interpretations of the possible significance of this "new" archaeological culture, the country's newspapers broke the story that the pieces were forgeries made by the locals of La Caleta (Narganes 2016; Severino 1968b:85–89; Vega 2015:55; for thorough overview of the media coverage see Pérez Guerra 1999). Luis Chanlatte Baik, who helped to expose this industry, famously called Los Paredones an "archaeological myth" in the escalating media coverage; the scandal came to be known as "the most spectacular fraud in the history of the country" (Severino 1968a:92–93; 1969b:139), a "Frankenstein" creation (Mañón Arredondo 1969:145). Chanlatte claimed to have traced the first examples back to 1946 (Severino 1968b:87), indicating an unexpected time depth to the industry, preceding even the first excavations of

1950, something also hinted at by Boyrie Moya (1952:181), where he noted the first carvings brought to the National Museum by the La Caleta residents in 1948 were so unusual they were initially considered forgeries. Chanlatte had interviewed the local artists who, due to economic hardship, admitted to turning to the creation of forgeries—though, in their eyes, they viewed their creations as "an authentic Dominican folk art" (Severino 1968b:85). He identified the carvers who were involved (including the mastermind behind the endeavor, Benyí, one of the original "diggers" in the 1950 excavations) and listed the telltale signs of a forger's art—from a lack of patina to clear metal tool marks on the sculptures' surfaces and a mud coating meant to obscure these (Severino 1968a:94). According to Chanlatte, "an experienced archaeologist could not fall for this innocent fraud" (Severino 1968a:94)—though a fair few did, including his colleague and mentor Boyrie Moya, director of the Instituto de Investigaciones Arqueologicas, with whom Chanlatte worked in Los Paredones from the 1950s. Perhaps out of respect for his work, the issue of forgeries emerged publicly only after Boyrie Moya's death in 1967, some two decades after the first questions were raised about the unusual carvings.

Such public exposure, which essentially challenged the authority of the Instituto (Ugarte 1969c:103), not to mention the judgment of wealthy collectors, whose purchases contributed to the escalation of the practice, was quick to elicit reaction, descending into something akin to a telenovela in the media. It was to grip national imagination—and newspaper columns—for several months, and the exchanges grew increasingly heated and emotive (and debates still continue—e.g., Vega 2015). Experts emerged to claim the pieces were real, for "reasons of pure logic," and to urge the government and learned societies to mount a defense of "what is as ours as the air we breathe" (Joaquín Priego in Ugarte 1969c:103–104). The prominent collector García Arévalo found it "absurd that people with archaeological awareness dare to make definitive judgements about the Paredones complex without relying on laboratory analysis and taking as dogma the statements of peasants and craftsmen to shield their theory" (in Severino and Ugarte 1969:123)—a clear questioning of Chanlatte's faith in his informants. Indeed, collectors were particularly vocal about what they felt was a clear attack on their investments, not to mention their discerning "eye" (see also Alvarez et al., chapter 2 in this volume). Some thought that "a collector can distinguish at first sight an authentic piece from a false one," and that there was "no doubt about the authenticity of a great number of pieces recovered from the caves since 1950"; indeed, despite the overwhelming counterevidence, they concluded that 100% of the pieces appearing between 1950 and 1967 were authentic, and forgeries started only after this point (see A. Fernández 1969a:157; Ugarte 1969b:164; see Walsh 2005:17 for a critique of the connoisseur's "eye").

Even the carvers—some of whom informed on the practice—complained of Chanlatte's exposé: Benyí, particularly, argued that the public denouncement discouraged collectors to "continue investing large amounts in the acquisition of pieces that Chanlatte, as an expert, was called to judge" (Ugarte and Severino 1969:128). Indeed, in the wake of the press release, several artists tried to assure the media that the Los Paredones carvings were authentic, and that many would continue to be found (Ugarte 1969d:96). The carvers expressed concerns that the collectors would ask for their money back (and one prominent collector had apparently requested this—Ugarte 1969b:164; see also A. Fernández 1969a:160), and that they would face legal charges for selling new pieces as antiquities. The situation was delicate; both archaeologists and collectors paid the carvers' bills—and the artists clearly did not want to lose their trade with either. Boyrie Moya paid two pesos for the first Los Paredones piece, purportedly found in a cave in 1948 by a campesino named Robles (Ugarte 1969d:97): two pesos was a fair amount of money at that time, and with such incentive the man had hopes of finding more— unsurprisingly, he (and others) did (Ugarte 1969d:97). Many other campesinos were in Boyrie Moya's employ during the cave excavations (and likely had been in Herrera Fritot's employ in 1945, when the neighboring site of La Caleta was being excavated; in fact, Benyí remained an unofficial guard of the site in his later years—Pérez Guerra 1999:17). According to Benyí, it was easier "to look for pieces than to make them" (Ugarte 1969d:98). Herein lies the ethical quandary central to the Paredones scandal: looting a site was considered less straining than creating forgeries, though both occurred to fulfill the needs of various parties. Further, pieces either made or acquired were openly sold in tourist shops—if real, this illicit trade in antiquities breached several heritage laws; if false, it completely muddled understanding of Dominican prehistory. No one stood to profit and, ultimately, it was the damage to the cave sites (where prehistoric charcoal had apparently been recovered) that hindered a concrete assessment on the presence of a genuine "Los Paredones" material culture (Morban Laucer in Ugarte 1969c:102).

Despite this backlash from various sectors, Chanlatte stood his ground. In an interview for *El Caribe*, he noted that "those who have invested thousands of pesos in the acquisition of these pieces will not surrender without a fight, and some, the most stubborn, will resort to any type of defense as long as the value of their collections is kept high" (Severino 1969a:114). Collectors, he noted, "pay a few pesos to locals to search for pieces by digging arbitrarily in the aboriginal settlements and cemeteries, thus destroying the stratigraphies and all the scientific information that these regions contain . . . and causing irreparable damage to scientific investigations" (Severino 1969a:114). In addition to encouraging the looting of sites for prized pieces, collectors made "declarations that create[d] a confusing and very dangerous situation for . . . the field of archaeology" (Severino 1969a:115)—notably, classifying the Paredones material as genuine, according to their "eye," and so distorting understanding of the past. It was a public challenge on tenuous grounds: who knew more about the prehistory of the region—collectors, who handled artifacts acquired via looters, or archaeologists, who—as the Paredones scandal later exposed—could be equally misled into believing they were excavating undisturbed contexts? Morban Laucer, the author of *Los Paredones: Un Santuario Prehistorico*, entered the media fray, admitting that he was initially deceived, but that to remain silent in "the maelstrom [that] seems to want to drag me down with its fury" was ethically impossible (Severino and Ugarte 1969:121). Based on his own subsequent review of the Paredones material, he concurred with Chanlatte that these were forgeries carved with metal tools.[6] Given Morban Laucer's history with the Paredones material, it was perhaps not surprising that he laid the blame squarely at the feet of the forgers: "I find it reprehensible the attitude assumed by those who are dedicated to selling the pieces as 'legitimate' . . . [it is] a deception" (Severino and Ugarte 1969:122). In future years, Morban Laucer was to become one of the most vocal critics of the forgery industry in the Dominican Republic, with very little sympathy for the campesino turned forger, no matter how desperate their economic circumstances (Morban Laucer 1989).

The claims and counterclaims escalated under media scrutiny, and a clearer picture only began to emerge after the National Commission for Development ordered a study of the situation in late January 1969 (roughly a month after the newspapers broke the story) and reassured the campesinos that they would not be legally prosecuted. The La Caleta community was assured that the pieces were now of "great value" because they represented the first appearance of a popular art form: "the important thing is that a Dominican folk art has been born for the first time. It is necessary to protect and sponsor it, not to persecute" (Ugarte 1969b:163). Further, the government was willing to concede a dedicated space at the airport terminal for artists to sell their pieces to tourists (A. Fernández 1969a:160). Also mentioned was the possibility of an exhibition of the Paredones pieces, which would "credit the true authors—the contemporary artisans who dedicated themselves to these labors" (A. Fernández 1969a:163).

With these reassurances, Benyí finally opened up, disclosing that his involvement with the deception started back in 1946, when he had started carving neo-artifacts—what he called "muñecos" ("dolls") (Anonymous 1969:218; A. Fernández 1969b:167–174). He confessed that he was responsible for a material culture that, for more than two decades, "impersonated [the] indigenous"[7] (Ugarte 1969f:171), and that the reasons for this were purely economic. "I had to continue living and feeding my 10 children and, as I did not want to steal, I had the idea of carving pieces with the stone from the caves. Since nobody helped me, I had to help myself" (Ugarte 1969f:171). Benyí also admitted he had "brought Boyrie Moya the first objects, and that for some time he worked without anyone noticing" (Ugarte 1969f:171)—one of the earliest pieces was an anthropomorphic stalagmite carving, for which Boyrie Moya paid him 10 pesos (Rodríguez Velez 1982:250–251).[8] From this point forward he started making amulets, necklaces, spatulas, and other carvings— essentially everything except ceramics (Rodríguez Velez 1982:251). Once the media furor died down, and particularly in light of the government's promised support, Benyí revealed some aspirations, including the expectation that he would soon be named professor of sculptural arts (Anonymous 1969:220); he envisioned a massive production of "authentic" Benyí pieces for the national interior design market; the scale necessitated convening an international conference to regulate the trade of the artworks, establishing a quota system similar to the nation's key exports of sugar, coffee, and tin (Anonymous 1969:221). It would appear that the media—like the government—had swung in favor of the carvers. As one reporter noted (A. Fernández 1969b:169): "it is true what Benyí says, the pieces are now more beautiful [than the] indigenous art, and above all, the manufacture of these pieces provides sustenance to more or less 1,600 poor Dominican people. Long live the Taínos!" Indeed, it was a matter of pride for Benyí that his workforce spanned much of the local community: "from here [La Caleta] to Guayacanes, almost everyone lives from the fruit of my idea" (Rodríguez Velez 1982:249).

But this positive spin about the birth of a national folk art lost some of its momentum when the true scale of the deception emerged in the 1980s, when Benyí finally confirmed the rumors that neo-artifacts were not just *sold* to archaeologists—they were *planted* for them to find (Moanack 1980:245–246; Rodríguez Velez 1982:252). Critically, these were not simply shoveled in from the surface but involved a much more elaborate intervention to keep the overlaying stratigraphy intact. The "artifacts" were introduced via tunnels by a man crawling in to place them at specific points below the surface; once finished, the hole was covered over with earth and packed down to give the appearance of an undisturbed area. In Benyí's own words, it was dangerous work: "It was a risk, of life or death, because the terrain could yield and crush me [in the tunnel], but it was [done] to avoid the embarrassment that would happen if they discovered [my work]." With the upper surface intact, "nobody knew that, underneath, you had worked the land; naturally they chose [undisturbed areas] and when digging . . . found the pieces" (Moanack 1980:246). Further, prior to being buried, the pieces underwent an "antiquing" process that involved a concoction of cave soil, mud, and about 20% lime, which was then heated to convincingly coat the neo-artifact and then worked over by hand to create a patina (Rodríguez Velez 1982:253). In all, it was a complex enterprise that emerged out of a clear understanding of how archaeologists worked and what they looked for (cf. Santos 1983:258; Ugarte 1969:207)—it catered, in a very sophisticated way, to these "clients." Excavations were, in many ways, the forgers' training grounds: "They worked . . . on Taíno cemeteries, they became familiar with the archaeological vocabulary [i.e., ancient styles], they learned the value of the objects found in the ground and they understood the high regard that some people had for relics of extinct cultures. [They were therefore] not alien to archaeological investigations . . . and cunning as they are and harassed by the needs of daily sustenance, they knew how to make use of the knowledge acquired" (Ugarte 1969e:207).

This history of duplicity made for an uncertain future for the new "folk art": "The fact that a gigantic deceit has given rise to a collective art of extraordinary quality is an unprecedented phenomenon in the history of archaeological fraud" (Ugarte 1969e:206), and it is "impossible to predict the course this will take, but even if the carvers take other courses in their lives, their valuable, abundant and beautiful work will remain as the testimony of a strange art born spontaneously in hiding" (Ugarte 1969e:209). Some thought that their "value will increase with the passing of the time, as much or more perhaps than if they were pieces made by a disappeared race" (Ugarte 1969e: 209). Benyí claimed that the forged pieces were so "beautiful" that no one wanted the authentic indigenous pieces anymore (in Ugarte 1969b:163), and that "when I die, [my pieces] will have the same value as Indian [pieces] today" (in Moanack 1980:247). In fact, the predictions of a lauded new art form quickly disappeared, just as the pieces themselves disappeared from view: the material was packed in storage boxes, and shut in storage facilities, or simply discarded. Today, the Museo del Hombre Dominicano has Boyrie Moya's massive display panels featuring hundreds of artistically arranged Paredones pieces, many now damaged, some loosely thrown in cardboard boxes with countless others (Figure 1.7). But the ramifications of Paredones went beyond the emptying of collectors' cabinets: there was a much wider disquiet that had a direct effect on the cultural sector. One contemporary Dominican artist, ceramicist Thimo Pimentel, whose work is heavily inspired by indigenous iconography, points to it as a watershed moment: "after Paredones I disconnected from indigenous themes. I disconnected because I was disappointed with the [falsifications]. From then on, I never wanted to know more about archaeology" (Pimentel in Ulloa Hung 2018:88). It would be well over a decade before Pimentel returned to the subject matter again (Ulloa Hung 2018a:88).

The Paredones scandal shook the archaeology community to its foundations, brought public awareness not only of ancient, but contemporary, artistic movements, and had a ripple effect across the island nation and beyond. The whole affair was entangled with the histories of prominent Dominican

Figure 1.7. *Left*: small section of Boyrie Moya's Los Paredones displays. (Courtesy Peabody Museum of Natural History, New Haven, Connecticut.) *Center and right*: Boyrie Moya's collection in storage at the Museo del Hombre Dominicano. The panel in the image on the lower right can be seen displayed on the lower middle shelf on the archival photo on the left. (Courtesy Museo del Hombre Dominicano; photo: Joanna Ostapkowicz)

families and their legacies as well as exposed prejudices of both class and race and undercurrents of academic in-fighting with serious ramifications for the field. That artifacts were planted within an archaeological site, and excavated under the direction of professional archaeologists who believed them authentic, called into question the entire discipline as a science—but then no one had anticipated such deception. Between 1946 and 1968, a new art form did indeed emerge (Vega 2015), specifically inspired by people's perceptions of what archaeologists were interested in, and what collectors desired. Further, it aligned to what this market wanted most: an artifact with good provenience to a known site. It was an audacious, highly entrepreneurial venture, and a scandal that remains a sore point in Dominican archaeology. Even after such public exposure, the La Caleta artists "refined" their work and went on to produce a "New" Paredones style that was sold well into the 1970s to tourists; indeed, it is offered today at the roadside stands in the vicinity of the airport (not, as promised by the government, within the airport itself). There is little information about this explosive history at these roadside stands, and one could drive past without realizing the impact of these carvings on the national consciousness of the late 1960s. As Rodríguez Velez (1982:249) writes, "the carved figurines . . . now look at us from the side of the road, gleaming in the sun and stripped of all mystery, and seem to remind us, amused, that once they played a prank on us."

FORGERIES OF THE 1960s–1970s:
"THE PHANTOM IN OUR DARK NIGHT"[9]

Fernando Morban Laucer, one of the few Dominican scholars who has written on the issue of forgeries post-Paredones, placed the start of the commercial boom, unsurprisingly, in the late 1960s—though there were hints, at least on neighboring islands, of a much earlier start to the enterprise (Herrera Fritot 1942; Rouse 1942:44—see Valcárcel Rojas et al., chapter 7 herein). Writing in 1968, García Arévalo (1968:66; emphasis added) noted that counterfeiters "have, in recent years, perfected their skills, [such] that the escalating scale has infected the great majority of private collections with *errors and contradictions.*" He cites a few specific examples in the Dominican Republic, including a resident of Yaque whose pieces (small figurines, carved of a compact, black stone with steel tools) have infiltrated the "best" collections in Santiago, and Macao Beach residents who were dedicated to repairing old ceramics and building new ones, mixing the original temper with cement, white sand, and clay dust (García Arévalo 1968:66). He further notes that in Guayacanes, Juan Dolio, Rubio, Las Cabuyas, Higuito, La Magdalena, Cucama, and Jube there are specialist forgers who have perfected their skills to such a degree that they can imitate the most varied forms of the best known originals, enhancing the designs to make them more "showy." They are skilled in most media, including shell, bone, and ceramics; the ceramics they cover with dirt to hide traces of their work (García Arévalo 1968:67; Severino 1968a:95). García Arévalo was not the only collector uneasy with this traffic; others were calling for a commission to draw guidelines to define what is authentic versus false, to "purify existing collections" (Pimentel in Ugarte 1968:113).

What led to this increase in forgeries? The 1965 Dominican civil war had many consequences, including inspiring a nationalism that increased interest in the prehistory of the island, which resulted in numerous publications, exhibitions, and conferences. The focus brought greater exposure to archaeological research and interest, in which some saw profitable possibilities. A more sophisticated approach to the forger's craft emerged, including, as Morban Laucer (1989:56) noted, "many tricks used by these criminals in their excessive desire for profit and unhealthy purpose to defraud the unwary." Difficult-to-work stones were specifically chosen to both impress and command high prices; drills and polishers were used to work the material, which was then finished by hand to erase modern tool marks. A variety of techniques were employed to achieve a patina and color, including fire, metallic pigments, and vegetable dyes such as the use of coconut shell boiled with sour lemon; lead acids from old car batteries were used to treat fresh woods to give them an antique appearance (Morban Laucer 1989:56–57). Pieces were also buried in precolumbian sites, as was clear from the Los Paredones fiasco, and specific areas were known as hot spots for the production of counterfeit artifacts, including La Caleta and San Pedro de Macorís. Together with the increased looting of archaeological sites to feed market demand, this situation created an unprecedented level of destruction and subterfuge. Morban Laucer (1986:57–58) did not mince his words when he concluded that "criminals invade with impunity private collections and institutions dedicated to science with counterfeit works. . . . The campesino has become a looter and destroyer of archaeological objects, stimulated by the high prices paid by native and foreign traffickers, who have moved like an international mafia with impunity in this illicit business, despite [the existence of] legal instruments that punish these infractions. Large and valuable pre-Columbian cemeteries have been destroyed, most of the time in front of the indifference or complicity of the authorities in charge of watching over the application of the law."

1980s: MUSEUM COLLECTIONS OF "NOT OBVIOUS FAKES"

By the 1980s, the art market and even museums were beginning to acknowledge a problem; several turned to the doyen of Caribbean archaeology at the time, Irving Rouse, to pass judgment on the authenticity of suspect pieces (see Ostapkowicz and Colten, chapter 8 herein). In 1981, an opinion was sought on a droopy-eyed, ungainly, and unusually weathered *duho*.[10] In 1984, a museum inquired about a complete Boca Chica–style water vessel in its collections, which Rouse suspected was a cobbled together reconstruction of various fragments from authentic vessels, something he noted was not uncommon. His response mentioned "a thriving industry in fakes in the Dominican Republic at the present time; vendors hawk them from roadside stands on the highway between Santo Domingo and its airport."[11] Two years later, a letter from a prominent auction house spelled out their uncertainty over two consigned pieces, noting that there were numerous forgeries circulating on the East Coast since recent Taíno exhibits, and asking his opinion.[12] Rouse had seen the collection before—the owner had sought out his opinion as well—and noted in his response that these were "part of a collection of about a dozen specimens, most of which were obviously forgeries." He concluded that the two pieces in question were "most likely to be authentic but I cannot be sure about them. All I can say is that they are not obvious fakes."[13] Setting aside the ethical issues of advising on precolumbian material assigned to an auction house for onward sale (which at the time would not have raised the ethical questions that it does now), Rouse's comments essentially underscored the growing concern: forgeries were getting sophisticated, and collectors were acquiring pieces by the dozens, and these eventually would enter museum collections as a single lot. One example is a large collection exhib-

ited at the Museo Chileno de Arte Precolombino, complete with a glossy catalog (Torres 1991)—two means to turn a dubious collection "authentic" in the
eyes of the public.

In the late 1980s, a brief mention in the journal *African Arts* noted Taíno
forgeries being made in Cape Haitian, Haiti: "A couple of young men, 28–
30, are producing works which were originally copied from photographs, and
now, having lost the photos, are producing 'Taíno style' images from memory.
These works are of a high standard, and although clearly unauthentic to an
expert, are convincing to the rare visitors. The forgers, or copiers as they call
themselves, sell these works through the guides at the hotels. There is a clear
intention to deceive the visitor by saying 'they were dug up by farmers out
of town.' . . . The interesting point here is that African-descent carvers are
producing Taíno Indian style works—is this forgery, copying or tourist art?"
(Dick-Read 1988).

1990s BOOM: QUINCENTENARY EXHIBITIONS
AND THE INCREASING SOPHISTICATION
OF FEIGNING AUTHENTICITY

It was the 1990s that marked a seismic shift in the trajectory of Taíno forgeries. The Columbian quincentenary, with its blockbuster Taíno exhibits
in Paris (Kerchache 1994) and New York (Brecht et al. 1997) brought the
Caribbean—as the historic gateway to the New World—into the national
narratives in full force. No exhibit of precolumbian art and archaeology was
now complete without a token Taíno piece, at the very least a stone collar or
trigolith (three-pointer cemí). Museums were scrambling for pieces to display and willing to accommodate pieces of less than scrupulous backgrounds,
or overlook the occasional stylistic oddity. Given that the study of Taíno iconography was (and still is) only emerging, the field was wide open and could
easily encompass the variety of material in circulation at the time. The acquisition sequence for the most part followed a simple formula: collectors were
largely guided by commercial art galleries, which made it their business to
secure quintessential examples of "Taíno" art. These pieces would sell for undisclosed sums and disappear into private hands until they reemerged behind
the glass vitrines of museums, uncritically propelled into the rarefied world
of curated examples of a vanished art for the paying public. But this was far
from a vanishing art—it was a deception growing in sophistication and complexity. It would seem that few museums were immune, from illustrious art
museums such as the Quai Branly (Delpuech 2016:47) to important university
research institutions, such as the Peabody Museum of Natural History (see
Ostapkowicz and Colten, chapter 8 in this volume)—yet these are the institutions that safeguard authenticity in the public's eye. Whatever is displayed

or featured in their glossy catalogs must have been vetted and therefore must be genuine. Once a piece passed into this realm, its position seemed assured.

Since the 1990s, it would appear that the floodgates had opened, and the range of neo-artifacts began to expand in new, entrepreneurial ways, made in a wide variety of styles, including borrowings from Oceanic and African arts—anything to cater to perceptions of what non-Western/tribal art should be. Western aesthetics and perceptions of the "primitive" guided the art (e.g., Pasztory 2002, and see Geurds, chapter 9 herein). There are faithful—or at least close—copies of well-known pieces, such as the composite, anthropo-morphic snuff tube in the García Arévalo collection (e.g., Kerchache 1994:82–83). If imitation is the sincerest form of flattery, then this piece, recovered from the heavily looted site of La Cucama, Dominican Republic (Ortega 2005), has inspired many reinterpretations—a quick search on the internet has found at least a dozen examples of varying skill in museums, private collections, and online sales. This little industry of reproductions, which people presum-ably purchase as "genuine" pieces, appears largely unaffected by the Inter-national Council of Museums' (ICOM) red list for Dominican patrimony (ICOM 2013:Figure 12), which specifically uses the García Arévalo snuff tube as an example of ceremonial artifacts at risk of illicit trafficking.

Many artifacts featured in the Paris and New York museum catalogs (Brecht et al. 1997; Kerchache 1994) have been replicated—faithfully, unfaithfully, and now with a growing confidence in combining stylistic elements from vari-ous artifacts to create new styles. Indeed, the hands of individual artists can easily be detected across a spectrum of different materials and artifact types. One particularly prolific artist is heavy handed on two-dimensional art, fill-ing almost every nook and cranny with spiral and triangle designs; droopy eyes featured in numerous neo-artifacts speak of the oeuvre of another art-ist; another uses stones featuring marbling and natural cracks to mimic the appearance of age (Figure 1.8). Concerningly, even human remains are be-ing reworked into saleable curiosities—such as a cranium in a Haitian col-lection, engraved with what has been interpreted as a lizard, the whole likely inspired by the art of Rapa Nui's (Easter Island) *moai kava kava* wood carv-ings, which feature very similar skull decorations. Parallels have long been drawn between Rapa Nui carvings and the skeletal art of the Taíno (see, for example, Kerchache 1994:155), and hence this would have been an easy con-nection for an entrepreneurial artist. This implies that the cranium—which may be quite recent in date—was dug up, carved, and then sold, potentially as a commissioned piece, to collectors.

While many of these pieces can easily be dismissed on stylistic and ma-terial qualities alone, there is a growing number of increasingly sophisticated forgeries, specifically aimed at giving the illusion of uniqueness and ancient

Figure 1.8. Collection of recent forgeries in the backroom storage of the Museo del Hombre Dominicano. The stylistic overlap across the group suggests that they were made by the same artist or "school," and all are carved of marbled, cracked limestone used to enhance the "aged" look. The anthropomorphic carving at the back measures 49 cm in height. (Courtesy Museo del Hombre Dominicano, Santo Domingo; photo: Joanna Ostapkowicz)

patina that continues to convince "connoisseurs" and museums alike. This is a direct result of the forces driving the antiquities market. The short phase in the mid-1990s (after Kerchache's 1994 *l'Art Taïno* exhibit), which saw a rise in forgeries that attempted to create exact copies of "old" collection pieces, is over; it seems demand is now for the unusual, and the forgers working over the last two decades have honed their skills in the various art styles and can cater to market demands. Indeed, so convincing are some of the forgeries that they are sometimes mistaken by border control authorities as the genuine article and repatriated back to the source island, as was the case recently of 67 pieces being returned by US Customs Enforcement to the Dominican Republic (Latin American Herald Tribune 2008; see also Alvarez et al., chapter 2 herein). Of course, if there is any doubt, it is best to err on the side of caution, as dealers sometimes include a few genuine pieces in a shipment, in the hopes that they will slip through in a shipment of "replicas"; distinguishing between the genuine and the forged in such situations is becoming increasingly difficult. But if a carving manages to infiltrate the United States or Europe and enter a commercial gallery, a whole barrage of studies and expert opinions geared to convince the buyer of the genuineness of the piece comes into play. It is not unusual now for galleries to attempt to turn "science" to their advantage: wood carvings, particularly pieces that would demand premium prices, such as pseudo-cohoba stands and duhos, undergo radiocarbon dating, though critical aspects such as sample location and chain of sample custody often remain unclear, and even results as recent as the mid-nineteenth century are used confidently to support the "authenticity" of an artifact.

More concerningly, forgers have been known to reuse old architectural wood, which can provide a date far more in keeping with the desired time range than modern woods. It is not possible to date stone carvings, but it is not uncommon to see "official" certificates purporting that the item in question is authentic based on a variety of vague judgments on patina and manufacture. So long as it does not appear to be made with modern tools it is deemed authentic, which ignores the well-known forger's trick of initially working the material with modern tools, then finishing with stone tools by hammering, pecking, and abrading to give the appearance of an ancient artifact. Other aging techniques—such as burying a stone carving for months in moist acid soil saturated with urine and dung or burying it in shallow limey earth and then building a fire over it—have been documented among Mexican forgers since at least the 1950s (Kelker and Bruhns 2010), and similar techniques are being used among forgers in the Caribbean (see Hanna, chapter 5 herein). Remarkably, even if modern tool marks survive this treatment, they are explained away as a result of recent cleaning of the artifact with a brush—as was the case for a trigolith, which in 2010 was offered at auction for a mere €30–40,000 starting price.

This illustrates the growing business in authenticating fresh goods to the market—that is, the more scientific the techniques used, in spite of their results, the seemingly more authentic these pieces become. If this convinces buyers, it may well convince museums, and a couple of exhibits and catalogs later, this is an established piece with a well-documented history and provenance, which gets used in art history and anthropology courses as a fine example of "prehistoric" art.

INSPIRATION: TAÍNO ARTISTIC ROOTS

While the 1940s saw a rise in forgeries, it also marked the start of "neo-Taíno art"—an art form taking inspiration from the past, but with a trajectory firmly set on the future. Critically, there was no intention to deceive, just an interest in incorporating indigenous aesthetics into the industrial arts and contemporary nationalistic endeavors. In Puerto Rico, Adolfo de Hostos (1939) published a volume titled *Industrial Applications of Indian Decorative Motifs in Puerto Rico*, which set out two-dimensional prehistoric designs for use in modern ceramics, textile industries, wood carving, and architectural features. The premise was straightforward: nothing was more Puerto Rican than the indigenous arts, influenced entirely by the local environment and spurred by the innate creative abilities of the island's first inhabitants, uninfluenced by colonial baggage. The subtext of this, of course, denies the strong influences of African heritage in particular with preference given to indigenous cultures long thought extinct and so conveniently idolized. Several initiatives followed in the subsequent years, in the Dominican Republic and in Puerto Rico, but it wasn't until the work of Yugoslavian artist Ivan Gundrum that the impetus was taken in a new, entirely innovative direction. Gundrum had worked in Havana's Guarná Institute in the early 1950s, reproducing and restoring Taíno artifacts; he had an intimate knowledge of the basic art forms and was hired by Emile de Boyrie Moya to come to the Dominican Republic and design for the newly established Cooperativa de Industrias Artesanales (COINDARTE) (Grupo Guamá 1944; Herrera Fritot 1946; Vega 1987). His templates would be turned into carvings in wood, bone, stone, amber, and gold by cooperative artists, but Gundrum himself was best known for his ceramic masterworks, clearly inspired by the past but reinterpreted for the modern age, in creations entirely unique to the artist (Figure 1.9; see also Valcárcel Rojas et al., chapter 7 in this volume).

Figure 1.9. Selection of Ivan Gundrum Ferich's artwork displayed at the Museo Etnologico del Grupo Guamá, Lyceum, Havana, in 1946 (Herrera Fritot 1946).

Fast forward to today, and, in García Arévalo's (1987:13) words, "the pre-Hispanic archaeological heritage constitutes an inexhaustible source of inspiration, interpretation and expression for contemporary artists" (see also García Arévalo 1988:36; Vega 1987). While tourist shops are filled with mass-produced ceramic souvenirs of Taíno figures and bowls as well as large-scale, hand-crafted replicas of high-profile museum pieces (Figure 1.10), artists such as Daniel "Guayacan" Silva are creating exceptionally detailed art forms methodically true to precolumbian originals, yet they are also taking their deep knowledge of the art and reinterpreting it via new creations (see Oliver, chapter 3 in this volume). Silva's works are made in efforts to better understand and explore indigenous technical skills—he creates ceramics using traditional techniques, laboriously grinds stone to make ornaments, and fashions gourd containers that are both practical and beautiful; there is never a question that these are anything other than modern reinterpretations by a well-known and respected artisan. Wood carver Saúl "Guatú" Perez Soler's Taíno-inspired designs can be seen in an exceptional reinterpretation of a duho, bringing the human form to the fore (Figure 1.11). Such work—which is based on Gautú's credo that "craftsmanship has to be evolutionary [and] creative" (Premio 2012:12)—has garnered him accolades, including the Innovator in Preserving

Figure 1.10. *Left*: Cohoba stand depicting twinned cemis seated on a duho, originally found in Samana, Dominican Republic. (National Museum of Natural History, Smithsonian A042662-0, on loan to the Museo del Hombre Dominicano, acc. 1981: MHD-A-000221–9-M). *Center*: wood replica, shop in Zona Colonial, Santo Domingo, Dominican Republic. (Photo courtesy Joanna Ostapkowicz). *Right*: ceramic replica, imported from the Dominican Republic, in a shop in Viejo San Juan, Puerto Rico. (Photo courtesy Joanna Ostapkowicz)

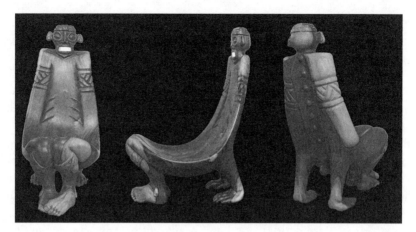

Figure 1.11. Three views of a duho by Puerto Rican artist Saúl Perez Soler. (Courtesy Saúl Perez Soler)

Traditional Arts award (2011) from the Instituto de Cultura Puertorriqueña; he also has his very own vintage-style "cartel," or poster (a historic advertising media in Puerto Rico), which includes the slogan "indigenous carvings, industrial development company." While Silva reconstructs indigenous artistic traditions and Soler puts a modern spin on iconic designs, others, such as Jaime Suárez, incorporate indigenous art forms as a springboard for completely novel designs, which have become icons of modern Puerto Rican art. *Totem Telurico* (Figure 1.12), commissioned as part of the 1992 quincentenary celebrations, and positioned in Viejo San Juan's Quincentennial Plaza, is, according to the artist, less a monument to the 1492 encounter and more a "monument to the land, which keeps in its bowels the story of who we are" (Fullana Acosta 2016). Made of ceramic fragments, including the occasional archaeological example found by workmen as the plaza was being built, it touches directly on Puerto Rico's archaeological past, conceived as a column of earth rising to expose the indigenous world that is buried, visually juxtaposed against the colonial and cultural imposition that the surrounding architecture of the Old City brings (Fullana Acosta 2016). Indeed, working in clay, Suárez broke with the Western tradition that monumental art had to be in bronze and marble—it was a subtle, tactile creation that, like totem poles on the Northwest Coast of North America, is conceived of as a living thing that grows old, its broken sections a testament to a life lived. What these three Puerto Rican artists expose in their work is the relevance and legacy of indigenous arts today to inspire creativity, reflection, and insight. Of course, this is not uniquely a Puerto Rican approach; it parallels the artistic production and aims of many island nations—from the Dominican Republic (e.g.,

Figure 1.12. *Totem Telurico* by Jaime Suárez erected in Viejo San Juan's Quincentennial Plaza to mark the Columbus quincentenary celebrations. (Photo courtesy José R. Oliver)

García Arévalo 2019:320; Ulloa Hung 2018a, 2018b) to Dominica (Waldron 2019:349), and beyond. There are multiple and varied reasons for this incorporation, spanning recognition of indigenous heritage in self-representation (e.g., Guitar et al., 2006:56, Figure 5; see Ulloa Hung and Valcárcel Rojas 2016) to national identity (e.g., Oliver 2005:280, Figure 7.28; Oliver, chapter 3 herein; Rodríguez Ramos and Pagán Jiménez 2016:103, Figure 8). Such broad relevance shows the sheer impact of this iconic imagery that, as Dávila (2001:49) notes, is linked to the "tenacity and resilience of memory, as an active realm in permanent transition, subject to constant reinvention and manipulation . . . indeed the Taíno was never forgotten. The Taíno was always implicated in new myths, uses and practices."

CONCLUSION

What is clear from these varied examples is that indigenous arts are alive and well in the Caribbean. We have seen two sides of this coin. On one side are pieces crafted to mimic the genuine or authentic precolumbian article, specifically and profitably created to deceive. Here the "real" is created on a nuanced knowledge of not only the artform and archaeology but also of the desires of the market—collectors and, through them, ultimately museums. It is an art form entirely entangled with people's interest in the past (both from the perspective of the maker and the consumer), and profitable to those who "pull it off." In the Dominican Republic, people speak of generations of families working in this field, and some take great pride if their artwork makes it into a museum display or catalog. On the other side of the coin are artists who are inspired by the past, but who view their artwork as an entirely contemporary interpretation, reinvented for a new audience, reengaging with select elements of indigenous art or concepts in the service of self—and national—identity. Here, "artifacts" are not the end point in themselves, replicating the illusion of authenticity, but the foundation for diverse reinterpretations of past and present, with implications for the future.

NOTES

1. Current work by Reniel Rodríguez Ramos is looking into untangling the history of the Nazario collection (see Rodríguez Ramos 2019).

2. Morban Laucer (1968:3) has this as 1949.

3. Mañón Arredondo (1969:148) noted that Boyrie Moya's presentation caused some surprise among the congress participants: "All those vistors were surprised by the Paredones pieces, but no kinship or affinity was found with the archaeological cultures of Mesoamerica nor any anthropological interpretation of possible origin. Despite the presence of Herrera Fritot and [José M.] Cruxent, John Goggin and [Herbert H.] Krieger, almost all reserved their opinions and none of them were remarkably interested, before those statuettes or idols with a typology [so] different from the other Antillean archaeological lithics."

4. For example, Rouse to Chanlatte Baik 1969, PMNH Rouse Archives; see Ostapkowicz and Colten, chapter 8.

5. Rouse, who took the radiocarbon sample himself when visiting the Los Paredones excavations in 1967 (Rouse to Boyrie Moya, January 18, 1967, PMNH Rouse Archives), noted in a letter to Bernardo Vega: "This date is much earlier than expected: I had thought that it would be somewhere between 750 and 1500 A.D. This was also your uncle's [Boyrie Moya's] opinion. . . . When a radiocarbon date is contrary to expectation, it must be suspected, because there are so many chances for error" (Rouse to Vega, June 19, 1967, PMNH Rouse Archives; see Ostapkowicz and Colten, chapter 8). Radiometric methods were relatively new techniques at this time, and it is not surprising that Rouse questioned the date; though equally, Rouse had a general mistrust of radiocarbon determinations if they differed from what he expected based on ceramic typologies. This is not the only radiocarbon date from a Paredones cave (see further discussion in Ostapkowicz and Colten, chapter 8).

6. Others also investigated the pieces: in 1963, Caro Alvárez sent one Paredones piece to the Smithsonian for examination and was informed that it was modern based on the fact that it was carved with metal tools (Ugarte 1969f:173). In 1969, at the

height of the controversy, Veloz Maggiolo (1969:175) sent 12 pieces to the Instituto Central de Conservation de Madrid for analysis, though it is unclear what the results were—they do not appear to have been published.

7. "Benyí . . . afirmó que el se hacía responsible, 'pase lo que pase,' de la creacíon de la cultura que durante más de dos décadas se hizo pasar por indígena."

8. This appears to be a different incident from the one mentioned earlier, where a campesino by the name of Robles received two pesos for the "first piece" seen by Boyrie Moya (Ugarte 1969d:97).

9. García Arévalo (1968) wrote of the many issues facing the cultural sector in his *Crisis Arqueologica* article, including the "great problem of forgeries," which he referred to as "otro fantasma más a nuestra oscura noche" (García Arévalo 1968:65).

10. Rouse correspondence, November 18, 1981, Rouse Archives, PMNH.

11. Rouse correspondence, October 22, 1984, Rouse Archives, PMNH.

12. Rouse correspondence, January 24, 1986, Rouse Archives, PMNH.

13. Rouse correspondence, February 6, 1986, Rouse Archives, PMNH.

2

Archaeological Heritage Market and Museums in the Dominican Republic

Arlene Alvarez, Corinne L. Hofman, and Mariana C. Françozo

Cultural heritage in the Caribbean evokes images of tropical landscapes, music, food, and traditions, rarely broaching the way material culture from the Amerindian past is valued or perceived in these tourism-driven countries. Peter Siegel and Elizabeth Righter (2011), in a compendium on the status of heritage protection in the Caribbean, highlighted the major issues for most islands when considering archaeological heritage protection and development. The conservation challenges in the region include legal frameworks that are hardly enforced; poorly conducted archaeological research; and the competing interests of development initiatives, tourism expansion, and heritage protection (Siegel and Righter 2011; Siegel et al. 2013). There is, moreover, a region-wide gap in research that focuses on how Caribbean heritage collections have formed, how they contribute to the formation of cultural products—such as museums and crafts—and how vulnerable they are to the forces of the antiquities market.

For hundreds of years, objects have been amassed with the desire to transmit information though systematic classification (Schulz 1994; Zytaruk 2011). In the formation of royal curiosity cabinets, world exhibition fairs, public and private museums of past centuries, and virtual museums in the twenty-first century, acquisitions and sales of cultural objects have played a role in creating collections that raise cultural awareness. The sale of cultural material is of global importance because of looting and illegal trafficking of cultural goods (Borodkin 1995). The cultural value assigned to portable pieces in collections is what transforms an object into a desired commodity for individuals in the market (Appadurai 1994; Kersel 2012; Pearce 1990, 1994a, 1994b). Collectors' tendencies to gather particular kinds of objects reflect what they think is valuable (Baekeland 1994: 206) and directly affect the commodification of certain antiquities by defining the terms of supply and demand.

Despite having legislatively recognized looting as early as 1903, the Dominican antiquities market is rarely discussed in public forums or the media. This chapter looks at the collecting practices in the Dominican Republic and focuses on the composition of the local antiquities market. It examines how collections have formed and how the legislative framework has allowed the market to operate in the country.[1] As the lack of context continues to dominate the formation of local museums and private collections, the impact on how communities connect with indigenous heritage is also analyzed. Lessons learned are considered to determine how the heritage community can motivate the implementation of feasible public policy as well as internal institutional and ethical private policies to discourage the acquisitions of looted material. The chapter ends with considerations on possible improvements to the way communities access heritage knowledge from collections on public display to those in exclusive private holdings.

LEGAL HERITAGE FRAMEWORK IN THE DOMINICAN REPUBLIC

The island shared now by Haiti and the Dominican Republic is geographically positioned as a key trading point in the Caribbean. European economic interests developed since 1492 include building a large capital, Santo Domingo, to house the first European governmental commercial controls and justice systems in the Americas. After independence from Haiti in 1844, the interest of cultural preservation focused largely on the conservation of colonial architecture, as evidenced in Decree 1134—dated February 3, 1870, the first piece of legislation designed to protect the remains of colonial buildings (Pina 1978; Prieto Vicioso 2011).

For the Dominican Republic, the initial pieces of heritage legislation also reflect an early need to protect Amerindian archaeological sites from being further looted indiscriminately. The legislation effort at the turn of the twentieth century considered that since "archaeological objects existing in Dominican land are national monuments to be preserved for the glory of the Republic . . . and many of the precious remains have left the country to enrich museums abroad" (Decree 4347 of 1903, paragraphs 1–3), people who found archaeological remains needed to be deterred from their search to find and sell objects. Articles 1 and 2 of the Decree 4347 explicitly define what archaeological objects are, where they can be found, and that they are the exclusive property of the Dominican nation—with the exception of private collections formed before the 1903 decree. It required that such private collections be registered officially, but to date, no record has been found listing collections of archaeological objects amassed before the initial legislation. The decree also specifically stipulated that a newly "found" object had to be declared, so that its "custodian" could be recognized for his/her contribution to the formation of the National Museum's collection.

The above dispositions were amended by the Dominican National Congress (Congreso Nacional de la República Dominicana, CNRD) in 1968 with Law 318 (CNRD 1968) regarding the Cultural Heritage of the Nation, prohibiting unauthorized archaeological excavations, and making mandatory the declaration of collections (CNRD, Law 318 of 1968, articles 12–13). The regulations for the Office of Cultural Heritage created the following year went on to stipulate that municipalities had to report "historic objects" (which included archaeological remains) under threat, and highlighted artifact sales as an urgent concern (Regulation No. 4195 of 1969, article 11 [CNRD 1969b]). Furthermore, Law 492, also introduced in 1969, indicated that the state could retain antiquities for the nation through the declaration of public utility and monetary compensation based on a legal appraisal (CNRD, Law 492 of 1969, articles 28–30 [CNRD 1969a]). Law 564 was created in 1973 for the protection and conservation of national ethnographic and archaeological objects. This law defined archaeological materials, reinforced the nation's ownership over current and future finds as well as artifacts in private hands, and imposed sanctions for violations (CNRD, Law 564 of 1973 [CNRD 1973]). It also extended the grace period for the registration of private collections to six months, after which these would be considered "clandestine" and subject to expropriation.

Despite over 30 years since Laws 318 and 564 and regulations 4195 came into effect, there are only a few documents that show sales transactions for archaeological objects and very general declarations of inventories, most made between 1971 and 1979; there are no records of official expropriation of private collections or any fine for violation of the law or lack of compliance with the regulations.

In the Dominican Republic, legislative documents since 1903 have recognized the cultural value in archaeological objects as collective representation for the nation (Pina 1978). "Archaeological relics obtained in the explorations" of archaeological sites, which were declared as monuments in 1913, had been destined for the formation of a national museum (CNRD, Law 5207 of 1913 [CNRD 1913]). In addition, as early as 1913, there was an acknowledgment of archaeological artifacts in private hands, which the state declared its jurisdiction over as part of the nation's heritage (CNRD, Law 520 of 1913 [CNRD 1913])—only later (in 1969) offering compensation (CNRD, Regulation No. 4195 [CNRD 1969b).

The language used in Dominican legislation suggests that a serious situation of archaeological depredation had begun by the nineteenth century. The repeated effort to document what was being found throughout the country, record what collectors were purchasing, forbid excavations to look for archaeological objects (CNRD, Law 318 of 1968, article 12), and to make available to the public objects found, indicates that archaeological objects were not being reported, sites were being looted, and that a sales market had been established.

The creation of laws in the late 1960s and of public and private museums in the early 1970s seems to have served as both a measure for controlling looting and increasing awareness of the historical and cultural value of the collected objects. Law 318 of 1968 was developed to help manage cultural resources and collections through a mandatory inventory, which obliged private collectors to declare their collections, make them available to the public, and declare any sales or purchases (CNRD, Law 318 of 1968 [CNRD 1968]). It also provided national universities and museums with official support for excavations with archaeological research goals as well as to foreign institutions under the authorization of the secretary of education and fine arts. In addition, it listed specific sanctions that included the potential of a minimum six-month prison sentence for violations to what the law specified, such as not declaring collections, illegal trafficking, damaging heritage objects, or excavating for archaeological objects without a permit (Espinal 2017; CNRD, Law 318 of 1968 [CNRD 1968]). Further legislative effort for the protection and conservation of national ethnological and archaeological objects stipulated confiscation, higher fines, and sanctions for undeclared sales, and where falsifications and reproductions of objects with intent to deceive became penalized, with up to a year of prison time (CNRD, Law 564 of 1973 [CNRD 1973])

At present, there are few archival standard systems in use for the heritage sector, with low-skilled staff and little supervision for the heritage departments dealing with archaeological issues. This limits the capacity to research the conditions that brought about the described heritage laws and regulations. With such a limited infrastructure for cultural heritage management, it is hard to understand the levels of threat to indigenous cultural material since colonial times, or the role of different interest groups advocating for the conservation of the cultural heritage of the Dominican Republic. Without good documentation, losses cannot be accounted for or tracked properly.

Law 41-00 of 2000 created what is now the Ministry of Culture and established its constitutional basis by indicating that Congress had the power to legislate "everything that had to do with the conservation of monuments and antiquity objects, and the acquisition of the latter" (CNRD, Law 41-00 of

2000, paragraph 3 [CNRD 2000]), again acknowledging an acquisitions market of heritage goods. In this latest law, the Ministry of Culture was charged with evaluating the current heritage situation and elaborating special protection plans (CNRD, Law 41-00 of 2000, article 47 [CNRD 2000]). After 19 years, the only recognizable manifestation of Law 41-00 is the creation of the National Museum Network (De Peña 2007), which developed a set of regulations for creating museums and emphasized standards based on the International Council of Museums Code of Ethics.

Increase in global concerns regarding the destruction of heritage across the world (Starrenburg 2018) are also reflected in the increased complaints from the Dominican public regarding the deterioration and destruction of archaeological sites, due mostly to negligence and tourism development (Espinal 2018). For legal heritage experts, the future seems bleak as constitutional statements have had no clear impact on cases between public protection and private ownership of tangible heritage (Espinal 2018, paragraph 7). In about 150 years of legislative drafting for heritage protection standards, the country, even as signatory of the 1954 UNESCO Convention for the Protection of Cultural Property in Armed Conflict (Gerstenblith 2010), could not implement its laws and regulations. As a result, the real loss of heritage cannot be accurately accounted.

HISTORY OF COLLECTING IN THE DOMINICAN REPUBLIC

The historical context of Caribbean indigenous heritage collections begins with the Spanish invasion of the Americas. The Spanish Crown started a new chapter of economic and territorial expansion when they funded Christopher Columbus's first expedition to find a new commercial route to Asia and the spice trade (Quesada 2004). The *Capitulaciones de Santa Fe* identified the economic gains of the endeavor, where Christopher Columbus was empowered to amass whatever significant materials were produced by the people he encountered and whatever precious metals he could obtain (Capitulaciones de Santa Fe 1492, paragraph 3). The commercial nature of the contract required the collection of new commodities from the discovered continent as gifts befitting the royal family (Russo 2011; Schnapp 2011; Vilches 2009). Starting in 1520, there were numerous displays of objects made by the indigenous peoples of the Americas, sent and inventoried by Hernán Cortés, some traveling in exhibition throughout different parts of Europe (Russo 2011; Schnapp 2011). However, many of these objects were misclassified through the centuries, often decontextualized by combining types of material without regard for their specific origins (Feest 1993; Johnson 2011). Many more ended up as personal gifts for the Crown's family members (Cabello Carro 1997:6–10; Cabello Carro 2008; Johnson 2011), and collections of Amerindian objects, such as the one gathered by merchant marine Antonio de Ulloa in 1752 during his travels, ended up as part of the Spanish Royal Cabinet of Natural History. This collection was put together with detailed instructions of how to catalog the objects and is considered one of the first inventories of an official collection (Cabello Carro 1997:11–13), though accessible only to scholars, rulers, and royal families.

The violent cultural destruction and near physical extinction of the indigenous populations during European colonialism transformed the identity of the indigenous settlers (Hofman et al. 2018; Valcárcel Rojas et al. 2013). Precolumbian settlements were often buried under European-imposed models of habitation in the new environment (Curet 2011). Such settlements have been unearthed by collectors and treasure hunters, contributing to the creation of a market of precolumbian artifacts (Curet 2011).

Until the middle of the twentieth century, the amateur nature of archaeological excavations in the Dominican Republic led to objects being taken out of context without information to reconstruct their provenience. Despite the growing professionalism of archaeological research and exhibition work in the country beginning in the 1970s, documentation of Dominican indigenous heritage collections has remained deficient—just as in many European museums where documentation remains scarce and research about indigenous collections is limited (see also Françozo and Strecker 2017).

The specific history of indigenous heritage collections in the Dominican Republic is difficult to establish because documentation is scarce. Colonial administration in the Caribbean did not contemplate the conservation of documents or the protection of the material heritage of the colony. Valuables were shipped to Europe, and no official entity conveyed to the local administration the importance of record-keeping (Cassá 1998). In addition, the lack of value assigned to keeping records in an island where literacy was minimal during the eighteenth and nineteenth centuries, the high rate at which legal and church documents were damaged and discarded due to climate, theft, administrative carelessness, and political instability contributed to a national documentation gap on many topics (Cassá n.d.).

The systematic compilation of historical records and legal documents in the Dominican Republic started only in the third decade of the twentieth century, with the National Archives founded in 1935. According to Roberto Cassá (n.d.), the current director of the Archivo General de la Nación (and the first person in the country to establish an archival cataloging system), there are hardly any documents predating the independence of the country in 1844 because the status of colony required sending most important documents to Europe. This also helps put in perspective the lack of information on heritage collections.

Although the history of indigenous heritage collections in the Dominican Republic has not been a common topic of study, the history of archaeology in Spanish-speaking Caribbean islands, such as addressed by Antonio Curet (2011), exemplifies how collections have formed in the country. The presentation of indigenous heritage collections at most museums in the Dominican Republic since 1972 reflects early classificatory tendencies of American and European archaeologists, as foreign support spurred research for decades (Curet 2011; Marechal 1998; Rouse 1977). New museology (Vergo 1989) brought criticism to static classificatory institutions for more concern about educational and social aspects in museums as well as to the forefront of exhibitions that dealt with social value, meaning, and politics (Stam 1993). Museums with indigenous heritage collections in the Dominican Republic have not updated the political nature of their displays, and many museum scripts remain based on classificatory research from the twentieth century. This has created a disconnection with communities by limiting the access to the cultural information that objects can help convey when interpretation strategies are not only designed for academics and people knowledgeable of Caribbean history.

Limited research regarding Caribbean collections, poor governmental policy and/or economic support, and low professional training for the management of collections in the Greater and Lesser Antilles has partly brought about a region-wide stagnation in the exhibition of cultural and natural objects that help narrate the deep history of the islands (Cummins 2004; Maréchal 1998). Nonetheless, the early recognition of archaeological artifacts in collections as cultural heritage in the legislative language pertaining to some Caribbean nations can be interpreted as initial attempts to recuperate indigenous cultural material as national riches with direct links to cultural identity (Jaramillo in Argaillot 2012; Hernandez Godoy 2014).

The historical unconsciousness of the Caribbean, as poignantly highlighted by Sued-Badillo, does not permit "an integral reconstruction of the social and material processes of the region" (Sued-Badillo 1992:600). Within a global context, this unconsciousness connects to the tendency of museums to amass major collections of objects largely lacking contextual documentation (Chippindale and Gill 2000; Sackler 1998). In the face of managing decontextualized objects, the ownership pedigree of an "art" piece—instead of its provenience—has been a main reference for the perceived value of the object (Chippindale and Gill 2000:467–468). This has been the treatment of indigenous heritage objects, often presented as art expressions of the first settlers in the Caribbean, with most objects displayed in exhibitions and catalogs lacking contextual documentation (Leon 2018).

Deficient official records that identify how collections were formed suggest several museums functioned with minimal collections management, or sometimes none at all, due to poor maintenance of the paper trail. Therefore, to understand the context of Dominican museums with indigenous cultural material, it is necessary to examine how they were formed (to the best of our knowledge), what information is available to the public, and the activities that are carried out to make collections accessible to the public.

MARKET PLAYERS

Collectors, defined as private individuals who look for and collect specific kinds of objects and select them to satisfy an urge (for pleasure, information, prestige, or investment) (Appadurai 1994; Baekeland 1994; Kersel 2012; Pearce 1994; Sackler 1998; Wendel 2007), had underpinned the trade of antiquuities in the Dominican Republic since before the start of the twentieth century (Pina 1978). There are also those collectors that, although they do not have a physical or institutional structure for displaying their collections, open their houses to students or allow scientists to study their collections (Figure 2.1). Local collectors also view their purchase of antiquities as a rescue effort to prevent the sale of objects to foreign markets.[2]

As we have seen from the legislative review, collectors have been acknowledged as important contributors to the formation of collections in the Dominican Republic. The country has seen some of its most important collections

Figure 2.1. Display of objects at collector's home in 2017, Laguna Salada, which is open to the public. Valverde Province, geographic area of study for the NEXUS 1492 ERC Project. (Photo courtesy Csilla Ariese)

made accessible—such as the creation of nonprofit educational institutions for national and international visitors to enjoy. The most active and longest-running private museums of such nature are Sala de Arte Pre-Hispánico in Santo Domingo, Centro León Jimenes in Santiago, and the Altos de Chavón Regional Museum of Archaeology in La Romana. The Museum of Dominican Man itself opened the twelfth of October 1973 and has a large portion of its inventory donated by the family of engineer and prominent collector Emile de Boyrie de Moya, who is considered to have helped pave the way to more scientific archaeological research in the country (Hoy Digital, March 14, 2004).

Some collectors have followed regulatory declarations, inventoried their collections according to the legislation—sometimes by government agencies—and have had educational programming that guarantees public access. But even with legal parameters in place, and the best intentions, no collection in the country with purchased items is free from the impact of looting, forgery, or fakes.

The enactment of heritage laws to convert cultural objects into state property took place from the mid-nineteenth to the early twentieth centuries in the hopes of discouraging the looting of sites (Gerstenblith 2010:174). Nevertheless, in countries where common law is applied, the law of finders, which may enable a finder to claim property title over a find if it goes unclaimed after public announcement, arguably could contribute to the price of an object (Wendel 2007:1024). Legal ownership allows looters and collectors to become part of an unregulated trade in the buying and selling of unclaimed finds.

Looters, those who intentionally and without authorization enter an archaeological site to find objects to eventually sell on the market, destroy the archaeological record (Gerstenblith 2010:174; Wendel 2007:76). They are enticed by the demands of the art market and are not easily deterred by prohibitory legislation that is often inconsistent and scarcely monitored (Borodkin 1995). The Dominican Republic lacks mechanisms to closely monitor those who enter archaeological sites illegally. With few heritage workers and few resources, there are many large and vulnerable sites that have not been studied or registered. Even well-known sites have been looted for decades with no controls or investigations made to catch repeat offenders.

Another major component of the market are forgers—skilled craftspeople who copy known objects or make them based on designs from looters, dealers, or what they hear collectors are looking for. Forgeries—copies made of known objects desired by collectors—are both a problem for the market and a response to its demand, since production is persistent. Forgeries are also an academic problem because they "deform and falsify our understanding of the past" (Jones 1994:94).

In many countries, the saturation of copied objects in the antiquities market escalates prices of unique finds (Borodkin 1995:384). In the Dominican Republic, instead of intensifying looting efforts to get real finds and obtain higher prices, what seems particularly common is that skilled forgers invent new design traditions (Figure 2.2). Some craftsmen created and sold enough invented materials that entire collections have been amassed by collectors under the impression that they have acquired unique archaeological objects. Locally, the desire for precolumbian objects also led to the development of new, Amerindian-inspired art forms (Vega 2014; see also Ostapkowicz, chapter 1 herein; Hanna, chapter 5 herein).

Some publications suggest archaeological forgeries have been around for more than a hundred years (Fewkes 1903), so it is safe to state that looting and forgeries have strongly influenced the country's collections, both private and public. There have been cases where a collector's trust in a dealer (either looters themselves or directly linked to one) is so well established that the relationship lasts for years, allowing the collector to purchase real and fake material over a long period.[3] When makers or dealers of forgeries were interviewed at length, some admitted having long-term sales relationships with known collectors and provided examples of what they sold (Figure 2.3).

Sales venues in the country also include open-air street markets that feature

Figure 2.2. Fakes purchased by Fernando Luna Calderón with the idea to establish a community-based museum of fake pieces. (Photo courtesy Arlene Alvarez)

Figure 2.3. Forgery from the eastern region of the Dominican Republic, 2015. (Photo courtesy Arlene Alvarez)

Figure 2.4. Fake objects and archaeological fragments for sale in an open-air street market in Santo Domingo's Colonial Zone, 2004. (Photo courtesy Corinne L. Hofman and Menno L. P. Hoogland)

a mixture of archaeological lithics, ceramic fragments, and neo-Amerindian sculptures (sold as if they were cultural objects) (Figure 2.4). In their purchase of these objects, collectors become active players of the trade. They often ask too few questions about the origin of the objects and tend to purchase moved by a self-justifying need to protect what they view as cultural heritage (Kersel 2012).

CONSEQUENCES OF THE TRADE

Part of the antiquity trade in the Dominican Republic relies on the continued interest of private collectors to expand their collections as well as local economic survival. This along with poor academic and scientific training to conduct archaeological field research are a few elements that fuel the antiquities market in the Dominican Republic—a market that few speak about in public.

There are behind-the-scenes talks of missing objects from public museum collections.[4] There are also forgery cases with an island-wide impact, such as the well-known Paredones in La Caleta, east of Santo Domingo (Vega 2014) (Figure 2.5), and the lesser known case of El Capá in San Juan de la Maguana.[5] The southern region has become associated with craftspeople who for decades have sold forgeries as archaeological pieces.[6]

In the case of Paredones, not only well-known collectors but also government institutions became major buyers of Ramón María Mosquea's ("Benyí") neo-Amerindian crafts (see Ostapkowicz, chapter 1 herein). Personal ac-

Figure 2.5. Fake objects related to the Cultura de los Paredones, 2018. (Courtesy Laura Alfau, Altos de Chavón Regional Museum of Archaeology)

counts from collectors tell how Benyí had participated in excavations and learned about the process used then for dating objects. Benyí initially looted objects and sold them to key collectors, establishing sales channels to subsequently sell fakes, he later confessed. He also admitted to crushing archaeological fragments and mixing them with pieces made by him in a sculpting style referred to as the "Paredones culture."[7]

A similar, but lesser known, account is that of the artisans of El Capá. Community members in San Juan de la Maguana province have described how a group of workers participated in archaeological digs during the 1980s and, after the work was done, looted similar sites where archaeological objects were found.[8] They sold them, and then, after they had no more objects to loot, started making fake pieces guided by the design they had observed in archaeological specimens, and what they understood collectors most wanted. Some members of this group are now part of a crafts association, Grupo de Artesanía Neotaíno, and have requested that the local government create a museum where they can showcase their work (Mendez 2011).

Over the years, based on different interviews with confessed forgers in the eastern region, community members, and collectors, their comments suggest a structure of how the Dominican antiquities market has emerged (Figure 2.6): (1) there are people who participate in excavations, who (2) recognize the demand for objects, (3) become more interested or knowledgeable about the value of archaeological pieces from precolumbian sites, and (4) then loot to sell to private collectors. When they run out of locally accessible looted material, (5) they start networking with others in the business, and (6) they become brokers of the archaeological material. (7) When they have people with ceramics or stone-crafting skills, the forgery begins, and (8) sales are established, sometimes lasting several years.

Neither public nor private Dominican museums have escaped the unregulated antiquities and forgeries trade. Acquiring private collections to form private museums or to expand public museum collections, as well as museum personnel acquiring objects to form personal collections, have been for decades an accepted norm in the country.

When interviewing forgers, the most skilled ones know where some of their forgeries have ended up—often in private collections or museums. In the case of the Altos de Chavón Regional Museum of Archaeology, sometimes looters arrived with cars full of stone and ceramic objects—a mix of archaeological and fake material—asking for a lump sum to leave everything at the museum. Due to the frequency of such visits, the museum developed a no-purchase policy in 2001. It now receives only about two or three requests per year about "found" objects that people want to sell. What has gone up however, are inquiries to help potential buyers determine whether the objects are real or fake (Figure 2.7).

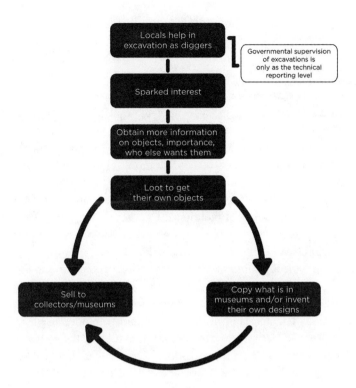

Figure 2.6. Diagram of the Dominican antiquities market. (Courtesy Laura Alfau)

Figure 2.7. Screenshot of digital inquiry from a buyer who wanted the Altos de Chavón Museum to authenticate the "artifacts" he was considering for purchase. (From the Altos de Chavón Regional Museum of Archaeology website, 2018)

MARKET ROUTES AND PROVENIENCE OBLIVION

Although exported antiquity sales are out of the scope of this chapter, there has been an increase of press coverage for confiscated objects related to indigenous archaeological material recuperated by US Customs (Cruz Tejeda 2011) (Figure 2.8). It takes a long time to process the return of confiscated material. There have been cases where it has taken years for national authorities to retrieve confiscated objects (Medrano 2011). There are no in-depth local investigations into who sold the antiquities in the Dominican Republic, who creates forgeries, or how the pieces were taken out of the country. Local media coverage does not mention the names of the people from whom the objects were confiscated, they only report on the returned objects (Cruz Tejeda 2011; Diario Libre 2016; Medrano 2011).

In such a typically contained and decontextualized environment, the indigenous heritage collections of the Dominican Republic still communicate through their traditional and outdated displays. Individually, the objects in the collections tell stories of utility, design, and technique used by indigenous peoples. Collectively, as archaeological evidence, the artifacts project knowledge of production and networks of economic exchange systems, beliefs, and values (Hofman and Hoogland 2011; Hofman et al. 2010). Just as heritage sites cannot be viewed as static, heritage collections (whether or not scientifically studied) are not static either and need to be considered as op-

Figure 2.8. Screenshot of article covering the news of the confiscated objects by the US Customs Department. (Reproduced with permission from Diario Libre; photo courtesy Arlene Alvarez)

portunities to reconnect with communities and generate greater appreciation of the past (Thomas 2016). The trade of real and fake archaeological objects hinders the possibilities for museums to improve the way collections are valued and accessed.

The focus on the collector, on the aesthetics of objects, or on the presentation of a people's culture in museum displays reveals, as Joyce (2013:302) describes, "power relations of the most subtle form, since they are reproduced by example, unanalyzed, inherent in how knowledge is experienced." Encouraging discussion on the benefits that collections yield in the Dominican historical spectrum, exploring the reasons collectors seek out archaeological material, and elucidating the values assigned to extensively collecting cultural material can all help address the lack of context and consideration for ethical issues within the current market system.

THE NEED TO ACT

Unregulated (or underregulated) antiquities markets contribute to the destruction of heritage sites. Museums can collaborate to influence educational policy, which can lead to the establishment of heritage and archaeology studies in the country; despite having plenty of potential areas for archaeological research, no Dominican universities currently have these higher education curricula. Capacity building of both museum staff and museum audiences can play an important role to aid in conservation efforts of archaeological sites and control of the local antiquities trade. For a variety of reasons, the centuries of neglect for indigenous heritage collections has caused meaning to be lost and objects to be disconnected from their place of origin and the communities that made them. Only a commercial value seems to connect both real and fake objects to the cultural narrative, which is not a priority in governmental regulation.

Museums with indigenous heritage collections have to become more active in helping control the trade by discouraging purchases, which should help minimize looting. Developing better ways in which the community's consciousness can be raised toward context-related scientific research is important to recuperate academic development in the Dominican Republic. We need communities near heritage-rich sites to be part of the protection effort. A crude reality of the country's antiquities market is the large collections open to the public that display mostly unprovenienced objects. Owners of these displays should be required to identify fake objects and seek professional advice before perpetuating unsubstantiated claims of archaeological provenience. A collective effort in the Dominican Republic could establish a network of trained professionals to advise public and private museums about objects worthy of further study. Some of these collections are in the care of individuals and institutions recognized by the government and are part of the national heritage viewed by thousands of visitors every year. Efforts to give context to decontextualized objects can help foster understanding about how objects are placed into a framework of the past. As it stands, fake objects in public Dominican collections communicate distorted cultural information. Through expert typological comparisons and examination of manufacturing and dating techniques, scientific measures could be used for distinguishing objects created by indigenous peoples from copies or invented designs.

The recent, heated debates within the Society for American Archaeology about the ethical considerations of archaeologists working with private collectors have brought to light the difficulties of navigating such engagement (Shott and Pitblado 2015). However, the fact that the Dominican Republic government endorses some private collectors in their efforts to make their holdings available to both the public and to research, and the fact that these are clearly understood as national (not private) patrimony on the island, there is an argument to be made about our collective responsibility to the accurate representation of the past. Engaging private collectors in the Dominican Republic and decontextualized collections can, in some instances, open up new avenues of investigation and make available genuine material culture now rarely encountered in the archaeological record. In this way, collections—whether private or public but, viewed collectively as national patrimony—can legitimately enter into discussions of precolumbian material culture, and in so doing complement local archaeological investigations. Collections open to the public, whether governmental or private, deserve further consideration for revising local cultural narratives as well as for improved analysis of designs at a regional level. Whether the recommended analysis is carried out or not is up to the requesting institution or individual. This would also help motivate collectors to update government registry requirements with at least basic inventory information of indigenous artifacts.

International recommendations that could be adapted to the Dominican Republic's market context include the formation of government agencies that work with land owners to regulate the discovery and sale of antiquities. This public-private approach could grant more control over how sites are affected and add value by creating more legitimacy in the provenience of materials (Borodkin 1995:412).

The Dominican Republic needs up-to-date, clear, and coherent cultural legislation that allows for an adequate regulation and management of cultural assets. Topics such as the history of cultural property in reference to how they end up in public and private collections can contribute to scientific and academic study. Regulations are also needed for the legal acquisition of cultural material, and sanctions must be enforced for illicit trafficking. The conservation of heritage through best practices that are on par with international standards needs to be developed. There is also a need to improve the capacity of municipalities, the Museum of Dominican Man, and the Center for the Inventory of Cultural Goods to provide technical assistance to museums that need to comply with regulations. This could improve the way information on collections is gathered, tracked, and provided to the public.

Formal higher education needs to be placed at the center of heritage conservation and protection efforts. A well-trained heritage workforce understands the conservation issues and threats and is ready to deal with cultural commercial activities that emanate from a poorly supervised antiquities market.

As a final note, it is necessary to highlight how important it is to de-bureaucratize processes for research, ensuring that governmental and private institutions lead in accordance with clearly defined laws and regulations, and that expert members of the cultural community can advise Dominican legislative power. This could create more binding public policies for the management and conservation of cultural heritage and achieve a better consistency of laws, with clear and implementable regulations and guidelines for the heritage community to have more responsible collecting practices.

ACKNOWLEDGMENTS

The research leading to these results has received funding from the European Research Council under the European Union's Seventh Framework Programme (FP7/2007–2013)/ERC-NEXUS1492 grant agreement 319209.

NOTES

1. This chapter stems from Arlene Alvarez's doctoral research, under the NEXUS 1492 ERC-grant agreement 319209 supervised by Corinne L. Hofman and Mariana C. Françozo.

2. Observation based on Arlene Alvarez's personal conversations with collectors.

3. Alvarez's interviews and informal conversations with collectors.

4. Alvarez, personal conversations with museum staff.

5. Alvarez, personal conversation with Anyelo Valenzuela, Province Director for Culture, San Juan de la Maguana.

6. Alvarez, personal conversations with cultural activists from San Juan de la Maguana.

7. Alvarez, informal conversations with a private collector who purchased pieces from Benyí.

8. Interviewed by Alvarez.

3

The Vibrancy of
"Taíno"-Themed Arts and Crafts

Identity and Symbolism in Modern and Postmodern Borikén

José R. Oliver

Taíno-themed arts and crafts by modern and postmodern *Borincanos*[1] are a common sight in Puerto Rico today. The following pages focus on the uses and meanings popularly attributed to Taíno arts and crafts, authenticity, and their implications in the formation of Puerto Rican identity. A small selection of Taíno-inspired modern and postmodern creations in various media are selected for discussion. These range from fine arts to mass-produced crafts, from texts (poetry) to performances. No claims are made as to how representative this sample is of the full corpus. Here, most of the examples under scrutiny are icons in the sense of a being (person, animal) or thing that is regarded as a representative (symbolic) of something or someone else (i.e., a likeness via simile; an image)—a sign that has a characteristic in common with the thing it signifies. It can be "iconic" by being a conventional exemplar, emblematic of a given icon (what/who it represents). The determination of authenticity (genuine) and unauthenticity (fake) as well as the interpretation of the symbolism and meanings of this corpus of material and performative culture require a consideration of how producers/creators and consumers/viewers regard their identities to be (e.g., Laguer Díaz 2014). It must also attend to the social-historical and situational contexts in which the images-persons-performers find themselves today. Achieving a situational context would require systematic, carefully designed *ethnographic* fieldwork—interviewing living craftsmen and women and consumers—as Ulloa Hung (2018b) has done in the Dominican Republic but that is yet to be accomplished in Puerto Rico. In its absence there is a real danger of forwarding unwarranted or unsupported generalizations inferred from a few examples and then extrapolated to the whole population. This is punctuated by my expectation that the norm in current *emic* understandings of these relationships is likely to be multivocal and vary with scale (from individuals and social segments to whole societies). Finally, the relationships of icons-people-contexts, their meanings and their symbolisms, inevitably will have undergone changes and transformations through time; solid explanations for change are historically contingent (*sensu* Gould 1989:283). Therefore, the generalizations and conclusions presented here should be regarded as tentative. The foregoing discussion focuses on Puerto Ricans inhabiting insular Puerto Rico, including Vieques, Culebra, and Mona (about 3.2 million), aware that the arbitrary exclusion of Puerto Ricans living in continental United States (about 5.1 million) and the wider world impoverishes the discussion.

AMID ANTI-INDIAN SENTIMENT, A HIDDEN POETIC TRUTH ETCHED IN STONE

A well-loved poem, "Pictografía," penned by laurate poet Juan Antonio Corretjer (1908–1985), eloquently conveys an important theme of this chapter: Boricua identity.[2] In it, Corretjer writes that he felt the bright sunlight falling on his forehead and was moved toward that hypnotic pictograph to "read" what a star engraved on the stone that morning. He does not know what ardent (fiery) *areíto* (ritual dance) presaged this encounter. Corretjer commands all Borincanos to gather their destiny from that pictograph that the sunlight has turned into stone (Figure 3.1) and states that neither the sun nor the rain, nor treason, will be able to erase what has been engraved on it. In other words, Borincano identity is permanently etched in stone, inerasable. For me, "treason" here means that not acting on the pictograph's revelation is tantamount to a betrayal; to deny one's own identity is treasonous. The iconic motif displayed by the petroglyph holds the key to discovering Puerto Ricanness. Corretjer notes that it is through the *areíto* that the message engraved in stone is to be apprehended and understood. He does not know what the message presaged; Borincanos will have to decipher it for themselves. Corretjer tells us that the destiny of Puerto Ricans lies in recovering their identity by "reading" what precolonial natives engraved in stone.[3] The *areíto* ceremony involved dancing and chanting, its lyrics reciting the history of the natives, especially the chiefly genealogy and rememorating the great deeds of the living caciques (chiefs) and their ancestors. While poetry is not strictly material, it equally has the power to elicit images (iconography). But Corretjer's call to find Borincano national identity in the past indigenous legacy (petroglyph) and in the heroic, historic figure of cacique Agüeibana (Corretjer 1990; cf. Sued Badillo 2008), was overshadowed by the anti-Indian Hispanophile intelligentsia (Sued Badillo 1978:16).

**Zamas Cave
Jayuya, Puerto Rico

"Sol de Jayuya" Motif**

Figure 3.1. Petroglyphs from Zamas Cave in Barrio Zamas, Jayuya, Puerto Rico. Two slightly different images of the popularly named "Sun of Jayuya" motif are visible in the panel (a close-up of one of them at the top). This motif is arguably the most popular petroglyph design reproduced in modern Taíno-themed arts and crafts. (Photo courtesy José R. Oliver)

As Sued Badillo (1978:16–17) noted, Corretjer's poetry (e.g., 1992, 1990) is quite exceptional in its positive portrayal of Taíno imagery, even when idealized in a period (starting in the 1930s) dominated by prejudiced historiographic portrayals of the *Indio*. These biased, negative images, lasting well into the 1950s, were inherited from the late nineteenth- to early twentieth-century scholarship. One such author was Cayetano Coll y Toste (1850–1930), whose hugely influential *Prehistoria de Puerto Rico* (1967 [1897]) echoed the early anthropological unilineal evolutionary discourse (i.e., the ladder of progress) that buttressed the racist ideology of imperialistic expansions of the era. Just as influential was Salvador Brau (1842–1912), whose earliest work of 1888 was also anti-indigenous, although his harsh rhetoric was significantly rectified in his 1907 work (Brau 1973, 2011; see Sued Badillo 1978:12). The following quotation is in stark contrast to the imagery of "Pictografía," where Indian wisdom is implicit: "The mental faculties of the *Borinqueño* [Indian of Borikén] correspond to those of the natural man in the Neolithic Period; with the proven inferiority of the Red race in contrast to the White race, in addition to the suppressing influences that the tropics effected upon ethnic mixing. *Mestizaje* [creolization] is favorable to certain races [only]. The intellectual development of the Borinqueño [i.e., *Indios*] was scarce, his [development] will be tardy, but his memory is felicitous, because he cultivated it in the recitals of the historic *areítos* [. . .] In this sense the savage [Indio] is at the level of a child; he is childish in his conceptions" (Coll y Toste 1967 [1897]:83–84; 102; my translation).[4]

A further prejudiced distinction at this time that had a long-lasting effect is the stereotyped dichotomy between two kinds of Indians: "The Carib of the Islands, eater of fresh [human] flesh, of bellicose instincts, sanguine, and cruel *antropófago* [cannibal] was the antithesis of the Arauca [Arawak], the aboriginal Antillean, consumer of flour [root crops], peaceful, hospitable, sweet and indolent" (Coll y Toste 1967 [1897]:57). The author argued that both "races" originated from one common stock in South America but diverged in "character" due to influences from the environment.

Of course, even if they had contemplated that Puerto Ricans inherited anything from the indigenous past, it certainly would not be the savage, bellicose, cannibalistic, uncultivated character of the Caribs, but that of peaceful and docile Taínos. They said that Taínos only resorted to (defensive) warfare when attacked. The reality and validity of Carib, particularly their cannibalistic attribution, is a matter of debate today. Sued Badillo (1978, 1995), for example, argues *Indios Caribes* to be a total Spanish fantasy created for political-economic reasons (i.e., justifying slavery). In contrast, Alegría (1971, 1976, 1981) defended their existence.

INDIAN, TAÍNO, AND CARIB: WHO? WHAT?

The terms *Indian*, *Taíno*, and *Carib* are today part of the vocabulary and discourse of Puerto Rican identity, but all are problematic conceptual and definitional categories. For the Spanish, the term Carib changed its meaning throughout the early colonial years. Since Isabella and Ferdinand's royal decrees of 1503 and 1511–1512 (Huerga 2006:163–171), legalizing the enslavement of *caníbales*, the term Carib acquired its most enduring, stereotypical features. Sued Badillo is in that sense correct. However, with this label Europeans lumped "real" human societies that inhabited both the Lesser Antilles and the continent (Guianas and beyond). As Curet (Epilogue, this volume) argues, the Carib concept "falsely homogenizes and misrepresents what in reality was a large diversity of identities and cultural practices." Discussions on the concept of Carib and its archaeological material culture correlates are ongoing (e.g., Whitehead 1995).[5] Still, no bioarchaeological evidence exists for cannibalism.

Instead, *Indio* (Indian), began its life with the famous misconception by Columbus of landing in the Indian subcontinent. The label stuck and was applied to all New World aborigines. It survives in the term Amerindian. Columbus's geographic error was corrected early on by chroniclers such as Las Casas with phrases like "the Indians from these our [and not the other] oceanic Indies" ("*los indios destas nuestras oceanas Indias*"; Las Casas 1875:28). The term *Indio* persisted, although it was often qualified: Indians of that town, province, island or region, or belonging to this or that cacique. Finally, the term *Taíno*, never used by the Spanish as an ethnonym, gradually came to rest side by side with *Indio* (e.g., Taíno Indian). The Spanish recorded *tayno* as meaning "good," while *nitayno* refers to an elite segment of society (Granberry and Vescelius 2004; Oliver 2009:7). Since 1836, "*tayno*" has been co-opted to designate a language (Arawakan family) and a type of people with uniform culture and practices. The label Taíno, in fact, disguises and misrepresents a diversity of identities and practices of natives from various parts of the Greater Antilles (Curet 2015). Although the terms Indian, Carib, and Taíno (or equivalents in Spanish) will continue to be used here, the reader should remain alert of their problematic conceptual baggage and be aware of how the popular, nonacademic understandings are at variance with that outlined here.

The term "neo-Taíno" is not used in this chapter, and for a good reason. It was first coined specifically for artistic movements in the 1940s, mostly related to commercial crafts (e.g., Herrera Fritot 1946). Since then "neo-Taíno" has come to be used to refer to contemporary indigenous people and their revival movements in the Caribbean and among its diaspora. While it may simply denote "chronologically recent," for many Puerto Ricans "neo-Taíno" is a loaded term that is deemed disrespectful, even pejorative, regardless of the context in which it is used.

THE MURAL *INDIA DE TANAMÁ*: THREE INTERPRETATIONS

Two fine art paintings (Figure 3.2) by artist José R. Oliver Aresti (1901–1979) introduce three interpretations of different native identities, which depend on historical context and the individual's knowledge of the subject. These paintings are part of a study (*boceto*) for a two-panel mural installed in the lobby of Hotel Tanamá (El Condado, San Juan), which no longer exists.[6] The artist repeatedly stated that the personages represented were indeed Caribs and Taínos. One scene, he explained, portrays a Taíno woman (Tanamá Indian) engaged in a ritual offering, next to a river, surrounded by petroglyphs (two

are from the Salto de Los Morones site, Utuado); next to her is a stone seat—
a depiction of a well-known carving (see Figure 3.2, top right). The other
scene, according to the artist, depicts the kidnap of the Indian of Tanamá (a
Taíno woman) by Carib Indians while a Carib-Taíno battle rages in the background. Until now, I had not questioned whether there was a historical personage named Tanamá or whether Tanamá was just a geographic reference
to match the hotel's name. The mural's native woman was either named India
Tanamá (i.e., her name) or India *de* Tanamá (i.e., Indian *from* the Tanamá region in Arecibo-Utuado, where a river of that name exists). This is a subtle
but telling difference. Further research indicates that there was no historically attested native named Tanamá or a battle registered for the region traversed by the Tanamá River. The painted scenes are, thus, not from a particular historical event but refer to several sixteenth-century Spanish accounts
describing such attacks and kidnappings in some detail (e.g., Huerga 2006).[7]

Figure 3.2. *Top left and bottom*: *Bocetos* (sketches) of two scenes for the mural *India de
Tanamá* formerly installed in the lobby of Hotel Tanamá, San Juan. Mural by José R.
Oliver Aresti (acrylic on canvas panel, 1963). (Photo courtesy Jorge Oliver). *Top right*:
Red marble seat from Los Coléricos, Arecibo. Sr. Soltero gifted it to J. R. Oliver Aresti
in the 1940s. It remained in the Oliver family until 1972 (Instituto de Cultura Puer-
torriqueña Collection, No. 3877; photo: José R. Oliver).

Oliver Aresti had as good a knowledge of the primary historical documents as any scholar of his generation (e.g., Oliver Aresti 1951).

Viewed by the likes of Coll y Toste and Brau, these scenes would reinforce the orthodox views: the Taíno woman as the victimized, noble savage while the ignoble, bellicose Caribs attacked the Taínos. One wonders how many contemporary viewers would still interpret it in such terms. Appreciating the paintings today, I am aware of the fallacy of the Taíno/Carib dichotomy. I know, for example, that the Taíno also engaged in kidnapping women (e.g., the case of Guacanagarí and Caonabo chiefs in Hispaniola [Oliver 2009:158]); that aggressive, not defensive, warfare is as much Taíno as it is Carib (e.g., Battle of Higüey, 1504; Rebellion of the Caciques of Puerto Rico, 1511); and that raiders coming from St. Croix and the Virgin Islands to kill, kidnap, and pillage natives and Spaniards residing on Borikén most likely comprised indigenous rebels from this island allied with Carib- and/or Taíno-speaking groups residing in, for example, Vieques or St. Thomas.

I see this painting today as the tragic consequence of armed, bloody conflicts among native peoples of all times and everywhere, not as a battle of "evil" Caribs versus "good" Taínos. Here the form (mural) is exactly as it was in 1963, but for me its meaning and symbolism changed through time and with increased knowledge. That is the power of artwork. As Franz Boas (1955) warned long ago, form and meaning (hence, interpretation) vary independently. Finally, Oliver Aresti indeed shared Alegría's and the Instituto de Cultura Puertorriqueña's (ICP) Three-Root Model of Puerto Rican identity. Oliver Aresti knew Alegría very well as he led the ICP's first paint and art restoration workshop (1955–1966) and later directed ICP's School of Plastic Arts (1966–1975).

MATTERS OF IDENTITY:
THE THREE-ROOT MODEL OF *PUERTORIQUEÑIDAD*

The Spanish-American War (1898) and the subsequent Paris Treaty (1899) resulted in the acquisition of Puerto Rico by the United States of America (Picó 1998). After nearly half a century, in 1948, the first popular vote resulted in Luis Muñoz Marín, a *Nuyorican*, being elected governor.[8] He spearheaded the US-PR *compact*[9] that created, in 1952, the "Commonwealth" of Puerto Rico or, more accurately, the Estado Libre Asociado (ELA), literally the "Free State Associated" with the United States (Morales Carrión 1983:267–282). One of Muñoz's priorities was to lift Puerto Rico from its poverty by shoring-up the public education program and strengthening higher education. The then chancellor of the University of Puerto Rico (UPR), Jaime Benitez, led its reform. These were largely inspired by the work of Robert Maynard Hutchins, president of the University of Chicago (Badillo 1998). Thus, "Occidentalism" (Western civilization) permeated the humanities curricula at UPR (e.g., fine arts, not popular arts). Indigenous history continued to be imparted in the same, tired Hispanophile tradition of the past decades (Sued Badillo 1978:19–20).

Yet, since the late 1940s, high quality social and anthropological research aimed at modern society, urban and peasant, was hosted by UPR. Some of the brightest American social science and anthropology scholars were engaged: Clarence Senior, Julian Steward, Harry Shapiro, Robert Manners, John Murra, Eric Wolf, Sidney Mintz, and Elena Padilla Seda. One research project culminated in the book *The People of Puerto Rico* (Steward et al. 1956; see Mintz 2011; Silverman 2011; and Wolf 1990:588–589 for retrospective appraisals). However, as Grodeau (2011) argued, following an initial critical reception, the book was thereafter ignored by Puerto Rican intelligentsia. It was perceived to weaken their advocacy for independence (from the United States) and objected to the book's "*presumed* questioning of [the validity of] a Puerto Rican 'national culture'" (Silverman 2011:182).[10] Indeed, UPR students were barely aware of this book (even through the 1980s) let alone of the impact it had elsewhere. Furthermore, none of these American scholars had even remotely considered whether Indian heritage had any bearing in the construction of Puerto Rican cultural identity, presumably because all indigenous traces were "erased" due to genocide in early colonial times. The question of "Indian-ness" was never put to Puerto Rican informants. This oversight and the uncritical acceptance of total extermination of natives are key grievances raised by the revival groups—self-designated as Taínos—since the late 1970s until today (Curet 2015; see also Feliciano-Santos 2011; Haslip Viera 2001; Haslip Viera 2013).

Inés Mendoza, a dedicated Independentist, concerned by UPR's Occidentalism (academic elitism), saw the need to counterbalance it by stimulating *popular* culture and national identity by engaging Puerto Ricans. Mendoza convinced her husband, Governor Muñoz Marín, to create an institution to promote, support, and rescue popular arts, crafts, theater, music, folklore, and literature. In 1955, the Instituto de Cultura Puertorriqueña was inaugurated with Ricardo Alegría as executive director (1955–1973). He became the sine qua non architect of Puerto Rican cultural policy. His influence continued as director of the Office of Cultural Affairs (1973–1977) and founder of the Centro de Estudios Avanzados de Puerto Rico y El Caribe (1976 2000). His legacy to Puerto Ricans cannot be underestimated (Hernández 2002). He was the first Puerto Rican to obtain postgraduate degrees in anthropology/ archaeology (master's degree at the University of Chicago; PhD at Harvard University).[11] Alegría has extensively published on anthropology, folklore, history, ethnohistory, and archaeology, including architectural heritage and conservation. His anthropological training and his nationalist sentiment sensitized him of the need to raise the profile of both the African (Herskovits's influence at the University of Chicago) and the Indian heritages. To this day, Puerto Ricans regard Alegría as the ultimate authority on indigenous history, archaeology included.

Alegría popularized the term *Taíno* among all Puerto Ricans, even though it is neither an ethnonym used by the natives nor by the Spanish to refer to them (Curet 2014). Taíno was first used in 1836 to refer to and encompass a broad group of natives linked by the Taíno language (Oliver 2009:6). In an interview, Alegría recalled that "even my father [José, an erudite journalist and writer] had said to me that I had invented those Taínos" (Hernández 2002:260). In hindsight, his father was close to the truth.

Alegría's long-lasting legacy is called the Three-Root Model (Curet 2015: 211; Curet this volume), represented in the ICP's official logo drawn by artist Lorenzo Homar (Figure 3.3). Following the views of the late nineteenth and early twentieth centuries, Alegría subscribed to the notion that Puerto Ricans are the result of a mixture of cultural and biological traits contributed by the Spanish, Africans, and Indians (the Taíno; seemingly not the Caribs). Unlike previous scholars, he rejected the notion of a tripartite-segmented so-

Figure 3.3. *Left*: Instituto de Cultura Puertorriqueña official logo by artist Lorenzo Homar. *Right*: detail of symbolic objects contributed by each racial/cultural root. The Spanish contributed Spanish language and literacy (Nebrija's grammar book) and the three crosses of the sails Santa María, La Pinta, and La Niña representing Christianity. The Indian/Taíno holding a *cemí* object, contributed crops (maize, tubers). The African brought music (drum), the labor (cutlass or machete), and *santería*-related feasts, represented by the horned mask of a *vejigante* (a devil/dragon-like personage). (Photo courtesy José R. Oliver)

ciety and instead argued for "a more homogeneous cultural substrate" (Curet 2015:211) that anchored a distinct, shared identity: the *Borinqueño* or *Puertorriqueño*. Identity is thus forged through a kind of synthesis, in accord with the democratic principles of this time and Alegría's own nationalistic values. But this idealized democratic, tripartite heritage hides inequalities on the ground (Laguer Díaz 2013). Not all inherited identities are equally valued. The logo itself depicts a male-gendered and implicit ranked hierarchy (Laguer Díaz 2014:50–62): the Spaniard stands at the center, with the Indian to his right and African to his left. This hierarchical arrangement echoes the Holy Trinity portraits of Western Christianity. Whomever stands to the right (Indian/Taíno) of "god" (Spanish) is of higher rank than the one on the left (African). Following the US colonial takeover of Puerto Rico, the effects of the cultural/racist dual opposition of "White/Black" (positive/negative values) lingered on. In time, the "Taíno/Indian" became a desirable alternative root identity for many Puerto Ricans: "to be neither black nor white but descended from a halcyon, genuine past with the deepest roots possible" in Borikén (Hanna, personal communication 2019) (Figure 3.4).

Figure 3.4. Young man in Taíno attire during the feast of Santiago Apostol (St. James Apostle) in Loíza Aldea, Puerto Rico, June 1998. He appears to echo chief Martín Veguilla's assertion that "everyone who is a Puerto Rican is a Taíno also." (Photo courtesy José R. Oliver)

Unquestionably, the idealized notion of synthesis in the Three-Root Model was heavily proselytized by the ICP. Alegría's *Historia de Nuestros Indios* (1950), later reprinted (1969) as *Isla y Pueblo* (*Noticias de Borikén*)—still in print (Alegría 1997)—reached all public and most private primary schools in the island and was widely read by adults as well.[12] It was distributed by the Division of Community Education of the Department of Public Instruction (DIVEDCO) that, since 1949, had in its graphic arts workshop some of the best artists of the island, many of whom would later join the graphics workshop of the ICP led by Lorenzo Homar (Tió 2003:70–197). Taíno, African, (Colonial) Spanish, and *jíbaro* (peasant)-themed graphic artworks not only embellished Alegría's many publications, but the iconography also became etched in the minds of readers. The Indian images once elicited largely from written text (mind's eye) are now constrained by the artist's creative representation and not just freely open to idiosyncratic imagination (Figure 3.5 *top*). Graphic images in books were used in the past (e.g., Fernández de Oviedo y Valdés; see Myers 2007) but sparingly until now. Unlike Spanish- and African-themed graphic arts, the Taíno-themed scenes were impressive because these images of natives were universally up to then inaccessible on account of their presumed total extinction, again a "fact" disputed by current Taíno groups and scholars (e.g., Oliver 2009; Valcárcel Rojas and Ulloa Hung 2018). Nonetheless, the text and its iconography were intended to educate Puerto Ricans, top-down, about their Taíno heritage, to instill pride in their indigenous cultural roots, without which the Three-Root Model would not work. Alegría's educative publications largely focused on the Taíno at the expense of African roots, as he thought that the native heritage was the least appreciated.[13] Alegría's (1969 [1950]:9) schoolbook text begins with the warning "that a Puerto Rican [individual] who, by ignorance, is contemptuous of the roots of his historic past, nonetheless has, in himself, a good part of the Indian heritage. On occasions, it is possible that he carries, in addition, some diluted drops of Taíno blood."

The ICP's evangelical fervor in disseminating the Three-Root Model worked its magic. Although lacking statistical support, it is deeply internalized by the majority of Puerto Ricans today. Like Curet (2015), I have often been told by Puerto Ricans that they are one-third of each; one, very seriously, said: "I am 33.3% Spanish, 33.3% Indian, and 33.3% African," to the decimal accuracy. At the same time, while some current Taíno groups accept a degree of creolization (in the form of *jíbaro* [countryside peasant]), others would not accept the idea of equal contributions enshrined in the Three-Root Model. Some groups argue that the core of their culture (or "deep structure," to use a linguistic, Chomskian analogy) is essentially indigenous (Curet 2015). Indeed, they argue that the historic *jíbaros* were in fact *Indios* or Taínos because

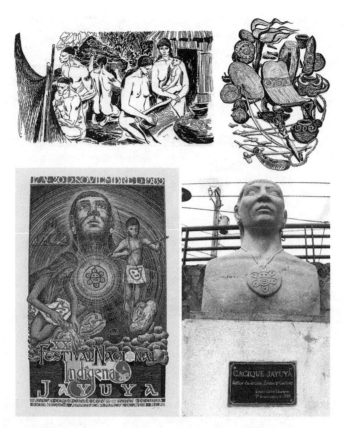

Figure 3.5. *Top left*: Daily activities of the Taíno by artist Antonio Maldonado. *Top right*: Taíno artifacts by artist Rafael Tufiño. *Bottom left*: Silkscreen (*cartel*) promoting the 20th National Indigenous Festival of Jayuya by artist Sixto Cotto (1989). *Bottom right*: Bust portraying the Cacique de Jayuya, erected in the town's plaza in 1969. This bust was the inspiration of Cotto's portrait in the silkscreen. (Photo courtesy José R. Oliver)

they only adopted what amounted to superficial traits from the other cultural components implied by the Three-Root Model (see Curet, 2014, 2015, for nuanced critical analysis of this complex topic, especially the problematic and varying concepts and values attached to *jíbaro*.) Be that as it may, it seems that *Borinqueño* identity is predicated on the fallacious notion of the (pre)existence of cultural "purity" that, once blended with other "pure" cultures/races, produced the *Borinqueño* or *Boricua*. As noted, the "blend" is not always conceived as resulting from equal proportions of Spanish, Indian, and African racial/cultural characteristics. The ICP's ideal, homogenizing identity ("I am equally one-third of each") sits uncomfortably with the racial/cultural tensions and inequalities that exist on the ground.

Figure 3.6. *Top*: enactment of the *areíto* by the Taíno Council Gua-Tu-Macua Borikén at the site of Caguana in 2013. *Bottom left*: detail showing Taíno *mayohabo* (log-drum) and a wooden figure with a plate (so-called *cohoba cemí*), with Caguana's original petroglyphs in the background. (Courtesy Miguel Rodríguez López). *Bottom right*: Cacique Martín Caciba Opil Veguilla with archaeologists Miguel Rodríguez López (*right*). (Courtesy Perry L. Gnivecky)

Martín Caciba Opil Veguilla (Figure 3.6), the leader of the Taíno Council Gua-Tu-Macua Borikén, rephrased the previous discussion in a somewhat different and interesting way: "We defend Taíno culture with 'cape and sword,' and we are promoters of the same [the Taíno culture], and with pride. It doesn't matter if the person is blonde and blue-eyed [or if] s/he has them [the eye color] mixed. *So long as you are Puerto Rican, you are Taíno also*"

(Veguilla, in Ruiz Mederos, 2019 video: 12:30–13:22 min.; my translation and emphasis).[14] The full interview in Ruiz Mederos's (2019) film reveals that, for Veguilla, Taíno is a distinct heritage with its particularly salient cultural traits, as is the case for African or white or Creole, but that regardless of such differences, *"everyone who is a Puertorriqueño is a Taíno also."* Like Corretjer's poem, it is up to the rest of the *Borinqueños* to discover for themselves their Taíno roots. While not all Taínos today may share Veguilla's view, he seems to imply that acknowledging variety (distinctive cultural traits) does not negate unity in terms of identity. The question remains whether Veguilla would also agree that everyone who is a Taíno is also a *Puertorriqueño* (see Figure 3.6). I strongly suspect he would respond affirmatively.

Despite the idealized democratic principle enshrined in the Three-Root Model, in practice the old stereotypes persist. The Spanish contribution to "civilization" is represented as superior, dominant, reified (Curet 2015; Laguer Díaz 2013, 2014). It ignores the diversity of cultural (and biological) "roots" present in Puerto Rico such as Haitian-French, Corsicans, Cubans, Dominicans, and even Catalans (arguably not "really" Spanish [cf. Elliot 2018]) who set roots here in the nineteenth and twentieth centuries as well as the large numbers of Amerindians (continental and insular circum-Caribbean) and Africans brought as slaves at the start of the colonial enterprise (Valcárcel Rojas and Ulloa Hung 2018). Each of the three "archetypes" reduce both diversity and variability, and ignore *disparity* (to borrow paleontological terminology), to essentialist, homogenized categories. Finally, Taíno was and still is popularly seen as static and unchanging. It temporally collapsed what, in fact, took over 5.5 millennia to emerge and involved much more cultural variability than is popularly assumed.[15] Cultural variability is borne out by much archaeological research, as exemplified by contributions in *The Oxford Handbook of Caribbean Archaeology* (Keegan et al. 2013), for example. Unless the public is well read on both the implications of archaeological finds and on the social-anthropological discussions of theories and epistemologies that inform notions of cultural mixture, hybridity, syncretism, and processes of creolization (e.g., Curet 2015; Duany 2003; Laguer Díaz 2013, 2014; Stewart 1999, 2007, 2011), the simpler Three-Root Model (its logical entailments as well as traps) will tend to trump the more nuanced, elaborate ones.

TAÍNO-THEMED ARTS AND CRAFTS: ICONOGRAPHY AND SYMBOLISM

The focus in this section shifts to illustrative examples of postmodern Taíno-themed arts and crafts whose formal iconography is overwhelmingly inspired by and reproduced from precolonial rock art designs. The examples illustrated here are from a brief period covering 1996 to 2008. We thus leave be-hind modernity and its early postmodern stirrings of the late 1960–1970s (e.g., Taíno revival, Afro–Puerto Rican "Black Power," feminist movements) that questioned received "truths" and have fully entered postmodernity, with its globalization, interconnectivity, intersubjectivity, and tendency to decon-struct what once was understood to be solidly constructed. Put simply, a re-ordering of the old order. But, as always, older notions can be resilient and can still sit, even if uncomfortably, with the new.

Taíno-Themed Crafts for Tourism and Popular Markets

Outside graphic art and paintings, replicas of a few aboriginal sculptures, such as three-pointed stones and miniaturized seats (*duhos*), were occasion-ally produced in the early 1970s by a few artisans, sold at convention centers, the defunct Adolfo de Hostos Museum, and the ICP's Museo del Indio Puer-torriqueño and its bookstore in Old San Juan. I have no recollection of seeing much Taíno-themed craftworks.[16] However, it seems that by the 1980s Taíno groups were busy crafting a wide range of Taíno-inspired artifacts (see Figure 3.5). Nonetheless, these artifacts were not made for market sale but primarily for internal consumption by Taíno groups. This all dramatically changed by the mid-1990s. In the *fiestas patronales* (patron saint feasts) taking place in interior mountain towns, stands selling Taíno-themed crafts began to appear regularly.[17] But a veritable explosion of this craftwork took place in 1999 at the start of an island-wide peaceful protest.

By the early 1990s, the Port of San Juan was host to the mega-cruise-ship tourism phenomenon, disgorging 2,000 and more (international, not just US) tourists per ship into Old San Juan, eager to buy souvenirs. San Juan, at the time, was the starting point of Caribbean cruise holidays, ensuring a steady supply of tourism. Shops in Old San Juan began to sell in earnest Taíno-themed craftworks aimed at tourists, consisting of jewelry, T-shirts, leather bags, glazed ceramic mugs, bookends, etched glass, and other house deco-rations, even personal business cards (Figure 3.7). Tattoo parlors also began to include petroglyph designs in their repertoire (for examples, google the phrase "taino tattoos"). Both tourists and Puerto Rican residents bought such crafts.

The popular success of sales of Taíno-themed crafts in the heyday of cruise ship tourism and during the Peace for Vieques protest movement resulted in the creation of more jobs and supplementary incomes for craftsmen and craftswomen. Indeed, kiosks and shops sprung up in that the most western cathedral of capitalistic consumerism: the shopping mall, with the behemoth of Plaza de Las Américas at its center.

Figure 3.7. Taíno-themed modern arts and crafts. *Clockwise from top left*: kiosk sells T-shirts with petroglyph designs in the Artisan Fair at Barranquitas (2001); tourist shop in Old San Juan displays leather bags with petroglyph designs; enameled bronze pendant with "Goddess" of Caguana and "Sun" of Jayuya motifs; original Caguana petroglyph; three pendants (epoxy casts) showing different petroglyph designs from a tourist shop in Old San Juan; two small silk screens on paper for sale at Plaza de Las Americas mall; tourist shop window display from Old San Juan, showing a variety of Taíno-themed crafts, from earrings, pendants, and ceramic mugs to reproductions of *duhos* (seats), pendants, and three-pointed stone *cemís*. (Photos courtesy José R. Oliver)

Daniel Silva's Taíno Art: Transmitting Knowledge and Skills

As everywhere, gifted master artists are in the minority. Rare are highly skilled and artistic productions of Taíno crafts based on deep knowledge—such as the work of Daniel Silva Pagán (Figure 3.8), an outstanding master of traditional crafts (see also Ostapkowicz, chapter 1 herein). Silva has intensively researched the original archaeological specimens from Puerto Rico. Many of the designs and motifs that serve as models come in fragments of pottery.

Figure 3.8. Boricua artisan Daniel Silva Pagán, San Juan, 2008. *From top left, clockwise*: carving an *higüero* or calabash (*Crescentia cujete*) into a receptacle; finished vessel with incised and pyroengraved designs based on Capá-style ceramics; Silva displaying a range of *higüero* vessels with Capá designs; vessel sits on direct fire with boiling water and a land crab (*Cardisoma* sp.). (Photos courtesy José R. Oliver)

Thus, he learned through practice the techniques involved in different stages of production by deconstructing the *chaîne opératoire* from the fragmented ceramics. He has aided and learned from archaeologists the methods for reconstructing (in drawings) vessel forms and their decorations. This entails an understanding of the aboriginal "grammar" rules for creating designs, such as symmetry, repetition, and alternation but, as claimed by Silva (2008), without sacrificing his own creative, artistic input.[18] The *higüero* or calabash (*Crescentia cujete*) vessels have their archaeological counterparts in the *cenote* of La Aleta in the Higüey region of Altagracia, Dominican Republic (Conrad et al. 2005). The calabash vessels do show scraped and incised (likely pyroengraved) decorations that characterize the style of Boca Chica (Taíno of Hispaniola) ceramics. In Puerto Rico *higüeros* have not (yet) been found archaeologically. Silva has instead made the reasonable assumption that the designs applied to ceramic vessels equally apply to similarly shaped organic containers. Silva's repertoire extends to ceramic vessels and stone sculptures as well. Rock art motifs do not seem to figure in his artwork. He is in the minority in this respect.

Crucially, Silva (2008) transmits his knowledge to the public. Unlike pottery, *higüeros* can be manufactured anywhere, thus while selling his artwork he often creates the vessels on site and addresses questions from the public. He has also organized workshops to teach and demonstrate his skills. His craft has been exhibited in various localities (especially museums and cultural centers) where he also creates them in situ. This contrasts sharply with the kinds of routine transactions between sellers (the artisans themselves or their intermediaries) and buyers of Taíno-themed crafts in artisan fairs and especially tourist shops. My impression is that meaningful conversations between buyers (especially foreign tourists) and sellers (especially intermediaries) about the significance of the Taíno crafts bought would be exceptional. Tourists generally buy these as souvenirs, to take home memories of their holiday. These Taíno-themed crafts, among many reasons, are bought for their design appeal, whose iconography is unique to Puerto Rico. I suspect that knowledge exchanged on Taíno craft symbols or meanings is very superficial. Likely, they are just one more interesting, appealing item on their shopping lists. Silva's approach to engaging the public is, for social scientists, educators, and students alike, a much more rewarding and enlightening experience that should be encouraged.

AN ICONOGRAPHY OF IDENTITY, PRIDE, AND DEFIANCE

Three banners were on display at the Festival de Artesanía (in 2001) in the mountain town of Barranquitas (Figure 3.9). That year coincided with the height of the Peace for Vieques (1999–2003) protest against the occupation

Figure 3.9. Banners combining petroglyph motifs and national flags in the Artisan Festival of Barranquitas (2001) during the Peace for Vieques protest movement against US Navy occupation of this island. The Independence flag is in the top register (white cross and a star in the top left square) and the Commonwealth flag is at the bottom (white star within a blue triangle on the left side). (Photos courtesy José R. Oliver)

of Vieques by the US Navy. Conflicting relationships between Puerto Ricans and the US government are par for the course of Puerto Rican life, but they periodically boil over, dramatically. As Barreto (2008:136) noted, "since the mid-1970s a grassroots Vieques peace campaign aimed at shutting down the Navy's bombing range has persevered. But for the most part it failed to captivate the hearts and minds of other Puerto Ricans." However, starting in 1999, Puerto Ricans, in vast numbers, had had enough of the presence of US Navy bases in Puerto Rico, and Vieques Island was both the fuse and the powder keg. Against the odds, they succeeded in expelling the US Navy in 2003. As Barreto explains, "The Vieques campaign that started in the spring of 1999 succeeded where its antecedents had not because Puerto Ricans in the traditional Caribbean homeland along with their ethnic kin on the U.S. mainland jointly consecrated the battle for Vieques into a *cause célèbre* for *puertorriqueñidad*—Puerto Rican-ness. That renewed notion of cultural identity was no longer dependent on conventional notions of territorial boundaries nor was it yoked to long-established notions of citizenship based on blind obedience" (Barreto 2008:147).

Against this backdrop, a veritable explosion of Taíno-themed symbols, frequently laced with national flags, appeared all over Puerto Rico and still remain popular to this day.[19] The Barranquitas' banners are but the most elaborate examples, and hence the most informative. The structural arrangement and choices of motifs are most relevant to interpret the iconographic symbols displayed and what they express in terms of Puerto Rican identity.

Two of the banners (see Figure 3.9, *left*) depict a central motif, the "Goddess of Caguana" and the "Sun of Jayuya," stylized but still good renditions of the original specimens from Caguana and Zamas Cave sites (see Figures 3.1 and 3.7 *bottom right*). In the top register is the flag of the (failed) pro-independence coup of 1868 against Spain (*Grito* [Revolt] of Lares; see Moscoso 2003; flag with white cross and star at top left); at the bottom is the official flag adopted by the Commonwealth of Puerto Rico in 1952 (García 1993:359; white star within a triangle). The central position of the icon, universally thought to be a powerful "goddess" of the ancient Taíno, structurally articulates Puerto Ricans with Independentist political leanings and those whose political proclivity lies either with the current status quo (Commonwealth) or, perhaps, with pro-statehood ambitions (i.e., becoming a "state" of the United States). However, the official Commonwealth flag also had its origins during the movement of independence from Spain in 1895 and later adopted by Nationalist Party, the reason why this flag had a tortuous history before becoming the Commonwealth's flag (Dávila 1996). Today it flies as a symbol of *Puertorriqueñidad* for all, regardless of political affiliation. Yet, it is not accidental that the independence flag is at the top register, rather than the bottom. It flies on high over everything. Note that no Afro–Puerto Rican motifs are in view here. One reason why a Taíno petroglyph is the central motif is because it is emblematic of the original, deeply "sedimented" root inherited by all Puerto Ricans and hence functions as an integrative device between politically segmented factions of society. The native heritage thus unites everyone in the shared identity of Boricua-ness.

The third banner, by a different artist, likewise displays petroglyph designs and the same flags, but the structural arrangement is different (see Figure 3.9, *right*). This banner is inscribed with the movement's other catchphrase, Peace for Borikén (the ultimate goal of the protest). Here the "Sun of Jayuya" (from Zamas cave) and another petroglyph are in the top and lower registers, framing the flags of Independence and Commonwealth. And, again, the Independence flag flies on high. While the source for the "Sun of Jayuya" is recognizable, the source of the other petroglyph is not. It does not matter, as both are symbols of the Taíno heritage. These examples show the crea-

Figure 3.10. *Left*: Printed T-shirt on sale at Barranquitas Fair (2001) is modeled after the "Sun" petroglyph (*right*) in its original site in Salto Arriba, Utuado. The boulder was bulldozed from its original location, shown above. The severely damaged boulder is presently on the grounds of the University of Puerto Rico–Utuado campus. (Photos courtesy José R. Oliver)

tive ways in which artisans co-opted Taíno symbols to iconographically express that "renewed notion of cultural identity" that Barreto spoke of, one of those precious moments in history when an entire population comes together as one. A T-shirt from a nearby stall in the Barranquitas' Artisan Fair expresses it in no uncertain terms. Again, the central motif of the "sun" is surrounded by two Commonwealth flags with the written message: "100% Boricua, Made in Puerto Rico" (Figure 3.10). In this instance, the sun icon is reproduced from the site of Salto Arriba in Utuado, the alternative to the sun motif from Jayuya.

THE VIBRANCY OF ICONS OF THE PAST AND THE PRESENT

Several petroglyphs have become iconic and the preferred choices for reproduction in today's Taíno-themed arts and crafts. However, their meanings and functions today are different from what they might have been in the pre- and early colonial periods (e.g., Hayward et. al. 2009; Oliver 2005). There is no recorded Spanish account describing how natives engaged with rock art or what the petroglyphs meant to them. The only glaring exception is to be found in Pané's fifteenth-century account of Iguanaboina cave in the territory of cacique Mauitatihuel ("Son-of-the-Dawn"; perhaps a mythical personage?) in Hispaniola. This cave "they held in great esteem and have [it] all painted in their fashion, without figures" (geometric designs only?) and from where they believed the Sun and Moon emerged (Pané 1999:16). Despite this vacuum, logical arguments have been proposed to elicit plausible interpretations of rock art (e.g., Hayward et al. 2009). Caguana's rock art (Figure 3.11)

Figure 3.11. Five petroglyphs located in the central section of the western row of monoliths in the main plaza of the civic-ceremonial center of Caguana. (After Oliver 2005; drawing and photo courtesy José R. Oliver)

is a pertinent example since some of its iconography is frequently reproduced in modern artwork (Oliver 1998, 2005, 2009, 2012).

The petroglyphs engraved in the central plaza's monoliths convey a specific "message" about how society should (ideally) be structured around the cacique as the legitimate leader of that community, if not polity. The five central petroglyphs (see Figures 3.7 *bottom right* and 3.11) depict a chief's face (identified by a *guaíza* pectoral) framed by a pair of high-ranked figures ("skeletal" features of an elder or ancestor) and by another pair of flesh-bodied figures of lower rank (no headdress, small ear spools, open eyes). This structural arrangement of the petroglyph personages is reproduced in the living society (ancestors/chief/descendants or grandparents/parent/children).[20] On either side of these five central images is a cast of zoomorphic and anthropo-zoomorphic figures that play a supportive role. Recall that the *areíto* chants, when performed in solemn occasions (Oliver 1998:95), consisted of reciting genealogical history and praising the deeds of living and ancestral chiefs, personages who are also present in the form of petroglyph figures. The petroglyph-studded plaza was the stage where the population around Caguana gathered to celebrate and reinforce identity and cohesion as a community.

These petroglyph-icons and other portable icons (three-pointed stones, *duho* seats, etc.) are likely to be imbued with a supernatural potency and power: *cemí* (literally meaning "sweetness"). However, it is unlikely that these icons were conceived as "gods" or the subject of "adoration" in the Western Christian sense. Regardless, these icons, especially the central five, have to do with group/community identity, cohesion and solidarity and, yes, under the watchful governance of the cacique. Take him/her out of society or remove the cacique petroglyph at the center of the row, and social as well as cosmological order collapses.

This civic-ceremonial center united the dispersed farmstead communities of the area, all the while each individual farmstead had its own small plaza with its own set of petroglyphs, as for example site Utu-27 (Rivera Fontán and Oliver 2001). Importantly, the iconographic arrangement and its potential functions and symbolism (as just outlined) are unique to this site. No other multicourt, civic-ceremonial site in Puerto Rico reproduces the same structural arrangement and set of icons, lending support to the argument that Borikén was not politically united under one paramount chief.[21] Different caciques and their communities displayed different icons (petroglyphs) and had different ways of arranging them around the plaza. One way or another, all these petroglyphs gathered within large central plazas of Borikén would have to relate to the rituals and ceremonies (e.g., *areítos*) taking place in them; the place and its contingent of icons brought people together as a community (or polity). Foreign guests would also recognize the iconography as distinctive of the hosts. Foreign guests must be included, since ball games (*batey*) often involved a visiting team (interestingly, ball courts do not have petroglyphs.) This brief description shows the contexts in which human beings and petroglyph beings were engaged, and thus their function and symbolism can be reasonably deduced.

The precolumbian functions and meanings of petroglyphs found in other contexts are likely to differ from those offered for Caguana. Some caves, for example, Juan Miguel (Cag-3), near Caguana, functioned as burial grounds, and thus cave rock art iconography and symbolism would be related to death (ancestors) and afterlife. Other caves lacking human burials, like Zamas, may be the loci of ritual performances linked to cosmological beliefs, as the Iguanaboina or Caçibajagua caves of Hispaniola suggest (Pané 1999; Stevens Arroyo 2006). In river contexts, petroglyph boulders may instead mark and commemorate important loci in the landscape where mythical or mythic-historical events took place.

Today petroglyphs perform different functions and have different social and symbolic meanings. There are significant differences with, for example, my interpretation of the banners from Barranquitas. Petroglyph images past and present, however, do broadly function to promote group cohesion and shared identity. These images remain vibrant: they are still powerful socio-political symbols of cohesion, of group identity, and of unity. But, obviously, the materials used (in banners, T-shirts, etc.), the techniques of manufacture, the contexts in which they are used, and the specific meanings and functions are different because of vast changes in society, politically, economically, and ideologically.

Taíno groups today perform *areítos* (see Figure 3.6) revived from historical documents that, unfortunately, still contain etic descriptions by Europeans of what they thought the natives believed they meant at that time. Also, the Spaniards often extrapolated one behavior, act, or belief to an entire population of a region and beyond, which comes around to the fallacious concept/category of *Indio* and later Taíno. For Taíno groups today, petroglyphs (such as Caguana's) are imbued with sacredness or a spiritual presence, to the point of some being referred to and treated as their Taíno-inherited "deities," albeit not how precolonial aborigines conceptualized them (Oliver 2009). In modern-day *areítos* performed in Tibes or Caguana, the original petroglyphs and the modern Taíno artifacts used in the ceremony (seen in Figure 3.6) are treated with a reverence different from other *Boricuas*. These Puerto Ricans may be aware that petroglyphs once were "religious" icons for the ancient Taíno, but this does not mean that they shared the beliefs held by modern-day Taínos. Nonetheless, such revival can be understood as an ongoing process akin to ethnogenesis, whereby new social groups, associations, or sodalities emerge. In this specific sense, it matters less the historical accuracy or logical reasoning by which cultural and biological elements for group identity are chosen (from a preexisting reservoir) or are argued to be inherited. What matters is that it works (praxis) today in maintaining group solidarity and identity, and in fighting for their rights. From their (emic) perspective, it is not an "invented tradition" (*sensu* Hobsbawm 1984), but the rescue of an authentic Taíno tradition that was "dormant" and suppressed by colonialism. From an etic, academic standpoint it is a case of Taíno heritage revival. This brings us to the overarching theme of this volume: authentic (real) or unauthentic (fake)?

REFLECTIONS ON AUTHENTICITY AND FAKERY

Short of reproducing archaeological specimens with the intention to deceive buyers and collectors, or the general public, none of the examples discussed here qualify as "fake" (see Ostapkowicz and Hanna, introduction to this volume). The Taíno-themed arts and crafts discussed are creative works that emulate, and are inspired by, the original archaeological objects and designs or by re-creating them (as objects or performances) from ethnohistorical sources. A good number of these artifacts are signed by the artist or bear the label of the company that produced it (e.g., Figure 3.7, Artaina label). Given this, it would follow that for many of today's Puerto Ricans, particularly self-designated Taínos, the Taíno-themed arts, crafts (e.g., "Sun of Jayuya"), and performances (e.g., *areíto, cohoba, batey*) arguably have become authentic Taíno symbols along with others (e.g., Commonwealth flag) that express *Boricua* identity. The *Concise Oxford Dictionary* defines "authentic" as an entity whose origin is undisputed. Derived from the Greek word αυθεντικός (*authentikós*), it also means principal, authoritative, and genuine.[22] However, the matter of what/who is or is not "authentic" is not straightforward and is both subjective and contextual. Culture heritage specialists, for example, have noted that there are "several different forms of authenticity which play a part in the dynamics of heritage and identities, and they are sometimes the cause of competition and debate" (Egberts 2014:24). These forms include authenticities of material and place (spatial context); there are also relational, creative, and referential authenticities. As Egbert notes, "Relational authenticity is the experience of authenticity through the personal engagement of individuals in historic events, places, or objects. . . . Creative authenticity refers to the artistic unicity or integrity with which an object or place is shaped. Referential authenticity is the contemporary reference to an historic event or historic practice that is consciously and self-evidently produced, as the annual commemoration of the Battle of Hastings (1066) in England [or the *areíto* performance in Caguana]" (Egberts 2014:25).

Relational authenticity is exemplified by the use of Taíno petroglyph designs and national flags during the Peace for Vieques (a historic event), but where clearly the materials (hemp textile, paint material, alphabetic writing) are, strictly speaking, unauthentic. Silva's gourds are a good example encompassing material (gourds) and referential (to precolonial practice) authenticities, but where the engraving tools for manufacture are not authentic. The modern performance of an *areíto*, with its chants and associated Taíno crafts, exemplifies all of these forms of authenticity mentioned. Here I guess that those self-designated Taínos would invariably claim the *areíto* to be an authentic Taíno performance, while I suspect that others witnessing such a ceremony may doubt or debate its authenticity. Certainly, some crafts such as earrings or T-shirts displaying petroglyph iconography are understood by all as being reproductions and, hence, not authentic in terms of materials and techniques of manufacture (including mass production), but authentic in that its design reproduces, even perpetuates, a precolonial Taíno symbol. But here what matters is not material (and technological) authenticity but rather the creative and relational authenticities: the petroglyphs display authentic formal designs that are counted as emblematic (iconic) of an indigenous Taíno heritage that underpins Puerto Rican-ness. In sum, authenticity/unauthenticity is *not always* a straightforward dyad, an all or nothing proposition.

Thankfully, Victorian-style archaeological collectors fueling the plundering of sites or the production of fake, truly unauthentic specimens are not a serious problem today for Puerto Rico as, for example, it is for the Dominican Republic (Alvarez et al., chapter 2 in this volume). Since Taíno heritage today is perhaps integral to Puerto Rican-ness, this sense of collective identity acts as disincentive (via peer pressure) on those local and foreign peoples who might venture in looting, hoarding, and/or illegal trading of archaeological patrimony. The popular success of Taíno-themed arts and crafts is an acceptable and fashionable means to display and legally "own" a piece of Taíno heritage, thus limiting, even suppressing, the need to acquire or trade in antiquities. Of course, illegal activities will never completely disappear (see Curet, Epilogue herein). However, for the reasons noted, the antiquities market is, for now, in decline compared to just half a century ago. Facebook, Twitter, newspapers, and other such popular media also contribute by shaming the culprits, although these tend to be largely reactive rather than proactive. More serious is the problem of the continued destruction of archaeological patrimony due to development projects and climate change. Both the ICP (national) and the State Preservation Historical Office (US federal) are simply understaffed and underfunded (especially ICP) to regulate patrimony effectively, albeit the staff do their best under the circumstances.

The concept of fake deserves a further comment. For example, the Taíno scenes depicting natives (elicited from historic texts) represented in paintings (e.g., Figures 3.2 and 3.5) or in modern *areíto* performances (Figure 3.6) could be accused of being fake/unauthentic; that is, of inaccurately representing or reenacting what transpired in the past. For these to be declared fake means that one must somehow demonstrate that the author's or artist's motive was, indeed, to deceive and misrepresent. Clear examples of falsifications with intentional deception were the sculptures of Paredones from the Dominican Republic, but others, such as Padre Nazario's stone artifacts, are more ambiguous, leaving the question (and intent) of fake or real, recent or old, open to debate (see Ostapkowicz, chapter 1 herein; Rodríguez Ramos 2019; see Swogger, chapter 6 herein for another example). Of course, ignorance (lack of knowledge, poor or misguided research) on the subject by modern artists (or performers) may lead to misrepresentations ("fake"), with all its attendant actions and reactions by the viewers at large, who may also lack the critical knowledge to discern between real or fake. Ignorance should and can be remedied.

CONCLUDING THOUGHTS

One practical way to fight ignorance is to find ways to arm—weaponize— *el pueblo* (the people) with the conceptual tool kit needed for critical thinking to make sense of the object/subject at hand. It does not suffice to "correct" misconceptions or misunderstandings the public (and academics) might have incurred. Academics do this regularly in specialist publications, but it is largely consumed by other specialists in that field. It really does not engage the *pueblo*. Popularizing scholarly work obviously does not entail "trivializing" it.

One problem is that top-down education policy, such as what Alegría and the ICP implemented, can end up imposing notions like the Three-Root

Model that are based on fallacious assumptions. "Bottom-up" (i.e., from the people to academia and institutions) would be, perhaps, a desirable approach to design effective educational strategies (and policies), but it still requires academics and researchers to weed out, among others, popular misconceptions, unsupported assumptions, uncritical reading of sources, and faulty logical reasoning. This would likely raise accusations that academic elites impose their views on *el pueblo*. We could start by rewriting and updating Alegría's *Historia de nuestros indios*, one directed at primary schools and another for adults. To this curriculum should be added histories of Afro–Puerto Ricans, a segment of the population that is essential to national identity and pride, yet even now is still badly neglected.[23] Success depends on academicians learning what are the pressing questions and issues that the public is keen to get answered and that still need to be addressed, particularly the young who are still open and eager to explore new or different ideas. In preparing the guidebook *Parque Ceremonial Indígena de Caguana* (Oliver 2012), an attempt was made to address the public's questions via a questionnaire given to visitors, but the publication itself lacked an explicit discussion of the conceptual tool kit that the readers would need for critical reflection. I narrated my interpretation of Caguana's ancient history but not how and why various conclusions were reached. Even so, it took nearly a decade to convince the ICP to publish this guide, thus implementation requires persistence and patience. And, while Alegría's 1950 textbook was free for all schools, mine is not.

In 2010, Rodríguez Álvarez published *Boriquén: Breve Historia de los Indios de Puerto Rico*. It is a slight improvement on Alegría's 1950 textbook, but it still suffers from uncritically accepting such concepts as Taíno. It does not provide the conceptual tool kit for a reader to appraise his/her version of history. It merely narrates history. By contrast, Robiou Lamarche's (2003) *Taínos y Caribes* book is well written and a far better researched treatise on the ethnohistory and archaeology of the Caribbean (not just Puerto Rico). Yet, like Rodríguez Álvarez, Robiou Lamarche also assumed the validity of the cultural categories of Taíno and Carib; it uncritically followed the normative culture historic paradigm set out by Rouse (e.g., 1992). Robiou Lamarche (2003:253–257) concluded with the welcome addition of the topic of "*reivindicación* (assertion) of modern indigenes." Nonetheless, this final, short section is purely descriptive and short on critical reflection.

We have yet to convince Puerto Rico's Department of Public Instruction (as Alegría did) of the importance of publishing updated school textbooks to incorporate in History of Puerto Rico curricula, particularly aimed at the young. It is one way that we can begin to topple lingering racial/cultural stereotypes so unhelpful and detrimental to Puerto Rico's social fabric. This also means not just to advise but to consult public school teachers and talk to the public and, in a word, to be inclusive not exclusive. Indeed, this is where the Institute of Puerto Rican Culture and the Department of Public Instruction could play a pivotal role.

ACKNOWLEDGMENTS

I am indebted to Joanna Ostapkowicz and Jonathan A. Hanna for their invitation to contribute and for their wise editorial comments that immeasurably enhanced this chapter. L. Antonio Curet also offered invaluable critiques and comments on previous drafts that made a big difference. I am most grateful to the anonymous reviewer who provided detailed, insightful comments and critiques that helped reshape the chapter to its current form. Data not accessible to me was graciously furnished by Miguel Rodríguez López, Perry L. Gnivecki, and Erika M. V. Segarra.

NOTES

1. Puerto Ricans have recently added Boricua to the older self-reference term Borincano/a or Borinqueño/a. These Hispanicized nouns derived from the Taíno (Arawak) word Borikén or Boriquén (Tejera 1977:220), the native name for the island. Both terms simultaneously refer to the person's individual identity and the island they belong to (though not their place of birth). In the nineteenth to early twentieth centuries, historians also used Borinqueño/Borincano to refer to the aborigines, in the sense of natives born in or from the island (i.e., "Indios Borincanos"). Boricua seems to evoke a much stronger emotion of Puerto Rican-ness.

2. For copyright reasons, the poem cannot be quoted here. It is ironic that this act of "erasure" goes precisely against Corretjer's sentiment in his poem where it warned against "erasing what is engraved in stone." His poem was and is clearly addressed to all Boricuas and is, in my view, a patrimony and heritage of all Borincanos. For the joy of experiencing "Pictografía," in its full glory, I encourage the reader to read it in Corretjer's anthologies (1970, 1977) or visit https://ciudadseva.com/texto/pictografia / and/or http://juanantoniocorretjer.blogspot.com/2010/05/pictografia.html.

3. I would have preferred to use the term "aborigines" instead of "natives." In the Latin sense "aborigine" means a "person, animal, or plant that has been in a country or region from earliest times" (https://www.etymonline.com). Instead, "native" means "born in," which is not implied in the term "aborigine." It stands to reason that not all precolonial peoples of Borikén were necessarily born on this island (i.e., not native), but they may have been there from earliest times (i.e., aborigine). However, among many English speakers today the term "aborigine" tends to evoke Australian Aborigine. To avoid any confusion, I refrained from using aborigine here.

4. In this period (1880s–1930s) the term Borinqueño was used in the sense of "Indian" from Borinquen; in time, Taíno would become the preferred term (Curet 2015; Oliver 2009:6). Before then, Taíno was sparingly used as a designation for aboriginal people. For example, only three instances occur in Brau's (1967) work.

5. Only recently have archaeologists uncovered a distinct ceramic complex (Cayo

Complex) directly associated with the historically attested Kalinago who spoke Island Carib (i.e., Arawak [Eyerí] and Carib [Kalipona] languages). Sites like Argyle, in Saint Vincent and La Poterie, in Grenada (Boomert 1986; Hoogland et al. 2011) yielded Cayo Complex ceramics that are said to share resemblances with late precolumbian ceramics from Hispaniola and Puerto Rico (Hofman et al. 2019:367–372), although settlement patterns differ. I remain dubious of such ceramic similarities.

6. José R. Oliver (1901–1979) was my paternal grandfather. To distinguish him I added his maternal surname, Aresti, although he never signed his artwork with it. The mural was dismantled by the Garrido family (owners), and one panel was taken to Majorca; three sketches painted on Morilla Co. cardboard panels survive in San Juan (two are depicted in Figure 3.2).

7. It is quite possible, but unconfirmed, that the scene may have resulted, in part, from a folk tale the artist collected in the Tanamá region, with mural details augmented by his research of historical documents.

8. Nuyorican ("New Yo[rk]-Rican"), was initially given by insular Puerto Ricans to a Puerto Rican born in New York City. Eventually it was extended to one born anywhere in continental United States.

9. Compact is a legal term, defined as an agreement between two states/nations on matters in which they have a common concern. Akin to, but not precisely, a contract.

10. Eric Wolf (1990:588) noted that "the original thrust of the project stemmed from Steward's attack on the assumptions of a unitary national culture and national character which then dominated the [anthropological] field of culture-and-personality. The project aimed instead at exhibiting the heterogeneity of a national society." Ironically (given our critique of Taíno/Carib), it is Steward's attack on cultural homogeneity that the Puerto Rican intelligentsia reacted against.

11. Alegría claimed he obtained his PhD in anthropology at Harvard in 1954 (see Hernández 2002:127–129), becoming the first Puerto Rican to do so. According to Harvard's online catalog, it was filed in 1973 (Curet, personal communication, 2019).

12. The current reprint of "Historia de Nuestros Indios" (e.g., Alegría 1997), however, is illustrated by Alegría's wife, Mela Pons de Alegría. While Alegría's wife was a competent illustrator, in my view, she lacked the high caliber graphics produced by the original DIVEDCO artists.

13. Although Alegría published some works on "African" roots (Alegría 1954, 1979), Afro–Puerto Ricans were not as visible in his publications; there was no *History of Our Africans* textbook as there was for *Our Indians*. However, with the ICP, he did support Afro–Puerto Rican arts and crafts (e.g., Castor Ayala's vegigante masks in Loíza), recordings/films and recitals by poets (e.g., Palés Matos, Juan Boria) and music (bomba and plena).

14. My direct transcription of the audio is "Defendemos la cultura taína a capa, y espada y somos promotores de la misma, y con orgullo. No importa si la persona es rubia de ojos azules [o si] los tiene mehclao [mezclados]. Después que seas puertorriqueño eres taíno también." The English subtitles in the video are not always accurate; for example, "violación" and "negros" [blacks] spoken by Veguilla appear in subtitles as "rape" and "Afro-Caribbean." One, understandably, aims to be politically

correct, but for "violation" to have the connotation of "rape" in Spanish it would need to have an adjective (violación sexual).

15. I stress again that Taíno is the label that culture historians and normative archaeologists had constructed ("invented") for classificatory and analytical purposes (e.g., Rouse 1992; critiques by Curet 2015; Oliver 2019; Rodríguez Ramos 2010). What emerged after 5.5 millennia cannot be reduced to this single classificatory noun, Taíno.

16. Specifically, between 1957 and 1971, when I resided in San Juan, I do not recall seeing sales of Taíno arts and crafts. The first crafts I became aware of (circa 1972–1974) were reproductions of three-pointed cemíes, crafted by Antonio Blasini and other unnamed artists, sold at the ICP store and at the Adolfo de Hostos Museum.

17. These feasts celebrate the town's patron saint and take place according to the saint's day as determined by the Catholic liturgy. These fiestas are not strictly Catholic. Parades, kiosks selling crafts, food, and drink, and even stands for betting on mechanical horse races were a common feature (mechanical horse races have long since disappeared). Traditional and modern music and poetry recitals fill the sounds of the town.

18. On occasion of the April–May 2008 exhibition of Silva's *higüero* vessels at the Centro de Estudios Avanzados de Puerto Rico y El Caribe in San Juan, the artist remarked that his work is not merely copying the archaeological designs. Speaking in third person, Silva observed that "our production is not limited to the reproduction of the decoration of Taíno objects, since the inspiration [creativity] of the artist has a free hand in creating motifs that show a personal 'stamp,' yet always following the patterns of Taíno design. The indigenous art, whether showing simple motifs or more elaborate or complex representations, always expresses movement and continuity; from the perspective of art it [the craftwork] is considered as an 'animated object' that possess its proper [own] existence" (Silva 2008:2; my translation).

19. Google "Taino artwork" to view a wide array of crafts on sale.

20. Just like Lorenzo Homar's ICP seal and the Romanic Christian art (e.g., Holy Trinity), the native artisan in Caguana also followed the same ranked right versus left structural arrangement with the important, focal, personage (the cacique) at the center.

21. The site PO-39 in Jácanas (Espenshade 2012:125–142), Ponce and Machuca (i.e., Tierras Nuevas) in Manatí include individual petroglyphs very similar in stylistic design to the high-ranking figures of Caguana, but the order (linear sequence) of the petroglyphs in the plazas is different and the style of the other accompanying petroglyphs are different.

22. For the Greek word for "authentic" I also consulted https://glosbe.com/el/en /αυθεντικό, and for its etymology, https://www.etymonline.com

23. I have barely touched on the African "root" topic, nowhere near as much as it deserves. It is as vast a topic as the Indian phenomenon. Likewise, I would have liked to write much more about creolization (*mestizaje*). The creolization phenomenon is not restricted to colonial or postcolonial periods. It is present from the start of the first waves of human migration into the Caribbean and continued unabated through its long precolumbian history.

4

Jamaican Cultural Material

Pilfered and Forged

LESLEY-GAIL ATKINSON SWABY

> One of the most noble incarnations of a people's genius is its
> cultural heritage, built up over the centuries by the work of its
> architects, sculptors, painters . . . and all the creators of form,
> who have contrived to give tangible expression to the many-
> sided beauty and uniqueness of that genius.
> —(M'Bow 1979:58)

JAMAICAN CULTURAL MATERIAL represents the intellectual, artistic, technological, and communicative talents and traditions of the various peoples who
made the island their home. This encompasses diverse populations that came
to Jamaica whether freed or by force—a mosaic that includes the biological
and cultural contributions of the Taíno, Spanish, Jewish, African, English,
Scottish, Irish, Welsh, Miskito, French, German, Indian, Chinese, Lebanese,
and others. Jamaica, like many other colonies of the British Empire, witnessed
the removal of cultural material from its shores, in part due to the extrac-
tive tendencies of the metropole. In centuries past, these cultural objects, in
particular, but not limited to, indigenous Taíno artifacts, served as objects of
curiosity in overseas museum collections. Since the late nineteenth century,
cultural objects have become increasingly desired by local private collectors.
The emergence of these local collectors (and the increased illicit trading of
objects to satisfy them) is just one part of the complexities facing the management of Jamaica's cultural material heritage. This has also given rise to not just
the raiding of heritage sites on the island but also to the production of forgeries. The failure to curb these illicit activities is exacerbated by the absence
of required legislation and implementation strategies. This chapter discusses

issues associated with the illicit movement of cultural objects in Jamaica and assesses the island's framework to resolve the problem.

JAMAICAN MATERIAL IN OVERSEAS COLLECTIONS

Modern archaeology was founded in the spirit of antiquarianism. The desire for "antiquities," or objects of curiosity, has served as the inspiration for some of the first collections of Jamaican material culture. One of the earliest collectors was Sir Hans Sloane, who came to the island as the physician to the Duke of Albemarle. Sloane stayed in Jamaica between 1687 and 1689 and amassed a collection that included flora, fauna, minerals, and other "curiosities" (Agorsah 1991:3; McAlpine 1994:22). New Seville, St. Ann, Guanaboa, St. Catherine, and the Blue Mountains are three recorded areas where Sloane recovered specimens and objects that helped to increase the size and value of his ethnographic collection (McAlpine 1994:22; Ostapkowicz 2015:94). Hans Sloane's *Catalogus Plantarum Quae in Insula Jamaica Sponte Proveniunt [Catalogue of Jamaican Plants]* (1696) contains an illustration of a precolumbian sherd from Jamaica, which is the first published record of a Jamaican artifact (Agorsah 1991). Sloane's collection subsequently became the foundation of the British Museum, established in 1753 (Trustees of the British Museum 2017).

From the late seventeenth century to early twentieth century, an unspecified number of Jamaican materials were taken from the island and are currently housed in overseas institutions such as the British Museum in London and the National Museum of the American Indian in Washington, DC. During the colonial period, there was no control of the movement of cultural material. Initially this movement of cultural property was centered on indigenous material, in particular religious artifacts such as Taíno wooden *cemís* that had been recovered from Jamaican caves. *Cemís* are often defined as depictions of deities, spirits, or ancestors, but they have a much deeper spiritual resonance that is not confined to carved form; they are understood to be supernatural forces that animate and influence the entire natural world (whether a tree or a hurricane) (Joanna Ostapkowicz, personal communication, 2019). Some of the most notable examples are the Carpenter's Mountain *cemís* that were discovered in 1792 in Vere, what is now southern Manchester (Aarons 1994:14–15). The three *cemís* were reportedly found with their faces turned to the east (Joyce 1907:403). On April 11, 1799, Isaac Alves Rebello, Esq., displayed the *cemís* in an exhibition for the Society of Antiquaries, London (Joyce 1907:404). The wooden figures were subsequently presented to the British Museum, where they remain today. Joanna Ostapkowicz and her colleagues have analyzed the Carpenter's Mountain *cemís* and other wooden artifacts from Jamaica housed in local and overseas institutions (Ostapkowicz 2015; Ostapkowicz et al. 2013).

THE CULTURAL AGENCIES: THE INSTITUTE OF JAMAICA AND THE JAMAICA NATIONAL HERITAGE TRUST

The Institute of Jamaica (IOJ) is the oldest cultural institution in Jamaica. It was established in 1879 by then governor Sir Anthony Musgrave "for the encouragement of Literature, Science and Art." According to Bernard Lewis (1967:5), from its inception the IOJ was regarded as "an organization designed to help the government in the advancement of culture in the island." The main functions as stated in the Institute of Jamaica Act of 1978 were the research, study, encouragement, and development of culture, science, and history; and the preservation of monuments such as national monuments for the public benefit, and the establishment of museums (Institute of Jamaica Act 1978:3–4).

The IOJ Act of 1978 was amended in 1985, 1995, and 2010. In addition to these functions, the institute was to "establish and maintain an institution comprising a public library, reading room, collection and preservation of cultural, scientific and historical works, illustrations, and artifacts" (Institute of Jamaica Act 1978:3–4). As a result of the institute's duties and functions, it subsequently evolved into an umbrella for many organizations and divisions. These include

- The Science Museum (now the Natural History Museum of Jamaica) (1879)
- The Museums Division (now National Museums Jamaica) (1895)
- The Junior Centre Division (1940)
- The Jamaica National Trust Commission (now the Jamaica National Heritage Trust) (1958)
- The African-Caribbean Institute of Jamaica/Jamaica Memory Bank (1972 and 1980)
- The National Gallery of Jamaica (1974)
- The National Library of Jamaica (1979)
- The Liberty Hall: The Legacy of Marcus Garvey (2003)
- The Simón Bolívar Cultural Centre (2015)

Under the responsibility of the IOJ, the first archaeological excavations took place in the 1890s. During this period, a number of the artifacts recovered from investigations were either donated or sold to overseas museums. This includes the cultural material from Norbrook, St. Andrew, excavated in the 1890s by Lady Edith Blake, wife of the then governor general. Blake's collection was later purchased by the Museum of the American Indian, Heye Foundation in New York (Cundall 1934; Howard 1950), which is now a part of the Smithsonian Institution's National Museum of the American Indian. Also in the 1890s, R. C. MacCormack, a government surveyor, commenced his exploration of 21 sites in Portland Ridge and Braziletto Hills in southern Clarendon (Howard 1950:38; MacCormack 1898:444). After MacCormack completed his excavations, he presented the bulk of his collection to the United States National Museum (USNM), now the Smithsonian Institution's National Museum of Natural History (Howard 1950:38). This tradition of donating collections to overseas museums continued into the early twentieth century. In some instances, overseas institutions funded research on the island and the artifacts were subsequently transported abroad (Cundall 1934; Fincham 1997; Howard 1950; Miller 1932). Only in a few instances were artifacts from these excavations housed at the Institute of Jamaica (Cundall 1934). At the time, there was no legislation restricting the movement, nor were procedures in place to encourage the return of excavated materials. It is uncertain whether a system was in place to encourage the sharing of the research results.

This situation is not unique to Jamaica and appears to be common across the region and among other colonized territories. Kenneth Ingram (1975:vii) highlighted the loss of other resources such as manuscripts: "rich sources of the social and economic history of the region are to be found in large collections of family estates . . . many of which have found themselves in overseas repositories and libraries by donation, deposit, or purchase." David Boxer (1946–2017), Jamaican artist, collector, preeminent art historian, and former long-serving director and chief curator of the National Gallery of Jamaica, highlighted the movement of Jamaican photography and furniture from the eighteenth and nineteenth centuries (Atkinson 1998:19). Boxer added that the "last wave of the movement of cultural property overseas was in the 1970s" as a result of political and economic factors (Atkinson 1998:19).

The late 1950s and early 1960s were a critical period in Jamaica, not just in terms of the island's political and national development (being on the cusp of independence from Britain) but for the establishment of cultural agencies and vehicles that have helped to promote and protect the island's cultural resources. During this period there was a resurgence of archaeological in vestigations at Port Royal and White Marl, and the first museum opened in 1961. The Folk Museum was opened in the stables of the Old King's House in Spanish Town, St. Catherine. This museum was subsequently renamed the Jamaican People's Museum of Craft and Technology, with an aim to reflect the lifestyle of the African Jamaican peasantry. A few years later, also in the parish of St. Catherine, the then Arawak Museum at White Marl was established in 1965. The IOJ's *Jamaica Journal,* which started publication in 1967, has also proven to be very influential in the preservation of Jamaica's heritage, as a medium of information to the public (Atkinson 1998).

The IOJ was also responsible for archaeological surveys, expeditions, exhibitions, and preservation policies. This was administered through the Jamaica National Trust Commission (JNTC), established in 1958. The JNTC, the predecessor of the Jamaica National Heritage Trust (JNHT), subsequently separated from IOJ and became an independent entity in 1985. The main objectives of the JNTC as detailed by the Jamaica National Trust Law of 1958 were "to preserve or restore monuments and places of historical or national interest" (Ministry of Development and Welfare 1967:1). The JNTC established a conservation unit that was developed as a necessary complement to ongoing research. The entity was also responsible for the listing of historic monuments, which were protected under the JNTC Act of 1958. From the outset, the focus was on historic structures and monuments. The listing of historic monuments was an extension of the work carried out by Frank Cundall, who served as secretary and librarian of the IOJ from 1891 to 1937 (Robertson 2014:120). As secretary of the IOJ, Cundall served on a committee to identify Jamaica's historical monuments and compiled a provisional list of historic and archaeological sites meriting protection that was first published in 1909 (Cundall 1909; Robertson 2014). The list of historic sites and monuments included 18 middens and 15 cave sites (Cundall 1909). The earliest attempts at developing a preservation policy for cultural resources were solely centered on structures and monuments.

The establishment of the JNHT expanded the mandate of the then JNTC. The JNHT is currently a statutory body under the Ministry of Culture, Gender, Entertainment, and Sport. The JNHT Act 1985 (Section 4:7) details the functions of the trust as follows:

(a) To promote the preservation of national monuments and anything designated as protected national heritage for the benefit of the Island;

(b) To conduct such research as it thinks necessary or desirable for the purposes of the performance of its functions under this Act;

(c) To carry out such development as it considers necessary for the preservation of any national monument or anything designated as protected national heritage;

(d) To record any precious objects or works of art to be preserved and to identify and record any species of botanical or animal life to be protected.

Based on the JNHT Act 1985, the entity is responsible for "identifying, protecting, restoring, and developing" Jamaica's heritage resources. This includes its responsibility "for all national and protected sites and monuments," which currently exceed 200 listed sites. The focus has been largely on historic sites and monuments. Artifacts are not protected individually but rather as a part of their associated site. According to the Jamaica National Heritage Trust (2009a:10), an artifact "can be declared or listed under the law"; however, "there are no accompanying regulations which ensure that the proper authorities are advised and that these artifacts are properly registered."

The JNHT attempts to be in accordance with international policies and standards in archaeology, historic preservation, and cultural resource management. These include the International Charter for the Conservation and Restoration of Monuments and Sites (Venice Charter) 1964, the Protection of the World Cultural and Natural Heritage Convention 1972 (ratification 1983), the International Council on Monuments and Sites Charter for the Protection and Management of the Archaeological Heritage 1990, and the Convention for the Protection of the Underwater Cultural Heritage 2001 (ratification 2011).

THE IMPORTANCE OF PRIVATE COLLECTIONS AND FOSTERING A WORKING RELATIONSHIP

Jamaican archaeological research grew out of the contributions of amateur archaeologists and private collectors (Keegan and Atkinson 2006). From as early as the late nineteenth century, the IOJ was aware of active private collectors of antiquities (Museum of the Institute of Jamaica 1895). J. E. Duerden, then curator of the IOJ Museum, appealed to the private collectors to lend or gift specimens for the public exhibition (Museum of the Institute of Jamaica 1895). Duerden's plea was successful, and the exhibition was realized. In 1895, Jamaica held its first exhibition showcasing the diversity of the island's indigenous material, which reportedly provided "evidence that many specimens of interest and importance are to be found in the possession of private individuals" (Museum of the Institute of Jamaica 1895). The associated private collectors also facilitated the IOJ Museum to study the artifacts, which resulted in the publication of the seminal "Aboriginal Indian Remains in Jamaica" (Duerden 1897). Ultimately, a number of the specimens from this exhibition were donated to the IOJ's Museum, now the National Museum Jamaica.

James Lee, a Canadian geologist who lived in Jamaica from 1951 to 1986, founded the Archaeological Club in 1965, later renamed the Archaeological Society of Jamaica (ASJ). The ASJ, in addition to having an active research program, created the newsletter *Archaeology Jamaica* and established an inventory system that has been instrumental to Jamaican archaeological scholarship. Lee mapped a total of 265 sites and collected material from 191 of them (Allsworth-Jones and Rodriques 2005). Lee's collection was possibly the largest private collection in Jamaica, which was donated (along with the accompanying documentation) to the University of the West Indies, Mona campus, in 2000 (Allsworth-Jones and Rodriques 2005). The analysis of the Lee collection led to the publication *Pre-Columbian Jamaica* (Allsworth-Jones 2008).

Another institution, the National Gallery of Jamaica (NGJ), provides an interesting case model of partnership between a government agency and private collectors. The NGJ has an active public education and acquisitions program, showcased in the 1992 exhibition *Arawak Vibrations: A Homage to the Tainos*, which contained pieces from both private and public collections. Although the NGJ is limited by government funding constraints, it is still able to acquire Jamaican pieces through a working relationship with, and assistance from, local private collectors. During the 1980s and 1990s, the NGJ had an informal partnership with private collectors to limit the movement of Jamaican art outside of the country. In this way, millions of dollars' worth of artwork had been acquired by the gallery mostly from the assistance of private collectors, according to the NGJ's then director, David Boxer (Atkinson 1998:36).

Although many private collectors will work with government cultural agents, some refuse. This is especially disappointing if the artifacts are from sites in which provenience can be confirmed. Archaeological material has the potential to provide crucial insight even if it is recovered out of context or through suspect methods; there are simply too many unanswered questions about Jamaica's past to not engage with such material. It is possible that a collector's negative attitude toward working with local authorities is due to the issue of ownership, since some collectors believe that the government will seize their property. Yet while the JNHT has the power to acquire sites deemed of national significance, the current legislation does not grant the trust with the power to acquire an individual's cultural property.

ANTIQUING AND THE TRADE OF ARTIFACTS

Antiquing seems to have become a thriving business in Jamaica. It is not unusual to find households with antique furniture or other items that have been handed down or acquired. Today there are antique shops scattered across Kingston. The Antiques and Collectibles Fair is an annual event that has been in existence for over two decades. According to Rowe (2011) the annual antique fair was established in 1992 after the *Antiques Roadshow* from the British Broadcasting Corporation (BBC) "crossed the Atlantic for the very first time. And it took place in Kingston, Jamaica." Rowe (2011) added that the BBC program gave the Jamaican collectors "tremendous encouragement."

This "encouragement" can be compared to a double-edged sword. On the roadside in certain areas of the capital, one can find vendors selling possibly illicit items ranging from bricks to copper boilers. According to the *Concise Oxford English Dictionary* an antique is defined as "a decorative object that is valuable because of its age" (Soanes and Stevenson 2004:58). Furniture and household items tend to be popular antique items. Antiquities are described as "objects or buildings from the distant past" (Soanes and Stevenson 2004:58). An artifact is typically a portable object that has been made, modified, and used by human beings. Artifacts have an extensive time line dating from at least 50 years to thousands of years ago. Another problem is that some of these antique dealers are misguided and believe that sale of these artifacts is "allowed as long as they remain in Jamaica" (Rowe 2011). This is particularly critical when some antique dealers are also selling artifacts that may have been looted from historic and archaeological sites.

The JNHT Act does not have a clear definition of an artifact; however, the act does make reference to "objects" in its definitions for national monuments and protected national heritage (1985:4–5). The JNHT Act (1985:4–5) details the national monument as follows:

> (a) any building, structure, object or other work of man or of nature or any part or remains thereof whether above or below the surface of the land or the floor of the sea within the territorial waters of the Island or within an area declared in an order made, under subsection (2) to be within the maritime resource jurisdiction of the Island;
> (b) any site, cave or excavation, or any part or remains thereof, declared by the Trust to be a national monument; "occupier" includes any person engaged in any development or maintenance works in, or over or under any national monument; "owner" means the person in whom is vested the freehold interest in the site of the protected national heritage.

"Protected national heritage," as defined by the JNHT Act (1985:4), is as follows: (a) any place name; (b) any species of animal or plant life; (c) any place of object (not declared by the Trust to be a national monument), designated by the Trust to be a protected national heritage.

UNESCO subdivides cultural heritage into intangible and tangible types (UNESCO 2017a). Intangible cultural heritage encompasses oral traditions, performing arts, and rituals. Tangible cultural heritage can be further subdivided into movable, immovable, and underwater. According to UNESCO movable cultural heritage includes works of art, coins, and manuscripts. Artifacts are recognized as cultural property. Immovable cultural heritage encompasses archaeological sites and monuments, including underwater cultural heritage such as "shipwrecks, underwater ruins, and cities" (UNESCO 2017a). The responsibility of managing cultural heritage is dependent on the frameworks present in the specific country. Based on the UNESCO definitions, in Jamaica the management of these cultural resources is the responsibility of three institutions: the IOJ, the JNHT, and the National Library of Jamaica. This management system is based on the types of cultural heritage governed within their acts and mandates. The focus of this chapter is on the archaeological resources, as such the two main institutions involved are the IOJ and JNHT.

According to UNESCO's definition, artifacts and antiques are types of cultural heritage. There is an overlap between prehistoric artifacts and antiquities, and likewise in the case of historic artifacts and antiques. One of the issues is distinguishing the associated context. Damien Huffer (2011) questioned the "legal and contextual differences inherent in the selling of archaeological 'antiquities' vs. ethnographic/historic 'antiques.'" Huffer (2011) added that "depending on the region and artifact type in question, there may be very blurry boundaries indeed between antiques and antiquities." The commentary highlighted that although local and global legislation may view artifacts, antiquities, and antiques as "one and the same," many of these artifacts have become isolated and "lifted from their contexts" (Huffer 2011). Huffer's article raised some key issues regarding how artifacts are valued—is this based on the provenience, association, manufacture, usage, age, or collection history (provenance).

The value of an object can be inherently subjective. To the layperson, an antique is anything old, while an artifact is also something old. The terms seem to be interchangeable. In the case of Jamaica, public education programs are needed to highlight these issues and thereby prevent the destruction of cultural heritage. Although human remains are not cultural objects, their treatment is an example of the problem. On the occasion when indigenous skeletal remains have been discovered by laypersons, they have been destroyed. A skull from a burial at Chancery Hall in St. Andrew, for instance, was destroyed by workers on the site in the belief that the person who recovered the skull was going to use it to perform obeah (Allsworth-Jones et al. 2006). Obeah is an African-derived spiritual system. It is defined as "the practice of harnessing supernatural forces and spirits for one's own personal use" (Giraldo n.d.). In Africa it is known as *Obeye*; however, in the Caribbean the system has many names, such as Obeah (Jamaica), *Voodoo* (Haiti),

Santería (Cuba), *Ju-Ju* (Bahamas), and *Shango* (Trinidad) (Giraldo n.d.). The practice has become infamous and is generally depicted in a negative light. It is typically associated with evil and self-interest; however, traditionally it was a source of strength and resistance for enslaved Africans in the West Indies (Giraldo n.d.).

From time to time, individuals may take in artifacts for identification to the JNHT or the IOJ. Obtaining clarification on the provenience of the artifact is usually a challenge. In the instances when the individuals choose to disclose the information, the authorities can only take the individual's word until the information is confirmed by a site assessment. In other cases the individuals do not wish to share the location. Currently, if an artifact is found on private property, it belongs to the landowners. Based on the existing laws, "artifacts remain property of owner of site who can dispose of cultural material at will" (JNHT 2009a:14). This freedom of disposal does not prohibit sale of the cultural property.

Although cultural agencies will encourage donations, they cannot force the private owners, nor do they offer a reward, since entities like the JNHT do not encourage valuating archaeological objects, as this is against archaeological ethics. Herein lies the problem, since many individuals who approach the cultural agencies with artifacts wish to determine authenticity, value, and compensation.

THE RAIDING OF SITES

In Jamaica there is no system to gauge an increase in illicit trade of cultural objects. Hypothetically, we can assume that the level of private collecting is on par with that of the nineteenth century; however, there is no way to determine the true scale. What is more apparent is that those selling illicit objects are less discrete, such as the roadside vendors mentioned previously. The convenience of the internet has also made anything and everything available, even the sale of artifacts.

The illicit trade of cultural objects is also the instigator of another critical problem—the raiding or looting of sites. Popular heritage sites—for example, the Taíno settlement at White Marl, St. Catherine; the first Spanish capital at Seville, St. Ann; and the underwater "pirate city" at Port Royal, Kingston—have had their share of looters for decades. For example, the site of White Marl, Jamaica's largest and longest-occupied Taíno village, was discovered around 1860. Its location was lost until the 1940s, when the construction of the main road to Spanish Town cut through the site. Ever since, White Marl has been continuously raided due to its location, political volatility, and the difficulty of controlling access to the site. During visits to the site today, fresh holes can be observed where looters have dug in search of artifacts.

The looting of sites is not limited to well-known heritage attractions. At Round Hill, a significant Taíno midden in a remote area of Clarendon, the JNHT found several areas of ad hoc digging (Jamaica National Heritage Trust 2007:49). The looters took the desired objects and left "hundreds of pottery sherds, decorated and undecorated pieces" scattered on the surface (Jamaica National Heritage Trust 2007:49).

Another example is the case of Falmouth, one of Jamaica's five historic districts notable for its eighteenth-century Georgian architecture. In 2009, the Falmouth Harbour was dredged for the construction of Genesis Claws, a cruise ship pier that was expected to accommodate two *Oasis of the Seas* mega-liners simultaneously. It was reported that numerous historic artifacts were recovered during the dredging process, which went to a depth of 11.5 m (37.7 ft) (Jamaica National Heritage Trust 2009b). A significant portion of the material was dumped in the sea about 9.7 km (6 miles) out from the dredging site, at a depth of 1 km (3,280 ft) (Jamaica National Heritage Trust 2009b). The remaining artifacts (onion wine bottles, ceramics, and metal objects) were taken from the site and sold illegally. The JNHT conducted a watching brief, which is a type of assessment undertaken during construction projects that seeks to protect, retrieve, and record archaeological resources. This investigation confirmed both the dumping of the artifacts and their theft by various individuals for eventual sale (Jamaica National Heritage Trust 2009b). Discussions with the contractors for the Falmouth project resulted in their assistance in curtailing the movement of additional objects. The investigation also revealed that the authorities had no clear estimate of the number of artifacts that were stolen and sold. No action was taken against the thieves, even though some blatantly admitted to stealing objects.

Historic structures are also vulnerable to vandals who salvage everything from floorboards to red bricks (Dalton et al. 2009:8). Even sites with protected status such as the Old Barracks in Spanish Town, St. Catherine, have been targeted. In the case of the Old Barracks, it was reported that bricks from the structure were extracted and sold. There have even been cases of grave looting at historical sites, such as at Pimento Hill, St. Mary, and at Point, Hanover. At these sites, looters took the grave goods and discarded the skeletal remains on the surface (Jamaica National Heritage Trust 2015:11).

Fortified sites, especially in the Hellshire Hills such as Fort Clarence and Dean's Battery, have also been looted. It seems that cannons and cannonballs are particularly valuable. This could also be a result of the scrap metal trade. From personal observation, a number of the cannons that once featured at these sites are missing and could have been stolen. The weight of the cannons alone suggests that these looters have an organized system of manpower to remove and transport these cultural materials.

At Seville, where a heritage site is under the management of the JNHT, the problem is not limited to the theft of cultural material but also to the infrastructure put in place to protect the site itself. The Seville property spans over 200 acres from the hills of St. Ann to the sea, divided by the north coast highway. The northern section seems to endure more traffic than the southern section, where the remains of Sevilla la Nueva is located. Sevilla la Nueva was the first capital of Jamaica under the Spanish from about 1509 to 1534 and contains the remains of the Governor's House and one of the earliest sugar mills on the island. The mill was excavated by Robyn Woodward and her team from Simon Fraser University (Woodward 2006). To protect the mill, a structure was built to cover it, but over time the thieves removed the plexiglass, the timber frames, and the shingles. It is clear the current security system in place at the site is inadequate.

The petroglyphs from the Canoe Valley Caves are another sobering case. Also known as the Bailey Spring Caves in Manchester, these sites were discovered in the early twentieth century (Lee 1990). The area contains three rockshelters that once housed the largest cluster of petroglyphs in Jamaica. Cave 1 was investigated by Martin and MacCormack in 1916, when approximately 35 petroglyphs were documented (Figure 4.1).The site was later mapped in 1965 by James Lee. By 1970, however, the petroglyphs in Cave 1 were severely damaged (Figure 4.2) when, according to Lee (1990:157–158), "a misguided person who sought to 'save' the carvings from possible damage by the construction of the new south-coast highway sliced off all the best petroglyphs by a rock saw and, though many are relatively unharmed, others were spoiled and the site as a unit has been ruined."

Caves 1 and 2 were reidentified by Philip Allsworth-Jones and George Lechler in November 2005. However the third cave reported in 1916 has yet to be found (Jamaica National Heritage Trust 2007). These rock art sites are currently a part of the Canoe Valley Protected Area, located in the parishes of Clarendon and Manchester. Collectively, the area has the largest concentrations of rock art on the island, with at least five petroglyph sites in the region. Although James Lee believed that these petroglyphs were taken for possible protective reasons, it seems suspicious that the petroglyphs were not handed over to the IOJ. Instead, they have disappeared, and it is not certain whether they even remain on the island.

What has been discerned from these situations is that, even if the artifacts or features are later handed over or acquired by the cultural authorities, determining provenience is difficult. Outside the case of the Canoe Valley Petroglyphs, most of these artifacts are undocumented, often making it impossible to identify them out of context. These actions diminish the amount of data that can be potentially retrieved about Jamaica's past, as well as af-

Figure 4.1. Petroglyph cluster at Canoe Valley Cave, Manchester. (Photo courtesy Estate of James W. Lee)

Figure 4.2. Section of the Canoe Valley Cave 1 where a number of petroglyphs were removed by a rock saw. The darkened areas, highlighted in figure, are where the petroglyphs were cut from the rock surface. (Photo courtesy Lesley-Gail Atkinson Swaby)

fect the integrity of the individual sites, and in the worst-case scenario lead to their destruction.

TAÍNO-INSPIRED ART, QUASI-TAÍNO ART, AND FORGERIES

Around the 1960s, possibly due to the White Marl research program, precolumbian peoples (Taíno) became a source of inspiration for some of Jamaica's notable artists. The Taíno "began to filter into the consciousness of the people," which is evident by the reproduction of Taíno motifs into contemporary Jamaican art (David Boxer, personal communication, 1999). Prominent artists like Carl Abrahams, Gaston Tabois, Osmond Watson (Figure 4.3), David Boxer, Karl "Jerry" Craig, Norma Rodney Harrack, and Anna Henriques have incorporated indigenous themes into their works. Thus, there has been a tradition for Taíno-inspired art. Reproductions of Taíno vessels have been used by museums and incorporated in displays on indigenous livelihood, however they are not always acknowledged as such (see also Swogger, chapter 6 herein).

Figure 4.3. *Afrowak Madonna* by Osmond Watson (1989). (The Lesley-Gail Atkinson Swaby Collection. Photo courtesy Lesley-Gail Atkinson Swaby)

For at least 30 years, there has also been an influx of Taíno forgeries. Private collectors seem to be especially targeted, as the sellers would not attempt to approach Jamaican cultural agencies. Thus the Jamaican authorities are unaware of the provenience or persons producing these fake pieces. The forgeries are primarily made of stone and are supposedly ceremonial celts, axes, metates, and *duhos*.

The stone artifact displayed in Figure 4.4 was observed in the collection of the late George Lechler. From personal observation, the object resembles a Mesoamerican metate, which is a flat or slightly depressed stone used to grind cereal, grains, and vegetables. This object, however, contrasts drastically from the few authentic metates recovered on the island, though these may be evidence of trade with Central America (Howard 1956). This particular object (see Figure 4.4) also does not display typical Ostionoid or Chican Ostionoid (Taíno) characteristics but is suggestive of a modern reinterpretation of an indigenous style. It may be a *duho*, which are the stools of the caciques (chiefs). These are primarily wooden, but coral and stone *duhos* have been found in other islands (Ostapkowicz 1998). If this object is a stone *duho*, it would have been without a back. The two *duhos* that have been found at Cambridge Hill Cave and Hellshire Hills are both wooden and have high backs. Thus, the Mesoamerican design, the stone medium, and "neo-Taíno" (new indigenous-style) imagery all suggest that the object in Figure 4.4 is a recent creation.

Since the 2000s some private collectors have attempted to authenticate a number of objects believed to be Spanish contact period Taíno artifacts (Banks 2012, 2013). Many of them are beautiful, reflecting great talent and

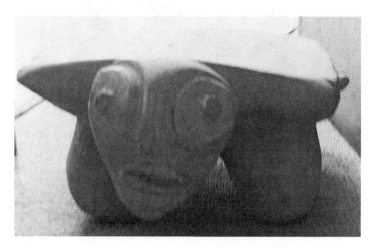

Figure 4.4. Possible fake stone duho or metate. (The George Lechler Collection. Photo courtesy Angus Mol)

skill. It is obvious, however, at least to the trained eye, that these are contemporary pieces. From personal observation, several are very similar to the artifacts featured in *Taíno: Pre-Columbian Art and Culture from the Caribbean* (Brecht et al. 1997), possibly attempts at duplicating the artifacts in the publication.

According to Banks (2012), "the imagery and evidence of tooling" suggest that the pieces were created after the arrival of the Spanish. Banks states that these objects have been recovered from the Dallas Mountains in St. Andrew, the Upper Yallahs Valley in St. Thomas, and Port Maria in St. Mary. This is particularly interesting because when questioned about the provenience of these artifacts in the past, this information was not forthcoming. Surface examination of the tool marks reveals metal tools were employed. The type of stone material used is also questionable. In the present case, it would be irresponsible for the Jamaican archaeological community to ignore issues such as questionable authenticity and no clear provenience. Perhaps if these objects were presented as Taíno-inspired art, the academic community would have been more receptive and interested in studying them. From observation, they display not only Taíno influence but also African and Mesoamerican.

In the past some collectors willingly purchased fake artifacts in hopes that something real and truly valuable would eventually be obtained (Figure 4.5). One particular collector has been adamant that these forgeries are real and seems determined to find a local or international academic who will validate

Figure 4.5. Possibly fake Taíno stone artifacts. (The George Lechler Collection. Photo: Lesley-Gail Atkinson Swaby)

his claims. In addition, it seems that this collector is also selling these fake artifacts, suggesting monetary gain to be a motivating factor in his persistence to "authenticate" them. Moreover, if the objects had looked authentic, the archaeologists consulted would have requested to see the site where they were recovered in order to determine vital data about the context. Withholding locational data only weakens the case. Authenticity and provenience are very critical factors, and researchers would need access to the site to investigate and conduct further research on the objects. The Aboukir cemís, for instance, were discovered originally in the 1940s in a cave in the hills in St. Ann. These wooden artifacts consist of a 168.4 cm anthropomorphic ceremonial staff, an avian sculpture with a canopy possibly used for snuffing a hallucinogenic powder, and a small anthropomorphic spoon (Saunders and Gray 2006). When the Aboukir cemís were to be handed over to the JNHT in 1992, the source site was investigated and the artifacts were assessed and proven to be authentic.

CONCLUSION

The preservation and protection of cultural heritage should not be limited to the built environment. There should be adequate and functional protection for all cultural resources. To date there is no antiquities law in Jamaica; the closest is the JNHT Act of 1985. This act of legislation is not strictly enforced and has no teeth to prevent and stop the looting of archaeological sites, nor is there a local system in place to curtail the illicit trade and movement of artifacts. In 1970, the Convention on the Means of Prohibiting and Preventing the Illicit Import, Export, and Transfer of Ownership of Cultural Property was created, but Jamaica has currently not ratified this convention (UNESCO 2017b). Andrea Richards (2012) discussed the movement of Jamaica's cultural property and made suggestions for how to regulate it. In the past, attempts had been made to develop a training course for Jamaica Customs Agency personnel to identify cultural material, but this has not yet been implemented.

There is currently no inventory of Jamaican artifacts outside of the JNHT, IOJ, and UWI databases. A system to gauge the amount of local collectors and obtain an inventory of their resources is also absent. Discussions on the amendments to the JNHT Act have suggested that all artifacts on the island should be registered with the JNHT (JNHT 2009a). It has also been suggested by the JNHT that all artifacts should belong to the government of Jamaica (2009a). It is doubtful that this recommendation will have strong support outside of the government institutions and agencies.

Several researchers have attempted to identify Caribbean archaeological collections in overseas museums (Françozo and Strecker 2017; Ostapkowicz 1998, 2015). It is not certain, however, if this information has been incorporated into the Jamaican databases. Recently, the Honourable Olivia Grange (2018), minister of Culture, Gender, Entertainment, and Sport, announced that Jamaica is developing a national register of cultural heritage places and objects. According to Minister Grange, the register will be developed through amendments to the JNHT Act (Jamaica Observer 2018), which has been under revision for the past ten years. It is hoped that the revised act will address these current shortcomings, provide adequate public education, and that the protection of archaeological artifacts will be considered an important cultural resource.

5

Spice Isle Sculptures

Antiquities and Iconography in Grenada, West Indies

Jonathan A. Hanna

Grenada is the southernmost island in the Antilles archipelago, roughly 90 miles from Trinidad and Venezuela (Figure 5.1). A former British colony, its people today are English speaking and predominantly of African and East Indian descent. Due to its historic dominance in global nutmeg exports, Grenada is often called the "Isle of Spice." At European contact, however, Grenada was known as "Camerhogne" (or "Camáhogne") by its Amerindian inhabitants (Breton 1999:204). Since 1962, five archaeological projects have worked to uncover the island's precolumbian record, identifying 87 precolumbian sites at present count (see summaries in Hanna 2017, 2018). The history of this archaeological work has had a unique effect on public awareness of Grenada's prehistory. This chapter explores the relationships between looters, collectors, archaeologists, and the general public in Grenada—from the seemingly endless looting of the Pearls site, to the various attempts at replica-making by archaeologists, to the ways in which the past is perceived and reinvented by the citizens of this culturally rich, economically poor, small island nation.

A LOOTER'S ART STUDIO

If there is one precolumbian site in Grenada that most Caribbean archaeologists are familiar with, it is Pearls (site #GREN-A-1) (Figure 5.2). Over 75 years ago, in 1943, construction crews graded the area (previously a golf course) for the island's first airport (Martin 2007), disturbing an enormous archaeological deposit. Perhaps Amerindian remains had been known from the Pearls area prior to this (hence its name, which was in common usage by the eighteenth century), but surely the extent of those remains was not.[1] Unfortunately, the artifacts overflowing from the backhoe piles sparked a free-for-all, and by 1956, artifacts from Pearls had made it to the British Museum

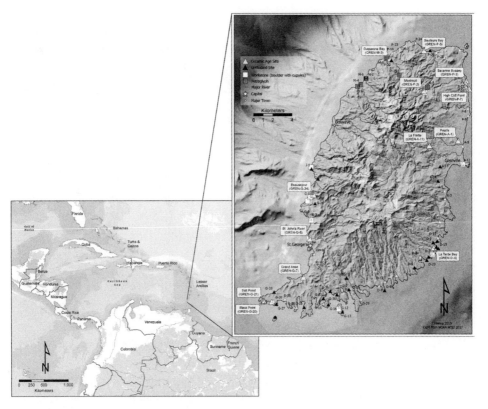

Figure 5.1. Prehistoric archaeological sites in Grenada. (Map courtesy Jonathan A. Hanna; base maps with digital elevation model [DEM] courtesy Environmental Systems Research Institute [ESRI] and National Oceanic and Atmospheric Administration [NOAA] and National Centers for Environmental Information [NCEI])

(British Museum 2018) and likely many other museums around the world. On nearby islands, Bright (2011:77) reports artifacts from Pearls on display in St. Lucia's Vigie Depot and Trinidad's National Museum and Art Gallery. Across Grenada, small private museums and displays (e.g., collector's houses, jewelry stores, and restaurants) invariably contain the zoomorphic adornos characteristic of the Pearls site. However, since all of these artifacts are un-provenienced (i.e., looted), we may never know their original provenience.[7]

Beginning with Ripley Bullen's excavations in 1962 (Bullen 1964), archaeological investigations at Pearls recovered ancient beads and pendants of exotic gemstones and non-native faunal remains sourced as far south as eastern Brazil and as far north as Vieques, Puerto Rico (Cody 1990; Giovas 2017; Hofman et al. 2011; Laffoon et al. 2014; Newsom and Wing 2004). Discoidal shells, lithic tools, bone pendants, and a highly decorative ceramic assem-

Figure 5.2. Pearls archaeological site (GREN-A-1) and previous excavations. FFR = Foundations for Field Research. (Map courtesy Jonathan A. Hanna; base map courtesy Environmental Systems Research Institute [ESRI])

blage of complete vessels and innumerable zoomorphic adornos have also been recovered. My 2017 survey confirmed the site to be one of the largest and longest occupied on the island, with radiocarbon dates delineating human occupation from AD 300 through AD 1300 and ethnohistoric evidence for continued occupation through AD 1649, when the French permanently settled the island (Hanna 2018). While there are other, equally significant archaeological sites, the size of Pearls and the attention it has received make it a standard proxy for researchers referencing Grenada's prehistory. Thus, from the unprecedented Amerindian site to the plantation-era windmill along the adjacent Simon River, to the 1970s revolution-era airplanes, Pearls encapsulates the entire history of Grenada. In this role, it is an ideal case study for the status of Grenada's heritage overall.

Following the closure of the Pearls airport in 1986, a playing field was graded north of the airstrip, destroying another large section of previously undisturbed material. At the same time, the USAID-funded Cocoa Rehabilitation Project (CRP) extracted truckloads of soil just east of the playing field area, effectively doubling the extent of disturbance overall. Despite the country's heritage laws at the time (e.g., the 1967 National Trust Act; see Byer, this volume), it took two years for the Grenada National Trust to stop the "soil" extraction (Cody 1990:40). Oddly, the soil at Pearls (a predominantly alluvial sandy loam with moderately high fertility), while adequate planting soil, is not the richest on the island, archaeological remains notwithstanding (see "Plains Sandy Loam" in Vernon et al. 1959:31); it is also the *same* soil type as Boulogne Estate, where it was sifted (Hanna 2017:31). It is unclear, then, *why* the CRP chose this exact location for soil extraction.[3] Indeed, the main effect of the extracted soil was not a revival of the cocoa industry (that would not happen for another two decades) but the creation of "faux archaeological sites" wherever that soil—and the artifacts it contained—was deposited (Cody 1990; Hanna 2017).

Around this time, local papers reported that carved "greenstones" (probably nephrite and serpentine) had been found at Pearls, fomenting an onslaught of looting described as "a jade rush" (Keegan and Cody 1990:5). Although efforts by archaeologists and government officials eventually attenuated the pace, looting at Pearls continues to the present day. Indeed, it is testament to the site's size and length of occupation that, despite this troubled history, a tourist can still drive up to the airstrip and buy a bag full of zoomorphic adornos, sandy loam still stuck in their crevices.

In early 2013, I joined John Angus Martin (then director of the Grenada National Museum, or GNM) on a visit to a looter's house at Pearls. The man was surprisingly candid with us, openly discussing his looting activities and showing us a stash of boxes under his board house containing complete vessels, adornos, and small beads and gemstones. He even demonstrated how he reconstructed ceramic vessels using a mixture of wood glue and sawdust (Figure 5.3), which was both surprisingly clever and a potential way to identify artifacts he had sold elsewhere (i.e., a kind of signature), including objects on display at the GNM. He also mentioned his relationship with a buyer in the United States, to whom he sent "boxes . . . every month or so." It would appear that trafficking at Pearls had returned to a level last seen in the 1980s.

When asked about making replicas, the looter complained that replicas did not sell, pointing to a pile of stone sculptures he had made from basalt and andesite. Some were half-buried while others were blackened from use as hearthstones (see Figure 5.3). The way they were presented gave the impression of neglect, but in hindsight, these sculptures were almost certainly buried and burned intentionally to create the appearance of antiquity. Unbeknownst to us at the time, we had stumbled onto a burgeoning new art form. These stone sculptures (and many others like them) eventually did sell quite well. And in some ways, they would also curtail the site's continued destruction by providing a viable alternative to looting.

On the streets of St. George's, Grenada's capital, several artists today sell

Figure 5.3. Looter's art studio: restoration via wood glue and sawdust (*top*), collection of sculptures enduring the elements (*middle*), and burning sculptures to add credibility (*bottom*). (Photos courtesy Jonathan A. Hanna)

the same stone sculptures we saw at Pearls, often marketing them as authentic precolumbian artifacts. Like adornos, these stone statuettes (made from basalt, andesite, and various greenstones) depict a mix of anthropomorphic and zoomorphic faces carved into oval and oblong stones. They typically have large, button-shaped eyes (sometimes multiple pairs), and puffy cheeks. Some are stylized variations of three-pointers, condor pendants, petroglyphs, and possibly even Suazan-type ceramic figurines (e.g., the Lavoutte Statue, see Hofman and Hoogland 2009:7), perhaps indicating some level of research by the artist (although they do not have any precolumbian precedent—see Discussion below). Some sculptors agree it would be better if these were valued as works of art in their own right, rather than considered forgeries, but "authentic" artifacts have more appeal (see Geurds, chapter 9 this volume). The other problem, however, is distribution: shop owners do not have the capital to pay for merchandise in advance, and artists do not trust them to allow consignment. This severely limits production, scale, and impact on the illegal antiquities market. Nonetheless, there are enough sculptors on the island that these art forms have become a ubiquitous part of the Grenadian landscape—a situation to which we now turn.

COLLECTING CAMERHOGNE

By 2016 (three years after visiting the Pearls looter), neo-Amerindian stone sculptures had overrun Grenada. Many local collectors had bought them by the barrel (believing them to be real),[4] the GNM also had several boxes of them (a few on display as authentic artifacts), and one could even find them embedded in the facades of buildings around St. George's (Figure 5.4).

One collector admitted some sculptures were probably fake, but they had to purchase everything in order to acquire the (authentic, precolumbian) ceramics that came with them, not to mention keeping the seller coming back—an issue other collectors had mentioned as well. Such comments are deceptive, however, because sellers are invariably poor and desperate for money (what Staley calls "subsistence diggers"; Staley 1993), so buyers have more control than they let on. Nonetheless, local collectors are now competing with external buyers in an ever-globalizing world, so having a wide variety (even an overstock) of antiquities could offer a competitive edge (Figure 5.5 outlines these basic relationships).[5]

In some sense, then, the amount of stone sculptures in a private collection represents that collector's involvement in the antiquities market. That is, regardless of authenticity, some objects are mere by-products—proxies for the total volume of antiquities that had gone through the collector's hands. Indeed, one collector who had hundreds of stone sculptures is well known to local authorities for antiquities dealing. Since collectors do not tend to be

Figure 5.4. Neo-Amerindian sculptures: in a building facade (*top*), in storage at the Grenada Museum (*middle*), and on display at a small museum in Sauteurs (*bottom*). (Photos courtesy Jonathan A. Hanna)

forthright about illicit deals, by-products like these might function (at the very least) as a general barometer for collecting habits and scale.

Given the volume of stone sculptures in some private collections, these objects may also be difficult to sell onward, whether because of their size or questionable authenticity. Other collectors have a similar overabundance of large, heavy items. For instance, one collector is believed by local authorities to have sold several historic cannons from the island, which are notoriously

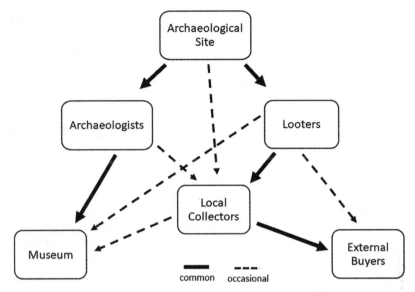

Figure 5.5. Flow of artifacts through the looter-collector-archaeologist network. (Courtesy Jonathan A. Hanna)

burdensome. Another has a sprawling collection of large copper vats left over from plantation-era sugar and cocoa production. Like stone sculptures, "coppers" are heavy, difficult to move, and may have little market demand.

Copper pots and cannons, of course, are authentic, historic artifacts, but stone sculptures are not. The collectors with hundreds in their yard were surprised to learn *none* were probably genuine antiquities. Perhaps it was a mistake to enlighten them, however, given the likelihood they would now refuse such neo-artifacts, thereby pushing the seller(s) back toward actual looting again. When serving as "authenticators" (inadvertently or not), archaeologists inherently maintain the standards for "authentic" precolumbian artifacts, which lessens the value of new creations, reinforcing the allure of authentic antiquities, and thus, in effect, encouraging the continued destruction of the very sites archaeologists aim to protect (see Ostapkowicz and Colten, chapter 8 this volume, for Irving Rouse's grappling with this issue).[6]

On this note, determining an unprovenienced object's antiquity contributes very little *new* knowledge to our understanding of the past. The determination is completely reliant on data from well-provenienced artifacts found elsewhere. Even basic provenience (e.g., island or site location), says nothing of how deep it was in the ground, what other objects it was associated with, what part of the site it was in, what part of a structure, the geochemistry of the soil, associated residues, associated fauna, associated seeds and botanicals, and so on—none of these can be reestablished (without archaeological documentation) once disconnected from their context. Even describing the style of an object as characteristic of a particular site is problematic—what if it was traded? For these reasons, constructive interpretation of the past neces-sarily relies entirely (with few exceptions) on archaeological provenience, not single objects (Coggins 1969). As the adage from a popular introductory text-book states: "It's not what you find, it's what you *find out*" (Thomas 1998:96).

ARCHAEOLOGISTS—A ROAD LINED WITH GOOD INTENTIONS

Returning again to 1962, Ripley Bullen, of what was then the Florida State Museum, surveyed Grenada and conducted limited archaeological testing across the island. His seminal report (Bullen 1964) laid the foundation for the island's ceramic typologies and for subsequent archaeological investiga-tions (e.g., the local types used in regional charts such as Rouse 1992:53).[7] However, since there was no national museum in 1962, there was no suit-able place to house the artifacts Bullen had unearthed. There were also no international heritage laws, so Bullen simply shipped ~25,000 artifacts from Grenada back to the Florida Museum of Natural History (FLMNH) (as well as type collections to the Yale Peabody Museum and the Smithsonian's Na-tional Museum of the American Indian), where they have safely remained ever since. To his credit, Bullen left roughly 5,000 artifacts on the island for the purpose of establishing a future museum (Bullen 1964:1–2). Unfortu-nately, that did not happen, and while a few dozen of Bullen's artifacts have since been identified in private collections (Hanna 2017:33), the vast majority have disappeared—there was simply no institution to maintain and protect them on the island. Meanwhile, the artifacts sent to the United States have remained in good stead, curated in sterile, pest-free, temperature-controlled facilities for half a century and available to study by successive generations of students (e.g., Donop 2005; Mistretta 2018).

In 1976, three American expatriates finally established a National Museum in Grenada (Dividend 1981; Whiting 1983:52).[8] One of these expats was an amateur archaeologist, Leon Wilder, who surveyed every beach in Grenada, recovering historic and prehistoric artifacts for display. Wilder found the iconic wooden canoe showcased at the GNM (apparently having washed up from South America), and he discovered a previously unknown series of petro-glyphs at Duquesne Bay. He also loved ground-stone artifacts and systema-tically collected 124 axes and 125 celts that he described in his only known report (Wilder 1980). Unfortunately, while the report meticulously analyzes the shape and color of each axe, it omits any mention of provenience, except a vague statement that they were all found in "the more lush, wet areas of the island where the biggest and tallest trees were found" (Wilder 1980:12)— ostensibly the island's interior but probably more a hypothetical than eviden-tial statement. In fact, the five axe proveniences that have been reported ar-

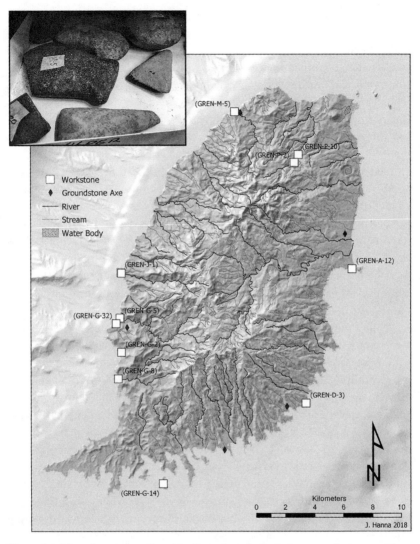

Figure 5.6. Map of stone axes found in Grenada and proximity to work stones, with inset photograph of stone axes in the Wilder Collection. (Map courtesy Jonathan A. Hanna with base map courtesy Environmental Systems Research Institute [ESRI]; photo courtesy Brittany Mistretta)

chaeologically in Grenada (yes, just *five*) are all from coastal areas, not the "lush, wet" interior (Figure 5.6).

Adding insult to injury, all of Wilder's 250 axes (and many other groundstone implements) were eventually removed from the National Museum and sent to the United States amid an argument with the family that later took over the GNM. Given the neglect shown to the collection (see the condition of the GNM's storage in Hanna 2017), this may have been understandable. Nonetheless, the end result was that, despite all he had done for Grenada's heritage, and however unintentional the repercussions, Wilder had single-handedly looted and exported *hundreds* of Grenada's precolumbian stone axes, without any semblance of documented provenience.[9] Reading his report, there is no doubt he wanted to preserve them for scientific research (hence, too, why they were eventually donated to the FLMNH, rather than sold for profit), but the manner in which they were acquired precludes all but the most superficial studies (e.g., see an attempt by Fandrich 1991).

Wilder likely did not understand the wider ramifications of his actions, but another archaeologist who worked in Grenada in the 1980s absolutely did. In 1994, Thomas Banks was accused of selling artifacts to local collectors and was eventually expelled from Grenada after nearly a decade of working there. Reports from his organization, Foundations for Field Research (FFR), show excellent archaeological methods and documentation, as do photographs of excavations and labeled bags deposited at the GNM. These same reports, however, hint at financial troubles, which may have been his motivation for selling some artifacts.

While the exact circumstances of the Banks episode are not known to the present author, with details provided only via personal communication with those present at the time, potential evidence of Banks's backdoor dealing recently appeared unexpectedly. While investigating the stone sculpture phenomenon, a local collector produced several objects that bore unmistakable resemblance to artifacts described in one of Banks's final reports. At the site of La Sagesse (GREN-D-1), Banks recovered numerous pendants and beads made from stone, shell, and bone, one of which was a circular shell disc carved with a punctated cross (Banks 1993). The items shown by the local collector appeared to be the same as those in Banks's report, including a carved shell disc with a punctated cross (Figure 5.7). When asked if the collector purchased these from Thomas Banks, the collector claimed everything was from Pearls. Yet the La Sagesse shell disc is especially suspicious, given its distinction as the only etched discoidal shell ever reported from Grenada. Was the collector, then, simply using Pearls (a site well known for its looting) as a cover, diverting attention from the *other* sites they have looted? Such is the malleability of provenience in the hands of collectors.[10] Banks broke the archaeological code of ethics, but perhaps we can be grateful he documented his finds before selling them into the oblivion of a private collection.

As for Pearls itself, one interesting (and more positive) intervention occurred in a workshop run by the archaeologist Henry Petitjean Roget in August 2000. Alarmed at the level of looting at Pearls seen during the 1999 Conference of the International Association for Caribbean Archaeology (IACA),

Petitjean Roget and IACA conducted a stone replica-making course at Pearls. This was intended to be the beginning of a series of workshops that would create a more virtuous cycle of sustainable economic activities based at the site, including plans for additional lapidary workshops, ceramic replica-making, and construction of a visitor's center (Petitjean Roget et al. 2000). Unfortunately, misunderstandings and arguments with local officials resulted in the program's cancellation. The Grenadian government then took a different tack, legalizing the sale of archaeological materials from Pearls under certain conditions (e.g., those from heavily disturbed areas)—what they called a "white market" (analogous to that proposed by Borodkin 1995). It is not known how many objects were sold in this way, nor whether there was any documentation about the objects that changed hands, but the scheme did not last long—the collectors continued to sell objects on the black market, undercutting what they saw as an unnecessary tax, despite the belief that authenticated provenience should *add* market value. Ultimately, the "white market" collapsed, and Pearls was again abandoned to the whims of collectors and looters.

Yet, while the IACA workshop was an initial failure, Petitjean Roget had still trained a dozen local people in stone replica production, some of whom taught others in their community. Indeed, the looter/artist mentioned at the beginning of this chapter had learned his replica-making skills from a neigh-

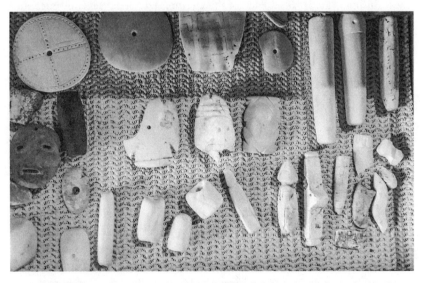

Figure 5.7. Drawer of a private collector with shell disks similar to those depicted in the Banks (1993) Report of Excavations at La Sagesse (GREN-D-1); other shell and bone tools in this collection likely originated at La Sagesse, among other sites. (Photo courtesy Jonathan A. Hanna)

bor who had participated. Herein lies the spark that set alight the recent proliferation of stone sculptures across Grenada.

What is so interesting about these modern stone carvings, however, is
how much they have taken on their own, idiosyncratic style. In a subtle (and
sometimes not so subtle) way, these objects depict modern Grenadian interpretations of Amerindian art. It is to this topic that we now turn in the final
section.

PERCEPTIONS OF THE PAST

As a former British colony, local perceptions of historical value in Grenada
are heavily influenced by British sentiments—for example, architecture, historical names and dates, and such—but this is combined with another, less
obvious Grenadian valuation system involving (among other things) memory.

On the morning of January 16, 1991, a large boulder slipped from a moun-
tainside in Concord, St. John's Parish, and landed on a moving public bus,
killing all nine people on board. As the worst vehicle accident in Grenada's
history, it remains in the minds of Grenadians today,[11] and the government
has since placed a memorial plaque marking the event along the Western
Highway.

Just down the road from the memorial, a local Rasta has created his own
monument to the victims by carving their portraits into a rock outcrop along
the main road (Figure 5.8). Each of the victims is depicted several times, and
the artist has since expanded his repertoire to include portraits of Maurice
Bishop, Fidel Castro, and Haile Selassie (respectively, the Grenadian revolutionary, the Cuban revolutionary, and the Rastafarian-revered former em-
peror of Ethiopia). Is it mere coincidence that these modern "petroglyphs"
occur not far from the cluster of Amerindian petroglyphs in Grenada's northwestern corner? Beyond the similarities in medium, the Concord portraits
also attempt to memorialize the dead, just as many precolumbian petroglyphs
have been interpreted (Wild 2003).

Unlike the Concord "petroglyphs," Grenada's stone sculptures have fewer
parallels in prehistory (see Discussion). There is some similarity with other
confirmed precolumbian mediums—for instance, two petroglyphs in Grenada have a somewhat similar style to the sculptures (Union and Mt. Rich)
(Figure 5.9). But Grenada's stone sculptures are best seen as local interpretations of Amerindian lifeways rather than anything grounded in archaeological research. This perception is succinctly captured in a placard at a small
museum in northern Grenada: "Some of these sculptures . . . may represent
a way of life, or an event, maybe a marriage, the birth of a child, a fertility
ceremony, death of a family member, an important or great event, a boun-
tiful crop, successful hunting skills, or a battle won." Given that these are all

Figure 5.8. Modern petroglyphs in memory of victims in the 1991 Concord bus accident. (Photos courtesy Jonathan A. Hanna)

Figure 5.9. Authentic stone sculptures? "Ceremonial Stone Hatchets" in Fewkes 1907, Plate XV (*top left*); "Stone Idols from Cuba" in Fewkes 1907, Plate LXXII (*top right*); likely original petroglyph at Mt. Rich (GREN-P-1, *bottom left*); likely original petroglyph at Union (GREN-P-28, *bottom right*). (Bottom photos courtesy Jonathan A. Hanna)

modern art (unbeknownst to the curator), this probably goes beyond the artist's vision, but it does offer an interesting window into how Amerindian values are perceived by the modern Grenadian public.

DISCUSSION

Neo-Amerindian Stone Sculptures in the Caribbean

At the 1975 International Congress for the Study of the Precolumbian Cultures of the Lesser Antilles (now IACA), Katheryne Kay (1976) presented a review of carved stones found throughout the Caribbean, of which several categories ("sculptured heads," "elaborate amulets," and "sculptured petaloid celts") appear to match the stone figurines seen in Grenada. They share some resemblance to "Macorís stone heads" (or "cabezas de Macorix") of Puerto Rico

(Oliver 2009), and some shell guaízas (Mol 2007), but there are major differences, too. As Oliver (2009:145) points out, "in contrast to the relatively flat guaízas, the [Macorís] stone heads are three-dimensional sculptures . . . [with] large, round, and deep eye orbits, and prominent bony cheeks that depict skeletal personages." Few of Grenada's sculptures have these hallmark "skeletal" features, often opting instead for puffy cheeks and smiling faces rather than gnashing teeth or grimacing mouths, not to mention the typical pedestal backing of Macorís (see Figure 5.30 in Waldron 2019). Thus, to be clear, the stone figures discussed here are not Macorís, nor anthropomorphic elbow stones, stone collars, trigoliths, and such, the authenticity of which is not under discussion here. But there are other examples of similarly dubious stones, as Kay's report indicates. Few of these appear to have archaeological provenience, although most were collected by antiquarians who did not typically document such details. It is notable, too, that some predate the Paredones affair (see Ostapkowicz, chapter 1 herein, and Alvarez et al., chapter 2 herein), despite bearing obvious similarities. Several suspicious "ceremonial stone hatchets" and "stone idols" in Fewkes (1907) were collected as early as 1903 (see Figure 5.9). These "stone idols" also bear resemblance to two "ceremonial celts" depicted in Joyce (1916:230; also referenced in Rouse 1964). Ostapkowicz (chapter 1 this volume) describes even earlier examples of forgeries. The inside cover of Bullen and Bullen (1972) also depicts an anthropomorphic stone sculpture from St. Vincent that was supposedly "dredged from the Kingstown harbor," while still others lurk amid museum collections everywhere (e.g., Waldron 2019:Figures 5.13 and 5.40). Atkinson Swaby (chapter 4 this volume) reports a similarly recent proliferation of stone sculptures in Jamaica, "discovered" solely by local collectors. None of these examples appear to have archaeological legitimacy and should be viewed with skepticism.

The pastime of deceiving elite foreigners is likely not a mid-twentieth century phenomenon (e.g., derived from Paredones), and the lack of provenience for so many anthropomorphic stone figurines in the Caribbean casts doubt on their occurrence in prehistory. As Fewkes notes for one in his publication: "more testimony would be desirable to establish fully its authenticity" (Fewkes 1907:179). Over 100 years later, we have good reason to be just as skeptical. Without an archaeological analogue for this artifact type (particularly the variations emerging in the Lesser Antilles), there is no legitimate foundation of knowledge to interface with. As is shown here, the vast majority (probably all) found in Grenada are recent creations.[12]

To be clear, such "fakes" are not the core problem. The producers of neo-Amerindian sculptures found a solution to two dilemmas: the legal risks of looting (at least in modern times, although fraud may carry legal risks as well), and the low profits of replicas. By calling their work "real," they created a sustainable resource for themselves. Among the options for material, stone is much easier to counterfeit than ceramics and much harder for archaeologists to discern, given their often-unconventional form. Even petaloid axes have been convincingly faked in large quantities (see Valcárcel Rojas et al., chapter 7 this volume). And for most consumers, these modern artifacts satisfy their desires for exotic works of art from the Caribbean. The problem arises when fakes end up on display in local and international museums as examples of precolumbian artifacts and interpreted as such (see also Swogger, chapter 6 this volume). But fakes ending up in museum displays is the fault of researchers, not artisans—again, interpretations of the past should generally not be based on unprovenienced artifacts.

THE CURRENT SYSTEM AND LESSONS FOR INTERVENTION

Until recently, buying antiquities in Grenada was mostly legal as long as they were not exported (except at the sites of Pearls and Grand Bay, Carriacou, which were specifically named in the 1990 National Heritage Protection Act). The new legislation, gazetted in July 2017, now levies a $10,000 fine for looting anything older than 50 years, but it has yet to be implemented (let alone enforced).[13]

Collectors argue that they are saving items that would have been destroyed or otherwise exported abroad. Absent effective government intervention, they may have a point. However, collectors are often unaware of where their artifacts actually came from, as made clear by the collector (above) who erroneously (though perhaps not unintentionally) claimed everything was from Pearls. Because an object's research value is intrinsically tied to its provenience, collectors are not actually preserving anything—they are simply bankrolling destructive looting. As Donna Yates adeptly points out in chapter 10 in this volume, shame is a perfect weapon against collectors because their collecting habits are motivated by prestige. "Calling out" offenders is therefore a highly effective (yet underutilized) tool against collectors and fellow archaeologists that run afoul.[14]

But just as importantly, stronger ties between archaeologists and communities are clearly needed. As has been seen with other public archaeology projects, the successful protection of heritage sites rests considerably on the surrounding community, whose members often play a role in looting and vandalism (Derry and Malloy 2003; Hofman and Haviser 2015). It seems clear that the rampant looting and neglect of many archaeological sites in the Caribbean (and developing world broadly) could be curtailed by such a grassroots approach to archaeological research. If archaeologists are to heed the call to "decolonize" archaeology (Oland et al. 2012; Orser 2012), we must be mindful of the intellectual gentrification and colonial overtones in our relationships with the (often underprivileged) people we interact with while "in the field." The more we act like keepers of some elite flame of knowledge, the more we marginalize the very people we need to engage. We must also be aware of the often-complex history of archaeological research in the countries we are working, since archaeologists sometimes contributed to the problem (e.g., Thomas Banks above).

Ultimately, Grenada's looting and forgery problems are a symptom and a sign of its development. As people's livelihoods are improved, they have become more interested in their island's history—an exemplary case of Maslow's (1943) "hierarchy of needs." Laws have been enacted to protect heritage sites across the island (see Byer, Appendix herein), but implementation has been slow. More proactive community engagement would empower local people to become stewards of their cultural heritage while also providing economic incentives (e.g., heritage tourism). In the process, such efforts would bring to light a new form of "folk art" brewing in the countryside for decades—a local reinvention of Amerindian aesthetics inspired by the past, forged in the present, and promising much for the future.

NOTES

1. In 1922, Fewkes (1922:119) mentions the similarity of (Saladoid-Barrancoid) adornos on Trinidad and Grenada, most likely referencing material from the Pearls site, although he does not specify the location. The name "Pearls" dates at least to the 1760s, when a bill of sale mentions the area "now generally known by the name of the Pearl Estate" (Proudfoot 1772). Many thanks to J. Angus Martin for this reference.

2. There are at least three other Saladoid-Barrancoid sites on the island (i.e., with similar artifacts), but they are much smaller, less extensive, and less well known than Pearls. Only Pearls has been consistently marked on maps of the island, no doubt encouraging both passive (e.g., tourist) and systematic looting. Since at least 1966 (DOS map #442, E703), maps of Grenada tend to have a symbol north of the Pearls airstrip that reads "Amerindian Remains [Here]."

3. While the CRP's soil extraction is documented in Cody (1990:40) and confirmed via personal communication with various members of the National Trust, as well as a worker at Boulogne (Hanna 2017:31), no mention of this extraction is made in the USAID reports (e.g., Fiester 1989; USAID 1991), suggesting the soil removal was an ad hoc initiative of Grenada's Ministry of Agriculture.

4. The term "local collectors" in this chapter refers to wealthier individuals (often elite expats of the United Kingdom and United States) engaged in purchasing antiquities from local looters and (occasionally at least) selling them onward to other buyers. They may profess they are salvaging artifacts from sites that will be destroyed, but they are far more involved in the market than avocational/salvage archaeologists. They have also done little to slow said destruction. Indeed, these collectors are neither interested in protection nor record-keeping/provenience, except for the purpose of looting more artifacts themselves "for fun."

5. Other common buyers are tourists and medical students studying at Saint George's University, an American medical school in Grenada. These buyers seek out precolumbian artifacts, apparently as mementos of their time in the Caribbean. However, these are likely the most naive buyers of antiquities, unaware of what Amerindian objects from archaeological contexts in Grenada look like and, presumably, the legal ramifications.

6. The act of writing this very chapter (and even this book) presents the same dilemma, of course, but the number of sculptures now on display in local museums (interpreted as genuine antiquities) has become a source of great misinformation. Ultimately, I hope that these pieces can be profitably sold as neo-Amerindian artworks. The fascinating story behind them, as recounted in this chapter, will hopefully add to their allure.

7. See Hanna (2019) for a revision of these local typologies.

8. Some of Bullen's artifacts were on display initially. However, arguments with the family that eventually took over the GNM led to their removal (similar to the Wilder case below, among others). About 100 of these have since been identified in the Cynthia Hughes Collection on display at the Westerhall Rum Distillery.

9. A large number of stone axes from Grenada (and Carriacou) were also collected by an earlier petroglyph enthusiast, Rev. Thomas Huckerby (1921; see also Fewkes 1922:49, 88), commissioned by George Heye, and now in the Smithsonian's National Museum of the American Indian. Many axes can also be found on display at local museums, including the Grenada National Museum, the Cynthia Hughes Collection at the Westerhall Rum Distillery, the Rome Museum, the Glebe Street Museum in Sauteurs, the museum at Belmont Estate, the Karaya Arawak display at Dodgy Dock, and private collections such as those owned by the Wilcox, Gaylord, and Taylor families—none have provenience beyond country of origin (and even that is an assumption).

10. Recent interest in this particular collection has resulted in highly detailed analysis of the ceramics and gemstones, among other things. The anecdote here highlights the fact that such time and attention would be better spent on artifacts with solid provenience. As shown, taking a collector's word that an artifact is from Pearls may not only lead to erroneous site associations but also chronological errors. As far as I know, the only gemstones with archaeological provenience from Grenada are the ~150 actually from Pearls described by Cody (1990), which are currently in storage at the Grenada National Museum. Moreover, such detailed studies serve as tacit "authentication" of private collections, adding to their perceived monetary value.

11. A common phrase in the English-speaking Caribbean is "if it pleases God"—used when referencing future events (e.g., "see you tomorrow, please god"). When asked why they say this, older Grenadians tend to say, "Lord can take you any time," and then mention things like car accidents and falling rocks—invariably referencing this specific bus accident in 1991.

12. None of the stone artifacts from Grenada reviewed by Wilder (1980) were carved faces or designs, nor are there examples from earlier fieldwork, as far as I am aware. Yet more systematic scrutiny of the provenience data for stone sculptures in

museum collections is duly needed, as we surely do not know enough of the range of Caribbean iconography to deem all "stone heads" without provenience as fraudulent.

13. The commonplace 50-year rule for protection neglects authentic modern artifacts (e.g., remains of the Grenadian Revolution and subsequent US invasion) that also deserve preservation. For instance, the two abandoned airplanes at the Pearls airport—a highlight for most visitors—are not technically protected under any law.

14. Unfortunately, this is not often possible for junior/less-established/nontenured scholars and/or those working on small islands—two cases where politics can sink promising careers.

6

Genuine Reproductions

Ethics, Practicalities, and Problems in Creating a Replica
of a Zemi from Carriacou, Grenada, West Indies

JOHN G. SWOGGER

WHEN IS A copy not a fake? In 2014, the Carriacou Archaeology Project, a joint venture between the University of Oregon and University College London, recovered a unique stone zemi at the Grand Bay site on the island of Carriacou, Grenada (Figure 6.1). A zemi—also spelled cemí—is an object associated with Amerindian spirituality. Many are depictions of deities, spirits, or ancestors; they take on a variety of shapes, including anthropomorphic, zoomorphic, or transformational. One category of precolumbian Caribbean carving often called a cemí features a triangular or three-pointed shape (these are sometimes referred to as "three pointers"). They are carved out of stone or wood, often small and undecorated but occasionally large and ornate, carved with faces and geometric designs. These objects may have been "regarded as numinous beings and believed to have supernatural, magic powers" (Oliver 2009:3). They are "not only the deities themselves but also . . . idols and fetishes representing them, which were made from the remains of ancestors or from natural objects believed to be inhabited by powerful spirits" (Rouse 1992:13). These beliefs are historically documented (Rouse 1992:13), and zemis in many forms have been found at sites across the Caribbean. The highly ornate examples are now often considered both "artifact" and "art" (Brecht et. al. 1997:23–24).

The zemi appeared at the very end of the 2014 season. Christina Giovas (now assistant professor at Simon Fraser University) was walking along the eroded edge of the Grand Bay site when she spotted, poking out from between some tree roots exposed by recent rain, the face of the zemi (Figure 6.2). Subsequent excavation revealed an area of burning and the remainder of the broken object. Its discovery was as astonishing as it was alarming. Erosion has

Figure 6.1. The island. (Drawing courtesy John G. Swogger)

always been a problem at the Grand Bay site, exacerbated by years of illegal sand mining. The project was always mindful of the sheer volume of material that erosion had already removed from the site; another day's rain with a few more inches of erosion, and the zemi might well have tumbled out of the soil and washed into the sea (Kaye et al. n.d.).

The zemi was a large stone object, broken (probably post-depositionally) into nine large fragments, one of which included the entire head of the object. Its discovery presented the project with something of a dilemma. The excavation was coming to an end, no more seasons were planned, and our archive of finds—including the zemi—had been moved to a storage unit at the edge of town in order to free up space in the Carriacou Historical Society Museum; out of sight—and, quite possibly, out of mind. But at the same time, the zemi was an exciting and unique artifact (Figure 6.3). Although plain three-pointer zemis had been found on the island—and although other decorated examples had been found on other, larger islands—nothing like this had ever been recorded on a small island like Carriacou before. And while the zemi was published in the project's annual report, it was felt important to draw attention more widely to the possibility that sites on Carriacou might be archaeologically "richer" than previously thought.

The decision to create casts of the zemi was made in order to facilitate simultaneous display of the object in both the Historical Society Museum on Carriacou and the National Museum on Grenada. It was hoped this would

Figure 6.2. The zemi. (Photo courtesy John G. Swogger)

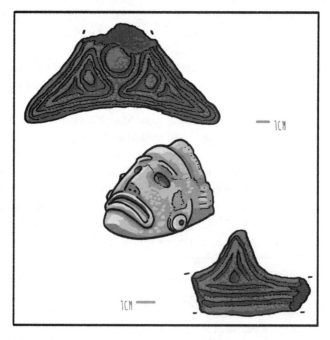

Figure 6.3. The artifact. (Drawing courtesy John G. Swogger)

allow both museums to advocate Carriacou as a place of particular archaeological significance, to stimulate scientific tourism and promote the research potential of the island to postgraduates. Furthermore, the story of the making of the casts—the transport of the original to the United Kingdom, the process of casting itself, and the return of both cast and original to Carriacou—was a unique public outreach opportunity. To us, the zemi was an artifact—like sherds of pottery, fragments of worked stone, or adzes made from conch shell. And we believed that, like any other artifact, the zemi could be used to engage public audiences with the archaeology we were carrying out on Carriacou. However, it has now become clear that, whatever our original intentions might have been, the presentation of a *cast* has raised some unanticipated—and potentially problematic—issues.

First, the original intention was that the museums would display the casts correctly labeled as copies, rather than as originals—and that the casts would be available for the public to handle, making their status as copies clear. This did not happen, raising the ethical question of whether the casts have moved from being mere "replicas" to being fakes; that is, are these now copies that work to deceive—however unintentionally or benignly—museum audiences?

Second, we intended that the casts would signpost the richness of the archaeology on Carriacou within the National Museum on Grenada and attract those interested in archaeology to Carriacou. However, those interested in the archaeology of Carriacou are not only tourists and archaeologists but also collectors and looters. The island is not wealthy and has no real means to protect its heritage against those who would illegally remove artifacts from known sites. Are these casts now functioning as the wrong kind of signpost, attracting the wrong kind of attention?

Lastly, because of the unusual nature of the original zemi, the casts themselves have inevitably developed an independent aesthetic appeal, reflected in requests by members of the team and the archaeological community for copies to use as teaching and display objects. While such copies contribute toward pointing out the archaeological richness of the island and its research potential, they also have the effect of adding new layers of economic and aesthetic value to the casts. What impact might this competing value have on the original artifacts, and can it be harnessed to further the original intention behind the making of the casts?

The journey of the zemi from artifact to art object, from find to fake, illustrates how archaeological practice and social context both assume and impose a multiplicity of identities on material culture. These identities are entangled, yet distinct, enabling archaeological objects to move from one milieu to another (as the illustrations that accompany this chapter aim to convey). While such complex and shifting identities may, indeed, prove problematic, they help illuminate the complexity and shifting identities that archaeology itself can assume. In so doing, they can help us negotiate those various identities in a way that gives our work and practice new meaning.

MAKING THE CASTS

Having approached the Carriacou Historical Society with our plans, the committee—headed by Randy Cornelius and the late Cosnel McIntosh—kindly gave permission for the zemi head to be loaned to me in 2014 for the purposes of casting. I was the project's illustrator, responsible for finds illustration as well as contributing to public outreach: helping with local museum displays, making posters and interpretation boards, and, latterly, creating comics about the project and its work (Kaye et al. 2009; Kaye et al. 2012). Although I had no direct experience producing such casts, I knew someone who did. I returned home to North Wales with the zemi head and began work with a colleague—Tony Meadows, a fellow archaeological illustrator turned sculptor—to produce a series of casts (Figure 6.4). I met with Tony in his cluttered, cramped studio, a shed filled with the mechanics and detritus of "art"—paint brushes and carving tools, clay and plaster, life drawings and maquettes. Tony works with Jesmonite—an acrylic casting material originally

Figure 6.4. The cast. (Drawing courtesy John G. Swogger)

designed for making decorative and architectural moldings. It is capable of taking a number of ancillary ingredients, including pigments and texturizers. Tony created several silicone molds and then created casts using a series of Jesmonite mixtures. These mixtures closely approximated both the original material and the variation in coloring that had resulted from the proximal in situ burning. The result was a set of casts that looked and felt very much like the original. Indeed, standing in Tony's studio, holding the original in one hand and a cast in the other, it was hard to know which was which. If you knew where to look, you could see faint marks where the two halves of the silicone mold joined; otherwise, the casting was so faithful that there was nothing to distinguish the original from the copy.

In the spring of 2015, I returned to Carriacou and Grenada, bringing with me a reproduction of the zemi head, which I presented to the director of the National Museum on Grenada and another that I presented to Carriacou Historical Society members Randy Cornelius and Cosnel McIntosh. At the same time, the original zemi was returned to the project's archive. That evening, I met Cosnel and Randy to watch the sunset and talk about the zemi. They were sufficiently impressed with the casting of the head that they readily agreed to casts of the remaining fragments. This would create a reproduction that showed how these fragments would all have originally fit together, and it would be much easier for the Historical Society to display than the originals. We quickly drew up a letter of permission to cover the making of the new castings, and I left the island the following day with the remainder of the zemi.

In addition to the casts that I presented to the National Museum on Grenada and to the Historical Society on Carriacou, Tony also made casts for the project's directors. These casts were intended to act as teaching and lecturing aids—but the directors also clearly appreciated them as aesthetic objects: they took pride of place on bookshelves and office desks. I, too, retained a copy, and it currently resides next to my drawing table. Clients comment on it when they visit my studio, and it is a great way to start conversations about the archaeology of the Caribbean. Another copy was presented to an archaeologist who works in a major museum in the United Kingdom, hopefully to encourage him to consider the island as a place for fieldwork. Tony, too, retains several slightly faulty casts displayed in his workshop. Although not featured in museums, these additional casts are also intended as "outreach" objects—but very clearly also have a display value that is more about aesthetics than archaeology.

Back in Wales, Tony found that casting the pieces of the body took somewhat more time than anticipated. Their small size, sharp corners and complex volumes meant that he had to design a rig that spun the molds in order to ensure the Jesmonite got into every nook and cranny. So it was not until spring 2017 that I returned to Carriacou with the new casts.

PROBLEMATIC COMPLICATIONS?

At this point I realized our intentions were going slightly astray. The story of the zemi was being complicated in three potentially problematic ways—ways that blurred our framing of the replica as a genuine "reproduction" and potentially raised several ethical red flags.

THE FAKE IN THE MUSEUM CASE

Our initial suggestion was that the replica zemis could be usefully employed in the museums on Carriacou and Grenada as part of a "hands-on" display. As they were replicas, not the real thing, they could be touched and handled freely and might encourage visitors to have a "closer engagement" with their Amerindian heritage. But while on Grenada, I discovered that the cast of the zemi head was now being displayed not as a hands-on object, not as a reproduction that would help understand the original—but in a museum case, behind glass, alongside other artifacts and with a label that simply read: "Three Pointer" Zemi—Troumassoid—Grand Bay, Carriacou (Figure 6.5).

Figure 6.5. The exhibit. (Drawing courtesy John G. Swogger)

In other words, there was no indication that this was not the original, but a cast; no information that would lead a visitor to understand that this was a replica, not the actual artifact. Whether by accident, ignorance, or omission, whoever had created that label had not identified the cast as such—and the verisimilitude that Tony had worked so hard to achieve now worked against it; there was no immediate way to tell that this was not the original without such a label. The end result was a displayed object that came uncomfortably close to being no longer a copy or a replica, but a fake or a forgery; the zemi and its label—whether unintentionally or not—worked to deceive.

The quality of the casting, the texture of the material, the parsimony of the label, and the barrier of the glass case all strongly suggest that the zemi head the visitor now sees in the National Museum is the genuine article. Indeed, as staff changes and relationships between the museum, the government, and archaeologists involved in the Grand Bay excavations slip further into the past, and the continuity afforded by professional memory consequently erodes, the false narrative implied by the label might eventually supplant its true identity.

Unintentional Signposting

On Carriacou, evidence for systematic and large-scale looting at Grand Bay was first noted in 2003—with deep cuts into the site, neat stacks of unwanted sherds left behind, and local reports of "bagloads" of material being removed from the site (Kaye 2003:132–133). It is unclear what might have been taken— but the evidence suggested that the looters knew what they were looking for and acquired it in large amounts. Such looting, while apparently not endemic to the island, might be framed within an economic milieu that also includes the mining of beach sand at Grand Bay—in other words, one that ascribes economic value to the island's archaeological heritage as just another "natural resource."

Comparative examination of privately held material on Grenada may provide some clues as to the focus of such looting activity. It is quite common, as a tourist, to see small collections of beach-combed artifacts on display in many hotels, bars, and restaurants—particularly those near beaches. Collections such as these vary considerably in scale and quality—some appear to be random collections of body sherds, selected without regard to any governing aesthetic or other criteria. But in displays at several popular tourist destinations most of the objects are ceramic adornos and pieces of carved stone that have human or animal faces on them. One is struck by the fairly obvious conclusion that it might be the presence of a face that lends a particular aesthetic value and desirability to an object, and may well be what prompted the inclusion of particular artifacts within the collection. Perhaps similar aesthetic criteria might explain looting behavior on Carriacou. There are certainly plenty of adornos at Grand Bay, ones with interesting faces, too—and, as we discovered in 2014, adornos are not the only artifacts at Grand Bay to have faces.

It was our intention to use the replica to highlight the archaeological significance of the site—the detail and quality of the carving, the molding of the features. We wanted the face of the zemi to signpost the richness of Carriacou generally and Grand Bay specifically to respectful tourists, to archaeologists, researchers, and scientists—but what if this face were to signpost the site instead to looters and collectors? The irony would be that, having worked so hard to protect the site from damage caused by sand mining and its accompanying erosion, we might actually be undermining our own efforts.

The Zemi on the Bookshelf

Photographs and illustrations are all very well, but there is no substitute in the teaching of archaeology for the real thing. You are more likely to convince students to join your field school or convince a PhD candidate to take up a research project if you can actually show them an example of what they can expect. And if, for practical reasons, you can't employ the actual artifact, then a high-quality replica will do.

This is what prompted us to commission Tony to create a series of casts of the zemi for the directors and staff of the project. We cannot take actual artifacts off the island, but having the casts on our office bookshelves allows us to have very different conversations with students, researchers, and colleagues about Carriacou, and give those conversations about its archaeology a very different emphasis. I brought my copy of the zemi cast to the 2018 meeting of the Society for American Archaeology for the original presentation of this chapter for exactly this reason.

But the cast would not be half as "useful" if it were just a shapeless lump of rock—the zemi head has an obvious visual appeal that we find engaging, and that adds layers of value—and meaning. Other Caribbean archaeologists have now begun to ask if they can purchase copies, attracted by the aesthetics of the item rather than any specific association with the discovery, the island, or the project. Such copies could no longer be considered teaching tools, they must be regarded as ornaments—signifiers of antiquity and erudition, sitting decoratively on the office bookshelf (Figure 6.6). While this may be understandable, it further complicates the values associated with the casts. We wanted to have copies of this replica because they were useful—but what if these copies are desirable simply because they look good? What happens when an archaeological object ceases to be interesting "just" as data and starts to become interesting because it is also something else—and what happens when it is archaeologists who are unwittingly encouraging that additional interest? There is a risk that the zemi as office ornament sends out conflicting signals

Figure 6.6. The ornament. (Drawing courtesy John G. Swogger)

about the private curation of artifacts, amplified by professional authority. In an age when the nature of "ownership" of cultural material is being questioned, challenged, and redefined in our institutions, awkward questions may be asked why a choice to display an Amerindian artifact on one's office bookshelf because it "looks cool" is not somehow a form of cultural appropriation. The meaning of the zemi displayed in my own office is itself ambiguous and subject to the same examinations: I work freelance; I do not teach in my office; what justifies my claim that the zemi is "useful" to me? There is always the risk that possession of a replica indicates a lack of understanding of serious background issues—that it symbolizes at best, ignorance; at worst, complicity. As such, I, like my colleagues, have then a responsibility to acknowledge (and communicate) the complex interplay of authenticity and aesthetics, functionality and decoration that contextualizes both the replica and its possession (cf. Brulotte 2012:131).

RECONSIDERATION AND OPPORTUNITY?

My return to Grenada and Carriacou in 2017 made me realize that these three unconsidered consequences blurred the meaning behind our original intention to produce the cast of the zemi. A combination of squeezed timetables and budgets—and also a lack of experience—meant that our exciting discovery and our fantastic casts raised a trio of potential ethical red flags. However, these also provide an opportunity for an interesting reconsideration of what a replica like our zemi means, and through such reconsideration suggest new ways in which replicas might be used to deepen—rather than worsen—local intersections with heritage in museums, the community, and the classroom.

The Zemi in the Museum

Perhaps it is not that the replica in the museum is being presented as "real"—but that we never considered how the replica could be presented as "fake" in the first place. After all, a museum is a place for "real" artifacts—not copies; how else should one understand an object in a museum other than as real—and priceless? To us, the fact that the cast was a replica meant that it was intrinsically of less worth than the original. But to a museum that does not necessarily have the capacity to commission such a replica, such a cast might well retain as much rarity value as the original; if it was damaged, lost, or stolen, the museum might have as little hope of replacing it as if it had been the original.

Looking back, as the person responsible for bringing the cast to the museum, and as the project's illustrator responsible for its public outreach, I should have realized that the cast might require as much—if not more—explanation than other archaeological artifacts in order to give it context. Such an explanation might serve to rebalance the asymmetric value ascribed to the replica by making it clear that this cast is potentially one of thousands, each costing less than $50 to make. Such an explanation, identifying the zemi head as a manufactured replica, might prompt a string of questions from museumgoers: the zemi is a replica—why? Who made it? How did they make it? Why isn't the real zemi on display? Where is the real zemi? Questions like these would have been a chance to answer a lot more than simply: "Three Pointer zemi—Troumassoid."

I recognize now that the real failure here is that the replica is perhaps less in danger of becoming a "genuine" forgery than a missed opportunity. The solution that immediately suggests itself to me is to seize the opportunity to produce some new and engaging informational content for the museum. Using as a basis the comic-strip series I have already produced on behalf of the Heritage Research Group Caribbean (Swogger 2018), I have started working with Tony Meadows on ideas for a display panel that—using a combination of sequential illustrations and 3D elements—will both explain the casting process and tell the story of who made the cast and why it was made in the first place. In other words, reconsidering the problematic identification might be an opportunity for visitors to the museum to learn about an aspect of the archaeological story that doesn't often get told, particularly in museums where budget constraints severely limit the storytelling and informational remit of gallery displays. And by extending the story to include a broad range of archaeological workers and the work they do, such an approach might be used to suggest educational and employment opportunities within archaeology beyond those normally visible in a small museum.

THE ZEMI BEYOND THE MUSEUM

Looting is motivated by the market value of ancient artifacts; collecting is motivated by aesthetic considerations. In both cases, it may be possible to explore the use of new technologies to "undercut" the market value of original artifacts and redirect desire toward new aesthetics. Tony's cast proves that it is both economically and practically feasible to create duplicates of objects like the zemi (Figure 6.7). If an adorno head can be sold once for $10 to a tourist on Grand Anse Beach, then twenty casts of an adorno head can be sold twenty times. The economics of looting make less sense if there is more value in selling copies than originals. Tony's casting took place in the United Kingdom—but casting does not have to. A small studio on the island would be a business opportunity that could be extended to other casting produc-

Figure 6.7. The souvenir. (Drawing courtesy John G. Swogger)

tion. As Jesmonite was originally designed to create decorative and architectural casts suitable for both exterior and interior use, a studio that casts archaeological replicas would not be limited to just such souvenir artifacts; the replicas could be part of a range of products and services. By linking casting of replicas to other business opportunities, the zemi represents the opening of a door not just to profit, but to skills and training.

If this were done in close partnership with the museum and various government ministries, added value might result through official sanction—sanction that could be integrated into publicity aimed at the potential local producers and tourist consumers. Moreover, rescue excavations could be organized at sites already targeted by looters and collectors, with excavated assemblages made available as originals to those producing casts—promoting a direct and safeguarded connection between economic benefit and heritage protection. The integration of 3D scanning and printing into the casting process would also bring the potential of new kinds of twenty-first-century technological training and skills opportunities. The involvement of local artists in developing their own creative responses could further extend this impact. Indeed, there have already been artists acting in this way, creating art objects—not quite fakes, not quite replicas, not quite copies, but a kind of creative entanglement with the archaeological past—based on material looted at the site of Pearls, for example. Just such an attempt was made during the 1990s with the encouragement of the International Association for Caribbean Archaeology (IACA), but the initiative lost momentum and ultimately proved to be unsustainable (see Hanna, chapter 5 this volume). However, developing long-term sanctioned approaches with an understanding of the existing market for artifacts in mind could redirect opportunistic participation and undercut the economic logic behind looting and collecting (cf. Brulotte 2012:55).

And, as the zemis on our mantelpieces suggest, "tourists" are not the only market to be served. There is clearly significant demand among archaeologists for objects that—aesthetically "ancient" but pragmatically "modern"—are actually more useful than the real artifact. Under official sanction, such a local production model could provide entire teaching collections of artifact casts to institutions interested in including Caribbean archaeology on their syllabi (see Valcárcel Rojas et al., chapter 7 herein, for an example from Cuba). Indeed, such an economically pragmatic model might well become a spur to engaging more scientific interest generally—exactly the original intention behind the casting of the zemi in the first place. Our replica zemi was produced outside the community from which the original came, with both economic and training benefit realized "overseas." But there are alternative models: in the American Southwest, Mexico, South and Central America, and the Mediterranean, replica-making is part of a package that brings local economic opportunities, facilitates skills training, and stimulates local creative engagements with processes and sources (Brulotte 2012, and see Geurds, chapter 9 herein). In such instances, the economic success of sanctioned replica-making has helped to transition the cultural economy beyond illegal looting to a creative reconnection with ancient culture.

THE ZEMI, "US" AND "THEM"

It would be interesting to explore how such creative engagements could be grown out of the existing creative practices that exist within archaeology: the visualization techniques, approaches and skills that we already harness for scholarship. After all, scientific illustrators and 3D modelers like myself already participate in this sphere of the cultural economy—fashioning craft replicas in a variety of media for market consumption. As an archaeological illustrator, my services and products may be purchased by universities and research institutions, but purchased they are. In terms of how I use my aesthetic skills and where I fit into an economic model, my practice is not that far removed from those of the tourist souvenir maker (cf. Bradley 1997:69–71) (Figure 6.8).

Figure 6.8. The creative engagement. (Drawing courtesy John G. Swogger)

Creative engagement with archaeology, history, and heritage is not just the preserve of the nonspecialist. Indeed, intelligently applied imagination is critical in expanding the horizons of archaeological thought beyond the trench, beyond the data. It has long been noted that the professional benefits of creative engagement with archaeology—though not unreported—often go unacknowledged. In other words, the value of "artistry, imagination, performance, playfulness, and enchantment as facilitators of the emergence and refinement of traditional archaeological method and theory" (Perry 2018:218) is hidden within disciplinary practice. But the creativity harnessed in the graphics, illustrations, paintings, and drawings employed in specialist publications is the same creativity that powers nonspecialist engagement.

There seems to be a gap here between the parallel engagements of specialist and nonspecialist creator that could be bridged—and perhaps we should be building that bridge. Perhaps we should engage with them, instead of expecting it always to be the other way around. Perhaps we archaeological illustrators, sculptors, and model-makers should shift the paradigm of the conversation by going out into the marketplace ourselves rather than expecting the souvenir makers to come to us. Indeed, perhaps facilitating public creative engagement with archaeological heritage should be an intrinsic part of public outreach—not just informing about the past, but demonstrating it by drawing on our own disciplinary heritage to make that past become part of contemporary creative practice (Swogger 2014). Instead of archaeologists "permitting" the use of archaeological originals as artistic inspiration (*contra* Brulotte 2012:90), archaeologists would actively demonstrate it; instead of "allowing" entrepreneurs to develop manufacturing techniques and artistic skills, archaeologists would actively share those they already make use of—skills and techniques like those Tony used in casting the zemi and that I used in drawing it. Such sharing of professional aesthetic skills between anthropological specialists and nonspecialists in host communities facilitate individual, personal engagements with the past (Hisashi 1996:iii). Rather than a specialist stewardship of heritage through the imposition of a dominant visual narrative with a selective, specialist perspective, in the service of a selective, specialist outcome, here is a path for a shared stewardship of heritage through multivocal, creative engagement and a multiplicity of forms. Such an approach already exists on Grenada, where the individual creativity of songwriting, storytelling, folklore, dance, and performance are harnessed in public festivals and celebrations such as the Spice Word Festival to help process the legacy of the revolution and intervention of the 1980s. This collaboration between individual engagement and public celebration already works to make difficult historical heritage "powerfully present" on the island (Puri 2014:259).

CONCLUSIONS

I have tried to use the questions thrown up by the casting of our "genuine reproduction" zemi and its unconsidered consequences to explore the possibility of new opportunities and new engagements rooted in disciplinary, economic, personal, and community creativity. Limitations of budget, expertise, and personal schedules meant that Tony and I embarked on making the zemi cast without identifying and making clear specific outcomes. Similar constraints mean that this chapter is a series of suggestions, rather than being an examination of lessons learned from an already-applied model. But such an approach does not have to be a limitation; instead, it can prompt a meaningful thought experiment—if these suggestions were to be used to create a model, what might it look like?

AN ASPIRATIONAL VISION

The rear courtyard of the National Museum is a hive of activity. In the rooms on the ground floor, small workshops turn out everything from pottery to covings, light fixtures to souvenirs. Each workshop employs a couple of people, creating castings, throwing clay, and carving stone and wood. Here on the table are a tray of ceramic lamp fittings, decorated with characteristic Saladoid curves and whorls copied from a reference library of archaeological reports. Once they have been fired, they will go to a hotel on Morne Rouge—a custom-designed order for refurbished rooms. In the workshop next door, two young artists put the finishing touches on a large mosaic panel. A government minister points out to a small group of foreign investors how the mosaic takes its inspiration from ancient Amerindian and contemporary African culture. One of the artists is a local teacher, and the plaque is destined to hang in his school in the north of the island.

Upstairs, above the courtyard, the rooms are full of school students making things out of clay and wire, papier-mâché and cloth. This week they have begun work on costumes for Carnival—one group is making new Shortknee tunics and masks; it is their turn to join in the Mas as new dancers. Another group is creating posters on large pieces of paper that describe the Shortknee Mas—these will be sent to the school in Mt. Royal on Carriacou, whose students will send back a description of their own Shakespeare Mas. Their teacher is talking with a visiting anthropologist, who cannot make notes fast enough. The anthropologist's students are enthusiastically helping to make new Shortknee "crowns"—a detail that has not been seen on the costumes since the 1960s and is being revived (Taylor 2009:Part2).

Back at the hotel on Grand Anse, a group of visitors from Guyana are clustered around a table set up in the lobby. Two potters demonstrate their skills, throwing and decorating replica ceramics—companions to those on sale in the hotel gift shop. A young archaeology student from Grenada talks confidently and knowledgeably about the ancient ceramics and how his group gives tours around the heritage of Mt. Rich—and, yes indeed, madam, we have a tour tomorrow. Would you like to sign up? (MYCEDO 2018).

And at the far end of the beach, just such a community excavation is taking place. Amid the music drifting from the bars, and under the curious gaze of visitors and locals alike, a huddle of local school children and diaspora kids from Peckham on a summer exchange program (Government of Grenada 2010), working alongside visiting archaeologists, are excavating the ghostly remains of a wooden boat in the sand by a new hotel development. "Was it abandoned here by pirates, slavers, or privateers?" the crowd asks. "None of these," says the young woman leading the community archaeology team—it's the remains of a fishing boat from the 1700s, perhaps damaged in a storm (Martin 2013:281). "My family used to be fishing folk in this part of the island," she says, "this is part of my heritage, and now it's part of my MA research."

Next to the excavation trench, an old man with a grizzled gray beard and long dreadlocks paints a picture on a small board perched on a rickety easel. With quiet precision he paints the boat not ruined and buried in twenty-first-century sand, but being hauled up the beach, battered but still afloat, its crew saved from the eighteenth-century storm. His style is uncomplicated and "naïve" (Mason 2005), but there is a real sense of place and time in the picture. "I'll pay you twenty dollars for it," a visitor says. "Thirty!" Another bids. The old man laughs. "This is for the museum," he says. "You'll have to paint your own!"

Such thought experiments are, in their own way, a kind of creative game; they are, of necessity, aspirational and idealized—perhaps even fanciful. But they are based in observations of things happening already on the island, as well as elsewhere, such as recorded by Brulotte (2012) and others (e.g., Hofman and Haviser 2015). Critically, however, this thought process allows us to see the future as unfixed and undetermined and to ask the crucial question: what if? What if we tried creative heritage projects on Grenada that were both ambitious in scale and interconnected across public, private, individual, and collective divides? What if we actively brought together heritage, art, sculpture, and archaeology—with entrepreneurship, training, and tourism (Figure 6.9)? What if we broadened our remit and went beyond museums and schools, onto the beach, or into the hotels? What if we thought about archaeology, material culture, education, jobs, and government on Grenada in an entirely different way? What if my colleagues on the island were to read this chapter and themselves think: what if?

As the references indicate, while the individual elements in this narrative

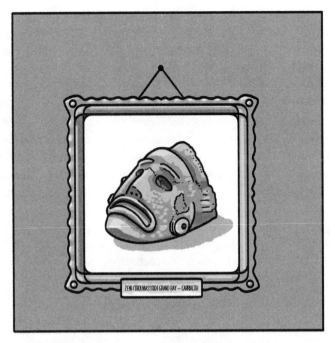

Figure 6.9. The conceptual hold. (Drawing courtesy John G. Swogger)

are all based on real elements situated within the broader archaeological and heritage setting of Grenada, this thought experiment allows us to "relax our conceptual hold" (Rowland 1976:48), and take the artifacts and data of archaeological research, and—using imagination and playfulness, performance, and enchantment—re-examine, re-present, and re-consider them within a narrative of professional practice (Perry 2018:218). Such a reconsideration suggests connections between elements—between visiting anthropological students and school craft projects, between carnival and revival of cultural practice, between artists and community heritage groups, between touristic development and marine archaeology. Currently, these individual elements are conceptualized as separate and discrete—but: *what if?* In some respects, I have already tried to embrace this idea of connections between disparate elements as an "aspirational vision" for heritage on Grenada in the final comic of a series produced for the Heritage Research Group Caribbean. Here, archaeology and carnival, craft projects and historic building conservation, economics and history are presented within a narrative of professional practice as equals (Swogger 2018:10).

Real—replica; art—artifact; genuine—reproduction: perhaps such binary definitions are not really what's important. Perhaps what is important is just the thing that so bothered me when I first saw the reproduction of the zemi inside the museum case: the ability of such objects to cross boundaries and, in so doing, usefully question the way we define them (Rowland 1976:44–51). However, archaeologists—with their professional interest in categorization and typology—may be discomfited by such interrogations (Perry 2018; cf. Hodder 2000:5 and Swogger 2000:151). There are issues to be considered that will inevitably shape the practical outcome of any *what if?* scenario.

There should, for instance, be more critical examination of my suggested roles for museums and archaeologists on Grenada with respect to the commodification of the past (cf. Stylianou 2013) and archaeology's lack of real-world "business acumen" when it comes to local heritage economics (cf. Koriech and Sterling 2013). Such critique should involve not only those with a background in local heritage but also those with a specific background in local economics. Acknowledgment must also be made that opening the door to what Radnoti (1999) calls artistic and archaeological "picaros" (tourist arts) may open the door to "real" fakes and "genuine" forgeries (Radnoti 1999). And such critique should involve not just archaeologists, art theorists, and art historians, but artists, collectors, and tourists.

Particular critical attention should also be focused on intersections with contemporary indigenous and descendant communities within the wider Caribbean (Joseph 1997; Martin et al. 2016). Despite the fact that Amerindian descendant communities have little living connection on Grenada (Martin 2013:297; UNHCR 2007), they nevertheless maintain a presence in the region (Caribbean News Now! 2018) and must be regarded as significant partners (Atalay 2012).

These are not trivial considerations—but our own boundary crossing and creative exploration of archaeological working provides us with a powerful tool not only to address these and other issues that the story of the zemi raises but also—as my thought experiment hopefully demonstrates—to look in new ways at public outreach aims, objectives, and project design. And, as I have indicated, such critical examination could help build collaborative practical partnerships with nonarchaeological specialists and community participants. Under such circumstances *what if?* could become: what next?

If presentation of the replica can be understood as a way to talk about the cast itself—not just what it was cast from; if the presentation of the replica can be harnessed as a way to expand the archaeological story; if the manufacture of the replica can proactively address issues such as looting; if the aesthetics implicit in its production can open the door to training and skills (and, yes, money)—then the story of our reproduction zemi becomes an opportunity to think imaginatively about the way the genuine zemi can create new meanings—and new opportunities—for archaeology on Grenada, beyond the narrow privileges of outsider interest.

7

Fakes, Copies, and Replicas
in Cuban Archeology

Roberto Valcárcel Rojas, Vernon James Knight,
Elena Guarch Rodríguez, and Menno L. P. Hoogland

The city of Santo Domingo in the Dominican Republic safeguards some of the earliest monuments of Spanish colonization in the New World. Among the imposing buildings, however, can be found souvenir vendors offering objects that, at first glance, appear so similar to genuine indigenous artifacts that an archaeologist lacking firsthand knowledge would be hard-pressed to recognize them as inauthentic. In a way, something of the conquered and suppressed indigenous peoples persists here among the symbols of Spanish colonial power, demonstrating the unusual courses that cultural persistence can take. These imitations are produced for different purposes, including numerous fakes destined for the collectors' market. Some of the fakes destined for the collectors' market are notable for their high quality and the high prices they command. Many are potentially works of art and, at the same time, instruments that inform us as much about the past, as reminders of indigenous creativity and technical skill, as they do about the present.

Such a situation also developed in Cuba, though without the scale of production, nor the perfection of neo-artifacts seen today in the Dominican Republic. The issue of reproductions/forgeries is a matter seldom discussed and generally underestimated in Cuban archaeological and museological research, perhaps because it occurred at a relatively early period and its development stopped almost completely in the middle of the twentieth century. Also lacking adequate assessment to date is the development in Cuba of an intriguing process of creating replicas for use in teaching and illustrating the archaeological record.

The dual cases of the Dominican Republic and Cuba in regard to fakes and copies of indigenous objects help to illustrate the diversity of paths taken by modern Caribbean peoples to forge and maintain links with their indigenous archaeological heritage and with a past that occupies millennia of regional history. In this chapter we offer a synthesis based on personal insights and a review of the largely understudied literature on replicas/forgeries in Cuba. The aims are to inform on the current Cuban situation in particular as well as to contribute to a regional perspective on the subject.

THE BROADER PICTURE: FROM TOTONAC CERAMICS TO THE MONUMENTAL ARCH OF PALMYRA

The superb fakes made by Mexican potter Brígido Lara have cast doubt on much of what was previously believed about the iconography of Totonac culture, and by extension, Maya and Aztec cultural material (Lerner 2001). Likewise, British art forger Shaun Greenhalgh's workshop successfully created falsifications in the most diverse materials, with a cultural scope that embraced Egyptian, Roman, Anglo-Saxon, and Assyrian themes (Hardwick 2010). These are just two of many examples that illustrate the fascinating and problematic character of fakes; they remind us of the enormous strength of creativity and human ambition and of the fragility of many historical and archaeological concepts. Some even see a poetic justice in these examples, whereby part of the society mocks and questions official knowledge, taking revenge—through the creation and sale of fake objects—for colonial plunder and the ambition of the elites (Lerner 2001). The case of the supposedly indigenous materials of Los Paredones in the Dominican Republic, which confused many archaeologists of the 1950s and 1960s and is still under debate (Pérez Guerra 1999:247; Vega 2015; see Ostapkowicz, chapter 1 herein, and Alvarez et al., chapter 2 herein), reveals to Caribbean researchers that this is a matter to be taken seriously, and underscores the fact that no region or culture is immune.

The difference between copies and fakes lies in the nature of imitation. Both seek to approximate the appearance of the original object, although the fake claims an authenticity that serves to deceive. Frequently, the faker does not try to reproduce a real object, but to create a new object that conveys the impression of belonging to a certain cultural or historical context. Here we are in the presence of artifacts that we could call *imitations*: "the construction of a new entity comprised of the imaginative fusion of the new and old works or artists" (Elkins 1993). Copies that seek to reproduce a particular piece also exhibit a range of accuracy or precision that may vary; when precision is high, we are in the presence of a *replica* or reproduction. Both imitations and replicas of original pieces have often been created with the intent of deceiving those who would acquire them as antiquities.[1]

From a Western perspective, the success of some falsifications has forced us to discuss the principles that define what is considered art, and the relationship between art and originality (Elkins 1993; Rubiano 2013). From an anthropological and archaeological perspective, the issue is complex because a fake can have an intrinsic value, which can increase in relation to the time and circumstances of its production and in its capacity to enlighten a certain historical period or society (Lowenthal 1992). However, fakes can negatively affect research, generate confusion, and lead to errors of interpretation that are far more serious than any inherent aesthetic or creative value (Gamble 2002; Jones et al. 1990).

Copies as a legitimate means of reproducing objects of aesthetic, historical, or commercial interest are documented from early times. During the European Middle Ages and Renaissance, copies of ancient sculptures, principally Greek and Roman, were made from plaster castings (Nichols 2006). The popularity of this practice gradually increased, coming to incorporate diverse subjects. It was linked to the art academies and to the collection by noble families of sculptures and antiquities. In the nineteenth century, the development of universities and museums gave a new impetus to this activity, situating it in the context of educational objectives and the construction of cultural visions supporting certain national projects developed in Europe (Frederiksen and Marchand 2010). Reproductions of body parts, using diverse materials, were also used in the study of medicine and anatomy at this time (Morell-Deledalle 2010).

Throughout the twentieth and twenty-first centuries the creation and use of copies or replicas of objects and monuments has been incorporated definitively in museology and in historical, anthropological, and archaeological research. For some authors, it is a vital resource and a legitimate part of the discourse of museums, entirely compatible with the handling of original objects (Morell-Deledalle 2010). Copies manipulated in the service of museum practice, or replicas that reproduce with high precision the features of genuine pieces or monuments, have various functions (Grove and Thomas 2016; Morell-Deledalle 2010; Yan 2010): they can complement museum exhibits or constitute in themselves the nucleus of the information presented to the public; they allow visualization of objects or monuments deteriorated or no longer extant, or that are in places inaccessible or inconvenient for visitation; they aid in the visualization of reconstructed spaces and objects, furthering an understanding of original forms and functions; and they operate as tools for didactic and educational ends and for cultural transmission. In addition, they provide an opportunity by which the original objects and monuments, by not being exposed, can be protected, conserved, and studied.

These replicas must be of an adequate quality and must be displayed in the most convenient way, identifying them as copies so that the public understands their nature (cf. Swogger, chapter 6 this volume). A key issue is that their creation must not jeopardize the integrity of the original object (ICOM 2017), a problem that new technologies seem to fully resolve. For example, a two-thirds scale replica of part of the Monumental Arch of Palmyra, destroyed by ISIL (Islamic State of Iraq and the Levant) in 2015, has been created using 3D printing and has been exhibited in different parts of the world, exemplifying the potential of these technologies in the face of present and future challenges to cultural heritage (Burch 2017).

The 3D printed replicas of archaeological objects are opening a new universe of possibilities. The capture of images and characteristics of objects using various techniques of digital photography and scanning in many cases practically nullifies the need for direct access to these objects, and any consequent alteration by contact (Santos et al. 2014). Additionally, 3D printing allows unprecedented fidelity in the creation of replicas. The availability of these models, which can be stored and distributed remotely in digital form, enhances the capacity for data recording and also the process of repatriation, as replicas may be transferred to indigenous communities or to the towns from which the originals came. Likewise, printing facilities reduce costs and increase the opportunity for multisensory interaction that enhances the comprehension of objects. These techniques enable an interaction with "artifacts," providing the potential to reach more varied audiences, including people of different cultural backgrounds and ages, or those with disabilities (Neumüller et al. 2014).

COLLECTING AND TRAFFICKING OF ARCHAEOLOGICAL OBJECTS AND FAKES IN CUBA

The first period of human occupation of Cuba is marked by the predominance of groups of fisher-gatherers, which in some cases managed cultigens (Chinique et al. 2019:113), who began arriving to the island at approximately 4000 BC. Between the seventh and eighth centuries AD, communities linked with the Arawakan language family of South America arrived. According to Cuban archaeological nomenclature they are known as *agricultores* or *agroalfareros* (agricultural ceramists) (Guarch Delmonte 1990; Tabío 1984). Irving Rouse (1992:7) includes them in the so-called Western and Classic Taíno groups. These communities controlled the greater part of the island in 1492 at the arrival of Christopher Columbus. Such a diverse and chronologically wide-ranging indigenous presence has generated an extensive material legacy that began to be recognized and collected in the nineteenth century. As of 2013, some 3,268 indigenous archaeological sites have been located on the island (Jiménez et al. 2018:42).

In the Cuban case, the production of fakes is clearly linked to the commercialization of antiquities and the development of artifact collecting. In the second decade of the twentieth century, within the framework of sessions of the Academy of the History of Cuba, there arose one of the first denunciations of forgeries on record; it was made by the Cuban anthropologist Fernando Ortiz, who gained the institution's support in raising awareness of this problem via the press (Estévez 2011).

In 1942, two important analyses (Herrera Fritot 1942; Rouse 1942) came to light that helped to address the issue of forgeries in the first half of the twentieth century. In 1941, the American archaeologist Irving Rouse visited the northern portion of the present provinces of Holguín and Las Tunas, one of the regions with the highest concentration of archeological sites of the agricultural ceramists communities on the island. His work took place throughout that year and consisted of an exploratory study of the indigenous archaeological sites of this area, including several excavations; the results were published in the book *Archeology of the Maniabón Hills, Cuba*. Rouse also exhaustively assessed existing information on this area and on Cuban archeology in general, which included direct examination of collections and the gathering of testimony from collectors. He prepared a valuable review of the history of research in this area and of the formation of collections from this part of Cuba (Valcárcel Rojas 2016a).

Rouse's (1942) work, which undoubtedly revolutionized Cuban archeology at the time, reported on the intensity of antiquities trafficking that had been reached in the region, particularly in Banes, which was directly related to an increase in collecting and indiscriminate excavation. In his opinion, this situation was accelerated in the 1930s, with many country folk dedicating themselves to digging for objects that were sold to collectors. He points out that antiquities had reached exorbitant prices for the time, due to high demand and competition among the owners of collections to obtain the best specimens. There were people recognized as diggers who had direct links with collectors who often acquired their pieces. Commercially motivated excavations had affected many sites, a phenomenon that Rouse considered difficult to stop.

Rouse's commentary reveals differences in the motivation for collecting at this time. For example, we have the case of José A. García Castañeda, then one of Cuba's most important collectors, who owned artifacts from the various cultures or indigenous societies that had settled on the island and studied the pieces from his own collection and published articles about them. He paid an excavator who worked at the El Yayal site, near the city of Holguín, for one year, specifically to bring him objects (Rouse 1942:38). Large quantities of materials were obtained that were unique at the time in characterizing the culture of the early colonial world and the process of indigenous adoption of European forms and objects. Castañeda maintained the integrity of the collection initiated by his father and always expressed an interest in forming a public museum. In fact, he exhibited his pieces in his house, which was constantly visited by students and researchers.[2] For other collectors, such as Dulce Baisi-Facci, a commercial interest is more evident. She formed two large collections from the same site (Potrero de El Mango, in Banes), whose continuous excavation she organized, and sold them to the Museo Montané in Havana (Rouse 1942:44–45). Regardless of this difference in motivation and cultural ideals, both practices, of course, had a destructive impact on archaeological sites.

In this environment, the manufacture of fake objects began to take hold, as can be recognized in many collections made during the period. In the case of Banes, hubs of forgery were located near the most important archaeological sites because of their size and richness; specifically, Potrero de El Mango, in the area of Mulas, and Yaguajay, later known as El Chorro de Maíta, in the zone of Yaguajay. The fakes were generally made from the materials more common at each site; thus in Mulas they were frequently made of bone, whereas in Yaguajay stone objects were more popular (Figure 7.1). In the Yaguajay area, one of the forgers was imprisoned for this kind of activity (Rouse 1942:70, 103, 106).

René Herrera Fritot (b.1895; d. 1968, professor of anthropology, official curator of the Museo Antropológico Montané at the University of Havana, and one of the most important Cuban archaeologists during the twentieth century), made a highly detailed and complete assessment on the subject of fakes, although he did not mention the origin or the owners of the collections

Figure 7.1. Imitations of archaeological objects of shell (*right*) and bone (*left*) from the Banes archaeological zone, Cuba, 2016. The largest piece measures 8 cm long. (Courtesy Lourdes Pérez Iglesias)

with which he dealt (Herrera Fritot 1942) (Figure 7.2). Like Rouse, he noted the strong relationship between forgery and collecting, a phenomenon that had reached notable proportions during the second and third decade of the twentieth century. Herrera Fritot speaks of an "archaeological fever" during that period, involving individuals who in many cases had formed private collections of archaeological artifacts.

The emergence of this "fever" is evident when we compare the number of collections of Cuban antiquities mentioned by archaeologist Mark Raymond Harrington, based on his visit of 1915, with those mentioned by Rouse in 1941. Harrington noted six private and three public collections in Cuba, as well as three others in the United States and several in Spain (Harrington 1935:69–85). In contrast, Rouse (1942:44–45), evaluating a relatively small area of Cuba, referenced 16 collections, formed mainly of materials from the Banes area, on the eastern side of the island. Most were located around the

Figure 7.2. René Herrera Fritot, 1968. (Courtesy Archives of Instituto Cubano de Antropología. Photo courtesy Ernesto Tabío Medina)

cities of Holguín and Banes, and many had been amassed in the 1930s. Some of these collections seem to have been created with the intention of selling them; in any case, it is unlikely that their owners were motivated by a love of archaeology. It is probable that some saw them only as a commercial resource.

According to Herrera Fritot (1942), collectors sought to boost the quantity of pieces they possessed. Prices depended on the personal appreciation of buyers, although these buyers often lacked the knowledge to determine the importance and authenticity of what they acquired. The demand for objects and their limited availability, as well as the prices they could attain, stimulated the production of fakes. Herrera Fritot (1942:10–11) classified these fakes into two types: unmodified, natural objects with suggestive forms, and those intentionally made. Among those intentionally made were both gross fakes and imitations of high quality. The forgers created stories about the places of discovery and often mixed fake objects with originals, which in the case of high-quality fakes could problematize their recognition. However, in Herrera's opinion, it was difficult to deceive a qualified archaeologist, who knew the indigenous materials in depth, as the variability of these was quite low and their features rather distinctive.

Herrera Fritot (1942) recommended being suspicious of pieces made of soft stone, as such pieces were not common in the archaeological record of any of Cuba's indigenous cultures; he suggested distrust of pieces lacking patina, indications of usewear, or breakage. He suggested studying the objects with care, looking within the incising and perforations for signs of metal tools. He also mentions, although it is not necessarily associated with the issue of fakes, the incorporation of African objects in some collections, or of indigenous pieces from other nonlocal cultures often obtained outside of Cuba.

Herrera Fritot's essay sought to alert collectors and also give them advice on the handling of objects to maintain their scientific value. He insisted on avoiding manipulations that on occasion were made with the erroneous belief that they would increase the value of objects, such as assigning proveniences (cultural origin or collection site) that were not known with precision, or retouching details to make the pieces more attractive. He also stressed the importance of preventing fake objects from being accepted, which would contribute to an erroneous image of indigenous materiality.

Falsified pieces made of stone were more common than the rare cases of faked ceramics (Herrera Fritot 1942:13–18). Among the stone fakes were several that suggested serial production due to their frequency and the repetition of certain characteristics: figures of sandstone with atypical traits, compositions, and postures, and pieces made of soft green steatite. Objects of this green stone were bought by various collectors, and even taken out of Cuba

(Herrera Fritot 1942:17–18). One of the collectors was taken to the site of an alleged "discovery" where he was shown recently "found" pieces. Herrera Fritot narrates the absurdity of the figures represented, wearing shoes and dressed in modern fashions, among other things. The most significant example, for the quality and quantity of objects produced by the same individual, was that of a set of faked petaloid axes. According to Herrera Fritot (1942:17), these were made in Pinar del Río province in westernmost Cuba using local marble, and they managed to deceive a renowned archaeologist who bought some of them. Individuals began to be suspicious due to their large quantity and excellent state of preservation. Thus, a detailed study was required, and several experts were consulted to discover the fraud.

A highly interesting case, reported several years after the publication of Herrera Fritot's article, was that of the collection of Augusto Fornaguera, located in Pinar del Río (see Figure I.9), which was reviewed by members of the Junta Nacional de Arqueología y Etnología in 1947. The published opinion (Royo 1948) mentions that the collection consisted of some 4,000–5,000 pieces, of which only 72 were considered genuine: seven of indigenous Mexican origin with the rest attributed to indigenous Cuban cultures. The evaluation considered aspects of style, kinds of materials, manufacturing technology, and presence of patina, among other characteristics. It described the fakes as "numerous and fantastic," it being possible to identify reptiles and anthropomorphic beings in various positions, ornate stone spheres, and artificial human skulls.

The expansion of collecting was undeterred. Forgeries probably continued unchecked as well, although we have not been able to locate data published on the subject after 1947.[3] The excavation of sites by looters who sold the pieces to national and foreign collectors, and to researchers either visiting or conducting studies in the country, was a practice that characterized the entire first half of the twentieth century in Cuba. This practice was more noticeable in areas of high archaeological potential and recognized presence of sites, such as Banes, Baracoa, Maisí, and the outskirts of the cities of Holguín and Santiago de Cuba. It came to the point that in 1964, researchers of the newly founded Centro de Antropología of the Cuban Academy of Sciences mentioned the partial destruction of many sites and their difficulty in locating undisturbed areas in archaeological localities (Tabío and Rey 1985:123, 184, 185).

Throughout the first half of the twentieth century, the Cuban government issued various legal decrees prohibiting the looting of archaeological sites to obtain archaeological objects as well as the exportation of pieces from the country (Hernández Godoy 2011; Junta Nacional de Arqueología y Etnología

1946). However, these decrees were rarely put into practice. With the Cuban Revolution of 1959, a policy of strong heritage protection radically changed the situation. The concept of private property, recognized in several previous heritage policies and which protected collecting, was deeply questioned and practically disappeared as part of a socialist-style social, political, and economic project. Very rapidly in this new environment, enormous support was given to the development of culture and science, seen as part of the national policy as resources to be defended and enriched (Núñez Jover et al. 2007). Archaeological heritage was perceived, politically and socially, as a national, progressive value whose protection and study was legally and institutionally organized—a process that continues up to the present time. From laws and decrees issued in 1977 and 1979, it was established that objects obtained from excavations of any kind or from casual finds were the property of the Cuban nation. The export of objects, always temporary, was regulated, as was their possession, transfer, and sale, and it was established that archaeological excavations could only be carried out by specialists (Consejo Nacional de Patrimonio Cultural 2002).

Personal possession of collections was strongly supervised, and the possibility of expanding these, or of establishing new private collections, was halted. The perception of archaeological collecting as a personal hobby, or as an economic activity, was entirely antithetical to new ethical and social values. In the midst of the fervor of the Cuban Revolution, new public museums proliferated and new research institutions were formed (García Perdigón 2014). The promotion of society and the nation above personal interests, and the real support given to groups interested in the establishment of museums and research, which in other times had been impossible dreams, stimulated the donation of the principal private collections to public institutions. Important examples were the creation of the Museo Indocubano Baní in 1965 from the collection of Orencio Miguel Alonso, and the donation of some of the largest collections in Cuba, including those of García Fería and the Grupo Guamá to the Cuban Academy of Sciences (Gómez and Martínez 2011; Rojas and Paris 2017; Vasconcelos et al. 2004:156).

In these circumstances, the commercialization and trafficking of archaeological objects were made illegal, and any stimulus to the production of counterfeits ended. Legal and social pressure, as well as the educational work of cultural institutions and museums, stimulated a significant reduction, and in some cases total cessation, of these activities.[4] This picture has begun to change. The economic crisis faced by Cuba in the last three decades greatly weakened archaeological work, which was never seen as a priority in shaping the national historical discourse (Valcárcel Rojas 2016b). This situation, together with material deficiencies of the museums network as well as the opening of the country to international tourism, have revived instances of looting and the sale of objects, although these do not, as yet, seem to be frequent.

REPLICAS OF ARCHAEOLOGICAL OBJECTS

The making of archaeological replicas as a means to record indigenous objects and so permit their museum display and study was a topic of interest for René Herrera Fritot, who spearheaded this approach in Cuba. Herrera Fritot had extensive professional training that included knowledge of geology, engineering, mechanics, geography, urban planning, architecture, museology, and physical anthropology, among others (Vasconcelos et al. 2004). He had worked as a technical draftsman, so he had skills in creating two- and three-dimensional reproductions (Rangel 2012:284), an ability that proved highly useful when dealing with iconographic aspects and typological evaluations of indigenous archaeological materials (see Herrera Fritot 1952, 1964).

In 1923, Herrera Fritot was appointed faculty assistant to the chair of anthropology at the University of Havana. In 1924, as part of this institution, he traveled to the United States, where for three years, in the National Museum of Natural History and the Museum of the American Indian, he completed studies and obtained training in techniques for mounting museum exhibitions, restoration, and reproduction of archaeological objects (Vasconcelos et al. 2004:155). In 1942, he was one of the founders of Grupo Guamá, an institution dedicated to archaeological and ethnological research that also had a museum (Museo Etnológico del Grupo Guamá) and a workshop for the reproduction of archaeological objects.

Grupo Guamá brought together the most important Cuban archaeologists, focusing not only on research and publication but also on the work of cultural advocacy, with emphasis on the presentation of exhibits and museum practice. Its artistic director was an internationally recognized sculptor, Ivan Gundrum Ferich (b. 1892; d. 1985). With extensive experience in the art of the ancient world, restoration, and conservation of art and museum pieces, Gundrum was thoroughly acquainted with techniques for making copies, and his artistic labors frequently re-created works of various styles, periods, and cultures. In fact, he owned a studio in Havana that specialized in the production of decorative accessories. He found a new source of inspiration in Caribbean indigenous artifacts and produced collections of copied pieces that are preserved in museums and institutions in Cuba, the United States, and the Dominican Republic (Haythorn 1984a, 1984b; Uyemura 1967). His incorporation of indigenous decorative and iconographic motifs as the basis of modern works became known as Neotaíno art (Herrera Fritot and Youmans 1946:13; Rangel 2012: 286) (Figure 7.3).

A key element of the exhibit work of Grupo Guamá was the use of copies

Figure 7.3. Ivan Gundrum with some of his Neotaíno sculptures. (Courtesy Marty Haythorn)

of archaeological objects created in their workshop. Herrera Fritot (1942:19) considered that scientific reproductions should derive directly from the original object in order to have the highest possible quality. They had to be precise in regard to dimensions, color, and materials. The purpose was to collect in their museum, for comparative study, a large assemblage of replicas representing the signature pieces found on the island. It was a strategy that also included an experimental component, particularly in the case of ceramics.

Gundrum created a large quantity of ceramic copies, in many cases following indigenous methods of manufacture, such that their principles of construction and decoration became important experimental archaeology studies (Uyemura 1967) (Figure 7.4).

Gundrum made copies of many of the ceramic vessels found at La Caleta site, in the Dominican Republic, for the museum of Grupo Guamá (see Herrera Fritot and Youmans 1946), helping strengthen the broader Caribbean profile of its collection. In 1955, he traveled to the Dominican Republic accompanied by the Cuban potter Luis Leal to collaborate with Emile Boyrie de Moya, director of the Instituto Dominicano de Investigaciones Antropológicas of the University of Santo Domingo (see Ostapkowicz, chapter 1 this volume), in the development of traditional craftwork with an indigenous theme (Rangel 2012:286). After the Cuban Revolution of 1959, Gundrum immigrated to Tallahassee, there working with Florida archaeologist Hale Smith in reproducing indigenous pottery vessels (Deagan 2010:20; Rangel 2012:286; Uyemura 1967). A collection of reproductions of precolumbian Gulf Coast pottery produced by Gundrum is preserved in the Tallahassee Museum of

Figure 7.4. Plaster molds made by Ivan Gundrum for his pieces of Neotaíno art. (Courtesy Marty Haythorn)

History and Natural Science (Figure 7.5). He also trained and inspired North American artists such as J. Martin Haythorn, who continued making reproductions and works based on indigenous artifacts (Haythorn 2005). The Cuban artist Ernesto Navarro also became involved in the manufacture of replicas from his work at the Museo Montané, an institution where he prepared a study of indigenous ceramic decoration of Cuba (Navarro 1973).

In 1967, the collection of archaeological artifacts of the Museo Etnológico of Grupo Guamá, as well as the equipment and molds from its reproductions workshop, were donated to the Academy of Sciences of Cuba (Vasconcelos et al. 2004:156). Herrera Fritot was involved in the founding of the Sección de Antropología Física and the Centro de Antropología of the new institution. Here, he consulted on the creation of a reproductions workshop and directed the artist who was to head this, Caridad Rodríguez Cullel (Figure 7.6). Following the techniques implemented by Grupo Guamá, and also using its molds, the workshop primarily worked in plaster reproductions (Gerardo Izquierdo, personal communication 2018; Rodríguez Cullel 2000).

The collaboration between Caridad Rodríguez Cullel (b. 1932; d. 2018) and Herrera Fritot began in 1963. Graduated in painting, modeling, and sculpture,

Figure 7.5. Potter Ivan Gundrum recreating Weeden Island pottery at the Tallahassee Jr. Museum, 1960s. (From State Archives of Florida, Florida Memory, https://www .floridamemory.com/items/show/233514, accessed August 14, 2019. Photo courtesy Richard Parks)

she became involved in the illustration of archaeological texts and in the restoration and recording of pictographs (see Guarch Delmonte and Rodríguez Cullel 1980; Tabío and Guarch Delmonte 1966). In 1968 she was artistic director for the construction of a life-size diorama of the iconic Cuban rock art site of Cueva Número 1 at Punta del Este (Rodríguez Cullel 2000) (Figure 7.7).

The theme of reproductions was part of the technical and methodological revival promoted by the Academy of Sciences of Cuba. As part of this drive, the use of new methods of recording data and presenting and disseminating information were encouraged, including film, photography, and scientific illustration. It was as a result of these circumstances that artist José Rogelio Martínez Fernández (b. 1934; d. 2014) developed his well-known paintings, reconstructing indigenous scenes based on ethnographic, ethnohistorical, and archaeological data (Cué and Fernández 2016). His images sought the highest possible accuracy and were based on data from physical anthropology (in the case of the individuals he depicted), on objects mentioned by historical sources from the time of the European conquest, and on objects recovered archaeologically (Figure 7.8).

Throughout the 1970s, Caridad Rodríguez Cullel continued her work in the manufacture of archaeological reproductions, receiving training in the use of polyester resins in modeling and the foundation of sculptures in sev-

Figure 7.6. Caridad Rodríguez Cullel (*far left*) during an exhibition of replicas of Cuban archaeological objects, 1970s. (From the Guarch-Rodríguez family collection, courtesy Elena Guarch Rodríguez)

Figure 7.7. Construction of a life-size diorama of the rock art site of Cueva Número 1 at Punta del Este, Cuba, under the direction of Caridad Rodríguez Cullel, 1968. (From the Guarch-Rodríguez family collection, courtesy Elena Guarch Rodríguez)

Figure 7.8. José Rogelio Martínez Fernández, 1968. (Courtesy Racso Fernández Ortega)

eral museums in Mexico as well as in Cuban companies dedicated to the production of plastics (Figure 7.9). Resulting from this work was the design of
a technological process that took advantage of various local materials to obtain higher quality and fidelity in replicas (which received awards from the
Academy of Sciences of Cuba in 1990). In 1986, she organized and directed
the Laboratorio de Reproducciones Arqueológicas as part of the Departamento Centro-Oriental de Arqueología (DCOA), a state-run archaeological
agency located in the city of Holguín, in eastern Cuba. Here she implemented
an ambitious program that allowed her (and the technicians she trained) to
create replicas of 462 objects, including the most widely recognized artifacts
of Cuba's indigenous heritage (Campos 2016:100; Guarch Rodríguez 2006).

The Laboratorio de Reproducciones Arqueológicas also worked on the
conservation and restoration of material obtained in the excavations carried out by the DCOA, but its most valuable accomplishment was, and remains, the creation of a wide collection of replicas and molds. Some molds
of Grupo Guamá were used, but the use of new materials and technology
obliged a detailed project of locating and copying objects throughout Cuba.

Figure 7.9. Caridad Rodríguez Cullel (*far right*) and José Manuel Guarch Delmonte
(*far left*) at the Instituto de Arqueología e Historia, México, 1970s. (From the Guarch-
Rodríguez family collection, courtesy Elena Guarch Rodríguez)

For this purpose, all the research institutions and archaeological museums of the country were visited, as well as most of the historical museums and a few private collections that still existed. The collection continued to be updated through the early 1990s, with a focus on making replicas of new finds (Figures 7.10 and 7.11).

The DCOA replica collection includes a large selection of ritual artifacts and body ornaments recovered on the island, coming mostly from agricul-

Figure 7.10. *Right*: replica of ceramic vessel in polyester resin, made by the Departamento Centro-Oriental de Arqueología laboratory. *Left*: original deposited in the Museo Indocubano Baní. (Photos courtesy Roberto Valcárcel Rojas)

Figure 7.11. Replicas of indigenous archaeological objects from Cuba manufactured by the Departamento Centro-Oriental de Arqueología laboratory, combining resins and various natural materials. (Collection of replicas of the Departamento Centro-Oriental de Arqueología, Holguín. Photo courtesy Roberto Valcárcel Rojas)

tural ceramists sites as well as references to the provenience of the originals and associated cultural data. The objects reproduced can be classified into the following categories: pendants with figural or geometric representations, hafted or ornamental axe heads, ornamented mortars and pestles, vomiting spatulas, idols and seated figures, wooden *dujos*, trays, and vessels, engraved pebbles, and numerous copies of ceramic vessels (see Figures 7.10 and 7.11). The DCOA possesses copies of the principal types of ear ornaments, beads, and inlays, as well as various decorated objects potentially used in bodily adornment. Numerous kinds of utilitarian artifacts belonging to various types of indigenous groups are also reproduced as well as pieces from other parts of the Antilles and some colonial artifacts found in indigenous Cuban contexts.

REPLICAS AS TOOLS FOR CULTURAL DISSEMINATION AND RESEARCH

The replicas produced by the DCOA have been incorporated into museum exhibitions in various parts of Cuba and in study collections of research institutions within and outside the island. The collection of replicas has served as a tool in support of aesthetic and iconographic research (Dávila 2017; Rodríguez 2000), as a source of inspiration for artistic creation, and as a vehicle for disseminating knowledge about indigenous societies and archaeological work. Replicas of archaeological pieces that have taken on iconic status, such as that of the anthropomorphic axe that constitutes the symbol of Holguín province, are given to people and institutions as recognition for their contribution to social development (Campos 2016; Guarch Rodríguez 2006). Other replicas are manufactured for sale in museums and cultural institutions.

The collection of replicas recently proved invaluable in an ambitious project that spanned seven years (2011–2018), with the aim of documenting and visually recording indigenous portable art and items of personal adornment of the late Ceramic Age in the Greater Antilles (Knight 2017, 2019, 2020). The completed database of 1,121 objects is, in turn, designed to serve as a digital resource for stylistic and iconographic studies where a large corpus is required for comparative work. The survey involved visiting 19 Cuban institutions at the national, provincial, and municipal level, collecting catalog data, measurements, and new high-resolution photographs for 496 artifacts.

In anticipation of this task, the DCOA collection of replicas showed its usefulness in providing an overview of the range of materials to be found in Cuban museums. All major categories of indigenous artifacts of personal adornment are found in the replica collection, from simple drilled stones to elaborately carved and engraved pendants of stone, shell, and bone (see Figure 7.11). Moreover, the DCOA replicas emphasize categories such as engraved *Oliva* sp. shell pendants that are found in greater proportion in Cuba than elsewhere in the Greater Antilles. Styles of anthropomorphic pendants and ear ornaments that are distinctively Cuban in their distribution are correspondingly well represented. Conversely, categories that are only sparingly found in Cuba are not well represented. In this manner, the DCOA collection of replicas provides a useful orientation to the kinds, styles, and relative frequencies of artifact forms present in Cuban museums, facilitating research on the original objects.

Although the database collection effort covered all of the major museum collections (and the most relevant smaller collections) of indigenous artifacts in Cuba, we nonetheless found that a surprising number of objects replicated in the DCOA collection could not be relocated. Many of these, undoubtedly, were copied from private collections or are otherwise unavailable today. Thus, the DCOA replicas are our only record of numerous Cuban pieces, some of key importance stylistically and iconographically. The precise nature of the replicas fortunately allows us to use the collection as a source of proxies for the missing pieces. In cases where the fullest possible corpus of objects in a given category is needed to provide a clearer picture of the range of variability, the DCOA replicas have a demonstrated ability to fill important gaps and thereby enrich the archaeological record.

Another place where the use of replicas made in the DCOA has played an essential role is at the museum of El Chorro de Maíta. This museum was built on the eponymous archaeological site, located in northeastern Cuba. The site was excavated by the DCOA in 1986 under the direction of José M. Guarch Delmonte (1996), revealing a central cemetery that held the remains of more than 133 individuals, most of them indigenous.[5] Thus, the museum not only displays replicas of archaeological objects but also replica human remains.[6] In fact, the main part of the museum's exhibit space (in a zone originally containing burials) is a diorama that reconstructs at full scale the exact location of each burial, maintaining the replica artifacts and skeletal remains as sets, with their correct orientations, dimensions, and colors, placed at their original depth (Figure 7.12). Although not all cases of skeletal remains are exact copies of the originals, the intent is to offer, as accurately as possible, a view of the positions in which they were found and the cultural materials found with them (Guarch Delmonte 1994; Valcárcel Rojas 2016c).

The presentation of replica skeletal remains dramatizes and strengthens the museum's narrative regarding the variety of social identities found among the burials. In addition, it provides a full-scale visual perspective of archaeological work and its techniques that traditional museum practices do not. The location of the replicas in an environment that reproduces the excavation within the same archaeological site provides a sense of integrity and originality of enormous strength, as on-site museums often do (Yan 2010). Additionally, it helps viewers to understand the relationship of the cemetery to the surrounding indigenous settlement, and the relationship of the latter to

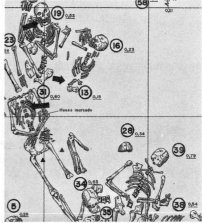

Figure 7.12. *Left*: Reproductions of human remains in the El Chorro de Maíta site museum. *Right*: drawing made during the archaeological excavation, which includes some of the human remains shown in the image on the left. (Photo courtesy Roberto Valcárcel Rojas; illustration courtesy Juan Guarch Rodríguez)

the natural environment. The copies of the remains (see Figure 7.12) offer a three-dimensional image that, combined with photographs, drawings, and excavation data, as well as a new osteometric study, have allowed the realization of taphonomic observations of great interest. The taphonomic analysis, carried out between 2009 and 2011 by Menno Hoogland and Roberto Valcárcel Rojas, concerned aspects such as the conditions of decomposition of the bodies, the peculiarities of their handling and placement within pits, the shapes of these pits, elements of constraint and containment of the bodies, their degree of articulation at the time of burial, the type of interment, whether primary or secondary, and details concerning the forms and dimensions of the graves, among other things (Valcárcel Rojas 2016c:179–190).

The fact that the DCOA removed the Chorro de Maíta human remains and curated them in a protected place has allowed their conservation and study using various approaches and archaeometric methods unavailable at the time of excavation. It is a form of management that respects the memory of these individuals and allows rereadings of the archaeological site, with the permanent possibility of reassessment. The wisdom of this strategy of removing and protecting the originals was also evident in 2008, when the site museum building was seriously damaged by Hurricane Ike, which took several years to repair. Replica skeletal remains of the site are still manufactured for use in other museums and cultural exhibitions (Figure 7.13).

The experience of the DCOA in creating expository dioramas has been applied to other archaeological indigenous sites. At the Bariay 2 site, also in the

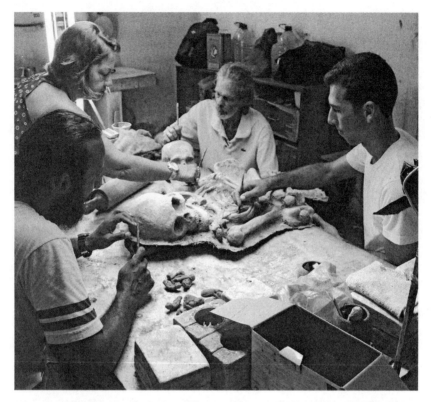

Figure 7.13. Working on the making of a reproduction of a human skeleton, Departamento Centro-Oriental de Arqueología laboratory, 2018. (Photo courtesy Roberto Valcárcel Rojas)

province of Holguín, an excavated midden area was reproduced at full scale on site (Campos 2016). However, difficulties in accessing financing, technical equipment, and raw materials have meant that this strategy has not enjoyed the popularity it deserves in Cuban museum practice and cultural dissemination. In recent years, the use of replicas has essentially ceased, and other advances in the manufacture of replicas, or in the digitization of objects and 3D printing, have not been adequately incorporated.

CONCLUSIONS

This analysis of fakes, copies, and replicas of archaeological objects in Cuba has been essentially an introduction, as there is still much to discuss and investigate. It shows the evolution of collecting and its negative impact in the first half of the twentieth century by generating the indiscriminate looting of sites and creating a market for archaeological objects. There were numerous complaints at this time from Cuban archaeologists about the removal of objects from the country (Hernández Godoy 2011). Both Rouse and Harrington purchased materials and exported valuable collections to US institutions, and access by foreigners to sites and materials became a contested point during times of increased nationalist sentiment.

At the same time, some Cuban archaeologists created their own collections, and several collectors became amateur archaeologists, overseeing excavations and publishing their finds. In general, this type of collecting was considered positive, conforming to the characteristics of archaeological practice and low level of professionalization of the discipline at the time. Archaeological activity with a scientific motive as well as artifact collection for commercial profit employed local people living near archaeological sites, often exploiting their poverty for cheap labor.

In this environment, forgeries were manufactured by people who lacked specialized knowledge concerning the forms, techniques, and materials used by indigenous people. These peculiarities, and the critical work of many archaeologists, limited the extent of widespread fraud. The authors of this chapter can verify the low percentage of fakes in Cuban archaeological collections compared to other Caribbean countries.

The matter of making copies and replicas as a long-term tradition with generational continuity, involving such researchers and artists as René Herrera Fritot, Ivan Gundrum, and Caridad Rodríguez Cullel, imparts a singular profile to the Cuban case. Its combination of archaeological, artistic, museological, and pedagogical perspectives generated a progressive, pioneering vision for the region and creative archaeological practice that sought to combine the technoscientific advances of the time with local solutions. The DCOA, through its collection of replicas and the creation of the exhibit space of the El Chorro de Maíta site museum, exemplifies this achievement.

In contrast to Cuban archaeology prior to 1959, the political, social, and cultural changes generated by the Cuban Revolution undoubtedly had a positive impact on the protection and study of Cuba's archaeological heritage, and consequently in governmental support for more socially responsible projects. The reduction of collecting, trafficking, and forging as well as the promotion of replicas as a tool for recording, researching, and presenting scientific and cultural information were significant and far-sighted achievements. Sustaining these advances and incorporating new technologies is the complex challenge for the continued management of Cuba's heritage in the twenty-first century.

ACKNOWLEDGMENTS

This chapter pays tribute to the memory of Caridad Rodríguez Cullel, René Herrera Fritot, Ivan Gundrum, and José Rogelio Martínez Fernández. The research leading to the results presented in this chapter was, for the first author, part of the ERC-Synergy NEXUS 1492 project, funded by the European Research Council under the European Union's Seventh Framework Programme (FP7/2007–2013)/ERC grant agreement No. 319209. We appreciate access to the DCOA of Holguín, Instituto Cubano de Antropología, and the El Chorro de Maíta site museum's archaeological collections and the help of their staff. We thank Lucero Arboleda (executive director of the Library of Instituto Tecnológico de Santo Domingo), Stephanie Akau, Martin Haythorn, Gerardo Izquierdo, Lourdes Pérez Iglesias, Esteban Maciques Sánchez, José Ramón Alonso Lorea, Racso Fernández, Juan Guarch Rodríguez, Stefanie Rodríguez, Amanda Moreno, and the State Archives of Florida, Florida Memory, and the libraries of the University of New Mexico and the University of Miami's Cuban Heritage Collection for their help in accessing images and bibliographic information.

NOTES

1. According to the *Cambridge Dictionary* a fake is a copy whose intent is to deceive. The entry for *falsificación* in the *Dictionary of the Royal Academy of the Spanish Language* also highlights criminal intent in the process. In both dictionaries, very high-precision copies are called replicas. Information accessed online December 18, 2018.

2. In 1962 José A. García Castañeda donated his archaeological collection to the Academy of Sciences of Cuba (Hernández Godoy 2011). Other types of goods that he collected and also donated were the basis for the creation of Holguín Natural Science Museum (Gómez and Martínez 2011; Rojas and París 2017).

3. A notable exception to this is the work of Fernández and colleagues (2013): while not focusing on the history of forgeries, the study investigates the authenticity of a collection of objects first acquired in the beginning of the twentieth century.

4. However, illegal activities at archaeological sites still persist, albeit on a small scale, often by people interested in archaeological matters, who organize collections that are usually small, or donate their finds directly to museums. A notorious case was the acquisition of a collection of wooden objects by fishermen in north-central Cuba, which led to the discovery of submerged and very well preserved indigenous structures at the Los Buchillones archaeological site (Calvera 1996; Valcárcel Rojas et al. 2006).

5. This cemetery, dating to the early colonial period, is one of the few found in indigeous sites in the Caribbean (Valcárcel Rojas 2016c). For the diorama, an area of the cemetery was selected that highlights the multicultural nature and European influence seen among the burials.

6. José M. Guarch Delmonte (see Figure 7.9) played a central role in the design of the El Chorro de Maíta museum, using replicas, and promoted and supported the creation of the DCOA Laboratorio de Reproducciones Arqueológicas.

8

"Seem[ing] Authentic[ity]"

Irving Rouse on Forgeries, a Museological Perspective

JOANNA OSTAPKOWICZ AND ROGER COLTEN

IRVING ROUSE (b. 1913; d. 2006), professor in Yale University's Department of Anthropology and curator at the Peabody Museum of Natural History (PMNH), is widely recognized as the doyen of Caribbean archaeology, establishing the classification system still in use today for the prehistory of the region (e.g., Keegan 2009:322; Keegan and Hofman 2017:17). He was at the forefront of Caribbean archaeology at a time that saw the escalation of site looting and forgeries (post-1930s), and his peripheral involvement in the Paredones scandal (Ostapkowicz, chapter 1 this volume; Alvarez et al., chapter 2 this volume) made him increasingly aware of the influence of archaeological heritage to those interested in profiting from the past. Growing uncertainty over the provenience of pieces in private collections and their authenticity brought many—including museums, auction houses, and private collectors—to seek his advice in distinguishing the genuine article from the fake. He also reviewed the PMNH's collection with an eye to identifying forgeries, and his comments still define some 124 pieces from Haiti, Dominican Republic, and Puerto Rico as "fakes." This chapter explores Rouse's growing concerns about forgeries in the region as documented in his work and correspondence, the latter now housed in the PMNH's Rouse Archives. It also explores the implications of curating forgeries in museum collections and their relevance to understanding the history of people's engagement with the past.

Rouse's first documented exposure to the issues of looting and forgeries was during his 1941 fieldwork in Banes, Cuba, where he noted the prevalence of looted sites and a thriving market catering to collectors of Amerindian antiquities (Rouse 1942; see Valcárcel Rojas et al., chapter 7 this volume). This environment, established in eastern Cuba since at least the 1930s, fueled the manufacture of forgeries to keep up with demand—what Rouse termed "Archaeology as a Business" (Rouse 1942:44). He rarely discussed the subject of forgeries in his later publications (but see Rouse 1992:164–165), though it is clear that he understood their potential impact on archaeological interpretations. The dangers of forgeries distorting material culture studies was a direct threat to what Rouse held most dear: clear, taxonomic classification, and therefore understanding, of archaeological material culture (Siegel 1996). Despite this, several forgeries entered the PMNH collections during his tenure, though they are clearly identified as such; perhaps Rouse viewed these as useful examples to further understanding of how to distinguish the forged from the genuine. He grappled with the issues of forgeries in his correspondence, largely a result of being drawn into discussions about what was "authentic" for the precolumbian Caribbean.

"APPROXIMATIONS" OF TAÍNO ART

The 1950s seemed to have marked the starting point for Rouse's archived correspondence on forgeries. In 1959, a collector of "Indian pottery and stones" from Santiago, Dominican Republic, sent an inquiry to the Smithsonian Institution, enclosing 41 photographs of precolumbian artifacts, including what he considered some rather unusual specimens. He requested an opinion specifically on these curiosities, including a particularly striking stone carving with three faces (featuring a bird, frog, and a human face on respective sides) purportedly recovered from Calaverna cave, Juncalito, Province of Santiago, circa April 1955 (Figure 8.1). The letter and images made their way through the Smithsonian and eventually were sent on to Rouse at the Peabody, given his expertise in Caribbean archaeology. Rouse concurred with the collector that the stone carving was "unique, both as to material, shape, and design. I would be inclined to regard it as a falsification since, while [some elements] approximate Taino designs, [the bird] is completely different and . . . looks Spanish."[1] As a caveat, however, he considered his comments tentative: "It would be necessary for me to examine the actual specimens before giving definitive opinions, especially as to whether there are falsifications." This cautious approach was characteristic of Rouse's careful assessment of most things and was a standpoint he would repeatedly return to as the escalation of forgeries continued unabated.

This correspondence is also important as it offers a concrete example of forgeries made before the Paredones watershed of 1968/1969 (see below and Ostapkowicz, chapter 1 herein). Indeed, some still hold that the material excavated at Paredones in the 1950s is authentic, and that forgeries did not emerge until the late 1960s as a response to the collector's market (A. Fernández 1969a:157; Ugarte 1969b:164; Vega 2015). This, however, is contrary to several references to Paredones material being forged as early as 1946, includ-

Figure 8.1. Three views of a three-sided stone carving purportedly from Calaverna cave, Juncalito, Province of Santiago, ca. April 1955. *Main image*: anthropomorphic head; *upper right*: bird; *lower right*: frog. (Rouse Archives, ANT.ARC.00121 2-12.36. Courtesy Peabody Museum of Natural History, New Haven, Connecticut)

ing an admission by the main forger to the creation of pieces in the 1940s (Severino 1968b:87). Indeed, the history of forgeries in the Dominican Republic is likely earlier than this, as the comparable Cuban situation demonstrates (Rouse 1942; see Valcárcel Rojas et al., chapter 7 herein); it is simply a matter of time before other examples come to light.

AN EMERGING PROBLEM

There is apparently a problem with the carvings from the Dominican Republic.

—Rouse to Paul Barker, April 9, 1968 (Rouse Archives, PMNH)

Rouse was in correspondence with the eminent Dominican archaeologist Emile de Boyrie Moya (b. 1903; d. 1967)—the first excavator of the Los Paredones caves, on the southern coast of the Dominican Republic (Boyrie Moya 1952; Vega 2015; for further details, see Ostapkowicz, chapter 1 this volume)— in the early 1960s, but would not meet him personally until 1967, on a trip to the Dominican Republic to consult about the Paredones material. In late 1966, Boyrie Moya invited Rouse to visit with him urgently to discuss the Paredones paper he had been working on,[2] an expansion of his initial 1952 article that brought the material to scholarly attention (Boyrie Moya 1952), and to discuss various archaeological "enigmas," including Paredones. Rouse was warmly hosted during his time there, but he only managed to get away from his Yale teaching obligations for four days—from January 11 to 15, 1967.[3] Despite the short duration of his visit, the time proved highly productive: it allowed Rouse to consult Boyrie Moya's Paredones collections (which were considerable; Figure 8.2) and discuss his findings, plan for the eventual publications, and even manage to assist with the excavations at the site of Cueva Universitaria No. 1, which would later yield a controversially early date (discussed below). He returned to the Peabody with a small group of photos from the excavation, dated January 12, 1967 (Figure 8.3), as well as some of the field finds—mostly ceramics with associated level designations—which now

Figure 8.2. Five views of Boyrie Moya's collection—only a small selection of the photographs held in the Rouse Archives. There are genuine pieces featured on certain shelves, but the Paredones materials dominate the displays, particularly the hundreds of "artifacts" artfully arranged on panels and scattered on tables and the floor. (Rouse Archives, ANT.ARC.00121 2-12.20. Courtesy Peabody Museum of Natural History, New Haven, Connecticut)

Figure 8.3. Images taken by Rouse during the January 12, 1967, Los Paredones excavations. He participated in the excavations at Cueva Universitaria during his four-day visit to the Dominican Republic. (Rouse Archive, ANTAR.020294, 020298. Courtesy Peabody Museum of Natural History, New Haven, Connecticut)

comprise 30 PMNH catalog entries. Among the artifacts also attributed to the Cueva Universitaria are two stone carvings (Figure 8.4) that Rouse kept uncataloged in his main study collection over the subsequent years (they were only accessioned in 2008/2009); associated information indicates that they were surface finds at the cave, though it is unclear whether they were recovered by Rouse or acquired in some other manner (in later correspondence, he mentioned two carvings given to him by Boyrie Moya—see below). Unfortunately, the field documents related to this small collection have not yet been found in the museum archives, but there is an ongoing effort to organize, index, and digitize Rouse's archival material, which may eventually locate additional information.

One of the outcomes of the visit to the Dominican Republic was an agreement for Rouse and José Cruxent (a long-term colleague of Rouse's, who also traveled to the Dominican Republic for the Paredones discussions) to assist with Boyrie Moya's manuscript, a draft copy of which is on file in the PMNH's Rouse Archives (ANTAR.042255). Indeed, shortly after the visit, Rouse noted: "As soon as Cruxent sends me the brief description of the Los Paredones material that he is preparing, I will put it together with extracts from Sr. de Boyrie's manuscript. . . . I hope that it will be possible for [the University of Santo Domingo] to publish this, as Boyrie's previous report does not give a very good idea of the nature of the material, particularly the later finds."[4] According to Rouse, the manuscript lacked "a classification and description of the material, which is most important since the reader needs to know the nature of the artifacts."[5] He also suggested omitting some of the theories currently in the manuscript, "for lack of detailed comparative study."[6]

Boyrie Moya, for his part, was awaiting the radiocarbon results that Rouse and Cruxent were running on excavated charcoal samples—his opinion was

Figure 8.4. Two carvings reportedly recovered from the soil surface of Cueva Universitaria, where Rouse excavated on January 12, 1967. Though Rouse knew they were fakes, he included them in his core study collection. *Left*: H: 14 cm, ANT.266200; *Right*: H: 17 cm, ANT.266199. (Courtesy Peabody Museum of Natural History, New Haven, Connecticut)

that Cruxent's samples would likely yield an earlier date (estimated ca. AD 600–1200) to those that Rouse took (estimated ca. AD 1200–1524), presumably based on the stratigraphy from which they were excavated. Unfortunately, Boyrie Moya passed away in May 1967, before the dates became available. The single date obtained by Rouse, despite its problems (see below), has been repeatedly used as evidence for the considerable antiquity of Paredones. Cruxent's radiocarbon date, published solely as a note in the journal *Radiocarbon* a year after the scandal broke, and to our knowledge not discussed in any subsequent publications, was dismissed entirely given the age (>32,000; IVIC-483).[7]

Rouse was in correspondence with Bernardo Vega, nephew of Boyrie Moya, in June 1967, and shared the long-awaited radiocarbon date he had just received from the lab:

> The date of the sample which bears the number Y-1850, is 1680 ± 100 years ago, i.e., 270 A.D. This date is much earlier than expected: I had thought it would be somewhere between 750 and 1500 A.D. This was also your uncle's opinion, as stated in his last letter to me.
>
> You are, of course, welcome to use this date in any way you see fit, but I would advise you to withhold it, at least until you receive Cruxent's date. When a radiocarbon date is contrary to expectation, it must be suspected,

because there are so many chances for errors. . . . Archaeologists are accustomed to accept dates which agree with their expectations, but when a date is contrary to expectation, it is the practice to suspend judgement until the date can be checked by analyzing another sample. In the present instance, it would be standard archaeological procedure to withhold the Yale date until it has either been disproved or validated by Cruxent's date.[8]

At the time, the family still had plans to publish Boyrie Moya's manuscript, including Rouse's and Cruxent's contributions—certainly Rouse had it firmly in mind in October 1967 when he declined an invitation from César García Victoria to undertake further research in the Dominican Republic. In his response, Rouse specifically notes various publication commitments, including preparing "a brief monograph" on the Los Paredones caves "in which so many sculptures have been found in recent years."[9]

Clearly, Rouse was thinking seriously about composing a statement on the "archaeology" of Los Paredones, but even at this point he was aware of the circulation of Paredones forgeries. Indeed, in April 1968, some eight months before the Paredones situation was fully exposed in the media, and in full, frank discussions about the issues with Frederick Dockstader, the director of the Museum of the American Indian (MAI; now National Museum of the American Indian, Smithsonian), he noted: "It is clear that Cruxent and I should produce a detailed study of the Boyrie Moya collection as soon as possible, and include in it a comparison with the presumed falsifications."[10] Commitments to his *World Prehistory* book kept him from taking up the task, and it would appear that the idea was dropped entirely once the scandal emerged in full force in the media.

In Dockstader, Rouse found a colleague well attuned to the proliferation of forgeries on the market. As director of the MAI, Dockstader had considerable experience in assessing private collections, given the quantity of material he considered for acquisition, let alone in his museum's holdings. He and his art world contacts—of whom he had many—were constantly reviewing private collections and those of professional dealers; their dubious involvement in this world would eventually (late 1970s) lead to Dockstader being dismissed as director, alongside the forced resignation of six of the museum's trustees during an investigation by the New York State Attorney General (Kelker and Bruhns 2010:53). In contrast to Rouse, Dockstader was an "old hand" at the wheeling and dealing of the precolumbian art world, and was well aware of the surge in forgeries during the mid-twentieth century. One account from the mid-1960s notes his disappointment in finding out an exceptional Nicaraguan figure was a forgery: "While in Spain I found to my genuine grief, that the large Nicaraguan figure is a fake . . . as a matter of fact, there is a major fake-factory going on. There seems little doubt of this, and I must confess I was thoroughly sold on the piece. Apparently the manufacturers have even gotten hold of the original pigments, etc., from which the ancient 'Ometepe' types were made, and turn 'em out wholesale . . . and expertly."[11] In another case dating to 1961, Dockstader was warned about a Mexican figure by a colleague who had witnessed some of the forgery techniques involved, and to whom he replied, "I cannot impress on you strongly enough the importance of the material you showed me, carved by Señor Tapia. I entreat you to note down on a card, or in some suitable manner, all the data concerning the manufacture of these items which you <u>know</u> to be of contemporary manufacture. You should indicate the source of the raw stone, the details concerning the transaction, the price paid for the work, the dating, in short, everything you can tell about this. I assure you this will be most valuable, because I know of no other single instance where such record has been maintained for material which in essence duplicates pre-contact materials."[12] Clearly Dockstader wanted to document the workings of the forger, to learn of the techniques used—something he would later appreciate through the media exposé on Paredones. All this trained his eye to see inconsistencies in style that might not be immediately apparent to others. In his dealings with Rouse, he sometimes gently nudged him to be more aware of this illusionary world. In a letter to him regarding some Caribbean "antiquities," he questions Rouse's assessment of some pieces as genuine: "I was astonished to get your letter of March 1, particularly after you had seen these polaroids. If they are indeed genuine I am even <u>more</u> astounded, and I feel we must both get together at an early date and examine the objects themselves."[13]

On January 30, 1968, Rouse visited Dockstader in New York, taking with him an assortment of suspect pieces and images: "1/ Cruxent's photographs of the carvings in the de Boyrie Moya collections, Santo Domingo; 2/ the two carvings given to me by Sr. de Boyrie Moya; 3/ the carvings and other material I excavated from the Cueva Universitaria for which we have obtained a radiocarbon determination of 270 AD; 4/ three carvings from a cave in Haiti sent for examination by Paul Barker, of the Gorham State College, Gorham, Maine."[14] While the conclusions of this meeting are not recorded in the correspondence, Dockstader did visit Rouse in March 1968, when discussions seemed focused on the Paredones materials. Afterward, Dockstader noted (emphasis added), "I am particularly happy that you now agree with me that the problem seems to be one of some genuine *but more false creations.* . . . It will be fun to see what happens with all of this now, particularly since some of it seems to be getting into art gallery outlets, which can only increase the supply and confuse the issue."[15]

Upon Dockstader's suggestion, Rouse visited the Cisneros Gallery, which stocked some of the Paredones sculptures, taking with him two of the sculptures he had acquired in the Dominican Republic (see Figure 8.4). There, he learned that the gallery owner "originally had six of the carvings from Santo Domingo, but had sold all but two, which he showed me. These were clearly fakes, in my opinion. . . . If I had seen the Cisneros specimens before talking with you, I think I would myself have been dubious about them. After our conversation, I'm sure they are falsifications."[16] Dockstader asked whether Rouse had noted these reservations to the gallery owner, to which Rouse replied (emphasis added): "I regret to say I did not tell Garcia that *you* felt his specimens were fakes. I did say that *you* were concerned about the authenticity of the entire group of Paredones carvings, upon which he remarked that he thought my two specimens showed evidence of working with iron tools, but I left it at that, unfortunately."[17] The reference to "you" in the letter clearly refers to Dockstader's opinion of the gallery collection (and likely, Paredones sculptures as a whole)—not Rouse's assessment. The exchange suggests that Rouse was still uncomfortable in making authenticity judgments on the Paredones artifacts, surprisingly so given his clear assessment of forgeries in Cuba (Rouse 1942:44–45).

Perhaps this uncertainty was a result of Rouse still holding onto the possibility that some of the Paredones materials were genuine. He was an archaeologist, and he had himself excavated at Cueva Universitaria, which yielded, among other things, Boca Chica–style ceramics (as identified in the correspondence and museum records by Rouse). He held discussions with archaeologists such as Boyrie Moya who had spearheaded the Los Paredones studies, with many years of excavations at the caves under his belt. Further, he joined the ranks of some of the most prominent contemporary Dominican archaeologists who were convinced that the material emerging from the excavations was the genuine article—among them Fernando Morban Laucer (1968) and Marcio Veloz Maggiolo (1968a, 1968b), who published their interpretations of this new archaeological "culture" shortly before the press exposed the fraud. Rouse, however, was more cautious—believing some to be real and many not. Indeed, in a letter to Morban Laucer in 1967, who referred to "La Cultura de los Paredones," Rouse notes, "I would prefer to say 'El Arte de los Paredones,' since I would not be surprised if this particular kind of stone carving turns out to be associated with one of the cultures known from dwelling sites along the coast of the Dominican Republic, such as Andel or Boca Chica."[18] In March 1969, shortly after the Paredones exposé, Rouse noted in a letter to Luis Chanlatte Baik (who had been instrumental in exposing the hoax a few months prior) that he "never . . . believed in [Boyrie Moya's] theory of a distinct Paredones culture. After looking at his material, however, I was convinced that there had been a separate Paredones style of stone carving. [My feeling is that the] Paredones style is merely a variant on the classic Taino style. For this reason, I had expected the radiocarbon sample we obtained at Cueva Universitaria to date between 1000 and 1500 A.D., i.e., from the time of the Taino, and was surprised that it turned out to be earlier."[19]

From the correspondence, it would appear that Rouse was, despite reservations, still attempting to make the Paredones material "fit" into his understanding of Caribbean archaeology. This stemmed in part from comparable limestone beads that he documented in the Bailey collection from Puerto Rico (Rouse 1961), though this material was acquired via a collector, and its context was not entirely clear; the main comparative point was simply that the same material (limestone) was used to make beads. Despite his discussions with Dockstader, in March 1968 Rouse wrote: "Summing up my impressions, I would say that I'm still convinced that most of the material in the de Boyrie Moya collection and in the possession of the other local collectors whom I visited is genuine, but agree with you that the material is now being falsified. It's going to be a job to determine which specimens are genuine and which are fakes, I'm afraid."[20]

All this came to a head in December 1968, when the media furor over the "archaeological myth" of Paredones began (see Ostapkowicz, chapter 1 this volume); it was to take center stage in the media over the course of several months (Pérez Guerra 1999). Chanlatte Baik, who Rouse met in January 1967 when his direct involvement in Los Paredones began, and who played a key role in exposing the forgery industry, sent several of the newspaper clippings to Rouse (Figure 8.5). To Chanlatte, Rouse responded, "We all owe a debt of gratitude to you for leading the struggle against the theory of a Paredones culture. You are to be congratulated that your observation that the carvings are simply a manifestation of contemporary popular art has been proved correct."[21] He copied the letter to Dockstader and Junius Bird, noting (emphasis added): "During the past year, a number of the Paredones carvings have been offered for sale in New York City, and the prospective purchasers have consulted either Dr. Junius Bird, of the American Museum of Natural History, or Dr. Frederick Dockstader . . . about them. Bird and Dockstader have, in turn, referred these people to me. As I looked over the material they were purchasing, I became convinced that many of them must be fakes. Bird and Dockstader went further than that; they were convinced that *all* the carvings were false."[22]

Despite this, Rouse concluded: "Nevertheless, I remain convinced that some carving of stalactites and stalagmites must have been done in the Pare-

Figure 8.5. News clippings (*El Caribe*, February 1, 1969) in Rouse's files, likely sent by Chanlatte Baik, titled "Los Paredones Culture Confirmed as Myth." (Rouse Archives, ANT.ARC.00189, 2-12.41. Courtesy Peabody Museum of Natural History, New Haven, Connecticut)

dones caves. The fact that we found refuse and potsherds, presumably of the Boca Chica style, in Cueva Universitaria where we dug, would seem to indicate this, and so also does the fact that all the stalactites and stalagmites in that cave had been cut off and that the cuts were covered by more recent accretions of limestone. It may be that the pieces cut off were used only for beads and pendants, like the ones we found in our excavation, but I would not be surprised if some of the carved figures are not also proved to be authentic. I cannot imagine the Tainos having carved only beads and pendants in the stalagmite material, when they also carved figures in other kinds of rock."[23] It should be kept in mind that when Rouse wrote this in 1969, he was wrestling to align his understanding of the archaeology of Paredones (based on his own experiences in excavating the site) with the emerging information about the forgeries; the revelations about the planting of neo-artifacts would only come to light over a decade later (see Ostapkowicz, chapter 1 this volume). His later notes on the Cueva Universitaria finds in the PMNH catalog, compiled sometime before his retirement, suggest an acknowledgment of disturbed contexts, and how this could impact on interpretations (see below).

To Dockstader, Rouse sent copies of the news clippings but was not entirely swayed by them (emphasis added): "As you will see, they bear out your conclusion about faking of the Paredones carvings. On the other hand, *I still think I was right in maintaining that some of the carvings are authentic*; otherwise the fakers would have been unable to develop their art. As I see it, the problem now is to discriminate between the authentic and fake carvings."[24] Dockstader remained dubious now that the scale of deception had been exposed in the national press: "I am still less convinced that you are right in your feelings concerning some of these particular carvings; I think the originals are to be found in a slightly different direction,"[25] a source he never explained in the correspondence.

And this remains one of the main issues with Los Paredones: the cave sites were so disturbed by looting and covert planting of artifacts that it will never be clear what the genuine archaeological material may have comprised. Indeed, the lead forger (Benyí) revealed that carvings were being made from the mid-1940s (Anonymous 1969:218; A. Fernández 1969b:167; Ugarte 1969f: 171; see Ostapkowicz, chapter 1 this volume) and from the photos in Boyrie Moya's seminal publication (1952:Plate 4) (see Figure 2.5) it is clear that forgeries were being "introduced" as early as the first archaeological investigations in the 1950s (whether directly planted or purchased as "accidental" finds is unclear, though the paper refers to "archaeological" pieces). With potentially such a long history of interference at the sites, much of what may have been genuine was likely completely disturbed. It is not inconceivable that even genuine pieces (e.g., ceramics) were placed within the upper strata of the excavated area to support the impression that the forged material was also genuine. At Cueva Universitaria, where Rouse was working, a scattering of genuine "Boca Chica" ceramic sherds was found throughout levels 1–3 (each comprising successive 25 cm spits), while a speleothem-carved pendant and beads were recovered in Level 2 (25–50 cm) (Figure 8.6).[26] Rouse identified the pendant and beads as "possible fake[s] plowed in site"; this was clearly intermixed within the ceramics. Further information regarding Rouse's interrogation of this issue has not been found, as yet, in the museum's archives— but his comments within the museum documentation suggest a clear questioning of the material.

While the Los Paredones exposé was emerging, the issue of forgeries was to escalate, and swiftly, with other examples. Shortly after being sent the news clippings by Rouse, Dockstader responded regarding a new group of dubious Haitian material, images of which were brought to him for authentication: "Hot upon the heels of your cordial letter and clippings concerning the Dominican objects, came some specimens and photographs from Haiti. . . . The material in [almost] every case . . . is of a brick-red clay, dabbed with a heavy coating of mud. As a matter of fact, I think they are made from old bricks, probably colonial material of the Eighteenth Century. . . . The story is that these and scores of other specimens of a similar nature were excavated during the demolishing of a church (hence my suspicion of the brick material) in the interior of the island; the specific site was not divulged. The owner has many more like them, but the person who brought these into the office was vague as to how many. The latter individual is convinced these are genuine. . . . I am convinced they are fakes."[27] Rouse was quick to reply: "It would seem that it

Figure 8.6. Excavated material from the Cueva Universitaria, Los Paredones, Dominican Republic, in the Peabody Museum of Natural History collections. *Left*: pendant and 13 cylindrical beads of speleothem stone dug from Level 2 (25–50 cm), and identified by Rouse as a "possible fake plowed in site," ANT 228148. *Right*: excavated ceramics and other material from Cueva Universitaria. The ceramic fragments were found in Levels 1–3 (0–75 cm below surface), with the pendant/beads recovered in Level 2 (25–50 cm), suggesting that the site was disturbed with planted artifacts, potentially including genuine sherds. (Courtesy Peabody Museum of Natural History, New Haven, Connecticut. Photos courtesy Roger Colten)

never rains but it pours. The photos of the specimens from Haiti seem to be blatant fakes and I wouldn't be surprised if there was some relationship to the fakes in the Dominican Republic. They don't look like any of the specimens in the Boyrie collection, but do resemble other specimens I have seen."[28]

For Rouse, the late 1960s proved a bit of a "baptism of fire" on the issue of Caribbean forgeries, particularly as he was implicated in the Paredones scandal. The newspapers running the story mentioned him by name—as the preeminent Caribbeanist who had visited only the year before, specifically to view the Paredones collections and to excavate one of the caves. In a letter to Bernardo Vega, who had sent him one of these news clippings, Rouse contested: "I would have preferred that the [newspaper] article had not mentioned me, in the light of the most recent revelations about the findings" (Vega 2015:55). Even with the escalating evidence for the scale of forgeries in the region (for Paredones alone, the number of carvings was estimated at over 25,000 by the late 1960s; Ugarte 1969:111), Rouse was quite cautious—even neutral—in his assessments of pieces, reluctant to be drawn into the quagmire. During this time, he never quite "outted" a collection (particularly that of a colleague) on his own judgment. Even in his letter to Paul Barker, who had sent him three Haitian carvings (which Rouse showed Dockstader during their meeting in January 1968), Rouse hedged his bets (emphasis added):

"Yours look authentic, but there is apparently a problem with the carvings from the Dominican Republic. Some of them, including the ones in the Boyrie Moya collection, also *seem authentic*, but it is evident that others are being falsified."[29] "Seem[ing] authentic[ity]" well defines a potential forgery, but on gentle and polite terms.

THE FORGER'S "URGE TOWARD ORIGINALITY"

The Rouse Archives do not appear to hold much in the way of correspondence on forgeries from the 1970s, apart from a collection of images sent to Rouse in November 1971, of pieces apparently from the Dominican Republic. Unfortunately, the original correspondence has not been located, but the series of photos features a range of modern carvings, apparently cut with power/rotary tools (Figure 8.7). The repetitive iconography in some of the figures—for example, the upraised arms in three carvings, the seated posture in another three—together with the blocky style of carving and unusual facial features suggest a carving production line, perhaps by the same artist or workshop of artists.

The subject reappears with renewed vigor in the 1980s. By this point (and

Figure 8.7. Selection of images sent to Rouse in November 1971. Note the similarity of some of the carvings. For example, the upraised arms of the last figure on the right, in the top row, are also featured in two figures in the bottom row. Large bones (possibly cow) were used to manufacture the figures in the bottom middle image. (Rouse Archives, ANT.ARC.00121, 2-12.22. Courtesy Peabody Museum of Natural History, New Haven, Connecticut)

on the verge of retirement), Rouse's assessments are more assured, though no less polite. Increasingly, members of the public would request his opinion on their collections, and in addition to growing confidence in forgery identification, Rouse also grew less hesitant to "authenticate" pieces. While this is ethically problematic today, and there are clear guidelines on why archaeologists should not engage with authenticating "artifacts" in private collections or on the market (see Ostapkowicz and Hanna, introduction to this volume), such was not the case in the past. One such request came in 1982, when a visitor to New Haven brought some carvings to show Rouse, two of which Rouse identified as "good examples of modern folk art, which are worthy of study as such but cannot be attributed to the Taino Indians."[30] In 1983, another four carvings were sent to Rouse for inspection; he responded: "I regret to say . . . that they are not authentic. . . . I must say that the modern artisans are becoming more skillful. However, they cannot resist the urge towards originality. In effect, they are developing a new form of folk art, which may some day become as valuable as the aboriginal art."[31] In May 1986, the same individual followed up with Rouse again regarding a vomiting spatula and an anthropomorphic wood carving, which Rouse had personally seen a year before. Rouse thought the spatula suspect, and there were some questions over the figure.[32] Images of other carvings from the same collection followed in September, to which Rouse responded that it was "difficult to determine whether all your artifacts are authentic. If they are not, they are excellent copies."[33] The two most impressive pieces—the vomiting spatula and carved wooden figure—were later offered at auction, though the auction house's due diligence brought them full circle back to Rouse, as the most recognized Caribbean prehistorian in the United States. His frank assessment noted that most pieces in the collection were forgeries, and the two in question he "could not be sure about. . . . All I can say is that they are not obvious fakes."[34]

In 1989, an art conservator approached Rouse with a query on the authenticity of a collection of stone carvings. The conservator noted that the limestone surface of the carvings was not marked by modern rotary tools or files, and rather featured signs of calcium deposits, erosion, and wear. Roots had even penetrated the holes within the stones. However, they did appear to feature an iron staining and had been covered with algae prior to being cleaned in a chlorine bath. The associated Polaroids (Figure 8.8) show modern anthro/zoomorphic carvings, yet the conservator's cautious assessments suggest that the forger's art has been masked sufficiently through burial and staining to give the illusion of antiquity. Rouse's response has not been found in the correspondence files, but the images were filed within a folder the labeled "neo-Taino art" in Rouse's handwriting.

In the same archive folder was found an intriguing group of images to-

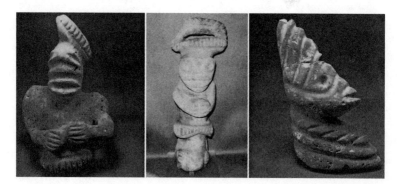

Figure 8.8. Three (of five) sculptures forwarded to Rouse in 1989 by an art conservator tasked with identifying whether the pieces were genuine. (Rouse Archives, ANT. ARC.00388. Courtesy Peabody Museum of Natural History, New Haven, Connecticut)

gether with an undated note. The images show a large assemblage of stone carvings (Figure 8.9). All are anthropomorphic, many in acrobatic poses, conforming to rounded, hammerstone, or celt-like shapes. There are no accompanying details to say where the figures came from, or whose collection this was—but it is clear from the unusual, uniform iconography that the figures were being made to loosely conform to perceptions of "indigenous art," though with added features and reinterpretations (e.g., the two conical projections emerging from the head of the figure in the lower central image in Figure 8.9). This "urge to originality," as Rouse called it, is something inherent in both midcentury (Paredones) and later forgeries—some of the most recent becoming more and more ornate and elaborate (for example, see Figure 1.8). These creations do not conform to, or directly copy, old pieces in museum or private collections but rather create their own aesthetic, revealing a recognizable "hand" of the artist/forger as seen through diagnostic treatments of the face or body. For example—as seen in several examples in Figure 8.9—an elongated rectangle of a nose, framed by small, coffee-bean eyes and mouth distinguishes a group of figures. In another group, the forehead and cheekbones are depicted as a raised semicircle. The uniform treatment of the hands, some with bent wrists, others with splayed fingers resting on the figure's belly—together with the oddly rounded legs—speak of a consistent, uniform style of carving. These elements are generally atypical of the highly stylized aesthetics of older carvings of secure provenance.

It is clear that in the 1980s several different styles of forgeries had come to light—some maintaining the Paredones aesthetic, others introducing new iconography, and yet others carved sufficiently well to raise questions even with someone as versed in the styles of the precolumbian Caribbean as Rouse.

Figure 8.9. Selection of images sent to Rouse, possibly in the 1980s. The unusual combination of facial and body features together with the stylistic uniformity spanning the corpus suggests mass manufacture specifically for the "market." (Rouse Archive, ANT.ARC.00388. Courtesy Peabody Museum of Natural History, New Haven, Connecticut)

Given the escalation of forgeries over the previous decades, it is not surprising that some pieces would eventually enter museum collections—and the PMNH itself was not immune.[35] The PMNH acquired a large collection of Caribbean artifacts in 1982, donated by Fred Olsen. This single accession holds the largest group (101 pieces) of cataloged "fakes" from the Caribbean at the Peabody Museum. Among this material were 82 forgeries purchased by Olsen from Paul Barker of Gorham State College in Maine. Virtually all of the Barker objects cataloged as fakes are said to be from Haiti. The Margaret Fay collection, acquired in the mid-1980s, also had material Rouse identified as forgeries.

By the 1990s, there was no denying that indigenous style neo-artifacts were an established "tradition" on Hispaniola (most of the examples documented in Rouse's files are from this island). Indeed, Rouse (1992:164) dedicated a short section in his widely accessible volume (*The Tainos: Rise and Decline of the People Who Greeted Columbus*, 1992) to the modern revival of indigenous arts, explaining that there were several reasons for its emergence—including the use of "Classic Taíno" designs as sources of distinctively local cultural inspiration/identity, particularly relevant to nationalist movements (e.g., García Arévalo 1988). Tourism, of course, spurred souvenir "copies" of ancient arts; the gaps in collectors' shelves created a market for increasingly sophisticated art forms, based on a knowledge of the genuine, but refined for more contemporary tastes (larger, more ornate pieces). Rouse noted: "Some specimens are crudely done, but the best are equal in quality to the aboriginal artifacts. . . . They differ in one or more ways: use of modern materials or techniques, modification of Taino shapes or motifs, and new combinations of modes of material, shape and decoration" (Rouse 1992:164). He illustrated three examples of "neo-Taíno" art in his volume (1992:Figure 40) (Figure 8.10), including one of the Paredones carvings currently in the PMNH collections. This is a quintessential Paredones sculpture, and perhaps this is the reason it was in Rouse's study collection, where diagnostic examples of Caribbean

Figure 8.10. Mock-up of Rouse's illustration of "Neo-Taino" art in his 1992 *Tainos* volume, using the original photos held in the Rouse Archives (compare with Rouse 1992:Figure 40, p. 165). *Left*: Paredones speleothem carving (ANT.266200), H: 14 cm; *center*: coral limestone anthropomorph; *right*: bone "vomiting" spatula, likely carved from cow bone. (Rouse Archive, ANT.ARC.00301, uncataloged photos, box 1; Courtesy Peabody Museum of Natural History, New Haven, Connecticut)

material culture were held. Although it is difficult to assess with certainty why Rouse retained fakes among diagnostic Caribbean artifacts, it may have been to demonstrate that such objects were in circulation or to make them readily available for discussion.

CONCLUSIONS

Through Rouse's collection and archives we have a window into nearly four decades of Caribbean forgeries. It is a filtered view, given that there was undoubtedly a wider spectrum of "artistic reinterpretations" in circulation at the time—but it is a view through the eyes of a Caribbeanist at the peak of his career, burdened with the responsibility of defining what was, to him, an unfamiliar world of forged "art" (precolumbian material culture, and by association its forged counterparts, had become the aesthetic pinnacle for the market from the early twentieth century; see also Geurds, chapter 9 this volume). Through his lens, we are able to document some of the variety and styles of Hispaniolan forgeries, and the resulting discussions that tried to make sense of this emerging, worrying trend. Rouse was largely reluctant to be drawn into the situation—reticent (in his correspondence) on the reasons why he identified some as "falsifications," while others, equally suspect, he tenaciously supported as genuine, despite the advice of colleagues. Perhaps private conversations were more direct, but on the whole, Rouse, despite his typically detailed, typological classifications of Caribbean archaeology based largely on material culture styles, preferred to leave the decisions on forgeries to colleagues like Dockstader, at least in the 1960s. Dockstader had his finger on the art market pulse and better understood the clever abilities of forgers to infiltrate the displays of moneyed collectors and (eventually) museums. Dockstader saw the most convincing, highly skilled Central and South American forgeries in the course of his work—creations that mimicked to an art form the iconography, stylistic characteristics, materials, and pigments used in the genuine pieces; what he saw in Paredones—and indeed many of the subsequent forgeries from the Dominican Republic and Haiti—were a long way from this sophisticated copying. In contrast, Paredones was the closest personal involvement Rouse had with the forger's world (he assisted in dating the site and was to help publish Boyrie Moya's work on the excavations there). He was drawn into what was essentially a deception, as were many of the most prominent Dominican archaeologists of the time, and the likelihood is that he resented being linked, even peripherally, with it. As an archaeologist, he had to trust what he pulled from the ground, but Paredones twisted the reality of this, particularly when Benyi's revelations about planting material emerged in the press in the 1980s. One need only examine the two Cueva Universitaria carvings in the PMNH collections, purportedly found on the "soil surface" of the cave, which Rouse excavated in January 1967, to realize how intimate Rouse was with the Paredones forgeries. He brought these to Dockstader, and to the Cisneros Gallery, and kept them close, in his main study collection—perhaps as a reminder of the increasing uncertainties over precolumbian Caribbean "art." With the escalation of the practice over the following decades, many sought out Rouse's opinion; he could never escape the question of what was "authentic" in a world of looted or forged collections—a situation that would increasingly impact his domain of carefully curated museum collections.

Museums maintain collections for education and research purposes. While the majority of objects in museums are authentic, some reproductions or forgeries could easily infiltrate the collections. Known fakes may be retained to further the education mission of the museum, or there could be complex ownership issues that limit the institution's options to deaccession the objects. This chapter demonstrates the importance of long-term preservation of collections, and, particularly, the archival material associated with them. We are fortunate that Rouse maintained a comprehensive archive of correspondence that provides a window into an important issue in Caribbean archaeology and history.

NOTES

1. Archival references are by last name and date of correspondence. Archive correspondence files, held in the Museum Support complex in West Haven, Connecticut, are organized alphabetically and by decades. Images are referenced according to their file number, and archive box. All images and archival information are reproduced with the kind permission of the Peabody Museum of Natural History, New Haven, Connecticut.

2. Rouse to Boyrie Moya, November 29, 1966, Rouse Archives, PMNH.

3. Rouse to Boyrie Moya, December 20, 1966, Rouse Archives, PMNH.

4. Rouse to Morbán Laucer, January 18, 1967, Rouse Archives, PMNH.

5. Rouse to Boyrie Moya, January 18, 1967, Rouse Archives, PMNH.

6. Rouse to Boyrie Moya, January 18, 1967, Rouse Archives, PMNH.

7. The comments for the sample are worth quoting in full: "Unidentified earth material (peat?) containing ca. 3% non-carbonate carbon taken 0.4 m below surface in cave E of Santo Domingo, Dominican Republic. . . . Statutes [*sic*] carved from stalagmites found in cave belonging to unknown complex. Sample assoc. with badly caclified bones whose organic carbon content was only 0.014%, lowest value we have seen for unburned bones. Fluorine content of bones was 0.15%. Coll. 1968 [*sic?*] and subm. by José Cruxent, who estimated age of complex at ca. 1000 yr. *Comment*: peat does not date culture. Bones, however, have a fuorine content that agrees with submitter's age estimation" (Tamers 1969:410). Two things are noteworthy here: fluorine dating measures the amount of fluoride buried bones absorb, which helps to provide an estimate or relative age, that is, the amount of time the bones have been buried; it

cannot provide a chronometric range. Also, the sample collection date is reported as 1968, rather than 1967, when Cruxent was in the field with Rouse and had taken the original sample; either this is in error or another sample was submitted at a later date. Our thanks to Jonathan A. Hanna for tracking down this date in the *Radiocarbon* lists.

8. Rouse to Vega, June 19, 1967, Rouse Archive, PMNH. See also Vega (2015), where Rouse's letter is translated into Spanish.

9. Rouse to García Victoria, October 31, 1967, Rouse Archives, PMNH.

10. Rouse to Dockstader, April 6, 1968, Rouse Archives, PMNH.

11. Dockstader to Francis Ross, November 10, 1964; MAI/Heye Foundation Records, NMAI.AC.001, Box 47, Folder 1, B 47.1.

12. Dockstader to Ross, March 22, 1961; MAI/Heye Foundation Records, NMAI.AC.001; Box 47, Folder 1, B 47.1.

13. Dockstader to Rouse, March 9, 1968; MAI/Heye Foundation Records, NMAI.AC.001; Box 47, B 47.3.

14. Rouse to Dockstader, January 25, 1968, Rouse Archives, PMNH.

15. Dockstader to Rouse, March 26, 1968, Rouse Archives, PMNH, emphasis added.

16. Rouse to Dockstader, March 15, 1968; MAI/Heye Foundation Records, NMAI.AC.001; Box 47, Folder 1, B 47.3.

17. Rouse to Dockstader, March 25, 1968; MAI/Heye Foundation Records, NMAI.AC.001; Box 47, Folder 1, B 47.3; emphasis added.

18. Rouse to Morban Laucer, February 18, 1967, Rouse Archive, PMNH.

19. Rouse to Chanlatte Baik, March 14, 1969; MAI/Heye Foundation Records, NMAI.AC.001; Box 47, B 47.3.

20. Rouse to Dockstader, March 25, 1968, Rouse Archives, PMNH.

21. Rouse to Chanlatte Baik, March 14, 1969; MAI/Heye Foundation Records, NMAI.AC.001; Box 47, B 47.3.

22. Rouse to Chanlatte Baik, March 14, 1969; MAI/Heye Foundation Records, NMAI.AC.001; Box 47, B 47.3; emphasis added.

23. Rouse to Chanlatte Baik, March 14, 1969; MAI/Heye Foundation Records, NMAI.AC.001; Box 47, B 47.3.

24. Rouse to Dockstader, February 23, 1969; emphasis added, Rouse Archives, PMNH.

25. Dockstader to Rouse, February 28, 1969; MAI/Heye Foundation Records, NMAI.AC.001; Box 47, B 47.3

26. Rouse to Boyrie Moya, January 18, 1967, Rouse Archives, PMNH. Rouse further notes that "I cannot be sure of the [Boca Chica] style of the pottery, since I found only plain sherds in levels 0.25–0.50 and 0.50 and 0.75."

27. Dockstader to Rouse, March 8, 1969; MAI/Heye Foundation Records, NMAI.AC.001; Box 47, B 47.3.

28. Rouse to Dockstader, March 14, 1969, Rouse Archives, PMNH.

29. Rouse to Paul Barker, April 9, 1968, Rouse Archive, PMNH, emphasis added.

30. Rouse, December 22, 1982, Rouse Archives, PMNH.

31. Rouse, June 19, 1984, Rouse Archives, PMNH.

32. Rouse, May 18, 1986, Rouse Archives, PMNH.

33. Rouse, October 16, 1986, Rouse Archives, PMNH.

34. Rouse, February 6, 1986, Rouse Archives, PMNH.

35. Understanding the nature of the anthropology collections of the Peabody Museum may put the Paredones material and other objects of ambiguous origin into a clearer context. The museum's anthropology collections include over 300,000 object catalog records representing an estimated 2,000,000 individual objects, plus some large archaeological collections being actively cataloged. The collections are derived from a variety of sources including Yale University faculty and graduate student research, donations, and bequests from Yale alumni and affiliates, donations by unaffiliated individuals, and a modest number of exchanges with other institutions. The majority of the collections were field collected by archaeological or ethnographic scholars affiliated with Yale University and/or the Peabody Museum.

While in the past collections with limited data were accepted as donations, more recently the anthropology division has developed acquisition guidelines emphasizing well-documented objects or collections with significant potential for research or education. This partly reflects the regulatory environment of international agreements such as the UNESCO Convention Concerning the Protection of the World Cultural and Natural Heritage (Geneva, 1972) and the Convention on International Trade in Endangered Species of Wild Fauna and Flora (CITES). Furthermore, limited storage capacity forces us to focus on collections with the greatest research and educational potential. Objects lacking good data have limited value in supporting the museum's mission of research and education.

Donations received in the past might contain objects of ambiguous origin, including some that are clearly reproductions or fakes. The term *fake* implies a conscious intent by the manufacturer to deceive, whereas a replica of an object or one made "in the style" of an authentic piece might be considered folk art. It is not uncommon for donations to include some authentic objects as well as tourist art.

9

Authenticity, Preservation, and Care in Central American Indigenous Material Culture

Alexander Geurds

Faking is to collecting what weeds are to gardening.
—Coe 1993:275

The understanding of "real" and "replica'" in the Caribbean and in parts of Central America is marked by a problematic entanglement of postcolonial nationalism, emerging indigenous identities, mass tourism, the trade in antiquities, and archaeological expertise. These overlapping fields all share a concern about authenticity and, specifically, the authority of voice to speak to what is authentic. The result is a difficult-to-navigate mix of essentialism, materialism, boundedness, heritage legislation, and individual objects. While a substantial argument was put forward in the social sciences on the fallacy of viewing authenticity as an either/or debate, instead convincingly arguing for a contextually grounded and processual emphasis on "authentication," this has yet to fully engage with the particular histories in the wider Caribbean and their varied contemporary developments. Here, I argue for attention to authentication processes taking place at either end of the illicit trade spectrum, albeit motivated by the uncomfortably distant social realities of seller versus buyer. This inequality of value, and how it is treated in the antiquities trade, is what is at the heart of the matter, as authentic becomes a function of a contested regimes of value. Ultimately, authenticity is an imprecise and dynamic concept, and as such it is mobilized by actors wanting to define it along particular intended lines. Those actors include collectors, auction houses, and archaeologists, but, as I will illustrate, equally so those looking to escape cultural marginalization and affect real socioeconomic implications (for insular Caribbean examples, see Ostapkowicz, chapter 1 herein; Hanna, chapter 5 herein).

As I write, there are 993 million Google hits for "authentic." This preceding sentence parallels what Cornelius Holtorf wrote in 2013 (Holtorf 2013:427), except for the number of Google results, which then tallied a meager 274 million. There may be a history of algorithmic developments to partly explain the additional 719 million results added in the span of roughly seven years (in fact, one does wonder), but it also underscores the increasing centrality of authenticity desires in both society and scholarship. Part of this importance awarded to authenticity is related to globalization, in the sense of time-space compression. That is, the potential for the mobility of objects and images has historically increased to such a degree that many places in the world are now linked physically or virtually, and the time it takes to communicate across such links has drastically decreased (Hodos et al. 2017).

It is a truism to say that the effects of such compression are widespread and cross into most aspects of life, and this has been put forward in a varied body of postmodern analysis, including, for example, tourism studies (e.g., Cobb 2014; Uriely 2005), material culture studies (Miller 2002; Stahl Brower 2012), and studies encompassing economics and identity (e.g., Comaroff and Comaroff 2009; Smith 2001). Such analyses are in themselves also of relevance to the study of the trade in precolumbian antiquities, as the material past plays a central role in tourism and identity construction. More to the point here, however, is that object mobility also becomes a function of authenticity desires in the commercial trade of precolumbian indigenous artifacts in the Caribbean and Central America, as is manifest in the continued procurement, either through looting or forging, of such objects to feed the demand of segments of the global antiquities and art markets.

I will illustrate that authentication processes are feeding the desire to collect "traditional" objects, including antiquities and tribal art, in part to feature alongside collections of early modernist works of art. At the other end of the spectrum, such traditional artifacts are increasingly difficult to procure, thereby increasing their relative demand and leading to replacement strategies of replicating and forging. At the same time, throughout Central America and the Caribbean, initiatives are put forward to stimulate or revive local practices of artisanal work, typically based on locally available materials and using traditional techniques. Such materials are seldom included in the wish lists of collectors, partly because they fail to comply with requirements to qualify as an authentic antiquity, including the anonymity of the maker and age. The value of antiquities, precolumbian, Amerindian, or otherwise, resides largely in their authenticity, as Donna Yates argues (Yates 2015a:72), and the authority to speak to objects' authentic nature is therefore a key feature in the commercial trade of antiquities.

If authenticity is the driver behind a value regime in the antiquities trade, then two questions may be asked. The first is what the value of "authentic" might be in cultural contexts that do not rely on the way Western thinking has devised it. This is a relevant consideration in the contemporary cultural and nation-state settings of the Caribbean and parts of Central America, and arguably even more so than in the case of objects from the Mediterranean world or the Near East. The second question is how the dynamic (or elusive) conceptual nature of "authentic" can be mobilized to favor local economic development and a more caring attitude toward material pasts. I use the word "care" here explicitly, to go beyond the Latin origin of "to curate" and in the sense of recent calls by Paul O'Neill and others to expand more traditional understandings of curating objects and sites to include a concern for and care of the world in a socially committed sense (O'Neill 2012). Originating in museum studies debates, curating is increasingly about what agentive, strategic roles museum curators can take on to value the renewed assertiveness of local traditions in a globalized art market. On a case by case basis, such a "caring" approach may provide new thinking on definitions of what is to be seen as authentic.

Being a concept determined by factors including age, provenance, aesthetics, and rarity, to designate an Amerindian antiquity as authentic is also to enable it to become iconic for particular constructed cultural ethnicities. Not surprisingly, these ethnicities are often the product of nineteenth-century efforts in cultural categorization of archaeological and ethnographic observations (Jones 1997:40–55). In turn, such categories are the domain of nation-states, eager to naturalize ideas of identity and national belonging. Such links between material culture, indigenousness, and national identity have been widely explored, both for the Americas (e.g., Benavides 2004; Kohl and Fawcett 1998) and elsewhere (e.g., Hamilakis 2009; Meskell 2011). Objects produced in the Caribbean and parts of southern Central America now circulate more readily across the globe, and archaeological objects dating to precolumbian times are no exception to this. While illicit looting, commodification, and movement of antiquities across nation-state boundaries is subject to a rule book of national, binational, and universal heritage legislation, the controlling mechanisms continue to fall short, and a significant market for particular object categories remains (see Byer, Appendix this volume).

PRIMITIVE ART

Since the early twentieth century, archaeological objects have been selected for their resonance with the clientele of auction houses and local tourism as complying with the rubric of "primitive art" (Myers 2006). The notion of primitivism and the wider invoking of archaeological materials in early modernist art and architecture is now a primary driver of the trade in precolumbian antiquities. Beginning in the early twentieth century and as an alternative to art nouveau, expressionists turned their artistic gaze toward what was referred to as "archaic" or "primitive" examples of art. Typically encapsulated in this broad anthropological (rather than art historical) category are objects from Central Africa, Melanesia, and Oceania as well as precolumbian objects. What specifically qualifies as primitive art is not clear cut (and therefore malleable in terms of authenticity), but adhering broadly to certain artistic responses of form, visual balance, materiality, texture, and abstraction (Rubin 1984). Today, the art produced in this early twentieth-century period are among the most sought after and commercially attractive, and the associated "primitive art," now renamed as "tribal art," is subject to what I call a "commodification slipstream," whereby the collector and modern art museums and galleries aim to acquire such ethnographic or archaeological objects in order to juxtapose them with the expressionist or surrealist art in question (Figure 9.1). As a consequence, tribal art is selling for significant prices at auction houses. It is wrapped in descriptive language tropes linking

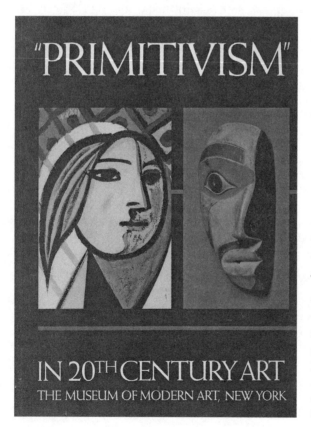

Figure 9.1. Book cover of *"Primitivism" in 20th Century Art: Affinity of the Tribal and the Modern*, edited by William Rubin (1984), the catalog accompanying the identically named exhibit at the Museum of Modern Art, New York. (Photo courtesy Alexander Geurds)

precolumbian objects and contemporary culture, such as the "spiritual unity" and "immortal passion for survival" that apparently links both its indigenous producers and contemporary buyers, or its strikingly "contemporary form" and apparent "plastic beauty from the mists of time."[1]

How the notion of primitive art affects the antiquities trade is difficult to quantify in numbers, networks, and flows of objects—something not necessarily surprising given the private nature of these trade networks (but for insightful attempts at this, see Brodie and Renfrew 2005 and articles in the *International Journal of Cultural Property*). The apparently straightforward question of who buys precolumbian antiquities is difficult to answer, because of the clandestine trafficking processes involved, essentially, a commodity chain sustained through flexible connections between local and global networks by which something murky and dirty morphs into something shiny and pleasant. Moreover, auction houses are famously founded on the principal that everyone can bid, publicly or anonymously, making the clientele for precolumbian antiquities difficult to chart. In the trade of antiquities, an object's origins may be obscure but its more recent biography is one of immaculate form, often surrounded by commercial curatorial care and the ascription of high economic and aesthetic value. This trajectory of the commodified artifact prompted James Clifford some time ago to critically speak of ethnographic objects as "travelers" discarding previous "lives" on their way to modern settings to assume the role of primitive art (Clifford 1988).

Beyond the apparent sensitive and clandestine elements to the trade in Amerindian antiquities, how such objects are received in gallery and collector circles is a discussion largely disconnected from how these precolumbian objects were made and used. These two veins of discussing Amerindian art, one being about reception and the other about contextualization, have little overlap. The former deals predominantly with an aesthetic analysis inspired by modernism, and the latter focusing on life history involving production, use, and eventual decay.[2] Where context and reception may meet is in the strategic construction of an object's authenticity, as such authenticating can happen through provenance and pedigree narratives as well as through technical material analyses. A focus on archaeological landscapes as well as on particular object features may help argue for or against an object's authenticity. An art historical focus on quality is in no way less needed than an archaeological emphasis on content and context, as both fulfill knowledge needed for authenticating an object.

As Coe argues in poignant style (1993), replicas in collections are like weeds in a garden. Most collecting is motivated by an exclusive desire to possess and display antiquity, rather than having to resort to visiting museums (see Price 1989 for an uncomfortable analysis of collecting primitive art), and objects passed off as antique when they are not, or assessed as singular when they are diachronic assemblages, will lose much of, if not all, their desirability. Authenticity of antiquities, when assessed by age determination, is inflexible. There is thus a perceived divide between precolumbian materials and those from colonial times, and this extends onward into more recent artisanal expressions. Such contemporary artisanal objects are typically viewed as folkloristic reinventions that speak little to wealthy collectors in the Western metropoles or parts of the Near East and Latin America, who are driven by authenticity desires.

The improving of local economies through replica production in Central America and the Caribbean is frustrated by the reliance on age for authenticity. This in turn jeopardizes archaeological contexts and continues to draw local archaeological heritage into the global modern art market, referring the very idea of replicas and their production to the tourist instead of the collector. The older, the better, the auctioneer will say, and this is of archaeological concern. What is also clear is that the current justification for protecting heritage, using archaeological arguments focused on context preservation, fails to impact both the supply and the demand ends of the Amerindian artifact commodity chain. In turn, the related goals of discouraging looting to protect archaeological sites and the safeguarding of Caribbean and Central American heritage in local settings are continually frustrated.

The authentic needs to be recognized and validated in precolumbian art, and therefore there is a particular role for the process of authentication. At present, this assessing and establishing of authenticity through expert knowledge typically takes place at auction houses and is the responsibility of regional specialists on staff at those companies. As discussed elsewhere (Kelker and Bruhns 2010; Yates 2015a:80–81), in those cases where this process errs in establishing an age and/or provenience and falsely attributes authenticity, a scandal, embarrassing to the auction house or museum, typically ensues. This is embarrassing due to apparently inadequate determination protocols and scandalous due to the financial loss of value for the owner, be it an individual collector or an institution. In other words, the question of authenticity is central to the value of art and antiquities at auctions (and in the art world in general), leaving no room for even the most sophisticated of replicas. Sophistication demonstrated through the highly skilled (re-)production of Amerindian objects is irrelevant to an understanding of authenticity based on age determination alone.

In the international art market, the authenticity concept is a central variable in the economic value regimes governing this global industry. Museums of anthropology or ethnology occasionally still have a role in this, but the advent of national and UNESCO heritage legislation and discussions of critical museology have prompted such museums to carefully consider their institutional position in light of colonial collecting histories and the long-time exclusion of indigenous communities (Geurds and Van Broekhoven 2013). This has led to considerable debates around authenticity in such museums, also due to its links to essentialist renderings of past cultures, and its current processes of redress, seeking out collaborations with indigenous communities (Colwell 2017; Golding and Modest 2010; Van Broekhoven et al. 2010). Modern art museums and galleries, however, are decidedly less involved in this critical debate on representation of culture, allowing for the continued search for authentic qualities in objects.

The recognition of the authenticating role played by the art world was argued in Arjun Appadurai's now classic edited volume on the commoditization of objects and the ongoing definition of authenticity in an age of industrial reproduction (Appadurai 1986). This inherently unstable or dynamic approach as to what makes something authentic is invariably conditioned by time, location, and material properties. Authenticating agents may ask *when* do we consider an object to be authentic, what might constitute a convincing precision of provenience, and how might an object have been made or assembled (Joyce 2013). Such unpacking of the authenticity concept is not new, having been discussed for the better part of the twentieth century, perhaps beginning with the oft-cited ideas of Benjamin (1968) and, more broadly, Herder (Berlin 1980), and remains of central relevance to heritage debates of global, national, and local scales.

The increasing sophistication, however, with which replicas are produced makes it likely that at least part of this demand can be met in ways other than looking for the original, and indeed replicas still represent a significant segment of existing private and public collections. The undeniable advantage of replicas over originals resides in their reproductive potential, whereas archaeological heritage is seen as a nonrenewable resource. A perhaps unforeseen consequence of the presence of replicas in the precolumbian antiquities market is that, combined with the difficulty inherent in authenticating objects from looted contexts, market value may decrease without the stamp of authenticity, as argued by Holtorf and Schadla-Hall (1999:234). But what does it mean when objects fail to be authenticated and then lose their value? I contend that this value ascription only occurs in environments where the authenticating happens, and it follows then that if different parameters of authenticity are employed, the value may be viewed differently. A useful example for this is the term "faithful reproduction" (Holtorf and Schadla-Hall 1999), which describes a widely accepted idea in the field of industrial technology where a person's engagement with the technological machine in question does not jeopardize the object's authenticity during replacement or repair.

Holtorf and Schadla-Hall use the example of Harley-Davidson, a motorcycle that might be considered less favorable by being both heavier and having less horsepower than most other brands. But remarkably, repairing and customizing actually adds to the authenticity of the object. Likewise, there are several examples of collecting practices that will value the biography of an object (say, a postal stamp or antiquarian book) over its authenticity, defined here as the conservation of its original state. These are examples of instances where authenticity is increased through historical association (say, a signed copy of a book). The element of rarity also plays a part here: authenticity is often also a function of an object's rarity, as long as the rarity does not cross into anomalous style when suspicions of falsification rise.

While the socioeconomic realities at the beginning and endpoints of the transnational trade in antiquities are stark, authentication processes can be observed at either end of this spectrum, albeit motivated by the uncomfortably distant social realities of seller versus buyer. The inequalities of value created in this network, and how it is treated in the antiquities trade, is a question whereby the authentic becomes a function of a political and economic regime of value. If we move the focus slightly away from the forensic identification of original (in this case precolumbian) objects, a potentially productive approach is found in asking how the microeconomic effects of replica production (and artisanship more broadly) are enabled or disabled through the nation-state and commercial actors involved in the trade network. In parts of the Caribbean and Central America, what is stimulated for the production of cultural knowledge and national identity formation is determined by nation-state policies. Such policies have historically contributed to the emergence of producers of precolumbian replicas, who are part of a trade network but are at the same time disconnected from the singular pricing at auctions. Ideas on authenticity in Amerindian objects originate in far earlier exotic renderings of the Americas and developed in historical settings marked by a troubling entanglement of neocolonial US foreign policy, as well as more recent episodes of civil war and economic disenfranchisement.

DEFINING PRECOLUMBIAN HERITAGE
IN CENTRAL AMERICA

The Western view of Central America's precolumbian past is one that was largely formed by eighteenth- and nineteenth-century explorers. These were generally well-to-do white males, often in diplomatic service and with ties to the museums that began to emerge in the middle part of the nineteenth century in the United States and Europe. Perhaps beginning with the monumental Maya site of Copán, situated in the extreme west of Honduras, and visited by John Lloyd Stephens and Frederick Catherwood in 1840, these views of a jungle with lost civilizations quickly gained popularity in the metropolitan centers of the United States and Europe (Evans 2004:44–87). Museums in particular started forming an integral part in transnational networks of precolumbian antiquities in which diplomatic posts functioned as collecting nodes. Much of this occurred unhampered by any form of legislative heritage management. While the Spanish colonial period had destroyed and looted an unfathomable amount of Amerindian objects from all across the Americas, the second half of the nineteenth century saw such materials become desirable through a mix of exoticism and aesthetics made possible by the wealth accumulation that accompanied the emergence of industrial capitalism in the United States and Europe. Moreover, the hands-on US foreign policy toward the American hemisphere enabled many US collectors to travel across Central and South America, sending crate after crate with precolumbian objects back to museums and institutions in the US northeast. Such "informal imperialism," to apply the phrase used by Margarita Díaz-Andreu (2007:167), even included visions of purchasing and displacing the entire site of Copán from Central America to New York.[3]

Initially, the reception of precolumbian objects in US circles was mostly centered on bewilderment toward the curious nature of such artifacts. Style, material, technology, and iconography seemed anything but compatible with the realism of materials of Greco-Roman origin, long valued in Western society.[4] Central America played a role in changing this rather poor view of precolumbian artifacts when increasingly, and helped by the advent of photography, individual objects came to be regarded as having artistic value, and the idea of forgotten urban ruins in Central America came to be appreciated as a corollary to the Romantic archaeological landscapes of Italy and Greece (Evans 2004). Such artistic juxtaposing effectively countered competing views of Amerindian societies as backward and simple when compared to Old World materials. This set the stage for the nostalgic views onto the material past in Central America—a perception needed for its archaeological record to become worthy of preservation and presentation as well as to find a place in the emergent collecting practices of the time and initiate an incentive to begin commercially exploiting precolumbian objects.

Transitioning into the twentieth century, systematic archaeological interest in Central American prehistory increased, initially stirred by private and public collections in the United States brought together as curiosities by industrialists active in the region. Among these, Minor Keith and Samuel Zemurray are perhaps the most well-known tycoon-collectors (Luke 2006:39; Steward 1964:160–168), but certainly not the only ones. It should be cautioned that Central America covers vast territories, many of which are challenging to access, with much of the region remaining lightly occupied even today. Systematic archaeological attention was restricted to a handful of excavations and surveys in more accessible areas or ones that were in the process of being commercially exploited (e.g., Hartman 1901, 1907; Yde 1938) and various typological studies were done on collections of ground stone and pottery objects, established by the aforementioned US industrialists (e.g., Lothrop 1926; MacCurdy 1911; Mason 1945). In one such study, the author characterized the links between archaeology and US industrial exploitation in Costa Rica in the following way: "Such unrifled cemeteries are as rare in America as are untouched tombs of the Pharaohs to the Egyptologist. . . . The unlettered residents, ignorant of the scientific value of the objects, flocked to the place, drawn by the lust of the treasure hunter. . . . Such would have been the fate of [the] Mercedes [site], but for the presence of Mr. Keith. Luckily for American archaeology, he was in the fortunate executive and financial position to stay the hand of the vandal, the treasure hunter, and souvenir seeker. . . . He was thus able to retain all the treasures, amounting to more than 10,000 pieces" (Mason 1945:199).

This quote illustrates both the magnitude of early twentieth-century collecting practices in the Central American republics under US foreign policy and the moral justification supporting it. Here, archaeological research and collecting were inextricably tied with networks of US cultural institutions, business interests, and emergent archaeology, with similar examples found in El Salvador, Costa Rica, Panama, and, to a lesser degree, in Nicaragua. This period is fairly well studied, as ample documentation surrounding such collecting is available, the direct outcome of the bureaucracy accompanying their registration, transport, and eventual accession to US museum collections.

After World War II, heritage legislation became gradually more effectively implemented in Central America, in comparable form to the Caribbean (Siegel and Righter 2011), and customs controls and provenance requirements were put in place in Western destinations of precolumbian artifacts. At the same time, the earlier mentioned art historical view of precolumbian objects, including those from Central America, became a more established school of thought, primarily in the United States (Coe 1993). Going back to the first half of the twentieth century, and influenced by expressionist painters and sculptors, notions of aesthetics and craftsmanship became more of a focus for US collectors. Midcentury US collectors became concerned with the style of objects offered to them, ranking objects along a scale of quality as well as making a distinction "between fakes and authentic objects" (Coe 1993:272). This was accompanied by the emergence of precolumbian art scholarship, stimulated by George Kubler at Yale University and art historical studies at Columbia University. Such connections between collectors, connoisseurs, archaeologists, and museum curators are now less present, effectively obscuring from archaeologists and heritage custodians how precolumbian objects are collected and what the underlying looting dynamics are.

The system underlying the handling and trading of precolumbian objects was one in which collectors were part of a network with antiquities dealers and museums playing a central role. Museums were part client to the dealers and part expert to private collectors, creating what James Clifford refers to as an "art-culture system" (Clifford 1988).[5] The preferences regarding object categories and materials were varied, but the foremost collectors seemed to emphasize precious stone and gold objects rather than pottery. Even though there are a plethora of precolumbian collections with a heavy emphasis on pottery, for Middle America (including Mesoamerica) this was primarily oriented toward ritual objects looted from, for example, west Mexican shaft tombs, stuccoed tripod vessels from Teotihuacán in the Basin of Mexico, Mezcala stone figures, and polychrome Maya vessels found in stone tombs at sites in the Maya Lowlands. The antiquities market in Central America, in contrast, was known to produce a considerable number of pendants and other bodily adornments produced in gold, alongside ground stone objects such as statues, mace heads, elaborate grinding stones, monumental stone spheres, and a range of jade-like greenstone pendants. What unites all these materials is their combination of high abstraction, geometric and spiraling forms, and a combined presence of zoomorphic and anthropomorphic elements expressing an ambiguity that complicates a straightforward iconographic reading.

A limited number of dealers, based out of Los Angeles and New York, established networks of clients and local contacts at different points in Latin America, invoking the help of US-based archaeologist-curators to authenticate materials under consideration for purchase. Auction houses were largely absent from collecting of precolumbian antiquities prior to the 1960s (Coe 1993:288), but firms such as Sotheby's increasingly focused on precolumbian antiquities since then, with overall decreasing numbers of objects for sale but with increasing prices (Tremain 2017:190–192). Authentication was a definite concern, as shown by the tight connections between collector, dealer, and archaeological expert, but how such authenticating took place is rather open, seemingly focused mostly on an object's style coherence and overall "convincingness" (see Ostapkowicz and Colten, chapter 8 this volume). Auction houses, in turn, operationalize authenticity proxies such as an object's pedigree, as expressed by previous appearances in exhibitions and scholarly publications, to allude to (but not guarantee) the authentic age and material properties of a precolumbian object for sale.

Apart from occasional reports on seized materials, the literature on more recent looting dynamics in Central America is predictably thin, with some additional studies available for Costa Rica (Aguilar Bonilla 2007; Boone 1993;

Heath 1973), which likely served as a "hub" for Nicaraguan looting as well. The US control over the Canal Zone in Panama likely also enabled a considerable shipping route from Central America to the United States and Europe. Dynamics of antiquities looting and trafficking in Central America were to some extent defined by national boundaries, but capital cities served as central nodes in such networks. As such, histories of looting precolumbian objects and the accompanying replica production are best examined per country. In this regard, Nicaragua presents a distinctive history, conditioned on the one hand by long-term US political involvement and business ties, but also featuring the Marxist-inspired cultural aspirations of the Sandinist FSLN party after 1979.

In the postrevolutionary period of Nicaragua, and building on prerevolutionary initiatives promulgated by the Banco Central de Nicaragua, government programs were designed to save and improve the work of artisans producing ceramics, both for utilitarian and decorative purposes. Such initiatives were emergent in Mexico at the time as well and were part of initiatives aimed at safeguarding and improving the technology used, for example, by pottery artisans. Community revitalization and the creation of a sustainable folk-art economy in Mexico were important reasons to conduct such programs aimed at establishing cooperatives run by the artisans themselves and producing objects using precolumbian materials and techniques (Carruthers 2001). This was similar to late twentieth-century government initiatives set up in Nicaragua in the 1970s and 1980s. Alongside ceramics, these efforts generally focused on fiber and textile materials, leaving ground and polished stone (popular in collector circles) out of view. This is understandable given the limited utilitarian use for such objects in contemporary indigenous settings. Grinding stones and *molcajetes* or stone mortars are the only ubiquitous object categories still in use today.

During the early 1980s, the newly established Sandinist government continued these workshop initiatives, in particular focusing on pottery. Work in the community of San Juan de Oriente is one of the most exemplary outcomes of these efforts, having produced high-quality pottery for almost 40 years now. As Les Field has argued, the production of such pottery was propagated with a threefold aim in mind, specific to postrevolutionary Nicaragua: to lessen the dependency on the import of vessels from abroad, cut out the exploiting middleman, and achieve an explicit revalorization for "national goods." The revalorization for "national goods" was deemed to lessen the hitherto dominating negative attitude toward local products, especially when compared with imported items and materials (Field 1999:105–106). Cultural policies designed by the Nicaraguan government since the 1980s were focused on controlling design, production, and distribution of artisanal goods, under the arguably rather ironic heading of bringing traditional indigenous material culture back to the residents.[6]

Importantly, potters today use different forms to show their skill, some seeking expressive styles, producing decorative vessels and plates. Others specialize in making pottery inspired by precolumbian examples as featured in publications (Figure 9.2). In particular, the 1979 Spanish edition of the 1926 publication *Pottery of Costa Rica and Nicaragua* by US archaeologist Samuel Lothrop gained popularity among some of the potters of San Juan. This two-volume book, published by the Fondo Cultural Banco de America, achieved considerable diffusion in Nicaragua (Lothrop and Meneses Ocón 1979) (Figure 9.3). It includes an early classification of polychrome and modeled precolumbian pottery and is profusely illustrated. It is still used today as visual inspiration for San Juan de Oriente potters (among others), leading to the production of ceramics that are decidedly more artistic creations than engineered copies.

This process, which uses two-dimensional illustrations of precolumbian

Figure 9.2. Precolumbian-inspired contemporary pottery, produced in San Juan de Oriente, Nicaragua. (Photo courtesy Alexander Geurds)

Figure 9.3. Book cover of *Cerámica de Costa Rica y Nicaragua*, the Spanish-language edition of Samuel K. Lothrop's 1926 illustrated study of precolumbian polychrome pottery from Pacific Nicaragua and Costa Rica. (Photo courtesy Alexander Geurds)

ceramics as artistic inspiration for the creation of unique neo-Amerindian objects, is different from the initial aim of replicating, and the historical background of national cultural policies has a decisive role in how such initiatives come about. A consideration of such regionally specific dynamics of artisanal industries is needed before being able to come to a more nuanced understanding of the trade in Amerindian objects, including both precolumbian artifacts and historic or recent artisanal objects. For San Juan de Oriente potters, what is an authentic vessel can be viewed in a number of ways (Field 2009), and the inspiration found in precolumbian objects was not intended to feed into the antiquities market, nor does it play a role there (Figure 9.4).

Figure 9.4. Don Alfredo Espinoza, expert potter from San Juan de Oriente, and one of his created pottery vessels. (Photo courtesy Alexander Geurds)

What this briefly illustrated case from San Juan de Oriente shows is that local practices of replica production and artisanal expression can fruitfully be explored to avoid adopting the metropolitan anthropological stance that tends to view contemporary local or indigenous practices relating to precolumbian pasts as a reenactment or government-instigated folkloristic revival. Regarding such practices of historical promotion and continued involvement in processes of identify formation in the diverse postcolonial settings of Central America and the Caribbean, such local craftsmanship in wood, clay, and stone provides an opportunity to engage a more nuanced understanding of communities making a living with these materials. Such appreciative views on local artisanship hold the potential to mobilize authenticity narratives and, in doing so, provide access to (inter)national collecting circles. Examples in the Americas where economic self-reliance is achieved through artisanal craft production include Pueblo pottery in the US Southwest (Babcock 1993) and Haida Gwaii wood and argillite carvings on the Pacific Coast of Canada (Ostrowitz 1999). In these instances, individual skill has become a factor of authenticity, subverting earlier notions on the anonymity of tribal arts as a requirement for authenticity.

DISCUSSION

Most archaeologies in Central America find themselves in what Oyuela-Caycedo (1994) has referred to as "State Archaeology," with emergent paths into a "National Archaeology," where in the former the patrimony narratives are largely univocal, in the latter a more inclusive dialogue is sought, calibrated by regional rather than national boundaries. In "National Archaeology," patrimony custodians and archaeologists have a professional duty to engage with cultural ideas as well as with microeconomic conditions at the local level, at times leading to the contestation of certain interpretations or heritage values. Rather than serving to reaffirm nation-state narratives, such dialogues are enabled by those interested in the material past, both stakeholders and archaeological professionals, and entail a local and a more disciplinary aspect, weighted appropriately according to the specifics of the material discussed.

The preservation of Central America's precolumbian material past is largely managed by state authorities, each setting out priorities in cultural representation. As was recently observed by Lena Mortensen (2016), patrimony legislation in Central America is itself not an objective process of deciding where protection of artifacts and archaeological sites ends and commercial or nationalist exploitation begins. Similar perhaps to cases in the Antilles, straightforward cultural patrimony narratives are often not available, as indigenous or local cultural forms are sometimes difficult to recognize.[7] For Honduras, the highly iconic monumental Maya site of Copán is the foremost cultural feature foregrounded in a univocal patrimony view, both in terms of research funding and links to tourism (Joyce 2008). In the case of Nicaragua, state priorities in cultural patrimony narratives do not rely, apart from a few exceptions, on precolumbian archaeological sites. This is partly related to the perceived inferior architectural aesthetics of local monumental sites and the overall modest volumes of surface structures. We can contrast this to Honduras, El Salvador, and, in part, Costa Rica, where certain sites with a history of investigation and restoration are actively protected. Some of these sites also authenticate a certain material past through visiting tourism flows and presentation on bank notes and postal stamps. Costa Rica and Panama have considerable indigenous territories along the Caribbean coastal regions, with local economies that include the production of artisanal products. In each of these Central American cases, the practical mandate of protection and preservation resides with the national institutes of culture or tourism. Beyond the particular histories of these cultural policies aimed at the precolumbian material world, the conviction to preserve the material integrity of sites and control the historical trajectory of objects promotes a distinctly scientific view of curatorial care. This is a selective caring system whereby some objects and sites are notably more valued than others, in turn suggesting that everything else (say, ceramic fragments or unimpressive small mounds) are somehow different and unsanctioned by the state, leaving such materials exposed and devalued.

Instead of having a primary focus on policing and protection, I would concur with proposals that, (a) seek to reduce markets for precolumbian objects (Yates, chapter 10 herein), and (b) seek to increase local audiences for these materials, creating a more inclusive, participatory collaboration between those who produce and use objects, applying traditional techniques and other audiences in Central America. Replica production of precolumbian artifacts is as old as collecting, and indeed the earliest cases of imitation and incorporation go back to precolumbian times (Hamann 2002).

Any discussion on the illicit trade in precolumbian antiquities has links to US foreign policy. Such relations have developed considerably from the times of John Lloyd Stephens, Ephraim Squier, and the long-term implementation of military and intelligence hegemonic strategies in, for example, Nicaragua (Whisnant 1995). The concerns of the United States now also take formal shape through cultural policy (Luke and Kersel 2012), channeled by the local embassies. While we may now look on the times of the "gentleman-explorer" as a quaint and antiquated past, contemporary archaeologies in Central America were dominated until not too long ago by North American and a handful of European scholars. With such foreign projects focused on site-based or regional research questions, national archaeology programs continued in a fragile state or focused largely on salvage and protection of heritage (Lange and Molina 1997). Again, this echoes to some degree the development of archaeology, heritage, and nation-state identity in parts of the Caribbean (see, for example, Curet 2011).

Collectors are driven in their collecting passion through a process of self-realization. Ironically perhaps, those looking to escape cultural marginalization and achieve economic autonomy in the circum-Caribbean region are facing the same challenge, albeit that the resources and wealth mobilized in this parallel process could not be further apart. Nonetheless, artisans still can effect real socioeconomic change in their local and national settings, as many case studies have shown. What the example of San Juan de Oriente in Nicaragua shows is the flexibility of enclosing strategies of the state: where the attention was to produce materialized examples of national (pre)histories, the potters instead developed their ideas based on Lothrop's museum collection study, incorporating individual and communal ideas of local history in giving shape to new pottery forms. Such pottery is obviously not precolumbian,

nor does it pretend to be. Rather, it is a contemporary product of a participatory and open-ended dialogue. Whether such objects should be protected
under national heritage laws I cannot say, but they are open to being cared
for, along similar lines as the communities that created them. In such conditions, archaeologists, local cultural institutions, and cooperatives can work together to create authentic objects that are neither fakes nor copies, but artistic
expressions based on ancestral traditions, in a similar vein to Pueblo pottery
or Haida Gwaii argillite carvings. The marginalization of certain communities in Central America and the Caribbean is a factor, but efforts to collaborate rather than merely protect could eventually be a healing force around
the circum-Caribbean.

CONCLUSIONS

The plurality of authenticity is now an acknowledged observation across the
fields of social science; multiple forms of the authentic are recognized, taking
shape in social worlds that are aware of the economic and political forces that
are exerted on them. Historically, we can adopt Clifford's notion of the art-
culture systems as "'machines for making authenticity." I described such systems previous to the 1970s and during the 1980s and 1990s as they affected
parts of Central America, pointing to the particular national histories that
often defy larger macroregional analyses and straightforward comparisons.
Differences in the voices of indigenous rights to self-determination and actively formulated lifeways further complicate transnational examinations of
artisan workshops focused on the indigenous material legacies. Networks for
precolumbian antiquities are inherently transnational, and the ways in which
both protective measures and market-reducing incentives are rolled out in
Central American nation-states differs widely.

From the early part of the twentieth century onward, both modern art museums and ethnographic museums continually played roles in such machines
of authenticating, although it should be noted that the UNESCO convention
of 1970 and the subsequent advent of critical museology have fundamentally
reshaped the role of ethnographic institutes and museums. Importantly, during this period auction houses also increasingly showed interest in what came
to be called "tribal art." Perhaps museums, heritage specialists, and patrimony
offices can find ways to subvert the authenticity machines that now dominate the black market of precolumbian antiquities. One such way of doing
so could be to open themselves up to national policies in Central America
and the Caribbean and voice their ideas in the particular historical settings
of each national context, following, for example, some of the existing work
from the Pacific Coast of Canada or on Puerto Rico. The encouragement of
local economies fueled by practices and materials with deep histories is not

helped by the rather dichotomous definitions of heritage and artisanal objects. The case of Nicaragua is illustrative of how specific such contexts often are, but also how resilient and innovative those who engage with these materials can be.

NOTES

1. These phrases are taken from the foreword to the Sotheby's catalog, published as a deluxe three-volume boxed set to accompany the infamous auction of the Barbier-Mueller Pre-Columbian Art Collection held in Paris in 2013 (Blazy 2013).

2. Alongside this, there is also considerable attention in archaeological analyses for the aesthetic potential of certain prehistoric art styles (Renfrew et al. 2004; Russell and Cochrane 2014) as well as the value of contemporary art for archaeological analysis (Renfrew 2006).

3. "To buy Copán!," John Lloyd Stephens famously exclaimed in his best-selling *Incidents of Travel in Central America, Chiapas, and Yucatan* (Stephens 1841:115). In setting out his plan, he intended to transport the site to New York and use it as a starting point for a museum that would address American antiquity on a hemispheric scale.

4. Illustrative for this are earlier eighteenth-century drawings of precolumbian objects and murals, mostly from Mesoamerica or the Andes, that were classicized or Egyptianized in their depiction (Hutson 2013:290–291; Pillsbury 2012:15–18).

5. This role gradually changed during the 1960s, culminating in the UNESCO Convention on the Means of Prohibiting and Preventing the Illicit Import, Export, and Transfer of Ownership of Cultural Property and its gradual adoption by countries around the world. Most Central American nations consented to this convention fairly early on, with Costa Rica following last in 1996.

6. As highlighted by Field (1999:106), this program was inspired by similar long-running programs in Mexico, revolving around the notion of popular arts. Such programs are problematic because they effectively are modernization models aimed at rural economies.

7. Violent colonial processes in the first decades after the arrival of European colonizers led to the extermination or displacement of indigenous society in large parts of the Antilles, to be followed by a range of European colonial regimes for several centuries (for an overview, see Siegel and Righter 2011).

10

Reducing the Market
for Illicit Cultural Objects

The Caribbean and Beyond

Donna Yates

THERE ARE TWO main crime issues related to Caribbean cultural objects presented elsewhere in this book: fraud, related to the faking of Caribbean pieces, and the theft, trafficking, and illicit sale of looted and stolen archaeological material. Here I discuss not the source of illicit or dubious Caribbean cultural objects, but the market for that material, and how market practices and market actors shield, negotiate, and neutralize wrongdoing. Ultimately, I argue that while measures to protect Caribbean cultural objects at source are worthwhile to discuss, a strategy of market reduction may be a more effective way of regulating the trade in this material. Taking into account the logistical realities of cultural heritage protection in many Caribbean jurisdictions, I assert that a market reduction approach is a realistic way to reduce the physical, social, and intellectual harms associated with forgery, theft, looting, and trafficking of cultural objects.

CRIME AND THE ANTIQUITIES TRADE:
MARKET AND MARKET ACTORS

In general, the trade in ancient and ethnographic cultural material is structured around the flow of objects from their origins, often in lower-income countries, for ultimate sale in higher-income countries. This mirrors greater global power imbalances and can thus be characterized as concentrating cultural heritage in the hands of those with the most power. While it is certainly the case that some antiquities markets are local, with source and sale occurring within the same region or even country, objects still move from the hands of the many to the hands of the few, from those without power to those with power, from the poor to the rich. The global illicit trade in antiquities largely depends on sources that, due to structural realities, are unable to protect their cultural assets, despite seemingly strong national law and policy.

There is nearly no completely legitimate source of antiquities,[1] with criminality of various kinds occurring at all points of the marketization pathway. While much discussion of this issue has focused on linking the destructive looting of heritage sites to the market (e.g., Brodie and Renfrew 2005; Coggins 1969; Elia 1997; Kersel 2007, 2008; Renfrew 2000) and ethnographic research into looting (e.g., Al-Houdalieh 2012; Antoniadou 2009; Kersel 2006, 2007; Matsuda 1998; Paredes Maury 1999; Van Velzen 1996), recent research has characterized the networks that move antiquities to market as organized crime (e.g., Alderman 2012; Bowman 2011; Campbell 2013; Chappell and Polk 2011; Davis and Mackenzie 2014; Dietzler 2013; Mackenzie 2011a; Mackenzie and Davis 2014; Tijhuis 2006) and market actors as engaging in a variety of activities that can be seen as white-collar crime (e.g., Adler et al. 2009; Bowman 2008; Brodie and Bowman 2014; Brodie et al. 2013; Mackenzie 2007, 2011b). This later-stage white-collar crime, and the actions of ambivalent white-collar market actors, serves to shield the antiquities trade from the type of scrutiny that one might normally expect from a market that can be so closely linked to theft, smuggling, and fraud.

The societal shielding of white-collar actors from the taint of dubious or criminal actions is a hallmark of white-collar crime, which is nonviolent crime that is able to be carried out due to an individual's public reputation or position of public trust. Further, there are particular features about the art market generally and the antiquities market specifically that serve to protect dealers and consumers of dubious goods. Speaking broadly, many practices and institutions of the modern antiquities market developed against the backdrop of the eighteenth- and nineteenth-century European "Grand Tour" voyages and the Age of Enlightenment, with period concerns such as sale confidentiality becoming embedded features in the trade. Critique of the antiquities trade's destructive effects on heritage sites and cultural knowledge, which gained considerable force in the 1960s onward, has been unable to counteract two centuries of opaque and unregulated art market practice. In most major antiquities market countries, sellers and auction houses are under no obligation to reveal the sources of the antiquities that they sell to anyone, nor are they required to identify their customers.

This creates a situation where buyers are unable to fully evaluate the legality and authenticity of an antiquity for sale. In this "gray market" (Bowman 2008; Mackenzie and Yates 2016), further trade practices have developed so that buyers are able to justify their purchases, despite the unknowns, which center on risk mitigation. Research into the development of interpersonal relationships in the antiquities market has shown that both collectors and dealers seek to consume antiquities of unknown and dubious origins while retaining plausible deniability and, thus, avoiding potential social or criminal penalties (Mackenzie 2006, 2007a, 2014). Market actors learn not to ask questions that might reveal problematic information and not to volunteer knowledge they have that might hint at theft, trafficking, or forgery. They also guide other market actors toward the creation of shared narratives about dubious antiquities. The illicit antiquities market, thus, protects and maintains itself, protecting market actors from consequences related to the consumption of illicit material. As I discuss in the next sections, market practice has developed to shield not only the people who operate in the market but also illicit and illegal antiquities from scrutiny.

LOOTED AND FAKE ANTIQUITIES

To be clear, the trafficking of looted antiquities is a transnational issue that connects heritage destruction in what are often lower-income countries to the art consumption practices of elites in higher or very high-income countries. Put simply, demand causes supply, and the willingness of white-collar actors to spend money on antiquities is the primary reason that looting in antiquities source countries exists. While the mechanics of the looting, trafficking, and illicit sale of antiquities falls outside the scope of this chapter (see Yates 2016 for a general overview and Mackenzie 2005 for a criminological perspective), it is worth noting some of the policy gaps that allow illicit artifacts to enter the market and the antiquities market practices that routinely obscure the illicit origins of artifacts for sale.

On the policy front, the major international conventions that form the basis for international policy in this area[2] are primarily concerned with protection of cultural heritage in situ and the return of a limited subset of looted cultural objects to their countries of origin. Neither disruption of trafficking nor disruption of the market are features of this framework. These conventions place the burden of preventing antiquities trafficking from occurring in the first place on source countries, many of which are economically unable to effectively respond to heritage crime (Yates 2015b); certainly this is the situation for many of the Caribbean nations (see, for example, Alverez et al., chapter 2 this volume; Byer, Appendix this volume). At the same time, they do not require antiquities market countries to fully police the market or curb demand, and they give no attention to the development of transnational anti-trafficking measures. A looted antiquity that leaves its country of origin, then, slips through the cracks and is unlikely to ever be returned. If the prevention of antiquities trafficking is the goal, then the effectiveness of local law becomes paramount.

When considering local/national antiquities protection law, it is important to note that although policy can be quite robust on paper, that does not
mean that it is effective. A well-written and well-intentioned antiquities protection law is meaningless if it is neither implementable nor enforceable, and
if the protection of heritage is not a government priority. This appears to be
the case in many Caribbean jurisdictions. I have characterized as "aspirational" those cultural heritage protection laws that appear to push for impec-
cable international-level standards for the prevention of looting and trafficking in places that do not have the police or customs capacity to maintain such
standards (Yates 2014, 2015b). These laws speak to an ideal that cannot be
practically achieved. In such circumstances, the policy is devalued by actors
at the source and within the market, as everyone knows that the law will not
be enforced. The result is little or no protection of antiquities on the ground
and no respect for the laws of source countries among market actors (see,
for example, Curet's Epilogue herein for discussion of a US museum curator
safeguarding, rather than denouncing, a broker of Puerto Rican "antiquities,"
despite being fully aware of Puerto Rican heritage laws). While one option
to explore is the crafting of better, more implementable local policy in antiquities source countries, I strongly advocate for the development of a parallel
approach that may be significantly more effective in preventing the trafficking of illicit and faked antiquities: market reduction (Brodie 2015; Mackenzie
2007b; Sutton 1998), which will be discussed later in this chapter.

Regarding the market practices that allow the trade to become saturated
with looted and trafficked material, perhaps none is more important than
the previously mentioned acceptance of absent, misleading, or outright false
provenance intended to shield market actors. Since the nineteenth century,
antiquities source countries have been enacting policy that clearly outlaws
the unauthorized extraction, export, and marketization of antiquities. While
these laws may not be effectively enforced, the movement of antiquities out
of the ground, out of the country, and on to the market is still illegal in most
cases. Yet with no parallel policy to curb market demand, antiquities remain
popular items for sale; they are a hot commodity with few legitimate sources.
For demand to be met, illicit or illegal sources of antiquities must be found.

Yet, unlike consumers of most other illicit commodities (e.g., narcotics,
arms, counterfeit goods, or people), antiquities buyers, as part of a Bourdieu-
sian quest for increased "cultural capital," require the ability to, as Velben
would say, "conspicuously consume." A primary purpose of a collected antiquity is, literally and figuratively, "for display," and to display a looted antiquity, the piece must be cleansed of the stigma of crime. Market acceptance
of absent and false provenance, then, becomes a laundering technique; it is
a method by which the market creates a shared false reality to self-preserve

and self-justify. Numerous analyses of antiquities sales have shown that accurate provenance information is not required for sale or provided for antiquities (e.g., Chippendale and Gill 2000, 2001; Davis 2011; Gilgan 2001; Levine and Martínez de Luna 2013; Yates 2006), and various prominent cases affirm that the market is willing to accept demonstrably false histories for looted artifacts (e.g., see Felch and Frammolino 2011; Watson and Todeschini 2007).

The antiquities market, then, does not and will not police itself with regard to stolen or otherwise illicit material. Provenance information related to ownership history and provenience information related to locational origins are optional across the trade and nearly nonexistent in the sales of many types of antiquities. For Caribbean antiquities, as for all types of antiquities, the result is a market saturated not just with looted artifacts that are indistinguishable from the very few legitimate artifacts available for purchase but also fake pieces that are indistinguishable from authentic ones.

Fake antiquities, alongside antiquities that are of questionable authenticity due to extensive "restoration" or modification to increase market value, are what consumers fear the most (Yates 2015a). Questionable authenticity, at least anecdotally, appears to contribute more to an antiquities consumer's rejection of a piece than the possibility of illegality; buyers of these items place extreme value on authenticity, prizing "genuine ancientness" and perceiving fakes as being without value (see Geurds, chapter 9 herein). Within a Caribbean context, if value is associated with the authentically ancient, it would be logical for dealers and buyers to favor objects with demonstrable find spots among Caribbean archaeological sites, reducing the risk of buying fakes. However, such well-provenienced Caribbean pieces are largely unavailable to the market, their excavation and export being illegal in most jurisdictions. As discussed, the type of provenience information that would reduce the chances of buying a faked antiquity would, in turn, reveal authentic antiquities to be definitively looted, and thus bar them from open consumption. This is a strange situation for the market to navigate. To get around this impasse, we often see incredible contortions to assert the authenticity of looted or faked objects (including forging letters from eminent Caribbeanists—see Curet, Epilogue, this volume)—a necessity if a seller wishes to obtain maximum profit for his/her investment. Commercial scientific testing, and more importantly the interpretation of scientific testing, becomes a marketing tool, a stand-in for secure proof that the object was found in situ at an archaeological site.

The prevalence of both fakes and illicitly obtained archaeological material within the antiquities market persists due to a continued market acceptance of the lack of legitimate provenance and provenience documentation. From the standpoint of the shared human endeavor to explore our past as part of our experience of individual and collective identity, we end up in a position where we have a tainted corpus of source material. Objects in private and public collections that are unprovenanced and perhaps fake have trickled into our understanding of the cultures of the Caribbean and elsewhere. Elizabeth Marlowe (2013) has referred to this foundation as the "shaky ground" on which our constructions of the past stand.

A MARKET REDUCTION APPROACH

I, along with others within the field of illicit antiquities research, have long argued that the illicit trade in cultural objects, be they fake or authentic, cannot be regulated effectively by policy or practice at source. Structural inequalities, economic failures, lack of access to development opportunities, natural disaster, and climate change all contribute to the context in which archaeological looting and trafficking occurs. Looting of archaeological sites in Caribbean and other countries is a symptom of greater societal challenges that cannot be solved though heritage training programs or targeted preservation laws. Incorporating heritage protection into greater efforts toward development may disrupt the illicit antiquities trade to some degree, but such an approach is best thought of as long-term. A far more effective approach may be to focus targeted anti-antiquities trafficking efforts on a less loftier goal than the economic and infrastructural changes required in antiquities source countries.

Professionals within heritage and preservation fields should focus on what we can reasonably influence: the antiquities market. While the antiquities trade is made up of white-collar individuals who occupy a place of social prestige and power in our society, we professionals also have a significant amount of social prestige and influence over the market. Professionals add value to the market by interacting with illicit antiquities in various ways: restoration, research, authentication, even denunciation. The market depends on this kind of professional participation to maintain validity among buyers (see Brodie 2011a and 2011b). If professionals give that value, we can also take it away. We can use our authority and expertise to make the purchase of unprovenanced antiquities from the Caribbean and elsewhere a socially unacceptable practice. We can be part of a market reduction approach.

To simplify Ayres and Braithwaite's (1995) concept of responsive regulation nearly to the point of nonrecognition (see Mackenzie 2011b for a thorough application to the antiquities trade), if our goal is to get people to comply with policy, we need to go beyond the black and white dichotomy of harsh criminalization versus total deregulation. Rather, we need to develop a range of social regulatory options that can be applied to the context of specific situations. This means options that, in most cases, encourage people not to offend by, for example, reaching out to potential offenders and encouraging them to not break the law, or even offering social rewards for compliance. Criminal sanctions would apply in only the most severe and most unrepentant cases. This is a particularly important aspect of such a regulatory model when dealing with white-collar crime, as white-collar actors are often able to avoid harsh sanctions anyway due to wealth, connections, or reputation.

The market end of the antiquities trade is entirely composed of white-collar actors, and some argue that those who flagrantly ignore the law and buy looted antiquities should be punished at least to the same extent as lower-income "looters." The reality is this is never going to happen. While a person looting an archaeological site in the Dominican Republic has a chance of being arrested, fined, or jailed, white-collar antiquities consumers who break the law are rarely punished. Any policy that "expects" white-collar antiquities criminals to face criminal sanctions is just as "aspirational" as source country laws that "expect" total site protection; both are ineffective. Responses that, instead, encourage compliance among white-collar antiquities consumers and punishes offenses with ostracism and social shame, however, may serve to reduce the market.

Just what form such market reduction initiatives should take is context specific, and should fit within local legal and social frameworks. However, for the sake of inspiration and adaptation, I offer some general ideas for market reduction approaches:

1. Mass public education in antiquities market countries about the trade in illicit antiquities, through popular media, websites, online courses, and such. The goal of such initiatives would be to make as many people as possible aware of the issue to foster a general societal unease about the consumption of antiquities as a commodity, leading to ostracism of offenders. A particularly effective example of such an approach can be seen in decades of public awareness campaigns against the consumption of elephant ivory.

2. Directly connecting the looting and trafficking of antiquities to harm and to loss, in as poignant a way as possible, and then sending that message through the previously mentioned mediums. Again, this has been effective in campaigns such as those to reduce the consumption of animal furs, whale meat, and the previously mentioned elephant ivory.

3. Reduction or elimination of professional cooperation with trade actors. This would include no restoring, authenticating, or publishing of unprovenancenced or unprovenianced material that entered museum or private collections after relevant heritage protection laws took effect in source countries, and being clear to all parties involved why.

4. Using that same authority to publicly undermine sales of illicit or unprovenanced antiquities. One method that has been gaining traction among some governments of source countries is to release a public statement from the ministry of culture in advance of a major antiquities auction. This statement indicates that a specific number of objects within the antiquities sale are fake but does not identify which ones are suspect. This serves to introduce doubt into the minds of buyers about all of the antiquities for sale and undermines the legitimacy of both the seller and the sale.

5. Naming and shaming of bad behavior among white-collar antiquities market actors, within the boundaries of local defamation law. We need to collectively overcome our tendency to be overprotective of the social status of elite wrongdoers. While such market actors will likely avoid criminal sanctions, we can still give them criminalized labels and thereby reduce the elite cachet that the collecting of unprovenanced antiquities retains in our society.

6. Pushing for more market transparency and oversight from dealers and auction houses. This might, under some circumstances, be done in collaboration with antiquities buyers who care a lot about authenticity. Approached in the right way, buyers might come to agree that an opaque market increases their own investment risks, as unprovenanced antiquities are often fakes. The potential for consumer-led antiquities market reform is underexplored.

7. Explore new technologies for replicating, experiencing, and participating in the understanding of antiquities. In particular, the development of creative ways for people to satisfy their legitimate love of these objects through means other than illicit consumption (see Swogger, chapter 6 this volume, for how replicas might be used in this way).

Our goal should be to develop a combination of formal policy and social initiatives at the market end of the antiquities smuggling chain that rewards good behavior with social accolades and distinctions and punishes bad behavior largely with social stigma. If people consume antiquities, at least in part, due to the social benefits of collecting, the social is where our responses should be focused and where we should develop our sticks and our carrots, so to speak. We need to make it socially unacceptable to collect unprovenanced and unprovenianced antiquities. And when I say this, I mean that our social focus must move beyond the big-name corporate sellers (the auction houses, the online platforms), to policy that has an effect on individual collectors. While this may seem harsh, it is worth remembering that buyers drive the market: auction houses/websites and dealers sell what they do, in this case unprovenanced and poorly provenienced Caribbean artifacts, because buyers are willing to pay for them. The goal, then, is not to make auction houses/sites and dealers avoid selling questionable antiquities—they have no business incentive to do so. The goal is to make potential buyers not wish to buy; this, then, will force a change in market practice.

Many approach the antiquities trade, and indeed the art market as a whole, as an inflexible entity whose policies and practices represent an unchangeable order; that the market is how it must be. Yet the norms that currently allow for the largely unchallenged sale of illicit, unprovenanced, and unprovenienced Caribbean cultural objects were developed to maximize dealer profit and shield key actors, not for any inherent structural reason. A "cleaned-up" antiquities market is, necessarily, a reduced antiquities market, as illicit material makes up a significant majority of what is available for sale. But that reduced market could represent an open and transparent marketplace that relieves consumers of the risk of buying loot or fakes and ensures that there is no market for illicit antiquities.

NOTES

1. In limited circumstances and in a handful of jurisdictions, some antiquities are legal to dig up and sell; this was the case with the Grenadian government legalizing the sale of artifacts from the site of Pearls, in Grenada, in the early 2000s (see Hanna, chapter 5 this volume). Other examples of this are antiquities found on private land in the United States. These situations are exceptions, not the rule, with the majority of antiquities source countries banning all extraction, marketization, and export.

2. That is, the 1954 Hague Convention for the Protection of Cultural Property in the Event of Armed Conflict; the 1970 Convention on the Means of Prohibiting and Preventing the Illicit Import, Export, and Transport of Ownership of Cultural Property; the 1995 UNIDROIT Convention on Stolen or Illegally Exported Cultural Objects; the 2001 UNESCO Convention on the Protection of the Underwater Cultural Heritage.

Epilogue

Real, Recent, Replica (Confessions of an Archaeologist/Curator/Puerto Rican)

L. Antonio Curet

WRITING ON REAL, recent, and replicated Caribbean artifacts is a challenge for me on a number of levels. Because of my position as a curator and a field archaeologist, Joanna Ostapkowicz asked whether I could address "the viability of engaging museum collections in studies, with all the dangers that this can bring." This troubled me not so much because of the nature of the issue, but because I have some strong feelings about it. And strong feelings in academia can mean taking things personally and with a strong passion, which inevitably leads to controversy.

Nevertheless, things took an unexpected and unsolicited turn. Before I started reading the chapters I was (and still am) certain that I know the main issues related to these topics and I thought I knew my position on all of them. However, once I began reading, I started seeing things from many opposite sides and noticing my own (and other peoples') biases and hidden assumptions/ premises. I am not referring necessarily to the authors' views, but to my own way of thinking. Some of these doubts/questions were triggered/inspired by some of the contributors, others from a critical approach toward some of the statements in the chapters. I began seeing the problems addressed here as multivalent and with a multiplicity of sides that I have not been able to organize in a rational way and much less solve. For that reason I use the word "confessions" in the title of this chapter; particularly, because I am questioning what I have been doing for most of my career and I have not been able to reconcile many of these views. This multiplicity of views is making me question my identities as archaeologist/curator/Puerto Rican; identities that ultimately and directly link to our subject of study, the archaeological record/ cultural heritage.

I begin the discussion with a series of stories of some of my experiences with the topics of this volume. In a way, this is to show the range of types of situations that arise when one is involved in this "business." It also shows contradictions and many gray areas. The rest of the essay is organized according to the identities I explore here, as listed in the title. Of course, they are written from my personal view. The idea is to show the plethora of problems involved with each of them. To complicate things, many of the issues I discuss overlap two or more of my identities. But, before I start I want to make it clear that I strongly believe that we need to protect and preserve the archaeological record and the cultural heritage and patrimony of people and that it is our duty to fight for their protection. Some of the comments below may seem to put into question this statement, but it is more in efforts to expose some of our contradictions, to clarify what exactly it is that we are defending versus what we *think* we are defending, and how some of our "ideals" can be naive or simplistic. Hopefully, everything will become clearer as the discussion progresses.

STORIES: LOSS OF INNOCENCE

My first story happened during my time as a member of the editorial board of *Latin American Antiquity*. The SAA has a strict policy of not publishing articles, photos, drawings, or descriptions of objects that have not been obtained under ethical circumstances (Society for American Archaeology 2018). At one point during my term, the editors brought to the board two manuscripts that focused on objects from a well-known institution. These objects were also part of well-known, private collections donated by wealthy and influential collectors, and that included many objects that may have been obtained under suspicious circumstances. However, for what to me seemed a black and white issue ended up in a long debate within a series of email exchanges between board members that lasted for weeks. The arguments were long and complicated. As I remember it, one issue was: where do we draw the line? Many of the larger and older museums have objects that have been looted, taken out of countries without the appropriate permissions, and so on. It is true that at one point in time, those practices were the standard of the trade, but does that make a difference? Even if we agree with that statement, in some ways, it is "easy" to say that objects obtained in 1910, for example, should be fine to publish because historically that was the standard at that time. But, how about the 1950s, when many countries already had laws protecting their archaeological heritage, but no strong international agreements existed? In addition, even if this was the "standard" at that time, does that make it right? Was it right for major museums to obtain objects from, say, Latin America, because of the colonial situation allowed it at that time?

Is it fine to publish those objects? Interestingly, some colleagues did not see any problem at all—why not publish the objects since we have them accessible already? Two other topics included in the discussion, among many more, was how the publications of such objects will enhance their commercial value and how some aspects of our discipline would be severely hampered if they did not include objects that had been removed from their contexts without what today we would consider proper recording.

The editors, in a skillful way, proposed a text addressing this issue in the publication guidelines of the journal, which has been revisited by later editors and today reads as follows: "Specifically, SAA will not knowingly publish manuscripts that provide the first descriptions of such objects. *In the case of LAQ, the editors are particularly wary of publishing images of looted artifacts that are in private collections or held by museums, whether or not they have been previously published*" (Society for American Archaeology 2018:7, emphasis added; see also Principle no. 3 in the SAAs Principles of Archaeological Ethics [1996]). This debate opened my eyes to the fact that the topics discussed in this book are more complicated than our zeal to protect the objects.

Besides promoting and doing research on collections, as a curator I also have to deal with requests for identifying or authenticating archaeological objects. Most of the time, the requests come from the US Immigration and Customs Enforcement (ICE) unit who occasionally intercept objects imported into the country. I normally decline requests from private collections, although I help some individuals who end up with mundane archaeological objects (e.g., sherds, stone axes) by accident or out of casual curiosity (e.g., inheritance, purchased in an auction). Occasionally, I get requests from colleagues at other museums with possible new acquisitions, in which case I tend to assist, with the premise that they are obtaining the objects in an ethical manner. However, in one occasion a colleague curator (and archaeologist) from a well-known and established art museum contacted me to authenticate an object that was brought to the United States from Puerto Rico and was being offered for purchase through an art broker. The object was a fake (probably made in Dominican Republic) and came with a faked letter supposedly from Ricardo Alegría, a well-known Puerto Rican archaeologist, "authenticating" it. I immediately informed this colleague about the Puerto Rican law and the illegality of selling Puerto Rican antiquities and even transporting the object outside the island without the government's approval. I also contacted the Instituto de Cultura Puertorriqueña to see how they wanted me to proceed. They asked me to obtain the name of the broker and, if possible, the name of the owner so they could send letters to inform them about the illegality of their actions and intents. When I contacted the curator/archaeologist, they refused to provide any information because they did not want to sour the relationship with the broker. My colleague declined even after I pointed out the ethical and legal issues involved. I asked my colleague to, at minimum, let the broker know about the illegality of the transaction; to my surprise, my colleague had already done so, but the broker was already fully aware of the Puerto Rican law and had proceeded regardless. Although I think my colleague's institution would not have purchased the object once they knew it was removed illegally from Puerto Rico (not to mention a fake), their zeal in protecting the museum's relationship with someone who blatantly disregarded the ethics of the discipline and the laws of the place of origin baffled me, and to this day still enrages me. Unfortunately, as mentioned in several of the chapters in this volume, situations like this happen more often than not, even in the most "respectable" organizations. Call me naive, but again, this opened my eyes to a situation I was not expecting: the enemy within.

Recently I met a colleague curator I have not seen for a while who had started working in a new job. This person is an art historian who has worked peripherally with Caribbean collections, and the job was to curate a collection owned by a multinational company that included some archaeological objects. However, this curator could not disclose the company's name or the location of the objects. My impression is that this collection is part of a practice of corporations to purchase antiquities as part of their art collections (e.g., see Appleyard and Salzmann 2012; Lindenberg and Oosterlinck 2010). My colleague was excited about the new job and the magnificent collection and eventually sent me photos of some amazing objects from the Caribbean I had never seen before. They may be fakes or authentic, but either way my impression is that these objects have been passing from one private collection to another under the radar of museums and governments. Again, I was conflicted. On the one hand, I did not know how these objects were acquired (whether legally or not), nor their history. All I knew for certain was that they are receiving a high level of treatment and care. On the other hand, was this job ethical? Looking back now, I do not think it was. However, what is at the core of this story is that in the whole conversation we had, I did not sense from my colleague any concern about the potential ethical dilemma of working with such a "secret" collection, which may have been obtained, in part, illegally. Nor, for my part, did I inquire further about the collections, or bring up the potential ethical problems related to this curatorial position.

ARCHAEOLOGIST

As mentioned in the volume introduction, the Principles of Archaeological Ethics of the Society for American Archaeology has several articles that deal with the preservation of the archaeological records in all its forms (i.e., site, artifacts, collections, field notes, and data). According to these principles, it is clear that the archaeologist's *first* duty is not toward the discipline or institutional affiliation, not even to the "owners" of the archaeological heritage, but to the archaeological record. As an aside point, in my opinion, this statement should also include our duty to protect the people who created such archaeological records. In other words, we should have the responsibility of not misrepresenting them or their descendants (if present) by misusing the data to (re-)create their history in an inaccurate manner. I know that all this seems basic and obvious, but while most of us will agree on these terms, in practice we often do not follow them. An example of this in the Caribbean is the use of the concept of Taíno, which traditionally has been used by almost all of us to refer to the identity of the native peoples from the Greater Antilles, Bahamas, and, at least, Virgin Islands. However, the term and concept have been strongly questioned and criticized recently (Curet 2014; Oliver 2009; Rodríguez Ramos 2010; Torres Etayo 2006) since it is an academic construct that falsely homogenizes and misrepresents what in reality was a large diversity of identities and cultural practices (e.g., Berman 2013; McGinnis 1997, 2001; Wilson 2001). Despite the fact that one has questioned these arguments, many are still misrepresenting the peoples of all these islands by using this concept in their publications in an indiscriminate manner without any explanation and ignoring its implications. Making things worse, it continues being used in popular media, misleading the general public, and perpetuating the simplistic view of the ancient peoples created by previous archaeologists.

Within the context of this volume, these ethical norms have three themes that I will explore in three examples. But, first, I start with another obvious statement that we need to keep in mind: archaeological fieldwork, independently of how extensive or intensive it is, destroys or distorts archaeological sites. And, because we can never recover all the information possible, we, too, destroy potential archaeological data. Considering this statement, then, archaeologists, in theory, should have a good reason to excavate, and always concentrate their efforts to minimize the degree of destruction. This is even more critical when we are working in places that are not our own country and, more important, when it is not our heritage or patrimony that we are destroying.

The first theme is that at least in *some sectors* of American archaeology there is an underlying consensus that to become an archaeologist one has to conduct excavations. I can give at least two examples of this perspective in academia. The first is that some universities or advisors still expect, and some actually require, doctoral candidates to conduct fieldwork for their dissertation project. I understand that many research questions may require fieldwork, but not all of them. Many topics can be handled by analyzing existing collections. I know of cases where students could not follow the topic of their interest because it involves only laboratory work and not fieldwork. The second example includes teaching and museums' positions requiring applicants to have an ongoing field project, again, emphasizing the field aspect of archaeology and eliminating "collection based or laboratory oriented" researchers from the pool of candidates.

Expectations and practices like these ones are not only discordant with the principles of archaeological ethics but also send the unintended message that archaeology is all about finding things and not an anthropological science. It erroneously implies that methodology and data collection is what defines the discipline.

What options other than excavating do we have? The answer is simple (and here I am wearing the curator hat, too): we have to start making use of object and archival collections in museums and in official depositories. Although many will argue that collections do not provide the important and critical information on context, this is only partially true and normally said from a biased and uninformed position (see further discussion in the following section). Suffice to say that many influential, successful, and impacting projects have been conducted using collections. Examples of these in the Caribbean include Jeff Walker's (1993) study of stone collars and three-pointers; José Oliver's (2008, 2009) study on semiotics and social organization; the study on collections of the British Museum (Oliver et al. 2008; Ostapkowicz et al. 2013); Boomert's (2000) study on interaction spheres in Trinidad; Vernon James Knight's (2020) ongoing project on personal ornaments; Joanna Ostapkowicz's work on wooden and cotton sculpture (e.g., Ostapkowicz et al. 2012; Ostapkowicz and Newsom 2012); Lawrence Waldron's (2016) focus on zoomorphic adornos; William Pestle's (2010) study of diet using stable isotope analysis; Jonathan Hanna's (2018) research spanning collections and *limited* excavations in Grenada, and many others.

Ignoring or underestimating the degree of destruction caused by archaeological excavations instead of using collections feeds a poor, unethical, and irresponsible practice. It perpetuates the vicious cycle of researchers giving preferential treatment to excavations when the answers to their questions may lie in the abundant collections in museums, and leads to the production of another collection that ends up collecting dust on shelves in museums or repositories. It is a vicious cycle. At the end of the day, then, why preserve the excavated materials? Unfortunately, many governments and cultural agencies in many countries have answered this in ways that many of us do not like: disposing of the bulk of their collections. Of course, they retain and curate the "best" artifacts, and in some cases, perhaps a sample of the more mundane ones. All these issues become more significant when considering that we are talking about the cultural heritage we are tasked with protecting. To be clear, however, the intention is not to blame the decision makers; the lack of storage space is a serious problem and solving it requires fiscal fortitude.

All this is to say that, despite being documented (*if* reports are produced at all—which is another potential ethical issue I am not discussing here), *unnecessary* archaeological excavations can be as damaging to the archaeological record and as unethical as looting for profit. After all, we (archaeologists) are profiting from the archaeological record. As graduate students we use it to acquire a degree and, eventually, get a good job, especially if a field project is required. And, we continue doing it to get promotions and prestige. So, although different in kind and degree, in some ways, like looters, we have an ulterior motive and interest in destroying the archaeological record. However, to make it clear, I am not implying or suggesting that excavations are not necessary. Excavations are often necessary. As one of the anonymous reviewers of this volume correctly stated: "the Caribbean [situation], where so many of the sites are coastal, essentially demands the recovery of archaeological materials lest they be lost to storms, erosion, impending sea level rise, development, and a host of other natural or cultural processes." The discussion above specifically targets *unnecessary* excavations and the state of mind in some archaeological circles that implies, consciously or unconsciously, that fieldwork makes the archaeologist. At the risk of repeating myself, methodology does not define a discipline. Archaeology is a social science (at least in the Americas), and excavation is just one of many methodologies and techniques used to achieve the scientific goals of the discipline: to understand and explain past human societies in all their forms. However, one point is true, considering the large number of collections available, the discipline/schools should be promoting among their students the use of museum collections for their graduate projects instead of promoting or even *requiring* fieldwork for degrees and jobs.[1]

MUSEUM CURATOR

While curiosity cabinets and the establishment of the earliest museums go back to the fifteenth and seventeenth centuries, respectively, it is only in the last century that the museological discipline has gotten rid of many "old habits" from that past. More importantly, museums have changed their missions, ethics, and goals. Now collections are not just feeding the fetishism of collectors, nor are they symbolic of the power of "civilized" empires. Now museums are more about protecting, preserving, and researching the collections, using them for education, representation, and appreciation, and making them accessible to the widest audiences both nationally and internationally.

Here I approach my curatorial position from two perspectives. The first one is, again, from the point of view of the value of collections for archaeological research. I concentrate, then, on the myths, misconceptions, and fallacies that roam among colleagues about the types and quality of information that can be obtained from them, or if it is possible to obtain any information at all. The second is from the perspective of the relationship of the curator with people outside the museum, primarily collectors and donors.

THE VALUE OF MUSEUM COLLECTIONS

There is a general feeling in the discipline of archaeology that museum collections cannot replace excavations since many of them do not have contextual data and, if they do, it is not specific enough. It is true that initially and for a long time most museums were interested mainly, if not solely, in objects. This is part of the fetishism present among the early antiquarians and museums (as discussed in several of the chapters in this volume) and, to be honest with ourselves, it is still present in our disciplines. Under these circumstances, collections are accompanied, at best, by basic information such as cultural affiliation and cultural region of origin (not necessarily origin of the object). A more specific context was not that important, with the exception of cases where a more localized provenience could increase significantly the social, monetary, or "historical" value of the object, and its uniqueness (e.g., a vessel from Pompeii or King Tut's tomb). However, these are generalized statements that hide what actually is a diverse degree of details in collection records. The research potential of each collection needs to be assessed individually. To show this, I present here three Caribbean collections from the predecessor of my home institution, the Museum of the American Indian (MAI), today the Smithsonian's National Museum of the American Indian (NMAI). All three were the result of excavations by "top" archaeologists of their times. The first is Jesse Walter Fewkes, who was an anthropologist on staff at the National Museum (today, the Smithsonian's National Museum of Natural History), but who, at least between 1912 and 1913, also did some work for MAI. The second is Theodoor de Booy, who worked in the Caribbean from 1911 to 1918. The third, Mark Harrington, a North Americanist who was sent to investigate eastern Cuba in 1915 and 1919.

Although the work of these three researchers overlaps in time and they knew each other, their field practices were considerably different. For example, the only one who may have excavated in a stratigraphic manner was Harrington, while Fewkes and de Booy excavated trenches with very little, if any, vertical or horizontal control. In terms of field notes, the most detailed ones are from Harrington and, to a lesser degree, Fewkes. De Booy's notes have yet to be found, but if his publications are a representative sample, his level of detail increased throughout his career (see Curet and Galban 2019). However, de Booy began working with specialists from other disciplines on his projects, for example, to identify faunal remains or the chemical composition of water from caves. Nothing like this was done by either of his two colleagues, nor did it become standard practice until relatively recently. The level of selectivity of collections also varied between the three of them. Harrington seemed to be the less selective, meaning he collected many more types of objects. However, de Booy's selectivity changed throughout his career, while Fewkes seems to have concentrated on objects with diagnostic features. Finally, both Fewkes and Harrington had worked in North America (including the American Southwest) where ethnographic and archaeological research went hand-in-hand, giving them a stronger anthropological perspective than de Booy. Thus, expectations of museum collections should be assessed individually and not assumed that they have little or no contextual information. True, some collections may require long and tedious archival work, but not much more than dealing with all the administrative and logistic work associated with fieldwork.

Today, things are considerably different in museums where provenance and provenience (see the volume introduction for the usage of these terms) are of utmost importance. Most museums with anthropological collections would not accept or purchase objects or collections without this information. Art museums are different, though. In addition, some museums have programs to obtain information on old collections retroactively. For example, NMAI has a program called Retro-accession (McMullen and Galban 2019), where a full-time researcher and curators are trying to reconstruct the biography of the objects/collections and, in some cases, provide contextual data of where the object was obtained originally. These may include date of acquisition, name of the collector or donor, provenience, and provenance of the object, how the collector obtained the objects, field notes kept in other institutions, letters that discuss the project if fieldwork was involved, reports and other documentation. In short, although much still needs to be done, procedures like these are providing information on collections and their histories and context that is useful for researchers (see Milosch and Pearce 2019 for other examples).

But, perhaps, more frustrating for a curator of archaeological collections is the outdated view many colleagues have of museum collections. In addition to these old and poorly documented collections, museums and other archaeological depositories also have collections obtained from more recent archaeological projects. Recent collections tend to be well documented and are accompanied by the original reports and field notes. This is where many of the materials obtained from salvage and academic projects end up. For the Caribbean, although some of these collections can be traced as far back as the mid-twentieth century, their numbers increase exponentially after the

1970s, when strong research programs were formed in the Greater Antilles and salvage archaeology became a legal obligation in places such as Puerto Rico (see the Appendix for development in other islands with the same effect). In these cases, some of these collections tend to include larger and more variable types of materials, including samples of charcoal, soils, and faunal and botanical remains, than previous projects.

Therefore, many collections in museums and depositories have the capacity to provide the information that can answer a plethora of research questions. It is time for archaeology to leave behind favoring fieldwork at the expense of museum work when the latter can provide the necessary information in a cheaper and faster way, and without further destroying the archaeological record/cultural heritage.

MUSEUMS, COLLECTORS, DESCENDANTS

Curatorship is entangled with the relationship museums have with collectors, art brokers or agents, and the descendants of the people whose material culture is represented in the collections. Although I started working in museums at a young age, my career as a curator began when I worked at a private, nonprofit museum. At that time, the Department of Anthropology had a formal group composed of people interested in anthropology and archaeology and included people from different backgrounds. However, many of them had their own private collections of antiquities. Sometimes the meetings of the group were held in a member's house, which provided the opportunity for them to show their collections. Interestingly, one of my colleagues mentioned that many of the collections had a good number of fakes. When questioned if he had told them, he responded (and I am paraphrasing), "Nooo! If I do, they'll complain or sue the broker or agent who sold it to them, who at the same time will sue the museum [and, perhaps, my colleague] for defamation."

At first, this relationship was a little uncomfortable to me; "perhaps, a remnant of the old days," I thought. But, was I naive or, more importantly, wrong? These type of relationships still persist today and are very common, in great part because of what is at stake. Collectors tend also to be big supporters and sponsors of museums: donating funds, unique objects, and even whole collections. Moreover, they also bring other potential donors and supporters to the museum. I hate to admit it, but it is a necessary "evil" in the environment we live. Even my institution, the Smithsonian Institution (NMAI), which is funded by the US government, still cannot operate at full capacity or, in some cases, survive at all without the support of private individuals.

Although museums and curators may need the relationships with collectors and others involved in the world of antiquity collections, this does not mean that we have to be unethical or "sell our souls." By this I mean we should not dilute or completely drop our ethical values. This does not mean that it is acceptable to authenticate objects from dubious collections, much less to visit and praise them. This behavior damages and counters all the efforts of colleagues, organizations, and governments at a local, national, and international level to stop the illegal traffic of antiquities. Even worse, it helps promote them. Doing that will put into question our integrity and ethics and, by association, those of the institution. Our names and those of our institutions, for example, can be used as proof of authentication and to increase the commercial value of the objects when trying to sell them. The potential effects can be more serious if the object was illegally obtained or fake. In addition, these situations can be complicated when considering that many objects are the culture heritage of contemporary people, especially the direct descendants of the culture that produced them.

However, I am not trying to imply that collectors are bad people. Many of them are people with a genuine interest of the past, the people, and their cultures. Their support of museums is done from an honest interest and belief that what museums do is a good and a necessary service to society. The comments above are more a word of caution. We need to be conscious of the ethical limits of a relationship of this kind and of the consequences of being lax. However, a relationship with individual collectors can also be seen as an opportunity for educating them and bringing them to par with the standards of the trade and international accords. I do not think most collectors fully understand the ethical, humanitarian, and moral issues involved in collecting antiquities and the impact their practices have. I truly believe that many times this relationship can be turned around as a positive opportunity to educate them. However, what I am saying is that it is possible, not that it will be easy. It will require a lot of effort, tact, and creativity from museum representatives to develop sensible strategies to accomplish such a relationship. This, by the way, can be an approach that complements in some ways the suggestions presented by Yates (chapter 10 this volume). Yes, doing this takes time and much work, but when considering what is at stake, it is worth it.

A final comment on collectors and the unethical and sometimes illegal practices of some curators and museums. When private collectors donate their collections, I believe that the curator and the museum have the ethical and legal responsibility of investigating and reconstructing the biography of the objects and determining, if possible, which were illegally obtained. They can report the pieces or, in the case they accept them, they should contact the country or indigenous descendants (see below) and begin the process of repatriation. Instead of doing this, more often than not, museums accept private collections from a stance of "don't ask, don't tell." We cannot continue staying quiet; to do so makes us accomplices. Even worse, because of our training and positions, we should be judged by higher standards, and that makes us even guiltier.

To end this section, I refer to communities of descendants of the people who produced the ancient objects in our collections. This is also a complicated issue. But, we have to start taking them into consideration when we do fieldwork, in the case of archaeologists, and when we collect, in the case of museums. I know some colleagues have already begun using "cultural sensitivity" in dealing with collections. But, I think that as a discipline, this is lacking in Caribbean archaeology. It is true that in many cases, it is difficult to determine who the actual descendants are—after all, it has been over 500 years of colonialism. To make things worse, in some islands, many people want to be Amerindian (as described for Puerto Rico below and in Oliver, chapter 3 herein). But, we have to start somewhere.

PUERTO RICAN

When the US Commonwealth of Puerto Rico was officially established in the 1950s, the island needed to create its own national identity (Dávila 1997, 2001). For this the government relied on Ricardo Alegría, who invented a "national identity" that promulgated the idea of the merging (creolization) of the three races and cultural traditions: "Indio,"[2] African, and European. Of course, this is a fallacy because, even though creolization happened, it was not as uniform or homogenous throughout the island as the "model" makes us believe, when even today racial categories such as white and black, which imply purity, are still used to describe or refer to people. Moreover, expressions such as European, "Indio," and African homogenize and simplify the multiplicity of cultural and biological groups that actually contributed to the formation of modern populations (see Oliver, chapter 3 this volume).

It is with the creation of this model that the "Indio" and the precolumbian history of Puerto Rico became democratized and proselytized. Eventually, the term "Indio" was replaced by the concept of "Taíno" (which is another fallacy, see Curet 2014, 2015), and their life, culture, and society was included in school curricula and textbooks. Alegría (1950) himself wrote a children's book and created the Centro Ceremonial de Caguana, the first archaeological park of the island. The mechanisms to implant this model were so effective that today representations of the indigenous past are present all over the island in a multiplicity of media. These include many contemporary artistic media and crafts such as tattoos, murals, paintings, carvings (Oliver 1998, 2005, chapter 3 this volume), films (Dávila 1997, 2001; Feliciano-Santos 2011:51ff), commercial logos, and festivals and other events dedicated to "Indian" themes (e.g., Festival Nacional Indígena de Jayuya and Festival en Las Indieras, Maricao).

However, the African side is hardly celebrated or even mentioned (at least, not as much as the "Indian"). A good example of this lack of interest or recognition was the first Afro–Puerto Rican museum, which was founded in the island in the 2000s and, according to colleagues, had to close its doors within five years because of the lack of support.

The "Indian" or "Taíno" became the symbol of the pure Puerto Rican. What can be more Puerto Rican than the original "Indians," the first ones to fight colonialism? In an unconscious and perhaps conscious manner the message is that the "abusive" Spanish and the "inferiority" of the Africans are not appropriate models/symbols of *puertorriqueñidad*. This bias is also present in academia, where we emphasize more the "Indian" and Spanish as subjects of study than the enslaved people and their descendants. Plantation houses or sugar cane factories are excavated, rebuilt, or remodeled, but not the slave quarters. They are ignored. We academics may speak of the institution of slavery, but very few actually discuss the enslaved people themselves, and the conditions of their lifeways, their cultural and social practices and legacy. And I have to confess that I am as guilty of this bias as anyone else.

This whole scenario has been complicated by studies in genetics, which introduced another variable into the already messy formula of identity and heritage. Initially, these studies showed that a large percentage of Puerto Ricans had indigenous mitochondrial DNA (Martínez-Cruzado 2013; Martínez-Cruzado et al. 2001), which led to people claiming indigenous descent. This happened even·with individuals who had strong African phenotypes. As a matter of fact, a man who phenotypically looked of African descent, stood up in a conference and praised geneticists because he always thought his family ancestry came from maroons, but his mitochondrial DNA results were indigenous and now he "knows" that he is Taíno. This is a clear example of how the supposed "authority" of hard science often trumps oral history or, maybe, a family tradition.

With this discussion I am not denying the contributions of indigenous culture to Puerto Rican culture. We definitely have some traditions that have been passed down throughout the generations. However, in reality, many of them are not distributed equally throughout the island; some regions having more evidence of mixtures than others. Other regions also have more African or Spanish influence. And, yet, these other influences are not represented in the same way in popular culture.

In terms of the cultural heritage, this means that its protection in the island gives preferential treatment to the precolumbian past. Even in school, more space is given in textbooks to the indigenous people, but little about slavery and even less about those people enslaved and their contribution to Puerto Rican cultural traditions. So, being a precolumbian archaeologist and after years of emphasizing the indigenous ancestry discourse, I look back and feel that while trying to educate people about the history of the island, I have been an accomplice to giving preferential treatment to the Amerindians at the expense of many other cultural and biological contributors. Nevertheless, what weighs even heavier on my heart is that it is not only me; this is the norm in Puerto Rico and, I suspect, it is happening to some degree in many other parts of the Caribbean. So, the question is not if we need to protect the cultural heritage, but whose cultural heritage are we preferentially defending? Or more to the point: whose heritage are we not protecting? But, even worse, by emphasizing one heritage over another, whose fictive legacy are we imposing on who?

CONCLUSIONS

I began this essay warning the reader of my conflicting thoughts. Some may think that many of these aspects may be the result of overthinking the topics, but a bigger and more dangerous strategy is to underthink it. More dangerous because we are academics, and in this world, we have an aura that we know better and that our knowledge is supposed to be more accurate. Therefore, what we say, do, and publish can and does have an effect on how people see (and create in their minds) their past and their "heritage."

My original intention was to address many of the issues presented in the previous chapters including ethics, the destruction of the archaeological record, falsifications, illegal trade of antiquities, and culture heritage from the different identities in my life. I thought it would be easy since the topics seem straightforward and we all know we have to protect the cultural legacy of our ancestors, both biological and cultural. But it is clear that this was a naive and simplistic perspective. While we agree with their protection, for some of us, in practice, our positions are lax, and we tend to drop our defenses. From interacting with collectors in manners that are unethical, to conducting unnecessary excavations, to defending zealously the precolumbian past while crassly ignoring (or even denying) the contributions of the huge African (and other peoples) component, it is clear how our prejudices and biases show up in an active, albeit unconscious, way. But, whether it is on purpose or not does not matter, the effects can be the same: it is still promoting illegal collections, destroying the archaeological record, and ignoring the protection of cultural heritage. Talking from a personal perspective, we all have the best of intentions and we agree with all the principles portrayed in this volume. However, many times our actions and responses to some situations betray us, and it is here where we need to work on bringing our biases to a conscious level and confronting them with our ethics.

It is difficult to propose some solutions to these problems, but it is clear that a multiple and diversified front is necessary. In many cases I believe that education is one of the key strategies (see, for example, Ostapkowicz and Hanna, introduction to this volume; Oliver, chapter 3 this volume), and here I am not referring to educating only the public and children. I am referring to educating the archaeologists, academics, museum curators, cultural workers, and so on. For example, I think basic courses on these topics should include a lesson on ethics—a topic I do not believe is taught in, for example, graduate schools in archaeology. Nevertheless, it cannot be just a lesson, it has to go beyond education; it is about inculcating this as a way of life, keeping it at a conscious level all the time. Other strategies have to deal with changing the "culture" in museums on how to handle relationships with collectors and the way we collect. A final example would be to promote among archaeology students the use of collections for research projects and perhaps even have a class to train them on collections-based research.

I also began this epilogue thinking that it would be a straightforward essay. However, starting from the request from Joanna Ostapkowicz to write a personal "soul" searching on how we do business (in museums and archaeology) as usual, the situation quickly became a surreal, multidimensional quagmire. It is difficult to find one's way in such a labyrinth, but I hope that the reflections herein offer some guidance for those also wearing these various hats, now and in the future.

NOTES

1. Several agencies and countries have already developed procedures to address this issue. According to Dominique Bonnissent (personal communication): "France's research policy, which is applied throughout the national territory, including overseas territories such as the FWI, is to consume less archaeological heritage by encouraging researchers to use existing collections to solve their scientific problems, as far as possible, rather than to carry out new excavations. However, this policy does not apply in the case of preventive archaeology where sites are irreparably destroyed and must therefore be excavated before destruction."

2. I use the term Indio and Indian in quotations here to differentiate Amerindians from those actually from India. I use "Indio" instead of other possible terms such as Amerindian because this is the term used by the model and most Puerto Ricans.

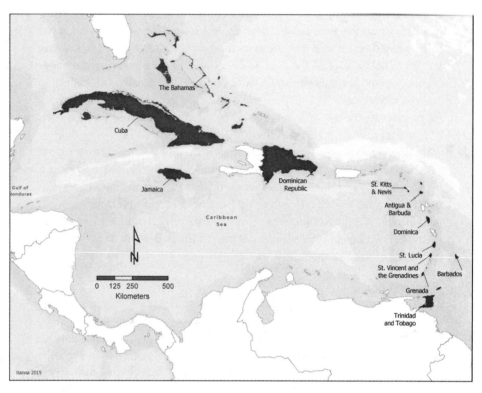

Figure A.1. Map of the Caribbean, with highlighted countries discussed in this chapter. (Map courtesy Jonathan A. Hanna; base map courtesy Environmental Systems Research Institute [ESRI])

Appendix

*An Overview of the Laws Governing Archaeological Heritage
in the English- and Spanish-Speaking Caribbean*

Amanda Byer

This overview of Caribbean heritage law examines the regulatory framework with respect to the archaeological heritage in the independent Spanish- and English-speaking Caribbean: Cuba; the Dominican Republic; Barbados; Jamaica; the Bahamas; the Organization of Eastern Caribbean States (OECS) members (Antigua and Barbuda, Dominica, Grenada, Saint Lucia, St. Kitts and Nevis, St. Vincent, and the Grenadines); and Trinidad and Tobago (Figure A.1). As a result, the following Caribbean countries subject to non-Caribbean law are absent: British protectorates (Anguilla, Turks and Caicos, British Virgin Islands, Montserrat); US territories (US Virgin Islands, Puerto Rico); French provinces (Martinique, Guadeloupe, St. Martin, Saint Barthelemy); Dutch territories (Aruba, Bonaire, Curaçao, Sint Maarten, Saba, St. Eustatius); and Venezuelan territories (Los Roques, La Orchila, Blanquilla, La Tortuga, Margarita). This review is not intended to be definitive or exhaustive; rather, it offers a snapshot of the main laws, their key features, and major implementation gaps. For readers wishing more comprehensive coverage, Siegel and Righter (2011) is a good starting point, as are the resources listed at the end section of this appendix. The latter resources include URLs for the laws mentioned here.

Heritage law is an important tool for identifying, classifying, protecting, and regulating heritage resources. As former Spanish and English colonies, these islands have inherited civil and common-law traditions, with modification on becoming sovereign nations. Because Spanish civil law and English common law are distinct legal systems, their terminology, administrative procedures, institutional arrangements, and protection mechanisms are very different. For instance, there is no common-law counterpart to the term "patrimony" as defined in the constitutional provisions of Cuba and the Dominican Republic that would protect heritage in the English-speaking Caribbean. Additionally, in the English-speaking Caribbean, the national trust is the premier institution empowered in law to identify, classify, regulate, and protect archaeological heritage. In Cuba and the Dominican Republic, there are other institutions charged with such responsibilities

Provided below are tables listing relevant laws in each country, organized by legal category, and highlighting key features of each law as well as noticeable gaps in legislation where applicable. The categories of heritage law considered for the purposes of this volume include antiquities legislation, legislation establishing heritage institutions (trusts, museums, and antiquities commissions), legislation governing archaeological sites such as parks and protected areas, nonheritage law with significant influence on heritage management, and implementing legislation of international cultural heritage law. Where countries are omitted, this means that there are no relevant laws that meet the category definition.

ANTIQUITIES PROTECTION

Background: Laws protecting antiquities specify means of protecting artifacts, such as inventories and lists, and outline procedures for conducting archaeological excavations, disposal, and exportation of any finds. The following countries have explicit antiquities legislation or address antiquities protection explicitly in the laws identified (Table A.1). Other countries may indirectly address antiquities protection via internal policies or institutional arrangements, or have draft laws not yet in force—these are not included here.

HERITAGE INSTITUTIONS: NATIONAL TRUSTS

Background: Trusts are colonial-era parastatal bodies found in the English-speaking Caribbean. They perform a variety of advisory, museological, educational, research, and monitoring functions. The law empowers trusts to compile inventories, acquire and manage heritage properties, and engage in public education initiatives. Some countries have modernized their laws since independence. In other cases, national trust laws share concurrent jurisdiction with modern museum, planning, and environmental legislation (Table A.2).

HERITAGE INSTITUTIONS: MUSEUMS

Background: Museums in the Spanish- and English-speaking Caribbean date to the colonial era. The earliest legislation in the English-speaking Caribbean to address museums was the product of education reform initiatives in the nineteenth century, which originated in legislation for public libraries with museum displays (Cummins 1992). Today, public and private museums are found throughout the region. This section focuses on museums with public functions, not privately incorporated entities. Thus, neither the many museums mentioned in chapter 2, nor the Carriacou museum in chapter 6, are described below, as there is no legislation supporting those institutions (Table A.3).

ARCHAEOLOGICAL SITES

Background: Laws establishing parks and protected areas can designate areas for protection based on natural, historic, or cultural value, and therefore have the potential to influence the management of archaeological sites. Management plans are the main mechanisms employed to manage such sites. There is usually an advisory body responsible for reviewing prospective parks and inventorying or managing the resources in these parks (Table A.4).

NONHERITAGE LAWS OF RELEVANCE TO HERITAGE MANAGEMENT

Background: Unlike the Spanish-speaking Caribbean, which has comprehensive legislation dedicated to heritage protection, the English-speaking Caribbean regulates heritage via laws that were not designed to necessarily protect heritage (Table A.5). Town and country legislation was established during the colonial era for the English-speaking Caribbean and regulated physical development. Some islands have replaced town and country laws with modern physical planning laws. Both types of laws regulate land resources, which include archaeological sites. This can pose a challenge for the protection of heritage resources, particularly those located on private lands. Barbados, Jamaica, Trinidad and Tobago, and St. Vincent and the Grenadines have retained town and country planning legislation with recent amendments. The OECS member states excluding St. Vincent have repealed these laws and replaced them with physical planning and development control legislation.

IMPLEMENTING LEGISLATION FOR INTERNATIONAL HERITAGE LAW

Background: Common-law countries require local laws to implement international treaties, such as the World Heritage Convention (WHC), but this can be a complex undertaking and depends on technical capacity to draft appropriate laws (Table A.6). Only Grenada has explicit legislation implementing the WHC. Other countries have similar laws in draft, or rely on interagency coordination of implementing projects to meet their obligations, or are in the process of building capacity to comply with international cultural heritage law.

TABLE A.1. PROTECTION OF ANTIQUITIES

	Title of law	Key features of legislation	Gaps in heritage protection
The Bahamas	Antiquities, Monuments, and Museum Act 1998	The Bahamas unites antiquities, monuments, and museum management in one law and centralizes heritage management previously undertaken by the National Trust and the Archives. Part IV of the Act outlines the permitting process for the excavation of archaeological heritage.	Penalties for damage to heritage are inadequate, and the quantum pre-scribed for fines is impractical as a deterrent to further destruction.
Cuba	The Constitution of Cuba 1976	Article 39 of the Cuban Constitution declares that Cuban culture and cultural patrimony are to be protected. A comprehensive system for the excavation and conservation of the archaeological heritage is outlined in Laws 1 and 2.	Extensive legal and institutional framework for heritage management can make the implementation process convoluted.
	Law 1, Law of Protection of Cultural Patrimony, August 1977	Laws 1 and 2 govern archaeological heritage: Law 1 covers the fundamental regulations in which cultural goods are defined "as the product of archaeological excavations and discoveries" (Art. 1[c]). The declaration also creates the National Register of Cultural Resources (Registro Nacional de Bienes Culturales), which requires registration of all the cultural goods of the nation (private or state collections), and regulates their exportation and importation.	Extensive legal and institutional framework for heritage management can make the implementation process convoluted (see Roberto Valcárcel Rojas et al., chapter 7, this volume).
	Law 2, Law of National and Local Monuments, August 1977	Law 2 establishes the National Commission of Monuments (Comisión Nacional de Monumentos), and has regulations for excavations and archaeological investigations. A new Subcommittee of Archaeology was established in 2003 under the National Commission of Monuments, with responsibilities for evaluating permit applications, updating the national register, and proposing sanctions for violations of regulations (Torres Etayo 2011).	Penalties for enforcement need to be strengthened (Torres Etayo 2011).

Dominican Republic	Law 41-00, June 6, 2000	Law 41-00 established a Council for National Culture as the agency coordinating cultural matters that, along with the Ministry of Culture, has oversight responsibility for public and private institutions involved with cultural matters. The Ministry of Culture therefore subsumed the Office of Cultural Patrimony (created in 1967), the Monuments Commission (created in 1972), and the authority of provincial, regional, and local commissions devoted to historical sites and monuments, thereby streamlining the institutional infrastructure for heritage (Prieto Vicioso 2011).	Lack of enforcement; poor documentation of artifacts in private and public collections, and limited monitoring capacity (see Alvarez et al., chapter 2 this volume).
	Constitution of the Dominican Republic (2015)	Articles 64 and 66 of the Constitution of the Dominican Republic reinforce State protection over the Cultural Patrimony of the Nation. Article 96 imbues the National Congress with the authority to establish the necessary framework for the conservation of the historic, cultural, and artistic heritage.	See implementation challenges with Law 41-00, above.
St. Kitts and Nevis	National Conservation and Environmental Protection Act 1987	St. Kitts addresses antiquities protection in Part IX of its conservation legislation and comprehensively addresses archaeological investigations.	The protective measures and incentives outlined in the legislation, such as tax incentives, technical advice, and use of equipment, are available for built heritage only.
St. Vincent and the Grenadines	Preservation of Historic Buildings and Antiquities Act 1976	St. Vincent is the oldest Commonwealth jurisdiction in the Caribbean with explicit legislation for the protection of antiquities. Section 4 charges the minister with the responsibility for listing heritage for protection.	The list itself has no statutory protection in the English-speaking Caribbean, and there is very limited provision for permitting and enforcement.

TABLE A.2. HERITAGE INSTITUTIONS: NATIONAL TRUSTS

Country	Title of law	Key features of legislation	Gaps in heritage protection
The Bahamas	The Bahamas National Trust Act	The Bahamas' trust makes provision for tiers of members, including student members. Its council may include non-Bahamian representatives, such as the New York Zoological Society, the Audubon Society, the Smithsonian Institution, the American Museum of Natural History, and the United States National Park Service. The trust also has powers to enforce protections for Trust property.	Inventories compiled by national trusts have no statutory protection. With the exception of Trinidad and Tobago, there are no criteria in the law for assessing Trust properties for protected status. Laws need to be rationalized to clarify the role of national trusts vis-à-vis museums, archaeological societies, cultural foundations, and cultural heritage nongovernmental organizations, which often have similar functions and mandates.
Barbados	Barbados National Trust Act 1961	Barbados' national trust is a member of the national World Heritage Committee (see final section) and collaborates with the chief town planner and the Barbados Museum on heritage matters.	
Grenada	Grenada National Trust Act 1967	Grenada's national trust sits on a number of committees, including the National Advisory Committee on Cultural Heritage established in law (see nonheritage laws section below).	
Jamaica	Jamaica National Heritage Trust Act 1958 (amended 1985)	Objects or places can be included under Jamaica's national protected heritage according to the first schedule to the act.	
Saint Lucia	Saint Lucia National Trust Act 1975	Saint Lucia's national trust works with planning authorities to develop permitting procedures for archaeologists and to advise on Environmental Impact Assessments, but these functions have not been formalized in regulations.	

Country	Title of law	Key features of legislation	Gaps in heritage protection
St. Kitts	Saint Christopher National Trust Act 2009	St. Kitts has the most recently established trust legislation with the most expansive remit, which replaced the Saint Christopher Historical Society. Properties may be recommended for protection and added to the act's schedule of Trust properties.	
St. Vincent and the Grenadines	St. Vincent and the Grenadines National Trust Act 1969	St. Vincent's national trust undertakes public awareness activities and works with visiting excavation teams, but this has not been formalized in regulation.	
Trinidad and Tobago	Trinidad and Tobago National Trust Act 2000	Trinidad and Tobago's act protects archaeological sites if they are declared properties of interest (Reid and Lewis 2011). The act also provides for classes of membership, though these are not as extensive as those contained in the Bahamian legislation.	

TABLE A.3. HERITAGE INSTITUTIONS: MUSEUMS

Country	Title of law	Key features of legislation	Gaps in heritage protection
The Bahamas	Antiquities, Monuments, and Museum Act 1998	Establishes the museum as a corporate quasi-governmental body responsible for cultural heritage management in the Bahamas. This consolidated the work of the National Trust and Archives (Pateman 2011).	Enforcement of penalties for destruction of heritage is weak. The upkeep of heritage resources on private property is not incentivized. Oversight for the entire archipelago (29 islands, 661 cays, and 2,387 rock formations) is limited in terms of human and financial capacity (Pateman 2011).
Barbados	Barbados Museum and Historical Society Act 1933	Barbados' law establishes a museum and historical society, not a national museum. Nevertheless, it functions as such in a de facto capacity. Barbados' museum has a good relationship with other heritage institutions on the island and sits on the national committee for World Heritage (see final section below).	The present museum's many (and exemplary) functions are not accommodated in legislation.
Dominican Republic	Law Number 318 of April 26, 1972.	Law Number 318 of April 26, 1972, created the Museo del Hombre Dominicano (Museum of Dominican Man), an institution responsible for precolumbian heritage.	Oversight and enforcement issues regarding supervision of archaeological sites and the trafficking of objects. There are challenges in the coordination of various actors (the museum, Ministry, and Immigration authorities) to effectively manage and monitor these sites (Prieto Vicioso 2011).
	Law 41-00	With the creation of the Ministry of Culture by means of Law 41-00 on June 6, 2000, coordination was mandated across state institutions that dealt with cultural issues. This action was initiated on February 14, 1997, with the formation of the Presidential Cultural Council (Decree 82-97).	

		Law 41-00 created the National Network of Museums, which is responsible for the protection, conservation, and development of existing museums and for establishing incentives for developing new museums in all areas of Dominican cultural patrimony (Prieto Vicioso 2011).	
Grenada	Grenada National Museum Act 2017	Grenada recently established a national museum in law and includes antiquities protection among its functions.	This law has been slow to implement (let alone enforce), and regulations need to be prepared to operationalize the museum's procedures. Capacity building is also needed in museum skills, archaeology, and heritage management.
Trinidad and Tobago	Trinidad and Tobago National Museum and Art Gallery Act 2000	Trinidad and Tobago's law establishes a national museum and art gallery. The National Museum is responsible for managing the national collection of artifacts and artwork.	There are no formal links with the archaeological heritage management process, such as excavations and registration of artifacts, or with the National Archaeological Committee.

Country	Title of law	Key features of legislation	Gaps in heritage protection
Antigua and Barbuda	Antigua National Parks Act 1984	Section 4 establishes the National Parks Authority, stating that the Authority is to protect, preserve, manage, and develop the historical and cultural heritage of Antigua and Barbuda. Section 10 makes reference to the conservation of archaeological sites.	Most countries do not have effectively functioning national park systems that are regularly updated and enforced. Although archaeological sites can be protected, the management system for these sites is often limited, unless laid out in a separate park-specific law. No clear criteria for designating archaeological sites as parks or protected areas exist, and park criteria tend to classify these sites as either cultural or natural sites, even though these sites tend to reflect both features.
	Antigua Environmental Protection and Management (EPM) Act 2014	The EPM Act updates park law and provides enhanced protection for archaeological sites by clearly defining the sites eligible for protection.	
The Bahamas	Antiquities, Monuments, and Museum Act	The Antiquities Monuments and Museum Corporation is responsible for restoring and preserving major heritage resources. Sites protected include historic forts, mansions, and marketplaces. No national park plan is in place, although a register of sites is currently being updated and refined.	
	Clifton Heritage Authority (CHA) Act	The CHA Act establishes an authority to manage and preserve the Clifton Heritage national park and historical site.	
Dominica	Dominica National Parks and Protected Areas Act 1975	Dominica's law requires parks to be unimpaired for use by future generations and requires consultation with communities associated with any proposed site before establishing a park.	
Grenada	Grenada National Parks and Protected Areas Act 1991	Section 5 of Grenada's act does not define "protected area," but states that protected areas may be established by order for the purpose of commemorating a historical event of national importance, or for preserving a historic landmark or place or object of historic, prehistoric, archaeological, cultural, or scientific importance.	

St. Kitts	St. Kitts National Conservation and Environment Protection (NCEP) Act 1987	Section 2 of the NCEPA clearly defines a historic site as a place that is historic by reason of an association with the past and part of the cultural or historical heritage of St. Kitts, which may include archaeological sites, historic landmarks, and areas of special historic or cultural interest.
St. Vincent and the Grenadines	St. Vincent and the Grenadines National Parks Act 2002	St. Vincent's legislation addresses the use of national parks for future generations. Section 23 lists prohibited acts in national parks, including the removal of archaeological or cultural material (section 23(1)(g)). This is the only park legislation that prohibits clandestine excavations, although it should be noted that in some of the islands referenced above, such offenses are addressed in other legislation.

TABLE A.5. RELEVANT NONHERITAGE LAWS

Country	Title of law	Key features of legislation	Gaps in heritage protection
The Bahamas	Planning and Subdivision Act 2010	Consolidates the law relating to town planning and makes provision for the prohibition of construction on land containing a significant archaeological resource.	
Barbados	Barbados Town and Country Planning Act 1968 (amended 1998)	Barbados is the only island in the English-speaking Caribbean to have conducted a nationwide archaeological assessment for its physical development plan. There is a well-developed institutional framework for using planning to integrate heritage management, including the Barbados Museum and the National Trust.	Where inventories are required, there are no criteria for the listing process and the list has no legal status.

Environmental Impact Assessments do not include compulsory assessment of heritage sites. Often there are no rules for regulating archaeological discoveries and no mechanisms for management (such as Archaeological Impact Assessments). |
Jamaica	Jamaica Town and Country Planning Act 1958, as amended	Jamaica's National Heritage Trust has prepared guidelines for Archaeological Impact Assessments, but these guidelines have not been adopted in Jamaica's planning law.	
St. Vincent and the Grenadines	St. Vincent and the Grenadines Town and Country Planning Act 1992	St. Vincent's act makes the planning minister responsible for compiling or adopting a list of heritage resources.	In recent years there have been policies introduced to consider heritage sites and flexible institutional arrangements in the form of expert consultations with the Trust or a local heritage nongovernmental organization. There is no consistent official guidance on procedures where heritage resources are identified in the course of construction.
Trinidad and Tobago	Trinidad and Tobago Town and Country Planning Act 1960 (amended 1990)	Trinidad and Tobago relies on the National Trust and the National Archaeological Committee to advise its work, but this is not captured in its planning law.	

| OECS member states excluding St. Vincent | Grenada Physical Planning and Development Control (PPDC) Act 2016 | Grenada makes the minister for planning responsible for compiling the list of heritage resources. Environment protection areas and heritage conservation areas may be declared.

 Section 39 of Grenada's PPDC Act established a National Cultural Heritage Advisory Committee (where the National Trust has representation) to review applications for development, but as it is advisory in nature its opinions are not binding.

 Other islands such as Barbados, Saint Lucia, and Trinidad and Tobago have similar arrangements with committees to review planning applications, but they are not established in law as in Grenada. |
| | S:. Kitts Development Control and Planning Act 2009 | St. Kitts makes provision for coordinating protection of archaeological sites with its conservation legislation, the NCEPA (see archaeological sites above). |

TABLE A.6. IMPLEMENTING INTERNATIONAL HERITAGE LAWS

Country	Title of law	Key features of legislation	Gaps in heritage protection
Grenada	Physical Planning and Development Control (PPDC) Act 2016	Section 38 of the PPDC Act 2016 explicitly states that the Planning and Development Control Authority functions as the national service for the identification, protection, conservation, and rehabilitation of the natural and cultural heritage of Grenada, in accordance with the UNESCO World Heritage Convention, to which Grenada is a party.	No regulations for implementing this section, such as criteria for assessment, compilation of a national inventory of sites, coordination with the National Museum for the retrieval of artifacts, etc. The advisory committee plays no role in implementing this convention, and there is no coordination with the Ministry of Culture.
Barbados		Barbados has not created implementing legislation, but the chief town planner chairs the national World Heritage Committee, under which a management plan has been put in place for Barbados' UNESCO listed site (Bridgetown and its Garrison). The Barbados Museum and National Trust also sit on this committee.	

CONCLUSION

The legal environment for managing and protecting the archaeological heritage of the Caribbean is strongly influenced by inherited legal traditions from Europe and Great Britain. However, while the Spanish-speaking Caribbean has had the institutional architecture for managing heritage in place since the nineteenth century—and progressively built on this framework—the legal framework in the English-speaking Caribbean is quite fragmented and in need of harmonization.

In both the Spanish- and English-speaking Caribbean there are challenges related to updating, implementing, and enforcing the law. Laws need to be updated to address the modern challenges of climate change and other environmental threats to the region. They also need to take into account the role of communities in interacting with and protecting heritage. Access to information and public education provisions in the law are important in this regard to ensure that the public is aware of threats to heritage and can hold public authorities to account where necessary, and to support community engagement with heritage.

Mechanisms for the protection of heritage such as lists, inventories, and registers must be given stronger legislative footing, and incentives to protect local heritage, such as tax incentives, need to be further explored. Heritage governance is also undermined by the enactment of laws establishing new heritage actors with concurrent jurisdiction for the same resources, which further obfuscates the roles and responsibilities of major stakeholders. Clarification of these roles and responsibilities, such as those of government agencies (e.g., planning authorities), museums, and national trusts is imperative so that there is a coordinated and institutionally streamlined approach to heritage management.

There are also challenges with implementation and enforcement of the law, even when there is robust legislation in place. Institutions established by law need to be fully funded and need to build the relevant technical capacity in order to effectively monitor and protect archaeological sites and gather data for inventories and registers. Significantly, there are no state archaeologists in government departments in the English-speaking Caribbean that are responsible for the archaeological heritage. Customs officials, police officers, and planners all have roles to play in the identification, retrieval, and protection of artifacts. Clear protocols must be in place to educate the public on their rights and responsibilities vis-à-vis archaeological sites and objects. A major gap is that Environmental Impact Assessments (EIAs) as currently outlined in the legislation do not take into account the existence of archaeological resources.

Unless these underlying challenges are addressed, it will be difficult to devise culturally appropriate measures to address trafficking and looting of cultural property in the Caribbean.

RESOURCES

Country-Specific Legislation

Online versions of heritage laws may be found at the following country-specific websites. Also included are sources for laws that apply to nonindependent territories of the Caribbean. Please note that these sites are not always up to date.

Antigua and Barbuda: http://laws.gov.ag/new/index.php
Aruba: https://www.overheid.aw/governance-administration/national
  -ordinances-laws_3901/
Bahamas: http://laws.bahamas.gov.bs/cms/en/
British Virgin Islands: http://www.bvi.gov.vg/file-type/legislation
Cuba: http://juriscuba.com/legislacion-2/leyes/
Dominica: http://dominica.gov.dm/laws-of-dominica
Dominican Republic: https://republica-dominicana.justia.com
  /nacionales/leyes/
Dutch Caribbean: http://www.dutchcaribbeanlegalportal.com/
France (French Caribbean): http://www.legifrance.gouv.fr
Grenada: http://laws.gov.gd/
Jamaica: http://moj.gov.jm/laws
Puerto Rico: https://estado.pr.gov/en/laws-of-puerto-rico/
Sint Maarten: http://www.sintmaartengov.org/Laws/Pages/default.aspx
Trinidad and Tobago: http://www.legalaffairs.gov.tt/Laws_listing.html
Turks and Caicos: https://www.gov.tc/agc/laws/annual-laws/2018
  -laws/2018-ordinances
US Virgin Islands: http://www.lawsource.com/also/usa.cgi?xvi
Venezuela (Venezuelan territories): http://www.leyesvenezolanas.com/

Other databases of interest:

Commonwealth Legal Information Institute: http://www.commonlii.org/
Environmental and planning laws of relevance: https://www.ecolex.org/
UNESCO database of national cultural heritage laws: https://en.unesco
  .org/cultnatlaws
World Legal Information Institute: http://www.worldlii.org/

References Cited

Aarons, George A.
    1994   The Jamaican Taino: The Aboukir Zemis Symbols of Taino Philosophy, Mysticism, and Religion. *Jamaica Journal* 25(2):11–17.

Adler, Christine, Duncan Chappell, and Kenneth Polk
    2009   Perspectives on the Organisation and Control of the Illicit Traffic in Antiquities in South East Asia. In *Organised Crime in Art and Antiquities*, edited by Stefano Manacorda and Duncan Chappell, pp. 119–143. ISPAC, Milan.

Agorsah, E. Kofi
    1991   Evidence and Interpretation in the Archaeology of Jamaica. *Proceedings of the 13th Congress of the International Association for Caribbean Archaeology (IACA 1989)*, edited by E. N. Ayubi and J. B. Haviser, pp. 2–14. Curaçao.

Aguilar Bonilla, Monica
    2007   The Pothunter's Livelihood: Huaquerismo and Costa Rican Law in Defense of the National Archaeological Heritage. *Anthropology of Work Review* 28(2):8–12.

Alderman, Kimberly L.
    2012   Honour amongst Thieves: Organized Crime and the Illicit Antiquities Trade. *Indiana Law Review* 45:602–627.

Alegría, Ricardo E.
    1950   *Historia de nuestros indios*. Departamento de Instrucción Pública, San Juan.
    1954   *La fiesta de Santiago Apóstol en Loíza Aldea*. Instituto de Cultura Puertorriqueña, San Juan.
  1969 [1950] *Isla y Pueblo (Noticias de Borikén)*. Libros para el Pueblo, no. 28. División de Educación de la Comunidad, Departamento de Instrucción Pública, San Juan.
  1971 [1969] *Descubrimiento, conquista y colonización de Puerto Rico*. Colección de Estudios Puertorriqueños. Editorial Corripio, Santo Domingo.
    1976   El ataque y destrucción de la ciudad de Puerto Rico (Caparra) por los indios caribes en el año 1513. *Revista del Instituto de Cultura Puertorriqueña*, No. 72.
    1979   *El Rey Miguel: Héroe puertorriqueño en la lucha por la libertad de los esclavos*. Instituto de Cultura Puertorriqueña, San Juan.

1981   Introducción: Las primeras noticias sobre los indios caribes. In *Crónicas de los indios caribes*, edited by M. Cárdenas Ruíz and intro- duction by R. E. Alegría, pp. 1–90. Editorial Universidad de Puerto Rico, San Juan.

1983   *Ball Courts and Ceremonial Plazas in the West Indies.* Yale University Publications in Anthropology 79. Department of Anthropology, Yale University, New Haven.

1997   *Historia de Nuestros Indios.* Ilustraciones por Mela Pons de Alegría. Colección de Estudios Puertorriqueños, San Juan.

Al-Houdalieh, Salah Hussein
2012   Archaeological Heritage and Spiritual Protection: Looting and the Jinn in Palestine. *Journal of Mediterranean Archaeology* 25:99–120.

Allsworth-Jones, P.
2008   *Pre-Columbian Jamaica.* University of Alabama Press, Tuscaloosa.

Allsworth-Jones, Philip, and Esther Rodriques
2005   The James W. Lee Arawak Collection, UWI, Kingston, Jamaica: Fact and Figures. In *Proceedings of the Twentieth Congress of the International Association for Caribbean Archaeology (IACA, 2003)*, pp. 296–305. Santo Domingo.

Allsworth-Jones, Philip, Anthony Gouldwell, George Lechler, Simon F. Mitchell, Selvenious Walters, Jane Webster, and Robert Young
2006   The Pre-Columbian Site of Chancery Hall, St. Andrew. In *The Ear- liest Inhabitants: The Dynamics of the Jamaican Taino*, edited by Lesley-Gail Atkinson, pp. 47–68. UWI Press, Kingston.

Alonso, J. R.
2018   *Pre-historia del arte Cubano: El inconsciente y la espiritualidad indu- cida.* Edición EstudiosCulturales2003.es. Miami. Available at http:// docplayer.es, accessed October 8, 2018.

Andrefsky, William, Jr.
1998   *Lithics: Macroscopic Approaches to Analysis.* Cambridge University Press, Cambridge.

Anonymous
1969   Benyí explica origen de sus esculturas, Listín Diario, February 17, 1969. In 1999 *Historia de los Taínos Modernos*, edited by Rafael Pérez Guerra, pp. 217–221. Taller, Santo Domingo.

Antoniadou, Ioanna
2009   Reflections on an Archaeological Ethnography of "Looting" in Ko- zani, Greece. *Public Archaeology* 8:246–261.

Appadurai, A.
1994   Commodities and the Politics of Value. In *Interpreting Objects and Collections*, edited by Susan M. Pierce, pp. 76–91. Leicester Readers in Museum Studies. Routledge, London.

Appadurai, Arjun (editor)
1986   *The Social Life of Things: Commodities in Cultural Perspective.* Cam- bridge University Press, Cambridge.

Appleyard, Charlotte, and James Salzmann
    2012   *Corporate Art Collections: A Handbook to Corporate Buying*. Sotheby's Institute of Art, New York.

Ariese-Vandemeulebroucke, Csilla E.
    2018   *The Social Museum in the Caribbean: Grassroots Heritage Initiatives and Community Engagement*. Sidestone Press, Leiden.

Ascher, Robert
    1961   Experimental Archaeology. *American Anthropologist* 63:793–816.

Atalay, Sonya
    2012   *Community-Based Archaeology*. University of California Press, Berkeley.

Atkinson, Lesley-Gail
    1998   *The Challenges of Heritage Restitution in Jamaica*. Unpublished thesis in Caribbean Studies, University of the West Indies, Mona Campus.

Ayres, Ian, and John Braithwaite
    1995   *Responsive Regulation: Transcending the Deregulation Debate*. Oxford University Press, Oxford.

Babcock, Barbara
    1993   Bearers of Value, Vessels of Desire: The Reproduction of the Reproduction of Pueblo Culture. *Museum Anthropology* 17(3):43–57.

Badillo, Pedro E.
    1998   Jaime Benítez, reformador de la universidad. *Boletín de la Academia Puertorriqueña de la Historia*, no. 55, pp. 47–55.

Baekeland, F.
    1994   Psychological Aspects of Art Collecting. In *Interpreting Objects and Collections*, edited by Susan M. Pierce, pp. 205–219. Leicester Readers in Museum Studies. Routledge, London.

Banks, Paul
    2012   Jamaica Stone Artifacts: If Replicas, Then of What and Made by Whom? http://www.academia.edu/, accessed November 18, 2018.
    2013   Jamaican Stone Artefacts: (Why) Is the Scientific Community Afraid of Them? https://www.academia.edu/, accessed November 18, 2018.

Banks, Thomas J.
    1993   *Project Reports Funded by FFR on Grenada, 1993*. Foundation for Field Research, Saint George's, Grenada.

Barker, Alex W.
    2003   Archaeological Ethics: Museums and Collections. In *Ethical Issues in Archaeology*, edited by Larry J. Zimmerman, Karen D. Vitelli, and Julie Hollowell-Zimmer, pp. 71–82. Altamira Press, Walnut Creek.

Barreto, Amílcar A.
    2002   *Vieques, the Navy, and Puerto Rican Politics*. University Press of Florida, Gainesville.
    2008   Vieques and the Politics of Democratic Resistance. *New Centennial Review* 8(1):135–154.

Benavides, O. Hugo

    2004   *Making Ecuadorian Histories: Four Centuries of Defining Power.* University of Texas Press, Austin.

Benjamin, Walter

    1968   The Work of Art in the Age of Mechanical Reproduction. In *Illuminations,* edited by Hannah Arendt, pp. 217–252. Schocken Books, New York.

Berlin, Isaiah

    1980   *Vico and Herder: Two Studies in the History of Ideas.* Chatto and Windus, London.

Berman, Mary Jane, Perry L. Gnivecki, and Michael P. Pateman

    2013   The Bahama Archipelago. In *The Oxford Handbook of Caribbean Archaeology,* edited by William F. Keegan, Corinne Lisette Hofman, and Reniel Rodríguez Ramos, pp. 264–280. Oxford University Press, New York.

Blazy, Jacques

    2013   *Pre-Columbian Art: The Barbier-Mueller Collection: 1. Mesoamerica.* Sotheby's, Saint-Honoré.

Boas, Franz

  1955 [1927]   *Primitive Art.* Dover Publications, New York.

Boomert, Arie

    2000   *Trinidad, Tobago, and the Lower Orinoco Interaction Sphere: An Archeologcial/Ethnohistorical Study.* Cairi Publications, Akmaar, Netherlands.

    1986   The Cayo Complex of St. Vincent: Ethnohistorical and Archaeological Aspects of the Island Carib Problem. *Antropológica* 66:3–68.

Boone, Elizabeth H. (editor)

    1982   *Falsifications and Misreconstructions of Pre-Columbian Art.* Dumbarton Oaks, Washington, DC.

    1993   *Collecting the Pre-Columbian Past.* Dumbarton Oaks, Washington, DC.

Borodkin, L.

    1995   Note: The Economics of Antiquities Looting and a Proposed Legal Alternative. *Columbia Law Review* 95(2):377–417.

Bowman, Blythe A.

    2008   Transnational Crimes against Culture: Looting at Archaeological Sites and the "Grey" Market in Antiquities. *Journal of Contemporary Criminal Justice* 24:225–242.

    2011   Organized Criminal Involvement in the Illicit Antiquities Trade. *Trends in Organized Crime* 14:1–29.

Boyrie Moya, Emile de

    1952   Las Piezas Arqueológicas, de material Travertinico, de las "Cuevas de Los Paredones" (Caleta II), República Dominicana. *Memoria del V. Congreso Histórico Municipal Interamericano,* I:181–186.

    MS   Arqueológia indigena de las cuevas de Los Paredones, Republica

Dominicana. Manuscript on file at the Rouse Archives, Peabody Museum of Natural History, ANTAR.042255.

Bradley, Richard
    1997   To See Is to Have Seen: Craft Traditions in British Field Archaeology. In *The Cultural Life of Images*, edited by Brian Molyneux, pp. 62–71. Routledge, London.

Brau, Salvador
    1973 [1888]   *Puerto Rico y su historia*. Editorial Edil, Río Piedras.
    2011 [1907]   *La Colonización de Puerto Rico*. Instituto de Cultura Puertorriqueña, San Juan.

Brecht, F., E. Brodsky, J. A. Farmer, and D. Taylor (editors)
    1997   *Taíno: Pre-Columbian Art and Culture from the Caribbean*. El Museo del Barrio and the Monacelli Press, New York.

Breton, Raymond
    1999   *Dictionnaire Caraïbe-Français* [1665]. Edited by Marina Besada Paisa and Jean Bernabé. Karthala: Editions de l'IRD, Paris.

Bright, Alistair J.
    2011   *Blood Is Thicker Than Water: Amerindian Intra- and Inter-insular Relationships and Social Organization in the Pre-colonial Windward Islands*. Sidestone Press, Leiden.

British Museum
    2018   Collection search: Grenada. British Museum. http://www.britishmuseum.org, accessed March 11, 2018.

Brodie, Neil
    2011a   Congenial Bedfellows? The Academy and the Antiquities Trade. *Journal of Contemporary Criminal Justice* 27:411–440.
    2011b   The Market in Iraqi Antiquities, 1980–2009, and Academic Involvement in the Marketing Process. In *Crime in the Art and Antiquities World: Illegal Trafficking in Cultural Property*, edited by Stefano Manacorda and Duncan Chappell, pp. 117–133. Springer, New York.
    2015   Syria and Its Regional Neighbors: A Case of Cultural Property Protection Policy Failure? *International Journal of Cultural Property* 22:317–335.

Brodie, Neil, and Blythe A. Bowman
    2014   Museum Malpractice as Corporate Crime? The Case of the J. Paul Getty Museum. *Journal of Crime and Justice* 37:399–421.

Brodie, Neil, Jessica Dietzler, and Simon Mackenzie
    2013   Trafficking in Cultural Objects: An Empirical Overview. In *Beni culturali e sistema penale*, edited by Stefano Manacorda and A. Visconti, pp. 19–30. Vita e Pensiero, Milan.

Brodie, Neil, Jenny Doole, and Peter Watson
    2000   *Stealing History: The Illicit Trade in Cultural Material*. The McDonald Institute for Archaeological Research, Cambridge. https://www.museumsassociation.org, accessed November 9, 2018.

Brodie, Neil, and D. Gill
    2003   Looting: An International View. In *Ethical Issues in Archaeology*, edited by Larry J. Zimmerman, Karen D. Vitelli, and Julie Hollowell-Zimmer, pp. 31–44. Altamira Press, Walnut Creek.

Brodie, Neil, and Colin Renfrew
    2005   Looting and the World's Archaeological Heritage: The Inadequate Response. *Annual Review of Anthropology* 34:343–361.

Brown, Mark
    2019   Jamaica Seeks Return of Artefacts from British Museum. *Guardian*, August 17, 2019, https://www.theguardian.com, accessed August 21, 2019.

Bruhns, Karen O., and Nancy L. Kelker
    2010   *Faking the Ancient Andes*. Left Coast Press, Walnut Creek.

Brulotte, Ronda L.
    2012   *Between Art and Artifact: Archaeological Replicas and Cultural Production in Oaxaca, Mexico*. University of Texas Press, Austin.

Bullbrook, J. A.
    1960   *The Aborigines of Trinidad*. Royal Victoria Institute Museum, Port of Spain.

Bullen, Ripley P.
    1964   *The Archaeology of Grenada, West Indies*. Social Sciences 11. Contributions of the Florida State Museum, University of Florida, Gainesville.

Bullen, Ripley P., and Adelaide K. Bullen
    1972   *Archaeological Investigations on St. Vincent and the Grenadines, West Indies*. Bryant Foundation, Orlando.

Burch, S.
    2017   A Virtual Oasis: Trafalgar Square's Arch of Palmyra. *International Journal of Architectural Research: ArchNet-IJAR* 11(3):58–77.

Cabello Carro, P.
    1997   *Museo de América*. Ministerio de Cultura, Madrid.
    2008   Colecciones españolas en el Caribe: Viajes científicos e inicios de la arqueología en las Antillas (siglos XVIII y XIX). In *El Caribe Precolombino: Fray Ramón Pané y el universo taíno*, edited by José Oliver, Colin McEwan, and A. Casas Gilberga, pp. 202–221. Ministerio de Cultura, Barcelona.

Calvera, J.
    1996   El sitio arqueológico Los Buchillones. *El Caribe Arqueológico* (1):59–67.

Campbell, Peter B.
    2013   The Illicit Antiquities Trade as a Transnational Criminal Network: Characterizing and Anticipating Trafficking of Cultural Heritage. *International Journal of Cultural Property* 20:113–153.

Campos, A.
    2016   La arqueología holguinera en su proyección comunitaria. In *Un rostro local para la Arqueología Cubana*, edited by R. Valcárcel

Rojas and J. A. Cardet, pp. 95–111. Editorial Nuevos Mundos—La Mezquita, Holguín.

Capitulaciones de Santa Fe

1492   Capitulaciones de Santa Fe. Edited 2012. Santa Fe, Spain. http://alcolonial.wordpress.com, accessed February 27, 2019.

Caribbean News Now!

2018   "Regional Indigenous and Tribal Peoples Hold First Meeting in St. Vincent." https://www.caribbeannewsnow.com, accessed February 26, 2019.

Carruthers, David V.

2001   The Politics and Ecology of Indigenous Folk Art in Mexico. *Human Organization* 60(4):356–366.

Cassá, R.

1998   *Historia social y económica de la República Dominicana.* Alfa y Omega, Santo Domingo.

n.d.   De los archivos en República Dominicana. Historia Dominicana Blogspot. http://historiadominicana.blogspot.com, accessed February 27, 2019.

CELAC

2014   Culture and Development: World Heritage in the Caribbean. https://whc.unesco.org, accessed January 30, 2019.

Chappell, Duncan, and Kenneth Polk

2011   Unraveling the "Cordata": Just How Organized Is the International Traffic in Cultural Objects? In *Crime in the Art and Antiquities World*, edited by Stefano Manacorda and Duncan Chappell, pp. 99–113. Springer, New York.

Childs, S. Terry

2003   Archaeological Collections: Valuing and Managing an Emerging Frontier. In *Of the Past, for the Future: Integrating Archaeology and Conservation*, edited by Neville Agnew and Janet Bridgland. *Proceedings of the Conservation Theme at the 5th World Archaeological Congress*, Washington, DC., pp. 204–210. Getty Conservation Institute, Los Angeles.

Chinique, Y., R. Rodríguez Suárez, W. M. Buhay, and M. Roksandic

2019   Subsistence Strategies and Food Consumption Patterns of Archaic Age Populations from Cuba: From Traditional Perspectives to Current Analytical Results. In *Early Settlers of the Insular Caribbean: Dearchaizing the Archaic*, edited by C. L. Hofman and A. T. Antczak, pp. 107–121. Sidestone Press, Leiden.

Chippindale, C., and D. W. J. Gill.

2000   Material Consequences of Contemporary Classical Collecting. *American Journal of Archaeology* 104(3):463–511.

2001   Collecting the Classical World: First Steps in a Quantitative History. *International Journal of Cultural Property* 10:1–32.

CIfA
    2014   Code of Conduct. Reading, UK. Chartered Institute for Archaeologists, https://www.archaeologists.net, accessed September 22, 2019.

Clifford, James
    1988   *The Predicament of Culture: Twentieth-Century Ethnography, Literature, and Art*. Harvard University Press, Cambridge.

Cobb, Russell (editor)
    2014   *The Paradox of Authenticity in a Globalized World*. Springer, London.

Cody, Ann K.
    1990   *Prehistoric Patterns of Exchange in the Lesser Antilles: Materials, Models, and Preliminary Observations*. Unpublished master's thesis, San Diego State University, San Diego.

Coe, Michael D.
    1993   From Huaquero to Connoisseur: The Early Market in Pre-Columbian Art. In *Collecting the Pre-Columbian Past*, edited by Elisabeth Hill Boone, pp. 271–290. Dumbarton Oaks, Washington, DC.

Coggins, Clemency
    1969   Illicit Traffic of Pre-Columbian Antiquities. *Art Journal* 29(1):94–114. DOI:10.1080/00043249.1969.10794675.

Coles, John
    1973   *Archaeology by Experiment*. Charles Scribner's, New York.
    1979   *Experimental Archaeology*. Academic Press, London.

Coll y Toste, Cayetano
  1967 [1897]   *Prehistoria de Puerto Rico*. Editorial Vasco Americana, Bilbao.

Colwell, Chip
    2017   *Plundered Skulls and Stolen Spirits: Inside the Fight to Reclaim Native America's Culture*. University of Chicago Press, Chicago.

Comaroff, John L., and Jean Comaroff
    2009   *Ethnicity, Inc.* University of Chicago Press, Chicago.

Congreso Nacional de la República Dominicana (CNRD)
    1903   Decreto Núm. 4347 que declara propiedad del Estado los objetos arqueológicos. Gaceta Oficial Núm. 1522 del 26 de diciembre de 1903. https://en.unesco.org, accessed February 27, 2019.
    1913   Ley 5207 que crea el Museo Nacional. https://en.unesco.org, accessed February 27, 2019.
    1959   Resolución No. 5219. Accessed at http://www.unesco.org/culture /natlaws.
    1968   Ley 318 de Patrimonio Cultural de la Nación. www.wipo.int.
    1969a   Ley 492 que declara varios yacimientos arqueológicos como monumentos nacionales en diversas provincias. https://en.unesco.org, accessed February 27, 2019.
    1969b   Reglamento Núm. 4195 sobre la Oficina de Patrimonio Cultural. https://en.unesco.org, accessed February 27, 2019.
    1972   Ley 318 que crea el Museo del Hombre Dominicano https://en .unesco.org, accessed February 27, 2019.

1973 Ley 564 sobre la protección y conservación de los objetos Etnológicos y Arqueológicos Nacionales. Gaceta Oficial Núm. 9315 del 8 de octubre de 1973. https://en.unesco.org, accessed February 27, 2019.

2000 Ley 4100 sobre la creación de la Secretaria de Estado de Cultura de la República Dominicana. www.wipo.int, accessed February 27, 2019.

Conrad, G. W., C. D. Beeker, and J. W. Foster

2005 Underwater Archaeology at the Manantial de la Aleta, Dominican Republic. In *Actas del XX Congreso Internacional de Arqueología del Caribe*, vol. 2, edited by C. Tavárez María and M. A. García Arévalo, pp. 703–710. Museo del Hombre Dominicano and Fundación García Arévalo, Santo Domingo.

Consejo Nacional de Patrimonio Cultural

2002 *Protección del patrimonio cultural: Compilación de textos legislativos.* Consejo Nacional de Patrimonio Cultural. Ministerio de Cultura, Havana.

Corretjer, Juan A.

1970 [1957] Pictografía. In *Yerba Bruja: Poemas*. Serie Biblioteca Popular, Imágen de Borinquén, vol. 4.

1977 [1957] Pictografía. In *Obras Completas de Juan Antonio Corretjer: 1: Poemas*, p. 299. Editorial Instituto de Cultura Puertorriqueña, San Juan.

1990 [1930] Agueibana. In *Primeros libros poéticos de Juan Antonio Corretjer*, study and compilation by Joserramon Meléndez. Ediciones Casa Corretjer, Ciales.

Cruz Tejeda, M.

2011 Reliquias tainas robadas en RD confiscadas en EE.UU. y PR. *Diario Libre*. 14 de septiembre, 2011. www.diariolibre.com, accessed February 27, 2019.

Cué, V., and R. Fernández

2016 Martínez: Sin un adiós, a su obra científica y artística. *Cuba Arqueológica* 9(1):60–62.

Cummins, Alissandra

1992 Exhibiting Culture: Museums and National Identity in the Caribbean. *Caribbean Quarterly* 38(2):33–53.

2004 Caribbean Museums and National Identity. *History Workshop Journal* 58(1):224–245.

2006 The Role of the Museum in Developing Heritage Policy. In *Art and Cultural Heritage: Law, Policy and Practice*, edited by Barbara T. Hoffman, pp. 47–51. Cambridge University Press, New York

Cummins, Alissandra, Kevin Farmer, and Roslyn Russell (editors)

2013 *Plantation to Nation: Caribbean Museums and National Identity.* Common Ground, Champaign, Illinois.

Cundall, Frank

1909 Historic Sites and Monuments Supplement to the Jamaica Gazette. *Jamaica Gazette*, December 23.

1934   *The Aborigines of Jamaica.* Institute of Jamaica Publications, Kingston.

Curet, L. Antonio

2011   Colonialism and the History of Archaeology in the Spanish Caribbean. In *Comparative Archaeologies: A Sociological View of the Science of the Past,* edited by Ludomir R. Lozny, pp. 641–672. Springer-Verlag, New York.

2014   Taíno: Phenomena, Concepts, and Terms. *Ethnohistory* 61(3):467–495.

2015   Indigenous Revival, Indigeneity, and the Jíbaro in Borikén. *Centro Journal* 27(1):206–247.

Curet, L. Antonio, and Maria Galban

2019   Theodoor de Booy: Caribbean Expeditions and Collections at the National Museum of the American Indian. *Journal of Caribbean Archaeology* 19:1–50.

Dalton, Ronald, Roderick Ebanks, and Heidi Savery

2009   *Cultural Heritage Management Survey, Archaeological Salvage Survey, Bluefields Gardens Development Area, Westmoreland.* Unpublished report.

Dark, Ken R.

1995   *Theoretical Archaeology.* Cornell University Press, Ithaca, New York.

David, Nicholas, and Carol Kramer

2001   *Ethnoarchaeology in Action.* Cambridge University Press, Cambridge.

Dávila, Arlene

1997   *Sponsored Identities: Cultural Politics in Puerto Rico.* Temple University Press, Philadelphia.

2001   Local/Diasporic Taínos: Towards a Cultural Politics of Memory, Reality, and Imagery. In *Taíno Revival: Critical Perspectives on Puerto Rican Identity and Cultural Politics,* edited by Gabriel Haslip-Viera, pp. 33–49. Markus Wiener, Princeton.

Dávila, B.

2017   *Formas y significados: El objeto portable ornamental-ceremonial reportado en el oriente de Cuba.* PhD dissertation, Universidad de Oriente, Santiago de Cuba.

Dávila Dávila, Ovidio

1996   *El centenario de la adopción de la bandera de Puerto Rico diseñada por don Antonio Vélez Alvarado, 1895–1995.* Sobretiro del Boletín Numiexpo '96. Sociedad Numismática de Puerto Rico, San Juan.

Davis, Dave, and Kevin Oldfield

2003   Archaeological Reconnaissance of Anegada, British Virgin Islands. *Journal of Caribbean Archaeology* 4:1–11.

Davis, Tess

2011   Supply and Demand: Exposing the Illicit Trade in Cambodian Antiquities through a Study of Sotheby's Auction House. *Crime, Law and Social Change* 56:155–174.

Davis, Tess, and Simon Mackenzie

2014   Crime and Conflict: Temple Looting in Cambodia. In *Cultural Prop-*

erty Crimes: An Overview and Analysis on Contemporary Perspectives and Trends*, edited by Joris Kila and Marc Balcells, pp. 292–306. Brill, Leiden.

De Booy, Theodoor
  1919   *Archaeology of the Virgin Islands*. Indian Notes and Monographs. Museum of the American Indian, Heye Foundation, New York.

De Hostos, Adolfo
  1939   *Industrial Applications of Indian Decorative Motifs in Puerto Rico*, designs by Matilde Perez de Silva. John C. Winstony, Philadelphia.

De la Cruz, Manuel Antonio, and Victor MI. Durán Núñez
  2012   *Artesanía Dominicana: Un arte popular*. Amigo del Hogar, Santo Domingo. http://identidadsanjuanera.blogspot.com.

De Peña, L.
  2007   *Manual de normas y procedimientos de la Red Nacional de Museos de la República Dominicana*. Reglamento de la Red Nacional de Museos. Aprobado por el Consejo Nacional de Cultural. Dirección General de Museos. Subsecretaría de Patrimonio Cultural. Secretaría de Estado de Cultura. Santo Domingo.

Deagan, K.
  2010   Cuba and Florida: Entwined Histories of Historical Archaeologies. In *Beyond the Blockade: New Currents in Cuban Archaeology*, edited by S. Kepecs, L. A. Curet, and G. La Rosa, pp. 16–25. University of Alabama Press, Tuscaloosa.

Delpuech, A.
  2016   Un marché de l'art précolombien en plein questionnement. *Les Nouvelles de l'archéologie* 144:43–50.

Derry, Linda, and Maureen Malloy (editors)
  2003   *Archaeologists and Local Communities: Partners in Exploring the Past*. Society for American Archaeology, Washington, DC.

Díaz-Andreu, Margarita
  2007   *A World History of Nineteenth-Century Archaeology: Nationalism, Colonialism, and the Past*. Oxford University Press, Oxford.

Dick-Read, Aragon
  1988   Fake Taíno Stone Carvings. *African Arts* 21(2):88.

Dietzler, Jessica
  2013   On Organized Crime in the Illicit Antiquities Trade: Moving beyond the Definitional Debate. *Trends in Organized Crime* 16:329–342.

Dividend
  1981   David Merriman, MB '36. *Dividend: The Magazine of the Graduate School of Business Administration*. University of Michigan, Ann Arbor.

Donop, Mark C.
  2005   Savanne Suazey Revisited. Unpublished master's thesis, University of Florida, Gainesville.

Doucet, Rachelle Charlier (editor)
  2015   *Sur les traces de nos ancêtres amérindienes: Actes du premier forum*

international sur le patrimoine amérindien. Fondation Odette Roy Fombrun, Pétionville, Haiti.

Douglass, Kristina, Eréndira Quintana Morales, George Manahira, Felicia Fenomanana, Roger Samba, Francois Lahiniriko, and Zafy Maharesy Chrisostome

2019   Toward a Just and Inclusive Environmental Archaeology of Southwest Madagascar. *Journal of Social Archaeology,* July, https://doi.org/10.1177/1469605319862072.

Duany, Jorge

2003   Nation, Migration, and Identity: The Case of Puerto Ricans. *Latin American Studies* 1:424–444.

Duerden, J. E.

1897   Aboriginal Indian Remains in Jamaica. *Journal of the Institute of Jamaica* 2(4):1–51.

Egberts, Linde

2014   Experiencing the Past: Introduction to Experience, Strategies, Authenticity, and Branding. In *Companion to European Heritage Revivals,* edited by Linde Egberts and Koos Bosma, pp. 12–29. Springer, London.

Elia, Ricardo J.

1997   Looting, Collecting, and the Destruction of Archaeological Resources. *Non-renewable Resources* 6:85–98.

Elkins, J.

1993   From Copy to Forgery and Back Again. *British Journal of Aesthetics* 33(2):113–120.

Elliot, J. H.

2018   *Scots and Catalans: Union and Disunion.* Yale University Press, New Haven.

Enrique Méndez, J.

2011   Los artesanos del Capá. *Identidad Sanjuanera* (blog). http://identidadsanjuanera.blogspot.com, accessed February 27, 2019.

Erlandson, Jon M.

2008   Racing a Rising Tide: Global Warming, Rising Seas, and the Erosion of Human History. *Journal of Island and Coastal Archaeology,* November, https://doi.org10.1080/15564890802436766.

Espenshade, Christopher T. (editor)

2012   *The Cultural Landscape of Jácana: Archaeological Investigations of Site PO-29, Municipio de Ponce, Puerto Rico.* Volume 2. Draft report submitted by New South Associates Inc. to the US Army Corps of Engineers, Jacksonville District, Stone Mountain, Georgia.

Espinal, E.

2017   *Legislación sobre patrimonio cultural dominicano: Apuntes de un taller.* Fundación Centro Cultural Altos de Chavón-Museo Arqueológico Regional, report on file at La Romana.

2018   50 años de gestión del patrimonio cultural en la República Dominicana: Balance de un recorrido. Revista Arquitexto. Patrimonio-Teoría y crítica. https://arquitexto.com, accessed February 27, 2019.

Estévez, J.
  2011   *La Academia de la Historia de Cuba: Panorama de su primera época,*
          1910–1962; El primer esplendor, 1923–1930. Available at www.ach
          .ohc.cu, accessed October 2, 2018.

Evans, R. Tripp
  2004   *Romancing the Maya: Mexican Antiquity in the American Imagina-*
          tion, 1820–1915. University of Texas Press, Austin.

Fandrich, Judith E.
  1991   Stone Implements from Grenada: Were They Trade Items? *Proceed-*
          ings of the XIII Congress of the International Association for Carib-
          bean Archaeology (IACA, 1989), pp. 162–166. Curaçao.

Farnsworth, Kenneth B.
  1973   *An Archaeological Survey of the Macoupin Valley.* Reports of Inves-
          tigations 26. Research Papers 7. Illinois Valley Archaeological Pro-
          gram, Illinois State Museum, Springfield.

Feder, Kenneth L.
  2017   *Frauds, Myths, and Mysteries: Science and Pseudoscience in Archae-*
          ology. 9th ed. Oxford University Press, New York.

Feest, C.
  1993   European Collecting of American Indian Artefacts and Art. *Journal*
          of the History of Collections 5(1):1–11.

Felch, Jason, and Ralph Frammolino
  2011   *Chasing Aphrodite: The Hunt for Looted Antiquities at the World's*
          Richest Museum. Houghton Mifflin, Boston.

Feliciano-Santos, Sherina
  2011   *An Inconceivable Indigeneity: The Historical, Cultural, and Interactional*
          Dimensions of Puerto Rican Taíno Activism. PhD dissertation, De-
          partment of Anthropology, University of Michigan, Ann Arbor.

Fell, Barry
  1987   Inscribed Stone Artifacts from Guayanilla, Puerto Rico. *Epigraphic*
          Society Occasional Publications 16:322. Midwestern Epigraphic
          Society.

Fernández, Alyeda
  1969a   Es probable salgan artistas Paredones, Listin Diario, January 31,
          1969. In 1999 *Historia de los Taínos Modernos*, edited by Rafael
          Pérez Guerra, pp. 157–161. Taller, Santo Domingo.
  1969b   Suena ser un artista, aprende y tiene exito, Listin Diario, February
          1, 1969. In 1999 *Historia de los Taínos Modernos*, edited by Rafael
          Pérez Guerra, pp. 167–169. Taller, Santo Domingo.

Fernández, Brinella
  1969   El hombre que confundio a los arqueologos, Ahora! February 17,
          1969. In 1999 *Historia de los Taínos Modernos*, edited by Rafael
          Pérez Guerra, pp. 209–217. Taller, Santo Domingo.

Fernández, R., D. Gutiérrez, J. B. González, and L. Dominguez González
  2013   *Los petroglifos de Santiago de Cuba y el personaje con los brazos en*

aspa: Un caso de obligatoria justicia. Available at www.rupestreweb .info, accessed September 2, 2018.

Fewkes, Jesse Walter

1903   Preliminary Report on an Archaeological Trip to the West Indies. In *Smithsonian Miscellaneous Collections*, XLV, Report no. 1429:112–133. Washington, DC. Available at https://library.si.edu, accessed September 29, 2019.

1907   *The Aborigines of Puerto Rico and Neighboring Islands.* Twenty-Fifth Annual Report of the American Bureau of Ethnology. US Government Printing Office, Washington, DC.

1922   *A Prehistoric Island Culture Area of America.* Annual Report 34. Bureau of American Ethnology. Smithsonian Institution, Washington, DC.

Field, Les

1999   *The Grimace of Macho Ratón: Artisans, Identity, and Nation in Late Twentieth-Century Western Nicaragua.* Duke University Press, Durham, North Carolina.

2009   Four Kinds of Authenticity? Regarding Nicaraguan Pottery in Scandinavian Museums, 2006–08. *American Ethnologist* 36:507–520.

Fiester, Donald

1989   *A Mid-Term Evaluation of the High Impact Regional Cocoa Rehabilitation and Development Sub Project (USAID Grant No. 538-0140.2).* Pan American Development Foundation, Washington, DC.

Figueredo, Alfredo E.

1974   History of Virgin Islands Archaeology. *Journals of the Virgin Islands Archaeological Society* 1:1–6.

Fincham, Alan G.

1997   *Jamaica Underground: The Caves, Sinkholes, and Underground Rivers of the Island.* 2nd ed. University of West Indies Press, Kingston.

Finlayson, Clive

2019   *The Smart Neanderthal: Bird Catching, Cave Art, and the Cognitive Revolution.* Oxford University Press, New York.

Fitzpatrick, Scott M.

2010   On the Shoals of Giants: Natural Catastrophes and the Overall Destruction of the Caribbean's Archaeological Record. *Journal of Coastal Conservation* 16(2):173–186. https://doi.org/10.1007/s11852 -010-0109-0.

Françozo, M., and A. Strecker

2017   Caribbean Collections in European Museums and the Question of Returns. *International Journal of Cultural Property* 24(4): 451–477. https://doi.org/10.1017/S0940739117000248.

Frederiksen, R., and E. Marchand

2010   Introduction. In *Plaster Casts: Making, Collecting, and Displaying from Classical Antiquity to the Present*, edited by R. Frederiksen and E. Marchand, pp. 1–10. De Gruyter, Berlin.

Fullana Acosta, Mariela
2016   El artista puertorriqueño ha moldeado una Carrera marcada por la experimentación y la pasión. *El Nuevodia*, November 13, 2016, www.elnuevodia.com, accessed February 25, 2018.

Gamble, L. H.
2002   Fact or Forgery: Dilemmas in Museum Collections. *Museum Anthropology* 25(2):3–20.

García, Osvaldo
1993   *Fotografías para la historia de Puerto Rico*. Ediciones Huracán, Río Piedras.

García Arévalo, Manuel Antonio
1968   Crisis Arqueológica, Listin Diario, August 9, 1968. In 1999 *Historia de los Taínos Modernos*, edited by Rafael Pérez Guerra, pp. 63–69. Taller, Santo Domingo.

1987   El Neotainismo Dominicano y la "Feria de la Paz." In *Arte NeoTaíno*, edited by Bernardo Vega, pp. 13–17. Fundacíon Cultural Dominicana, Santo Domingo.

1988   *Indigenismo, Arqueología e Identidad Nacional*. Museo del Hombre Dominicano/Fundación García Arévalo Inc., Santo Domingo.

2019   *Taínos: Arte y Sociedad*. Banco Popular Dominicano, Amigos del Hogar, Santo Domingo.

García Perdigón, J. R.
2014   La labor museológica de la Revolución cubana y el proceso de transformación en la proyección social de los museos en Cuba. *Intervención* 5(9):65–75. Available at www.scielo.org.mx, accessed October 8, 2018.

German, Senta C.
2012   Unprovenienced Artifacts and the Invention of Minoan and Mycenaean Religion. In *All the King's Horses: Essays on the Impact of Looting and the Illicit Antiquities Trade on Our Knowledge of the Past*, edited by Paula K. Lazrus and Alex W. Barker, pp. 55–68. SAA Press, Washington, DC.

Gerstenblith, P.
2010   International Art and Cultural Heritage. *Journal of International Law* 44:487–501.

Geurds, Alexander, and Laura Van Broekhoven (editors)
2013   *Creating Authenticity: Authentication Processes in Ethnographic Museums*. Sidestone Press, Leiden.

Gilgan, Elizabeth
2001   Looting and the Market for Maya Objects: A Belizian Perspective. In *Trade in Illicit Antiquities: The Destruction of the World's Archaeological Heritage*, edited by Neil Brodie, Jennifer Doole, and Colin Renfrew, pp. 73–88. Macdonald Institute Monographs, Cambridge.

Giovas, Christina M.
2017   Continental Connections and Insular Distributions: Deer Bone

Artifacts of the Precolumbian West Indies—A Review and Synthesis with New Records. *Latin American Antiquity* 29(1):1–17. DOI:10.1017/laq.2017.57.

Giraldo, Alexander
n.d.   Obeah: The Ultimate Resistance. https://scholar.library.miami.edu, accessed October 26, 2019.

Goebel, Ted
2015   Grave Consequences: Crossing the Line with Collectors. In *SAA Archaeological Record*, special issue: Pros and Cons of Consulting Collectors 15(5):29–32.

Golding, Viv, and Wayne Modest (editors)
2010   *Museums and Communities: Curators, Collections, and Collaboration.* Bloomsbury, London.

Gómez, D. J., and M. Martínez
2011   *Holguín: Coleccionismo y museos.* Editorial La Mezquita, Holguín.

Gould, Stephen Jay
1989   *Wonderful Life: The Burgess Shale and the Nature of History.* W. W. Norton, New York.

Government of Grenada, Official Website
2010   PM Thomas Makes Direct Appeals to Overseas Nationals to Invest at Home. www.gov.gd, accessed February 26, 2019.

Granberry, Julian, and Gary S. Vescelius
2004   *Languages of the Pre-Columbian Antilles.* University of Alabama Press, Tuscaloosa.

Grodeau, Islar Pilar
2011   The People of Puerto Rico: Past and Present Contemporary Reactions to the Book. *Identities: Global Studies in Culture and Power* 18:218–228.

Grove, L., and S. Thomas
2016   The Rhino Horn on Display Has Been Replaced by a Replica: Museum Security in Finland and England. *Journal of Conservation and Museum Studies* 14(1):1–11.

Grupo Guamá
1944   *Reproducciones de Iván Gundrum sobre Cultura Taína Indoantillana.* Lyceum, El Siglo XX, A. Muñiz y Hno., Havana.

Guarch Delmonte, J. M.
1990   *Estructura para las Comunidades Aborígenes de Cuba.* Ediciones Holguín, Holguín.
1996   La muerte en Las Antillas: Cuba. *El Caribe Arqueológico* 1:12–25.

Guarch Delmonte, J. M., and C. Rodríguez Cullel
1980   Consideraciones acerca de la morfología y desarrollo de los pictogramas cubanos. In *Cuba Arqueológica II*, edited by M. A. Martínez, pp. 55–76. Editorial Oriente, Santiago de Cuba.

Guarch Rodríguez, E.
2006   *Perfeccionamiento de la socialización de los resultados de las investigaciones arqueológicas en la provincia de Holguín.* Master's thesis,

Archives of the Departamento Centro-Oriental de Arqueología, Holguín.

Guitar, Lynne, Pedro Ferbel-Azcarate, and Jorge Estevez
2006   *Ocama-Daca Taíno* (Hear Me, I am Taíno): Taíno Survival on Hispaniola, Focusing on the Dominican Republic. In *Indigenous Resurgence in the Contemporary Caribbean: Amerindian Survival and Revival*, edited by Maximilian C. Forte, pp. 41–67. Peter Lang, New York.

Gutiérrez Calvache, Divaldo
2017   La teoría del origen neurofisciológico del arte rupestre y su introducción en Cuba. Notas reflexivas, *Cuba Arqueológica* 10(1):9–23.

Haber, Alejandro
2016   Decolonizing Archaeological Thought in South America. *Annual Review of Anthropology* 45(1):469–485. https://www.annualreviews.org.

Hajdas, Irka, A. J. Timothy Jull, Eric Huysecom, Anne Mayor, Marc-André Renold, Hans-Arno Synal, Christine Hatté, Wan Hong, David Chivall, and Lucile Beck
2019   Radiocarbon Dating and the Protection of Cultural Heritage. *Radiocarbon* 1–2. https://doi.org/10.1017/RDC.2019.100.

Hamann, Byron
2002   The Social Life of Pre-sunrise Things: Indigenous Mesoamerican Archaeology. *Current Anthropology* 43:351–382.

Hamilakis, Yannis
2009   *The Nation and Its Ruins: Antiquity, Archaeology, and National Imagination in Greece*. Oxford University Press, Oxford.

Hanna, Jonathan A.
2017   *The Status of Grenada's Prehistoric Sites: Report on the 2016 Survey and an Inventory of Known Sites*. Ministry of Tourism, Botanical Gardens, Grenada, DOI:10.18113/S1QG64.
2018   *Ancient Human Behavioral Ecology and Colonization in Grenada, West Indies*. PhD dissertation, Department of Anthropology, Pennsylvania State University, University Park.
2019   Camáhogne's Chronology: The Radiocarbon Settlement Sequence on Grenada, West Indies. *Journal of Anthropological Archaeology* 55:101075. DOI:10.1016/j.jaa.2019.101075.

Hardwick, T.
2010   The Sophisticated Answer: A Recent Display of Forgeries Held at the Victoria and Albert Museum. *Burlington Magazine* 152(1287):406–408.

Harrington, M. R.
1921   *Cuba before Columbus: Indian Notes and Monographs*. Museum of the American Indian, Heye Foundation, New York.
1935   *Cuba antes de Colón*. Colección de Libros Cubanos, Volume 32. Cultural S.A., Havana.

Hartman, Carl V.
1901   *Archaeological Researches in Costa Rica*. Royal Ethnographical Museum, Stockholm.

1907   *Archaeological Researches on the Pacific Coast of Costa Rica.* Memoirs of the Carnegie Museum 3(1). Carnegie Institute, Pittsburgh.

Haslip Viera, Gabriel

2013   *Race, Identity, and Indigenous Politics: Puerto Rican Neo-Tainos in the Diaspora and the Island.* CreateSpace Independent Publishing Platform, Scots Valley, California.

Haslip Viera, Gabriel (editor)

2001   *Taíno Revival: Critical Perspectives on Puerto Rican Identity and Cultural Politics.* Markus Wiener, Princeton.

Hatt, Gudmund

1924   Archaeology of the Virgin Islands. *Proceedings of the International Congress of Americanists* 21(1) 29–42.

Haythorn, M. L.

1984a   Ivan Gundrum's Life and Times Are Recalled. *Times-Enterprise,* March, Thomasville.

1984b   Artist Never Stopped Work. *Times-Enterprise,* March 30, p. 6, Thomasville.

2005   Symphony of Smoke and Fire: The Pottery of J. Martin Haythorn. *Florida Frontier Gazette* 5(1):2–4.

Hayward, Michele H., Lesley-Gail Atkinson, and Michael Cinquino (editors)

2009   *Rock Art of the Caribbean.* University of Alabama Press, Tuscaloosa.

Heath, Dwight B.

1973   Economic Aspects of Commercial Archaeology in Costa Rica. *American Antiquity* 38:259–265.

Hernández, Carmen Dolores

2002   *Ricardo Alegría: Toda una vida.* Plaza Mayor, Madrid.

Hernández Godoy, S. T.

2011   El patrimonio arqueológico y su protección jurídica en Cuba. *Anales del Museo de América* 19:258–267.

2014   Historia de la arqueología cubana desde una externalista de la ciencia (1847–1940). *Cuba Arqueológica* 7(1):5–19.

Herrera Fritot, René

1942   Falsificaciones de objetos aborígenes cubanos. *Memorias de la Sociedad Cubana de Historia Natural "Felipe Poey"* 16(1):5–20.

1946   *Arte Neo-Taíno en Cuba.* Museo Etnologico del Grupo Guamá, Lyceum Lawn Tennis Club, Havana.

1952   Arquetipos zoomorfos en las Antillas Mayores. *Revista de Arqueología y Etnología* 7(15–16):215–226.

1964   *Estudio de las hachas antillanas: Creación de índices axiales para las petaloides.* Comisión Nacional de la Academia de Ciencias, Departamento de Antropología, Havana.

Herrera Fritot, René, and Charles Leroy Youmans

1946   *La Caleta: Joya Arqueológica Antillana.* El Siglo XX, Havana.

Hirst, K. Kris

2018   Provenience, Provenance, Let's Call the Whole Thing Off. *ThoughtCo.* www.thoughtco.com, accessed January 7, 2019.

Hisashi, Endo
  1996   *Collective Works of Hijikata Hisakatsu—Myths and Legends of Palau.*
          Sasakawa Peace Foundation, Tokyo.

Hobsbawm, Eric J.
  1984   Introduction: Inventing Traditions. In *The Invention of Tradition,*
          edited by E. J. Hobsbawm, pp. 1–14. Cambridge University Press,
          Cambridge.

Hodder, Ian (editor)
  2000   *Towards Reflexive Method in Archaeology: The Example at Çatal-*
          höyük. Oxbow Books, Oxford.

Hodos, Tamar, Alexander Geurds, Paul Lane, Ian Lilley, Martin Pitts, Gideon Shelach,
    Miriam Stark, and Miguel John Versluys (editors)
  2017   *The Routledge Handbook of Archaeology and Globalization.* Rout-
          ledge, London.

Hofman, C., A. J. Bright, and R. Rodríguez Ramos
  2010   Crossing the Caribbean Sea: Towards a Holistic View of Pre-Colonial
          Mobility and Exchange. *Journal of Caribbean Archaeology,* special
          publication 3:1–18.

Hofman, Corinne L., Arie Boomert, Alistair J. Bright, Menno L. P. Hoogland, Sebastiaan
    Knippenberg, and Alice V. M. Samson
  2011   Ties with the Homelands: Archipelagic Interaction and the Endur-
          ing Role of the South and Central American Mainlands in the Pre-
          Columbian Lesser Antilles. In *Islands at the Crossroads: Migration,*
          Seafaring, and Interaction in the Caribbean, edited by L. Antonio
          Curet and Mark W. Hauser, pp. 73–86. University of Alabama Press,
          Tuscaloosa.

Hofman, Corinne L., and Jay B. Haviser (editors)
  2015   *Managing Our Past into the Future: Archaeological Heritage Manage-*
          ment in the Dutch Caribbean. Taboui 3, Sidestone Press, Leiden.

Hofman, C., and M. Hoogland
  2009   *Interim Report on the Results of the 2009 (May and June) Rescue*
          Excavations at the Lavoutte Site (Cas-en-Bas), St. Lucia. Leiden Uni-
          versity. Available at http://media.leidenuniv.nl, accessed January 2,
          2019.
  2011   Unravelling the Multi-Scale Networks of Mobility and Exchange in
          the Pre-Colonial Circum-Caribbean. In *Communities in Contact,* ed-
          ited by Corinne L. Hofman and Anne van Duijvenbode, pp. 15–43.
          Sidestone Press, Leiden.

Hofman, Corinne L., Menno L. P. Hoogland, Arie Boomert, and John Angus Martin
  2019   Colonial Encounters in the Southern Lesser Antilles: Indigenous
          Resistance, Material Transformations, and Diversity in an Ever-
          Globalizing World. In *Material Encounters and Indigenous Transfor-*
          mations in the Early Colonial Americas: Archaeological Case Studies,
          edited by Corinne L. Hofman and Floris W. M. Keehnen, pp. 359–
          384. Brill, Leiden

Hofman, C., J. Hung, E. Herrera Malatesta, and J. Sony Jean

2018   Indigenous Caribbean Perspectives: Archaeologies and Legacies of the First Colonised Region in the New World. *Antiquity* 92(361): 200–216. DOI:10.1518/aqy.2017.247.

Hollowell-Zimmer, Julie

2003   Digging in the Dirt: Ethics and "Low-End Looting." In *Ethical Issues in Archaeology*, edited by Larry J. Zimmerman, Karen D. Vitelli, and Julie Hollowell-Zimmer, pp. 45–56. Altamira Press, Walnut Creek.

Holtorf, Cornelius

2013   On Pastness: A Reconsideration of Materiality in Archaeological Object Authenticity. *Anthropological Quarterly* 86:427–443.

Holtorf, Cornelius, and Tim Schadla-Hall

1999   Age as Artefact: On Archaeological Authenticity. *European Journal of Archaeology* 2:229–247.

Hoogland, Menno L. P., Corinne L. Hofman, and Arie Boomert

2011   *Argyle, St. Vincent: New Insights on the Island Carib Occupation of the Lesser Antilles.* Unpublished paper presented at the 24th International Congress for Caribbean Archaeology, July 25–30, Martinique.

Howard, Robert R.

1950   *The Archaeology of Jamaica and Its Position in Relation to Circum-Caribbean Culture.* PhD dissertation, Yale University, New Haven.

1956   The Archaeology of Jamaica: A Preliminary Survey. *American Antiquity* 22(1):45–59.

Hoy Digital

2004   Emile de Boyrie de Moya pionero de la arqueologia. March 14. https://hoy.com.do, accessed October 3, 2019.

Huckerby, Thomas

1921   *Petroglyphs of Grenada and a Recently Discovered Petroglyph in St. Vincent*, edited by F. W. Hodge. Indian Notes and Monographs 1(3). Heye Foundation, Museum of the American Indian, New York.

Huerga, Álvaro

2006   *Ataques de los caribes a Puerto Rico en el siglo XVI.* Academia Puertorriqueña de La Historia; Centro de Estudios Avanzados de Puerto Rico y El Caribe; Fundación Puertorriqueña de las Humanidades, San Juan.

Huffer, Damien

2011   Antiques vs. Antiquities: A Case Study from Malta. http://savingantiquities.org/, accessed October 27, 2019.

Hutson, Scott

2013   "Unavoidable Imperfections": Historical Contexts for Representing Ruined Maya Buildings. In *Past Represented: Archaeological Illustration and the Ancient Americas*, edited by Joanne Pillsbury, pp. 282–316. Dumbarton Oaks, Washington, DC.

Ikhlef, Khalissa
    2014   Culture in Small Island Developing States. In *Culture and Development: World Heritage in the Caribbean*, pp. 16–21, UNESCO. https://whc.unesco.org, accessed January 30, 2019.

Ingram, Kenneth E.
    1975   *Manuscripts Relating to Commonwealth Caribbean Countries in United States and Canadian Repositories*. Caribbean Universities Press, Saint Lawrence, Barbados.

Institute of Jamaica (IOJ)
    1978   Institute of Jamaica Act. https://moj.gov.jm, accessed February 27, 2019. Jamaica National Heritage Trust.
    2007   *Canoe Valley Protected Area Clarendon/Manchester: Archaeological Appraisal Report*. Archaeology Division, Jamaica National Heritage Trust, Kingston.
    2009a   *Jamaica National Heritage Trust Act—A Review: A Document to Guide the Discussions of the Proposed Amendments to the Act*. http://www.jnht.com, accessed October 27, 2019.
    2009b   *Falmouth Cruise Ship Pier Watching Brief*. Unpublished report, Kingston.
    2015   *Pimento Hill, St. Mary*. Archaeological Appraisal Report, Jamaica National Heritage Trust, Kingston.

International Council of Museums (ICOM)
    2013   *Red List of Dominican Cultural Objects at Risk*. International Council of Museums, https://icom.museum, accessed October 17, 2016.
    2017   ICOM Code of Ethics for Museums, https://icom.museum, accessed February 17, 2019.

Jamaica Observer
    2018   *Jamaica Developing National Register of Culture Places, Objects—Grange*. September 18. www.jamaicaobserver.com, accessed October 15, 2018.

Jaramillo, L. 2004, in Argaillot, Janice
    2012   Cuba y el patrimonio cultural cubano y caribeño desde los principios de la Revolución. *Anuario Americanista Europeo* 10:1–19.

Jarvis, Kate
    2017   Maya Heritage: 150 Years of Preservation, https://blog.britishmuseum.org, accessed December 9, 2018.

Jiménez Santander, J., L. Torres de la Paz, D. Morales Valdés, and L. Jiménez Ortega
    2018   Las comunidades aborígenes de Cuba: Censo 2013. In *Cuba: Arqueología y legado histórico*, edited by J. Larramendi Joa and A. Rangel Rivero, pp. 41–47. Ediciones Polymita S.A., Guatemala City.

Johnson, C. L.
    2011   Aztec Regalia and the Reformation of Display. In *Collecting across Cultures: Material Exchanges in the Early Modern Atlantic World*, edited by Daniela Bleichmar and Peter C. Mancall, pp. 83–99. University of Pennsylvania Press, Philadelphia.

Jones, M.

1994   Why Fakes. In *Interpreting Objects and Collections*, edited by Susan M. Pierce, pp. 92–97. Leicester Readers in Museum Studies. Routledge, London.

Jones, Mark, Paul Craddock, and Nicolas Barker (editors)

1990   *Fake? The Art of Deception*. British Museum Press, London.

Jones, Sian

1997   *The Archaeology of Ethnicity*. Routledge, London.

Joseph, Garnette

1997   Five Hundred Years of Indigenous Resistance. In *The Indigenous Peoples of the Caribbean*, edited by Samuel Wilson, pp. 214–222. University Press of Florida, Gainesville.

Joyce, Rosemary E.

2008   Critical Histories of Archaeological Practice: Latin American and North American Interpretations in a Honduran Context. In *Evaluating Multiple Narratives: Beyond Nationalist, Colonialist, Imperialist Archaeologies*, edited by Junko Habu, Clare Fawcett, and John M. Matsunaga, pp. 56–68. Springer, New York.

2013   When Is Authentic? Situating Authenticity in Itineraries of Objects. In *Creating Authenticity: Authentication Process in Ethnographic Museums*, edited by Alexander Geurds and Laura Van Broekhoven, pp. 39–57. Sidestone Press, Leiden.

2019   Making Markets for Mesoamerican Antiquities. In *The Market for Mesoamerica: Reflections on the Sale of Pre-Columbian Antiquities*, edited by Cara G. Tremain and Donna Yates, pp. 1–15. University Press of Florida, Gainesville.

Joyce, Thomas. A.

1907   Prehistoric Antiquities from the Antilles, in the British Museum. *Journal of the Royal Anthropological Institute of Great Britain and Ireland* 37:402–419.

1916   *Central American and West Indian Archaeology: Being an Introduction to the Archaeology of the States of Nicaragua, Costa Rica, Panama, and the West Indies*. Cambridge University Press, Cambridge.

Junta Nacional de Arqueología y Etnología

1946   Legislación sobre arqueología aborigen, arqueología colonial: Declaraciones de monumentos nacionales y etnología. *Revista de Arqueología y Etnología* 1(2):12–23.

Kay, Katheryne

1976   A Survey of Antillean Sculptured Stone. In *Proceedings of the VI International Congress for the Study of Pre-Columbian Cultures of the Lesser Antilles* (1975 IACA), pp. 187–199. Guadeloupe, France (FWI).

Kaye, Quetta

2003   A Field Survey of the Island of Carriacou, West Indies, March 2003. *Papers from the Institute of Archaeology* 14:129–135.

Kaye, Quetta, Scott Burnett, Scott M. Fitzpatrick, Michiel Kappers, and John G. Swogger
    2009   Archaeological Investigations on Carriacou, West Indies, 7th July–
          9th August 2008. Fieldwork and Public Archaeology. *Papers from the
          Institute of Archaeology* 19:91–99.

Kaye, Quetta, Scott M. Fitzpatrick, Mary Hill Harris, and Michiel Kappers
    2012   Bowls and Burials—An Update from Grand Bay, Carriacou, West
          Indies, May–June 2011. *Papers from the Institute of Archaeology*
          21:91–100.

Kaye, Quetta, Scott M. Fitzpatrick, Christina Giovas, Mary Hill Harris, Michiel Kappers, and John G. Swogger
    n.d.   Archaeological Investigations on Carriacou (forthcoming mono-
          graph).

Keegan, William F.
    2009   Benjamin Irving Rouse. *Biographical Memoirs* 90:306–331. www.nap
          .edu, accessed November 16, 2018.
    2017   The Archaeology of the Caribbean. *Oxford Bibliographies.* Latin
          American Studies. DOI:10.1093/OBO/9780199766581-0191.

Keegan, William F., and Lesley-Gail Atkinson
    2006   The Development of Jamaican Prehistory. In *The Earliest Inhabitants:
          The Dynamics of the Jamaican Taino*, edited by Lesley-Gail Atkinson,
          pp. 13–33. University of the West Indies Press, Kingston.

Keegan, William F., and Ann K. Cody
    1990   *Progress Report on the Archaeological Excavations at the Site of
          Pearls, Grenada, August 1989.* Miscellaneous Project Report no. 44.
          Florida Museum of Natural History, Gainesville.

Keegan, William F., and Corinne L. Hofman
    2017   *The Caribbean before Columbus.* Oxford University Press, Oxford.

Keegan, William F., Corinne L. Hofman, and Reniel Rodríguez Ramos
    2013   *The Oxford Handbook of Caribbean Archaeology.* Oxford University
          Press, Oxford.

Kelker, Nancy L., and Karen O. Bruhns
    2010   *Faking Ancient Mesoamerica.* Left Coast Press, Walnut Creek.

Kerchache, J. (editor)
    1994   *L'art des sculpteurs Taïnos: Chefs-d'oevre des Grandes Antilles préco-
          lombiennes.* Musée du Petit Palais, Paris.

Kersel, Morag
    2006   *License to Sell: The Legal Trade of Antiquities in Israel.* PhD disserta-
          tion, University of Cambridge.
    2007   Transcending Borders: Objects on the Move *Archaeologies* 3:81–93.
    2008   The Trade in Palestinian Antiquities. *Jerusalem Quarterly* 33:21–38.
    2012   The Value of a Looted Object: Stakeholder Perceptions in the Antiq-
          uities Trade. In *The Oxford Handbook of Public Archaeology*, edited
          by Robin Skeates, Carol McDavid, and John Carman, pp. 253–272.
          Oxford University Press, London.

Knight, V. J.
2017 Database of Portable Representational Indigenous Art, Greater Antilles, with Notes on the Anthropomorphic Figurines. *Proceedings of the 26th Congress of the International Association for Caribbean Archaeology*, edited by Christopher B. Velasquez and Jay B. Haviser, Session 9: Art and Symbolism, pp. 1–16. SIMARC Heritage Series, No. 15, Saint Maarten, Lesser Antilles.

Knight, V. J. (compiler)
2019 *Database of Indigenous Portable Art and Personal Adornment, Late Ceramic Age, Greater Antilles.* University of Alabama Museums, Department of Museum Research and Collections. https://collections.museums.ua.edu.

Knight, Vernon James
2020 *Caribbean Figure Pendants: Style and Subject Matters; Anthropomorphic Figure Pendants of the Late Ceramic Age in the Greater Antilles.* Sidestone Press, Leiden.

Kohl, Philip I., and Clare Fawcett
1998 *Nationalism, Politics, and the Practice of Archaeology.* Cambridge University Press, Cambridge.

Kohl, Philip L, Irina Podgorny, and Stefanie Gänger
2014 *Nature and Antiquities: The Making of Archaeology in the Americas.* University of Arizona Press, Tucson.

Koreich, Hana, and Colin Sterling
2013 Archaeology and Economic Development. *Papers from the Institute of Archaeology* 22:158–165.

Laffoon, Jason E., Reniel Rodríguez Ramos, Luis Chanlatte Baik, Yvonne Narganes Storde, Miguel Rodríguez Lopez, Gareth R. Davies, and Corinne L. Hofman
2014 Long-Distance Exchange in the Precolonial Circum-Caribbean: A Multi-Isotope Study of Animal Tooth Pendants from Puerto Rico. *Journal of Anthropological Archaeology* 35(September):220–233. DOI:10.1016/j.jaa.2014.06.004.

Laguer Díaz, Carmen A.
2013 The Construction of an Identity and the Politics of Remembering. In *The Oxford Handbook of Caribbean Archaeology*, edited by W. F. Keegan, C. L. Hofman, and R. Rodríguez Ramos, pp. 557–567. Oxford University Press, Oxford.
2014 *The Historical Creation of Identities in Puerto Rico.* PhD dissertation, Department of Anthropology, University of Florida, Gainesville. ProQuest Dissertations.

Lange, Frederick W., and C. Mario Molina
1997 A Regional Approach to Cultural Preservation: A Central American Example. *Nonrenewable Resources* 6:137–149.

Las Casas, Bartolomé de
1875 *Historia de las Indias.* Volume 1. Imprenta de Manuel Ginesta, Madrid.

Latin American Herald Tribune
    2008   US Returns 67 Historic Artifacts to Dominican Republic, www.laht .com, accessed January 27, 2018.

Laughlin, Charles D., and Eugene G. d'Aquile
    1974   *Biogenetic Structuralism*. Columbia University Press, New York.

Lee, James W.
    1990   The Petroglyphs of Jamaica. *Proceedings of the XI International Congress of the International Association for Caribbean Archaeology* (IACA, 1985):153–161. Puerto Rico.

Leon, M. M.
    2018   Tesoros del Arte Taino: A pensar pensándonos. In *Tesoros del arte taino*. Centro Cultural Eduardo Leon Jimenes. 2nd ed., 6–11.

Lerner, J.
    2001   Brigído [*sic*; Brígido] Lara: Post-Pre-Columbian Ceramicist. *Cabinet Magazine* (2).

Levine, Marc N., and Lucah Martínez de Luna
    2013   Museum Salvage: A Case Study of Mesoamerican Artifacts in Museum Collections and on the Antiquities Market. *Journal of Field Archaeology* 38(3):264–276.

Lewis, C. Bernard
    1967   History and the Institute. *Jamaica Journal* 1(1):4–8.

Lewis-Williams, David, and David Pearce
    2005   *Inside the Neolithic Mind: Consciousness, Cosmos, and the Realm of the Gods*. Thames and Hudson, New York.

Lindenberg, M., and K. Oosterlinck
    2011   Art Collections as a Strategy Tool: Typology Based on the Belgian Financial Sector. *International Journal of Art Management* 13(3):4–19.

Lothrop, Samuel Kirkland
    1926   *Pottery of Costa Rica and Nicaragua*. 2 volumes. Museum of the American Indian, Heye Foundation, New York.

Lothrop, Samuel Kirkland, and Gonzalo Meneses Ocón
    1979   *Cerámica de Costa Rica y Nicaragua*. Fondo Cultural Banco de América, Managua.

Lowenthal, D.
    1992   Counterfeit Art: Authentic Fakes? *International Journal of Cultural Property* 1(1):79–104.

Luke, Christina
    2006   Diplomats, Banana Cowboys, and Archaeologists in Western Honduras: A History of the Trade in Pre-Columbian Materials. *International Journal of Cultural Property* 13:25–57.

Luke, Christina, and Morag Kersel (editors)
    2012   *US Cultural Diplomacy and Archaeology: Soft Power, Hard Heritage*. Taylor and Francis, New York.

McAlpine, Alistair
    1994   Hans Sloane: Collector, Scientist, Antiquary, Founding Father of the

British Museum. In *Sir Hans Sloane: Collector, Scientist, Antiquary, Founding Father of the British Museum*, edited by Arthur Mac-Gregor, p. 22. British Museum Press, London.

MacCormack, R. C.

 1898 Indian Remains in Vere, Jamaica. *Journal of the Institute of Jamaica* 2(5):444–448.

MacCurdy, George Grant

 1911 *A Study of Chiriquian Antiquities.* Memoirs of the Connecticut Academy of Arts and Sciences 3. Yale University Press, New Haven.

McGinnis, Shirley A. M.

 1997 *Ideographic Expression in the Precolumbian Caribbean.* Unpublished PhD dissertation, Department of Anthropology, University of Texas, Austin.

 2001 Patterns, Variations, and Anomalies in Ideographic Expression in the Precolumbian Caribbean. *Proceedings of the Eighteenth International Congress for Caribbean Archaeology* 2, edited by G. Richard, pp. 99–114. International Association for Caribbean Archaeology, Guadeloupe.

Mackenzie, Simon

 2005 *Going, Going, Gone: Regulating the Market in Illicit Antiquities.* Institute of Art and Law, London.

 2006 Psychosocial Balance Sheets: Illicit Purchase Decisions in the Antiquities Market. *Current Issues in Criminal Justice* 18:221–240.

 2007a Transnational Crime, Local Denial. *Social Justice* 34:111–124.

 2007b Dealing in Cultural Objects: A New Criminal Law for the UK. *Amicus Curiae: Journal of the Society for Advanced Legal Studies* 71:8–18.

 2011a The Market as Criminal and Criminals in the Market: Reducing Opportunities for Organised Crime in the International Antiquities Market. In *Crime in the Art and Antiquities World: Illegal Trafficking in Cultural Property*, edited by Stefano Manacorda and Duncan Chappell, pp. 69–84. Springer, New York.

 2011b Illicit Deals in Cultural Objects as Crimes of the Powerful. *Crime Law and Social Change* 56:133–253.

 2014 Conditions for Guilt-Free Consumption in a Transnational Criminal Market. *European Journal on Criminal Policy and Research* 20:503–515.

Mackenzie, Simon, Neil Brodie, Donna Yates, and Christos Tsirogiannis

 2019 *Trafficking Culture: New Directions in Researching the Global Market in Illicit Antiquities.* Routledge, London.

Mackenzie, Simon, and Tess Davis

 2014 Temple Looting in Cambodia: Anatomy of a Statue Trafficking Network. *British Journal of Criminology* 54:722–740.

Mackenzie, Simon, and Donna Yates

 2016 What Is Grey about the "Grey Market" in Antiquities. In *The Archi-*

tecture of Illegal Markets: Towards an Economic Sociology of Illegality in the Economy, edited by Jens Beckert and Matías Dewey, pp. 70–86. Oxford University Press, Oxford.

McMullen, Ann, and Maria Galban

2019   Lost and Found: Re-establishing Provenance for an Entire Museum Collection. In *Collecting and Provenance: A Multidisciplinary Approach*, edited by Jane Milosch and Nick Pearce, pp. 229–242. Rowman and Littlefield, Lanham, Maryland.

Mañón Arredondo, Manuel de Js.

1969   Porque no creo en la Cultura de los Paredones, Ahora! January 16, 1969. In 1999 *Historia de los Taínos Modernos*, edited by Rafael Pérez Guerra, pp. 144–154. Taller, Santo Domingo.

Maréchal, J.

1998   For an Island Museology in the Caribbean. *Museum International* 50(3):44–50.

Marichal Lugo, Flavia

1998   Biographies. In *Puerto Rico: Arte e identidad*. Hermandad de Artistas Gáficos de Puerto Rico, pp. 417–451. Editorial de la Universidad de Puerto Rico, San Juan.

Marlowe, Elizabeth

2013   *Shaky Ground: Context Connoisseurship and the History of Roman Art*. Bloomsbury, New York.

Martin, John Angus

2007   *A–Z of Grenada Heritage*. Macmillan Caribbean, Oxford.

2013   *Island Caribs and French Settlers in Grenada*. Grenada National Museum Press, St. George's.

Martin, John Angus, Joseph Opala, and Cynthia Schmidt

2016   *The Temne Nation of Carriacou*. Polyphemus Press, Chattanooga.

Martínez-Cruzado, Juan

2013   The DNA Evidence for the Human Colonization and Spread across the Americas: Implications for the Peopling of the Caribbean. In *The Oxford Handbook of Caribbean Archaeology*, edited by William F. Keegan, Corinne Lisette Hofman, and Reniel Rodríguez Ramos, pp. 470–485. Oxford University Press, New York.

Martínez-Cruzado, J. C., G. Toro-Labrador, V. Ho-Fung, M. A. Estévez- Montero, A. Lobaina-Manzanet, D.A. Padovani-Claudio, H. Sánchez-Cruz, P. Ortiz-Bermúdez, and A. Sánchez-Crespo

2001   Mitochondrial DNA Analysis Reveals Substantial Native American Ancestry in Puerto Rico. *Human Biology* 73:491 511.

Maslow, Abraham H.

1943   A Theory of Human Motivation. *Psychological Review* 50(4):370–396. DOI:10.1037/h0054346.

Mason, J. Alden

1945   *Costa Rican Stonework: The Minor Keith Collection*. Anthropological Papers 39, Part 3. American Museum of Natural History, New York.

Mason, Peter

    2005   "Canute Calliste" (obituary). *Guardian* (newspaper). November 25 2005, www.theguardian.com, accessed February 26, 2019.

Mathieu, James R.

    2002   Introduction—Experimental Archaeology: Replicating Past Objects, Behaviors, and Processes. In *Experimental Archaeology: Replicating Past Objects, Behaviors, and Processes*, edited by James R. Mathieu, pp. 1–11. BAR International Series 1035. Archaeopress, Oxford.

Matsuda, David

    1998   The Ethics of Archaeology, Subsistence Digging, and Artifact Looting in Latin America: Point and Muted Counterpoint. *International Journal of Cultural Property* 7:87–97.

M'Bow, Amadou-Mahtar

    1979   A Plea for the Return of an Irreplaceable Cultural Heritage to Those Who Created It. *Museum* 31(1):58.

Medrano, N.

    2011   Estados Unidos devuelve 59 piezas tainas a RD. Patrimonio, La Republica. Listin Diario. 19 de septiembre, 2011. https://listindiario.com, accessed November 4, 2019.

Meskell, Lynn

    2011   *The Nature of Heritage in the New South Africa*. Wiley-Blackwell, Oxford.

Miller, Daniel

    2002   Coca Cola: A Black Sweet Drink from Trinidad. In *The Material Culture Reader*, edited by Victor Buchli, pp. 245–263. Routledge, London.

Miller, Gerrit S.

    1932   Collecting the Caves and Kitchen Middens of Jamaica. In *Explorations and Field Work of the Smithsonian Institution in 1931*. Smithsonian Institution, Washington, DC.

Milosch, Jane, and Nick Pearce

    2019   *Collecting and Provenance: A Multidisciplinary Approach*. Rowman and Littlefield, Lanham, Maryland.

Ministry of Development and Welfare

    1967   *Ministry Paper No. 32 Jamaica National Trust Commission*. Ministry of Development and Welfare, Kingston.

Ministry of Justice

    1978   *The Institute of Jamaica Act*. http://moj.gov.jm, accessed October 20, 2018.

    1985   *The Jamaica National Heritage Trust Act*. http://moj.gov.jm, accessed October 20, 2018.

Mintz, Sidney

    2011   Did the Puerto Rico Project Have Consequences? A Personal View. *Identities: Global Studies in Culture and Power* 18:244–249.

Miranda, José David
 1998   Notes on the Development of the Ceramics in Puerto Rico. In
         Puerto Rico: Arte e identidad, Hermandad de Artistas Gáficos de
         Puerto Rico, pp. 315–321. Editorial de la Universidad de Puerto
         Rico, San Juan.

Mistretta, Brittany A.
 2018   Ripley Bullen's Grenada Ceramic Typology, www.bamarchaeology.com,
         accessed September 28, 2018.

Moanack, Gloria
 1980   Benyí o la agonia de un arte: Parte Segunda, Listin Diario, Septem-
         ber 20, 1980. In 1999 *Historia de los Taínos Modernos*, edited by
         Rafael Pérez Guerra, pp. 244–248. Taller, Santo Domingo.

Mol, Angus A. A.
 2007   *Costly Giving, Giving Guaízas: Towards an Organic Model of the
         Exchange of Social Valuables in the Late Ceramic Age Caribbean.*
         Sidestone Press, Leiden.

Morales Carrión, Arturo
 1983   The PPD Democratic Hegemony (1944–1969). In *Puerto Rico. A Po-
         litical and Cultural History*, edited by A. Morales Carrión, pp. 256–
         307. W. W. Norton, New York.

Morban Laucer, Fernando
 1968   *Los Paredones: Un santuario prehistórico.* Instituto de Investigaciones
         Antropológicas. Universidad de Autónoma de Santo Domingo,
         Santo Domingo.
 1989   Arte, falsificación, saqueo y destrucción. *Boletín del Museo del Hom-
         bre Dominicano* 22:51–63.

Morell-Deledalle, M.
 2010   The Copy as an Exhibit. Paper presented at the Annual Meeting of
         ICMAH-ICOM International Committee for Museums and Collec-
         tions of Archaeology and History. 22nd ICOM General Conference,
         Original, Copy, Fake: On the Significance of the Object in History
         and Archaeology Museums, Shanghai. Available at http://network
         .icom.museum, accessed December 18, 2018.

Mortensen, Lena
 2016   Artifacts and Others in Honduras. In *Challenging the Dichotomy:
         The Licit and the Illicit in Archaeological and Heritage Discourses*, ed-
         ited by Les Field, Cristóbal Gnecco, and Joe Watkins, pp. 56–74.
         University of Arizona Press, Tucson.

Moscoso, Francisco
 2003   *La revolución puertorriqueña de 1868: El Grito de Lares.* Editorial
         ICP, San Juan.

Museo del Barrio, El
 1981   *Los Tainos: A Visual Tradition.* An exhibit of modern and pre-
         Columbian images and decorations in contemporary use, 12
         March–14 May, 1982. El Museo del Barrio, New York.

Museum of the Institute of Jamaica

> 1895   *An Exhibition of Arawak Remains.* August 7, Museum of the Institute of Jamaica, Kingston. (Circular.)

Museums Association

> 2008   Code of Ethics for Museums: Ethical Principles for All Who Work for or Govern Museums in the UK. Museums Association, London. www.museumsassociation.org, accessed November 9, 2018.

MYCEDO (MYCEDO/Mt. Rich Carib Stone Interpretation Center)

> 2018   These are some of the visitors getting an on-site tour . . . they were well pleased and so they took photos with the tour guides . . . visit or contact us for bookings. Facebook, post and photos. July 2, 2018, www.facebook.com, accessed February 26, 2019.

Myers, Fred

> 2006   "Primitivism," Anthropology, and the Category of "Primitive Art." In *Handbook of Material Culture,* edited by Chris Tilley, Webb Keane, Susanne Küchler, Mike Rowlands, and Patricia Spyer, pp. 267–284. Sage Publications, London.

Myers, Kathleen Ann

> 2007   *Fernández de Oviedo's Chronicle of America: A New History for a New World.* University of Texas Press, Austin.

Narganes, Yvonne

> 2016   In Memorian: Luis A. Chanlatte Baik (1925–2016). *Diálogo.* December 13, 2016, http://dialogoupr.com, accessed December 15, 2017.

Navarro, E.

> 1973   *Motivos de arte en la cerámica indocubana.* Universidad de La Habana, Havana.

Neumüller, M., A. Reichinger, F. Rist, and C. Kern

> 2014   3D Printing for Cultural Heritage: Preservation, Accessibility, Research, and Education. In *3D Research Challenges in Cultural Heritage: A Roadmap in Digital Heritage Preservation,* edited by M. Loannides and E. Quak, pp. 119–134. Springer, Heidelberg.

Newsom, Lee A., and Elizabeth S. Wing

> 2004   *On Land and Sea: Native American Uses of Biological Resources in the West Indies.* University of Alabama Press, Tuscaloosa.

Nichols, M.

> 2006   Plaster Cast Sculpture: A History of Touch. *Archaeological Review from Cambridge* 21(2):114–130.

Núñez Jover, J., F. Castro Sánchez, I. Pérez Ones, L. F. Montalvo Arriete, A. Gallina, J. Núñez, and F. Montalvo

> 2007   Ciencia, tecnología y sociedad en Cuba: Construyendo una alternativa desde la propiedad social. In *Innovaciones creativas y desarrollo humano,* edited by A. Gallina, V. Capecchi, J. Núñez Jover, and L. F. Montalvo Arriete, pp. 185–209. Editora Trilce, Montevideo.

Odell, George H.

> 2000   Stone Tool Research at the End of the Millennium: Procurement and Technology. *Journal of Archaeological Research* 8(4):269–331.

2001   Stone Tool Research at the End of the Millennium: Classification, Function, and Behavior. *Journal of Archaeological Research* 9(1):45–100.

Oland, Maxine, Siobhan M. Hart, and Liam Frink

2012   *Decolonizing Indigenous Histories: Exploring Prehistoric/Colonial Transitions in Archaeology.* University of Arizona Press, Tucson.

Oliver, José R.

1998   *El centro ceremonial de Caguana, Puerto Rico: Simbolismo iconográfico, cosmovisión y el poderío caciquil taíno de Boriquén.* Vol. 727, International Series. British Archaeological Reports, Oxford.

2005   The Proto-Taíno Monumental *Cemís* of Caguana: A Political-Religious "Manifesto." In *Ancient Borinquen: Archaeology and Ethnohistory of Native Puerto Rico*, edited by Peter E. Siegel, pp. 230–284. University of Alabama Press, Tuscaloosa.

2008   El universo material y espiritual de los taínos. In *El Caribe precolombino: Fray Ramón Pané y el universo taíno*, edited by José R. Oliver, Colin McEwan, and Anna Casas Gilberga, pp.136–221. Ministerio de Cultura, Ajuntament de Barcelona-Institut de Cultura, Museu Barbier Mueller, and Fundación Caixa Galicia, Barcelona.

2009   *Caciques and Cemí Idols.* University of Alabama Press, Tuscaloosa.

2012   *Caguana: Legado histórico.* Editorial ICP, San Juan.

Oliver, José R., Colin McEwan, and Anna Casas Gilberga (editors)

2008   *El Caribe Pre-Colombino: Fray Ramón Pané y el Universo Taíno.* Ajuntament de Barcelona—Instituto de Cultura, Barcelona.

Oliver Aresti, José R.

1951   *Aportaciones a la historia de Arecibo: De la "fundación" o no "fundación" de Arecibo.* Unpublished manuscript, Open Access, www.academia.edu.

O'Neill, Paul

2012   *The Culture of Curating and the Curating of Culture(s).* MIT Press, Cambridge.

Orser, Charles E.

2012   An Archaeology of Eurocentrism. *American Antiquity* 77(4):737–755. DOI:10.7183/0002–7316.77.4.737.

Ortega, Elpidio J.

2005   La Cucama. In *Compendio General Arqueologico de Santo Domingo*, Vol. 1, pp. 71–77. Academia de Ciencias de Republica Dominicana, Santo Domingo.

Ostapkowicz, Joanna

1998   Taíno Wooden Sculpture: Duhos, Rulership, and the Visual Arts in the 12th–16th Century Caribbean. PhD thesis, University of East Anglia, Norwich.

2009   3D Laser Scanning the Pre-Hispanic Caribbean Sculptures. Liverpool Museums, www.liverpoolmuseums.org.uk, accessed February 28, 2019.

2015   The Sculptural Legacy of the Jamaican Taíno, Part 1: The Carpenter's Mountain Carvings. *Jamaica Journal* 35(3):52–59.

Ostapkowicz, Joanna, Fiona Brock, Alex C. Wiedenhoeft, Rick Schulting, and Donatella Saviola

    2017a   Integrating the Old World into the New: An "Idol from the West Indies." *Antiquity* 359(91):1314–1329.

Ostapkowicz, Joanna, Fiona Brock, Alex C. Wiedenhoeft, Christophe Snoeck, John Pouncett, Yasmin Baksh-Comeau, Rick Schulting, Philippe Claeys, Nadine Mattielli, Mike Richards, and Arie Boomert

    2017b   Black Pitch, Carved Histories: Radiocarbon Dating, Wood Species Identification and Strontium Isotope Analysis of Prehistoric Wood Carvings from Trinidad's Pitch Lake. *Journal of Archaeological Science: Reports* 16:341–358.

Ostapkowicz, Joanna, Christopher Bronk Ramsey, Fiona Brock, Caroline Cartwright, Rebecca Stacey, and Mike Richards

    2013   Birdmen, Cemis and Duhos: Material Studies and AMS ^{14}C Dating of Pre-Hispanic Caribbean Wood Sculptures in the British Museum. *Journal of Archaeological Science* 40(12):4675–4687.

Ostapkowicz, Joanna, Christopher Bronk Ramsey, Fiona Brock, Tom Higham, Alex C. Wiedenhoeft, Erika Ribechini, J. J. Lucejko, and Samuel Wilson

    2012   Chronologies in Wood and Resin: AMS ^{14}C Dating of Pre-Hispanic Caribbean Wood Sculpture. *Journal of Archaeological Science* 39:2238–251.

    2019   *Taínos: Arte y Sociedad*, Banco Popular Dominicano, Amigos del Hogar, Santo Domingo.

Ostapkowicz, Joanna, and Lee Newsom

    2012   Gods . . . Adorned with Embroiderer's Needle: The Materials, Making, and Meaning of a Taíno Cotton Reliquary. *Latin American Antiquity* 23:300–326.

Ostrowitz, Judith

    1999   *Privileging the Past: Reconstructing History in Northwest Coast Art.* University of Washington Press, Seattle.

Oyuela-Caycedo, Augusto (editor)

    1994   *History of Latin American Archaeology.* Avebury, Aldershot.

Pané, Fray Ramón

1999 [ca. 1495]   *An Account of the Antiquities of the Indians.* Introductory Study, Notes, and Appendixes by J. J. Arrom. Translated by S. G. Griswold. Duke University Press, Durham, North Carolina.

Paredes Maury, Sofia

    1999   *Surviving in the Rainforest: The Realities of Looting in the Rural Villages of El Petén, Guatemala.* FAMSI Report. Available at www.famsi.org, accessed February 28, 2019.

Pasztory, Esther

    2002   Truth in Forgery. *RES* 42:159–165.

Pateman, Michael P.

    2011   The Bahamas. In *Protecting Heritage in the Caribbean*, edited by Peter E. Siegel and Elizabeth Righter, pp. 1–8. Caribbean Archaeology and Ethnohistory. University of Alabama Press, Tuscaloosa.

Pearce, S. M.
    1990   *Archaeological Curatorship*. Smithsonian Institution Press, Washington, DC.

Pearce, S. M. (editor)
    1994a   *Museum Objects: Interpreting Objects and Collections*. Leicaster Readers in Museum Studies, pp. 9–11. Routledge, London.
    1994b   *The Urge to Collect: Interpreting Objects and Collections*. Leicaster Readers in Museum Studies, pp. 157–159. Routledge, London.

Pearson, James L.
    2002   *Shamanism and the Ancient Mind: A Cognitive Approach to Archaeology*. AltaMira, Walnut Creek.

Pérez Guerra, Rafael (editor)
    1999   *Historia de los taínos modernos: La verdad del arte lítico*. Los Paredones de la Caleta, República Dominicana. Taller, Santo Domingo.

Perry, Sara
    2018   Why Are Heritage Interpreters Voiceless at the Trowel's Edge? A Plea for Rewriting the Archaeological Workflow. *Advances in Archaeological Practice* 6(3):212–227.

Pestle William J.
    2010   Diet and Society in Prehistoric Puerto Rico, an Isotopic Approach. Department of Anthropology, University of Illinois at Chicago.

Petitjean Roget, Henry, Gerard Richard, and Lesley Sutty
    2000   Pearls Amerindian Settlement: First Phase Preliminary Study and Evaluation. International Association for Caribbean Archaeology (IACA), Guadeloupe, France (FWI).

Picó, Fernando
    1998   *1898: La guerra después de la guerra*. Ediciones Huracán, Río Piedras.

Pillsbury, Joanne
    2013   Perspectives: Representing the Pre-Columbian Past. In *Past Represented: Archaeological Illustration and the Ancient Americas*, edited by Joanne Pillsbury, pp. 1–48. Dumbarton Oaks, Washington, DC.

Pina, P.
    1978   *Legislación dominicana sobre museos y protección del patrimonio cultural, 1870–1977*. Ediciones Museo del Hombre Dominicano, Santo Domingo.

Pinart, Alphonse Louis
    1890   Note sur les pétroglyphes et antiquités des Grandes et Petites Antilles (manuscript). Rare Book and Manuscript Library, University of Pennsylvania, Ms. Coll 700, Item 211, http://dla.library.upenn.edu, accessed November 24, 2018.

Pitblado, Bonnie L.
    2014   An Argument for Ethical, Proactive, Archaeologist-Artifact Collector Collaboration. *American Antiquity* 79(3):385–400. https://doi.org/10.7183/0002-7316.79.3.385.

Poupeye, Veerle

2019a   The Wheels of History: Museums, Restitution, and the Caribbean—
Part 1. https://veerlepoupeye.wordpress.com, accessed May 12, 2019.

2019b   The Wheels of History: Museums, Restitution and the Caribbean—
Part 2. https://veerlepoupeye.wordpress.com, accessed May 12, 2019.

Premio a la Excelencia Artesanal

2012   *5.0 Premio a la Excelencia Artesanal Instituto de Cultura Puertorriqueña.* San Juan.

Price, Sally

1989   *Primitive Art in Civilized Places.* University of Chicago Press, Chicago.

Priego, Joaquin

1967   Sublime Ideal, Listín Diario, January 21, 1967. In 1999 *Historia de
los Taínos Modernos,* edited by Rafael Pérez Guerra, pp. 111–113.
Taller, Santo Domingo.

Prieto Vicioso, E.

2011   Dominican Republic. In *Protecting Heritage in the Caribbean,* edited
by Peter E. Siegel and Elizabeth Righter, pp. 35–45. University of
Alabama Press, Tuscaloosa.

Proudfoot, Edmund

1772   Edmund Proudfoot and Thomas Proudfoot, Esquires to Thomas
Smith, Esqr., Mortgage for Securing . . . (docket title). Hamilton
College, New York. M214. Proudfoot, Edmund, fl. 1772. Beinecke
Lesser Antilles Collection, http://beinecke.hamilton.edu, accessed
December 14, 2018.

Puri, Shalini

2014   *The Grenada Revolution in the Caribbean Present: Operation Urgent
Memory.* Palgrave Macmillan, New York.

Quesada, M. A.

2004   Isabel la Católica: Perfil politico de un reinado decisivo. In *Isabel la
Católica: La magnificencia de un reinado; Quinto centenario de Isabel
la Católica, 1504–2004,* edited by Sociedad Estatal de Conmemora-
ciones Culturales, pp. 33–48. Junta de Castilla y Leon, Valladolid.

Radnoti, Sandor

1999   *The Fake: Forgery and Its Place in Art.* Rowman and Littlefield, Oxford.

Rainey, Froelich G.

1940   *Porto Rican Archaeology.* Scientific Survey of Porto Rico and the Virgin Islands 18(1). New York Academy of Sciences, New York.

Rangel, A.

2012   *Antropología en Cuba: Orígenes y desarrollo.* Fundación Fernando
Ortiz, Havana.

Reid, Basil A., and Vel Lewis

2011   Trinidad and Tobago. In *Protecting Heritage in the Caribbean,* edited by Peter E. Siegel and Elizabeth Righter, pp. 125–133. Caribbean
Archaeology and Ethnohistory. University of Alabama Press, Tuscaloosa.

Renfrew, Colin
    2000   *Loot, Legitimacy, and Ownership: The Ethical Crisis in Archaeology.* Bristol Classical Press, Bristol.
    2006   *Figuring It Out: What Are We? Where Do We Come From? The Parallel Visions of Artists and Archaeologists.* Thames and Hudson, London.

Renfrew, Colin, Chris Gosden, and Elizabeth DeMarrais (editors)
    2004   *Substance, Memory, Display: Archaeology and Art.* McDonald Institute of Archeological Research. University of Cambridge, Cambridge.

Renfrew, Colin, and Ezra B. W. Zubrow (editors)
    1994   *The Ancient Mind: Elements of Cognitive Archaeology.* Cambridge University Press, Cambridge.

Richards, Andrea
    2012   Regulating the Movement of Cultural Property Within and Out of Jamaica. In *Caribbean Heritage*, edited by Basil A. Reid, pp. 356–366. University of the West Indies Press, Kingston.

Rivera Fontán, Juan, and José R. Oliver
    2003   Impactos y patrones de ocupación histórica jíbara sobre componentes Taínos: El sitio "Vega De Nelo Vargas" (Utu-27), Barrio Caguana, Municipio De Utuado, Puerto Rico. *Proceedings 20th International Congress for Caribbean Archaeology* 1:1–14. Museo del Hombre Dominicano and Fundación García Arévalo, Santo Domingo.

Robertson, James
    2014   Cundall, Frank (1858–1937). In *Encyclopedia of Caribbean Archaeology*, edited by Basil A. Reid and Grant R. Gilmore III, pp. 120–121, University Press of Florida, Gainesville.

Robiou Lamarche, Sebastián
    2004   *Taínos y Caribes: Las culturas aborígenes antillanas.* Punto y Coma, San Juan.

Rodríguez, C.
    2000   Apuntes sobre la figura del murciélago en la iconografía prehispánica de Cuba. *El Caribe Arqueológico* (4):94–99.

Rodríguez Álvarez, Miguel
    2010   *Boriquén: Breve Historia de los Indios de Puerto Rico.* Editorial Nuevo Mundo. CreateSpace Independent Publishing Platform.

Rodríguez Cullel, C.
    2000   *Autobiografía.* Archives of Departamento Centro-Oriental de Arqueología, Holguín.

Rodriguez Ramos, Reniel
    2010   *Rethinking Puerto Rican Precolonial History.* University of Alabama Press, Tuscaloosa.
    2019   *La colección de las piedras del Padre Nazario.* Ediciones de la Universidad de Puerto Rico–Recinto de Utuado, Río Piedras.

Rodríguez Ramos, Reniel, and Jaime R. Pagán Jiménez
    2016   Sobre nuestras indigenidades boricuas. In *Indígenas e indios en el*

Caribe: Presencia, legado y estudio, edited by Jorge Ulloa Hung and Roberto Valcárcel Rojas, pp. 97–114. Instituto Tecnologico de Santo Domingo, Santo Domingo.

Rodríguez Velez, Wendalina

 1982 Despues de la Aventura: Benyí, HOY, June 23, 1982. In 1999 *Historia de los Taínos Modernos*, edited by Rafael Pérez Guerra, pp. 249–256. Taller, Santo Domingo.

Roe, P.

 1997 Epilogue: The Beaded Zemi in the Pigorini Museum. In *Taíno: Pre-Columbian Art and Culture from the Caribbean*, edited by F. Brecht, E. Brodsky, J. A. Farmer, and D. Taylor, pp. 164–169. Monacelli, New York.

Rojas, I., and M. París

 2017 *José Agustín García Castañeda: Un científico holguinero del siglo XX.* Editorial La Mezquita, Holguín.

Rouse, Irving

 1939 *Prehistory in Haiti: A Study in Method.* Yale University Publications in Anthropology 24, New Haven.

 1942 *Archaeology of the Maniabón Hills, Cuba.* Yale University Publications in Anthropology 26, New Haven.

 1952a *Porto Rican Prehistory: Introduction; Excavations in the West and North.* Scientific Survey of Porto Rico and the Virgin Islands 18(3). New York Academy of Sciences, New York.

 1952b *Porto Rican Prehistory: Excavations in the Interior, South and East; Chronological Implications.* Scientific Survey of Porto Rico and the Virgin Islands 18(4). New York Academy of Sciences, New York.

 1961 The Bailey Collection of Stone Artifacts from Puerto Rico. In *Essays in Pre-Columbian Art and Archaeology*, edited by S. K. Lothrop, pp. 342–355. Harvard University Press, Cambridge.

 1964 Prehistory of the West Indies. *Science*, new series, 144(3618):499–513.

 1977 Patterns and Process in West Indian Archaeology. *Journal of World Archaeology* 7(1): 1–11.

 1992 *The Taino: Rise and Decline of the People Who Greeted Columbus.* Yale University Press, New Haven.

Rowe, Marcia

 2011 Antique Dealers Celebrate 20 Years. *The Gleaner.* http://jamaica-gleaner.com, accessed October 26, 2019.

Rowland, Kurt F.

 1976 *Visual Education and Beyond.* Ginn, London.

Royo, F.

 1948 La colección Fornaguera. *Revista de Arqueología y Etnología* 2(6–7): 99–107.

RPA

 2019 Code of Conduct. Baltimore, MD: Register of Professional Archaeologists. https://rpanet.org, accessed May 24, 2019.

Rubiano, A. H.

2013   *Arte y falsificaciones: El mito de la originalidad*. Master's thesis, Universidad Nacional de Colombia, Bogotá.

Rubin, William

1984   *"Primitivism" in 20th Century Art: Affinity of the Tribal and the Modern*. Museum of Modern Art, New York.

Ruíz Mederos, Rafael (film director)

2019   Interview segment with Martín Caciba Opil Veguilla. In *Eat, Drink, Share Puerto Rico Food—Barbacoa Taína*, minutes 3:02–13:22. YouTube, accessed July 29, 2019, https://www.youtube.com.

Russell, Ian A., and Andrew Cochrane (editors)

2014   *Art and Archaeology: Collaborations, Conversations, Criticism*. Springer, New York.

Russo, A.

2011   Cortes's Objects and the Idea of New Spain. *Journal of the History of Collections*. Advance Access published January 21, pp. 1–24.

Sackler, E. A.

1998   The Ethics of Collecting. *International Journal of Cultural Property* 7(1):132–140.

Sandis, Constantine

2016   An Honest Display of Fakery: Replicas and the Role of Museums. *Royal Institute of Philosophy Supplement* 79:241–259.

Santos, Danilo de los

1983   Artes plásticas, Hoy, March 12, 1983. In 1999, *Historia de los Taínos Modernos*, edited by Rafael Pérez Guerra, pp. 257–260. Taller, Santo Domingo.

Santos, P., S. Pena Serna, A. Stork, and D. Fellner

2014   The Potential of 3D Internet in the Cultural Heritage Domain. In *3D Research Challenges in Cultural Heritage*, edited by M. Ioannides and E. Quak, pp. 1–17. Springer, Berlin.

Saraydar, Stephen C.

2008   *Replicating the Past: The Art and Science of the Archaeological Experiment*. Waveland Press, Long Grove, Illinois.

Saunders, Nicholas, and Dorrick Gray

2006   Zemís, Trees, and Symbolic Landscapes: Three Taíno Carvings from Jamaica. In *The Earliest Inhabitants: The Dynamics of the Jamaican Taino*, edited by Lesley-Gail Atkinson, pp. 187–198. University of the West Indies Press, Kingston.

Sax, Margaret, Jane M. Walsh, Ian C. Freestone, Andrew H. Rankin, and Nigel D. Meeks

2008   The Origins of Two Purportedly Pre-Columbian Mexican Crystal Skulls. *Journal of Archaeological Science* 35:2751–2760.

Schiappacasse, Paola

1994   Colecciones arqueológicas de Puerto Rico en cuatro museos del este de los Estados Unidos. Master's thesis, Centro de Estudios Avanzados de Puerto Rico y el Caribe, San Juan.

Schiffer, Michael Brian

2009   Ethnoarchaeology, Experimental Archaeology, and the "American School." *Ethnoarchaeology: Journal of Archaeological, Ethnographic, and Experimental Studies* 1(1):7–25.

Schnapp, A.

2011   Ancient Europe and Native Americans: A Comparative Reflection on the Roots of Antiquarianism. In *Collecting across Cultures: Material Exchanges in the Early Modern Atlantic World*, edited by Daniela Bleichmar and Peter C. Mancall, pp. 58–78. University of Pennsylvania, Philadelphia.

Schulz, E.

1994   Note on the History of Collecting and of Museums. In *Interpreting Objects and Collections*, edited by Susan M. Pierce, pp. 175–187. Leicester Readers in Museum Studies. Routledge, London.

Schwartz, Hillel

1996   *The Culture of the Copy: Striking Likenesses, Unreasonable Facsimilies*. MIT Press, Cambridge.

Sellen, Adam T.

2014   Anatomy of a Fake. *Ixiptla* 1:151–164.

Semenov, Sergei A.

1964   *Prehistoric Technology*, translated by M. W. Thompson. Barnes and Noble, New York.

Severino, Manuel

1968a   Califica de mito arqueológico llamado Arte de los Paredones, El Caribe, December 28, 1968. In 1999 *Historia de los Taínos Modernos*, edited by Rafael Pérez Guerra, pp. 92–95. Taller, Santo Domingo.

1968b   Motivos Indigenas popularizan arte, El Caribe, December 20, 1968. In 1999 *Historia de los Taínos Modernos*, edited by Rafael Pérez Guerra, pp. 85–89. Taller, Santo Domingo.

1969a   Sugiere mesa redonda entre los arqueologos, El Caribe, January 14, 1969. In 1999 *Historia de los Taínos Modernos*, edited by Rafael Pérez Guerra, pp. 114–118. Taller, Santo Domingo.

1969b   Muestran inconformidad por forma integrar grupo, El Caribe, January 27, 1969. In 1999 *Historia de los Taínos Modernos*, edited by Rafael Pérez Guerra, pp. 138–141. Taller, Santo Domingo.

Severino, Manuel, and María Ugarte

1969   Respalda investigación autenticidad Paredones, El Caribe, January 16, 1969. In 1999 *Historia de los Taínos Modernos*, edited by Rafael Pérez Guerra, pp. 119–127. Taller, Santo Domingo.

Shott, M. J., and B. Pitblado (guest editors)

2015   Pros and Cons of Consulting Collectors. The SAA Archaeological Record. *Society for American Archaeology* 15(5):11–39.

Siegel, Peter E.

1992   *Ideology, Power, and Social Complexity in Prehistoric Puerto Rico*. PhD dissertation. State University of New York, Binghamton.

1996   An Interview with Irving Rouse. *Current Anthropology* 37(4):671–689.

2011   Preface: Intersecting Values in Caribbean Heritage Preservation. In *Protecting Heritage in the Caribbean*, edited by Peter E. Siegel and Elizabeth Righter, pp. vii–xi. University of Alabama Press, Tuscaloosa.

Siegel, Peter E., and Elizabeth Righter (editors)
2011   *Protecting Heritage in the Caribbean*. University of Alabama Press, Tuscaloosa.

Siegel, Peter E., Corinne L. Hofman, Benoît Bérard, Reg Murphy, Jorge Ulloa Hung, Roberto Valcárcel Rojas, and Cheryl White
2013   Confronting Caribbean Heritage in an Archipelago of Diversity: Politics, Stakeholders, Climate Change, Natural Disasters, Tourism, and Development. *Journal of Field Archaeology* 38:376–390.

Silva Pagán, Daniel
2008   *Higüeras: Arte Taíno*. Unpublished manuscript prepared for the exhibition *Higüeras: Arte Taíno* at the Centro de Estudios Avanzados de Puerto Rico y El Caribe, San Juan, April.

Silverman, Sydel
2011   Introduction: The People of Puerto Rico Project Sixty Years Later. *Identities: Global Studies in Culture and Power* 18:179–184.

Sloane, Hans
1696   *Catalogus Plantarum Quae in Insula Jamaica Sponte Proveniunt (Catalogue of Jamaican Plants)*. Impensis D. Brown, London.
1707   *A Voyage to the Islands Madera, Barbados, Nieves, St. Christophers, and Jamaica with the Natural History of the Herbs and Trees, Four-Footed Beasts, Fishes, Birds, Insects, Reptiles etc.*, vol. 1. Printed by B. M. for the author, London.

Smith, Anthony D.
2001   Authenticity, Antiquity, and Archaeology. *Nations and Nationalism* 7:441–449.

Soanes, Catherine, and Angus Stevenson
2004   *Concise Oxford English Dictionary*. 11th edition. Oxford University Press, Oxford.

Society for American Archaeology
1996   Principles of Archaeological Ethics, www.saa.org, accessed February 28, 2019.
2018   Editorial Policy, Information for Authors, and Style Guide for *American Antiquity*, *Latin American Antiquity*, and *Advances in Archaeological Practice*. https://documents.saa.org, accessed on February 26, 2019.

Stahl Brower, Ann
2012   Material Histories. In *The Oxford Handbook of Material Culture Studies*, edited by Dan Hicks and Mary C. Beaudry, pp. 150–172. Oxford University Press, Oxford.

Staley, David P.
1993   St. Lawrence Island's Subsistence Diggers: A New Perspective on

Human Effects on Archaeological Sites. *Journal of Field Archaeology* 20(3):347–355. DOI:10.1179/jfa.1993.20.3.347.

Stam, D. C.

1993   The Informed Muse: The Implications of "The New Museology" for Museum Practice. *Journal of Museum Management and Curatorship* 12(3):267–283.

Starrenburg, S.

2018   Cultural Heritage Protection: A Truly "Global" Legal Problem? Völkerrechtsblog September 5, 2018. DOI:10.17176/20180919-181637-0. http://voelkerrechtsblog.org, accessed February 27, 2019.

Stephens, John Lloyd

1841   *Incidents of Travel in Central America, Chiapas, and Yucatan.* 2 vols. Harper and Brothers, New York.

Stevens Arroyo, Antonio M.

2006   *Cave of the Jagua: The Mythological World of the Taínos.* 2nd ed. University of Scranton Press, Scranton, Pennsylvania.

Steward, Watt

1964   *Keith and Costa Rica: The Biography of Minor Cooper Keith, American Entrepreneur.* University of New Mexico Press, Albuquerque.

Steward, Julian H., Robert A. Manners, Erik Wolf, Elena Padilla Seda, Sidney W. Mintz, and Raymond L. Shelley

1956   *The People of Puerto Rico: A Study in Social Anthropology.* University of Illinois Press, Urbana.

Stewart, Charles

1999   Syncretism and Its Synonyms: Reflections on Cultural Mixture. *Diacritics* 29(3):40–62.

2007   Creolization: History, Ethnography, Theory. In *Creolization: History, Ethnography, Theory*, edited by C. Stewart, pp. 1–25. Left Coast Press, Walnut Creek.

2011   Creolization, Hybridity, Syncretism, Mixture. *Portuguese Studies* 27(1):48–55.

Stylianou, Elena

2013   Broadening Museum Pedagogy: An Art Intervention at the Archaeological Museum of Cyprus by Angelos Makrides and Phanos Kyriacou. In *Mediterranean Art and Education: Navigating Local, Regional, and Global Imaginaries through the Lens of the Arts and Learning*, edited by J. Baldacchino and R. Vella. Sense Publishers, Rotterdam.

Sued-Badillo, Jalil

1978   *Los Caribes: Realidad o fabula.* Editorial Antillana, San Juan.

1992   Facing Up to Caribbean History. *American Antiquity* 57(4):599–607.

1995   The Island Caribs: New Approaches to the Question of Ethnicity in the Early Colonial Caribbean. In *Wolves from the Sea*, edited by N. Whitehead, pp. 62–89. KITLV Press, Leiden.

2008   *Agüeybana El Bravo.* Ediciones Puerto, Colombia.

Sutton, Mike
    1998   *Handling Stolen Goods and Theft: A Market Reduction Approach.* Home Office Research Study 178. Home Office Research and Statistics Directorate, London. http://webarchive.nationalarchives.gov.uk, accessed February 28, 2019.

Swogger, John G.
    2000   Image and Interpretation: The Tyranny of Representation? In *Towards Reflexive Method in Archaeology: The Example at Çatalhöyük,* edited by Ian Hodder, pp. 143–152. Oxbow Books, Oxford.
    2015   Ceramics, Polity, and Comics: Visually Re-presenting Formal Archaeological Publication. *Advances in Archaeological Practice* 3(1):16–28.
    2018   The Grenada Heritage Comics Facebook Public Group. Photos include ten comic strips. www.facebook.com, accessed February 26, 2019.

Tabío, E.
    1984   Nueva periodización para el estudio de las comunidades aborígenes de Cuba. *Islas* (78):35–52.

Tabío, E., and J. M. Guarch Delmonte
    1966   *Excavaciones en Arroyo del Palo.* Academia de Ciencias de Cuba, Havana.

Tabío, E., and E. Rey
    1985   *Prehistoria de Cuba.* Editorial de Ciencias Sociales, Havana.

Tamers, M. A.
    1969   Instituto Venezolano de investigaciones científicas natural radiocarbon measurements IV. *Radiocarbon* 11(2):396–422.

Taylor, Caldwell
    2009   The Story of the Shortknee Part 1/2. https://spicemasgrenada.com, accessed June 8, 2020.

Tejera, Emilio
    1977   *Indigenismos.* Editora de Santo Domingo, Santo Domingo.

Thomas, David Hurst
    1998   *Archaeology.* 4th ed. Harcourt Brace College Publishers, San Diego.

Thomas, N.
    2016   *The Return of Curiosity: What Museums Are Good For in the 21st Century.* Reaktion Books, London.

Tijhuis, Antonius Johannes Gerhardus
    2006   *Transnational Crime and the Interface between Legal and Illegal Actors: The Case of the Illicit Art and Antiquities Trade.* PhD dissertation, Leiden University.

Tió, Elsa
    2003   *El Cartel en Puerto Rico.* Prentice Hall, Mexico City.

Toftgaard, Casper J.
    2017   The Huecan Style in the US Virgin Islands—"Old" Evidence from the National Museum of Denmark. *Proceedings of the XXVII Con-*

gress of the International Association for Caribbean Archaeology (2017 IACA). St. Croix.

Torres, Constantino

1991   *Taíno: Los descubridores de Colón.* Museo Chileno de arte precolombino, Santiago.

Torres Etayo, Daniel

2006   *Tainos: Mitos y realidades de un pueblo sin rostro.* Asesor Pedagógico, Mexico City.

2011   Cuba. In *Protecting Heritage in the Caribbean*, edited by Peter E. Siegel and Elizabeth Righter, pp. 9–14. Caribbean Archaeology and Ethnohistory. University of Alabama Press, Tuscaloosa.

Tremain, Cara G.

2017   Fifty Years of Collecting: The Sale of Ancient Maya Antiquities at Sotheby's. *International Journal of Cultural Property* 24(2):187–219. DOI:10.1017/S0940739117000054.

Tremain, Cara G., and Donna Yates

2019   *The Market for Mesoamerica: Reflections on the Sale of Pre-Columbian Antiquities.* University Press of Florida, Gainesville.

Trustees of the British Museum

2017   Sir Hans Sloane. www.britishmuseum.org, accessed October 21, 2019.

Ugarte, María

1968   Explica motive imiten piezas indigenas, El Caribe, December 26, 1968. In 1999 *Historia de los Taínos Modernos*, edited by Rafael Pérez Guerra, pp. 90–92. Taller, Santo Domingo.

1969a   Aparecen cerca de 25 mil piezas, El Caribe, January 11, 1969. In 1999 *Historia de los Taínos Modernos*, edited by Rafael Pérez Guerra, pp. 111–113. Taller, Santo Domingo.

1969b   Declaración cambia fase de polemica, El Caribe, January 31, 1969. In 1999 *Historia de los Taínos Modernos*, edited by Rafael Pérez Guerra, pp. 161–167. Taller, Santo Domingo.

1969c   Se comprueba autenticidad pieza, El Caribe, January 4, 1969. In 1999 *Historia de los Taínos Modernos*, edited by Rafael Pérez Guerra, pp. 100–106. Taller, Santo Domingo.

1969d   Defienden autenticidad los Paredones, El Caribe, January 1, 1969. In 1999 *Historia de los Taínos Modernos*, edited by Rafael Pérez Guerra, pp. 96–99. Taller, Santo Domingo.

1969e   Los Paredones: Fenomeno artistico sin precedentes, El Caribe, February 15, 1969. In 1999 *Historia de los Taínos Modernos*, edited by Rafael Pérez Guerra, pp. 206–209. Taller, Santo Domingo.

1969f   Confirman como mito cultura los Paredones, El Caribe, February 1, 1969. In 1999 *Historia de los Taínos Modernos*, edited by Rafael Pérez Guerra, pp. 170–174. Taller, Santo Domingo.

1969g   Estima arte auténtico caso de los Paredones, El Caribe February 3, 1969. In 1999 *Historia de los Taínos Modernos*, edited by Rafael Pérez Guerra, pp. 181–182. Taller, Santo Domingo.

Ugarte, María, and Manuel Severino
    1969   Remite archivos, El Caribe, January 18, 1969. In 1999 *Historia de los Taínos Modernos*, edited by Rafael Pérez Guerra, pp. 127–132. Taller, Santo Domingo.

Ulloa Hung, Jorge
    2018a   El Sello de Thimo. *Ciencia y Sociedad* 43(2):83–95.
    2018b   Legado indígena: Cerámica y artesanía en la República Dominicana. In *Indígenas e indios: Presencia, legado y estudio*, edited by Jorge Ulloa Hung and Roberto Valcárcel Rojas, pp. 369–423. INTEC-Editora Búho, Santo Domingo.

Ulloa Hung, Jorge, and Roberto Valcárcel Rojas (editors)
    2016   *Indígenas e indios en el Caribe: Presencia, legado y estudio*. Instituto Tecnologico de Santo Domingo, Santo Domingo.

UNESCO
    2017a   *Illicit Trafficking of Cultural Property*. www.unesco.org, accessed November 17, 2018.
    2017b   *Jamaica Non-Ratified Convention*. http://portal.unesco.org, accessed December 6, 2018.

UNHCR/Refworld
    2007   World Directory of Minorities and Indigenous Peoples—Grenada. www.refworld.org, accessed February 26, 2019.

Uriely, Natan
    2005   The Tourist Experience: Conceptual Developments. *Annals of Tourism Research* 32:199–216.

USAID
    1991   *Final Evaluation—Eastern Caribbean Cocoa Rehabilitation and Development Project (USAID Grant No. 538–0140.2)*. USAID, Barbados. http://pdf.usaid.gov, accessed January 2, 2019.

Uyemura, K. J.
    1967   *The Artistic Works of Ivan Gundrum: With Particular Reference to His Reproductions of Clay Artifacts of the Florida Gulf Coast Indians*. Master's thesis, Florida State University, Tallahassee.

Valera Castillo, Yamel, and Faustino Peralta Montero
    2012   República Dominicana: Las artesanias una tradicion de origen Taíno. In *Estado del arte del sector artesanal en Latinoamerica*, edited by Adriana Patricia Uribe Uran, pp. 165–180. Ciencia y tecnología para el desarrollo (CYTED), Programa Iberoamericano. Universidad Simón Bolívar, Barranquilla.

Valcárcel Rojas, R.
    2016a   Irving Rouse en Maniabón. In *Un rostro local para la Arqueología Cubana*, edited by R. V. Rojas and J. A. Cardet, pp. 55–60. Editorial Nuevos Mundos–La Mezquita, Holguín.
    2016b   Los caminos de la arqueología en Cuba y Holguín. In *Un rostro local para la Arqueología Cubana*, edited by R. Valcárcel Rojas and J. A. Cardet, pp. 153–174. Editorial Nuevos Mundos–La Mezquita, Holguín.

2016c   *Archaeology of Early Colonial Interaction at El Chorro de Maíta, Cuba*. University Press of Florida, Gainesville.

Valcárcel Rojas, R., J. Cooper, J. Calvera, O. Brito, and M. Labrada
2006   Postes en el mar: Excavación de una estructura constructiva aborigen en Los Buchillones. *El Caribe Arqueológico* 9:76–88.

Valcárcel Rojas, R., A. Samson, and M. Hoogland
2013   Indo-Hispanic Dynamics: From Contact to Colonial Interaction in the Greater Antilles. *International Journal of Historical Archaeology* 17(1):18–39.

Valcárcel Rojas, Roberto, and Jorge Ulloa Hung
2018   Introducción: La desaparición del indígena y la permanencia del indio. In *De la desaparición a la permanencia: Indígenas e indios en la reinvención del Caribe*, edited by Roberto Valcárcel Rojas and Jorge Ulloa Hung, pp. 5–39. INTEC-Editora Búho, Santo Domingo.

Van Broekhoven, Laura, Cunera Buijs, and Pieter Hovens (editors)
2010   *Sharing Knowledge and Cultural Heritage: First Nations of the Americas; Studies in Collaboration with Indigenous Peoples from Greenland, North and South America*. Sidestone Press, Leiden.

Van Velzen, Diura Thoden
1996   The World of Tuscan Tomb Robbers: Living with the Legal Community and the Ancestors. *International Journal of Cultural Property* 5:111–126.

Vasconcelos, D. E., L. Á. Urgellés, and H. Jiménez
2004   Doctor René Herrera Fritot. *Gabinete de Arqueología* 3:154–160.

Vega, Bernardo
1987   *Arte NeoTaíno*. Fundación Cultural Dominicana, Santo Domingo.
2014   Los Paredones: ¿Arte precolombino o falsificaciones contemporáneas? *Hoy Digital*. June 14. http://hoy.com.do, accessed February 27, 2019.
2015   Los Paredones: ¿Arte precolombino o falsificaciones contemporáneas? *Boletín Museo del Hombre Dominicano* 46:49–59.

Veloz Maggiolo, Marcio
1968a   *Interpretación socio cultural del arte de Los Paredones*. Instituto de Investigaciones Antropológicas de la Universidad de Autonoma de Santo Domingo, Santo Domingo.
1968b   Paredones: Una nueva cultura antillana, Revista: Mundo Hispano, Madrid, November 1968. In 1999 *Historia de los Taínos Modernos*, edited by Rafael Pérez Guerra, pp. 78–85. Taller, Santo Domingo.
1969   Sobre Paredones: Una respuesta a Luis Chanlatte, Ahora! February 3, 1969. In 1999 *Historia de los Taínos Modernos*, edited by Rafael Pérez Guerra, pp. 174–181. Taller, Santo Domingo.

Vergo, P. (editor)
1989   *The New Museology*. Reaktion Books, London.

Vernon, K. C., Hugh Payne, and J. Spector
1959   *Grenada*. Soil and Land-Use Surveys no. 9. Soils Research and Survey Section, Regional Research Centre, Imperial College of Tropical Agriculture, Trinidad and Tobago.

Vilches, E.

2004   Columbus' Gift: Representations of Grace and Wealth and the Enterprise of the Indies. *Modern Language Notes* 119(2):201–225.

Waldron, Lawrence

2016   *Handbook of Ceramic Animal Symbols in the Ancient Lesser Antilles.* University Press of Florida, Gainesville.

2019   *Pre-Columbian Art of the Caribbean.* University Press of Florida, Gainesville.

Walker, Jeffery B.

1993   Stone Collars, Elbow Stones, and Three-Pointers, and the Nature of Taino Ritual and Myth. PhD dissertation, Department of Anthropology, Washington State University, Pullman.

Walsh, Jane MacLaren

2005   What Is Real? A New Look at Pre-Columbian Mesoamerican Collections. *AnthroNotes* 26(1):1–7; 18–19.

Watson, Peter, and Cecilia Todeschini

2007   *The Medici Conspiracy: The Illicit Journey of Looted Antiquities from Italy's Tomb Raiders to the Word's Greatest Museums.* Public Affairs, New York.

Wendel, P. T.

2007   Protecting Newly Discovered Antiquities: Thinking Outside the "Fee Simple" Box. *Fordham Law Review* 76(2):1015–1063. http://ir.lawnet.fordham.edu, accessed February 27, 2019.

Whisnant, David E.

1995   *Rascally Signs in Sacred Places: The Politics of Culture in Nicaragua.* University of North Carolina Press, Chapel Hill.

Whitehead, Neil (editor)

1995   *Wolves from the Sea*, edited by N. Whitehead, pp. 62–89. KITLV Press, Leiden.

Whiting, John S.

1983   Museum Focused Heritage in the English-Speaking Caribbean. UNESCO Technical Report PP/1981–1983/4/7.6/04. UNESCO, Paris. https://unesdoc.unesco.org, accessed February 3, 2019.

Wild, Kenneth

2003   Defining Petroglyphs from the Archeological Record. *Proceedings of the XXI Congress of the International Association for Caribbean Archaeology* (IACA, 2002). Santo Domingo, Dominican Republic.

Wilder, Leon W.

1980   Stone Artifacts of Grenada, West Indies. Grenada National Museum.

Wilson, Samuel M.

1993   The Cultural Mosaic of the Indigenous Caribbean. *Proceedings of the British Academy* 81:37–66.

2001   Cultural Pluralism and the Emergence of Complex Societies in the Greater Antilles. In *Proceedings of the Eighteenth International Congress for Caribbean Archaeology*, edited by G. Richard, pp. 7–12. International Association for Caribbean Archaeology, Guadeloupe.

  2007   *The Archaeology of the Caribbean.* Cambridge University Press, New York.

Wolf, Eric
  1990   Distinguished Lecture: Facing Power—Old Insights, New Questions. *American Anthropologist* 92(3):586–596.

Woodward, Robyn P.
  2006   *Medieval Legacies: The Industrial Archaeology of an Early Sixteenth-Century Sugar Mill at Sevilla la Nueva, Jamaica.* PhD dissertation, Simon Fraser University, Burnaby.

Yan, B.
  2010   Significance of Originals and Replicas in Archaeological Site Museums with a Case Study of the Han Dynasty Site Museums in China. Paper presented at the Annual Meeting of ICMAH-ICOM International Committee for Museums and Collections of Archaeology and History. 22nd ICOM General Conference. Original, Copy, Fake: On the Significance of the Object in History and Archaeology Museums, Shanghai. http://network.icom.museum, accessed December 14, 2018.

Yates, Donna
  2006   South America on the Block: The Changing Face of Pre-Columbian Antiquities Auctions in Response to International Law. Master's dissertation, University of Cambridge.
  2014   Church Theft, Insecurity, and Community Justice: The Reality of Source-End Regulation of the Market for Illicit Bolivian Cultural Objects. *European Journal on Criminal Policy Research* 20:445–457.
  2015a   "Value and Doubt": The Persuasive Power of "Authenticity" in the Antiquities Market. *PARSE* 2:71–84.
  2015b   Reality and Practicality: Challenges to Effective Cultural Property Policy on the Ground in Latin America. *International Journal of Cultural Property* 22:337–356.
  2016   The Global Traffic in Looted Cultural Objects. In *The Oxford Research Encyclopedia of Criminology and Criminal Justice* (online). Oxford University Press, Oxford. DOI:10.1093/acrefore/9780190264079.013.124.

Yde, Jens
  1938   *An Archaeological Reconnaissance of Northwestern Honduras: A Report of the Work of the Tulane University–Danish National Museum Expedition to Central America 1935.* Middle American Research Institute, Publication 9. Tulane University, New Orleans.

Zytaruk, M.
  2011   Cabinets of Curiosities and the Organization of Knowledge. *University of Toronto Quarterly* 80(1):1–23.

Contributors

Arlene Alvarez is a visiting fellow within the CaribTRAILS project for the KITLV/ Royal Netherlands Institute of Southeast Asian and Caribbean Studies and an affiliated PhD researcher at Leiden University's Faculty of Archeology Nexus 1492 project. Her research interests include heritage management, community participation, and social development. As director of the Altos de Chavón Regional Museum of Archaeology in the Dominican Republic for 19 years, she was in charge of all aspects of collections care, community outreach, and educational development. She also served as a coordinator for the Swedish-African Intercontinental Museum Network where she collaborated in several projects between museums from Africa, Asia, Latin America, and Sweden.

Lesley-Gail Atkinson Swaby is a Jamaican archaeologist, educator, and publisher. Her research interests are Taíno and Afro-Jamaican archaeology, rock art, and cultural contact studies. Atkinson Swaby is the editor of *The Earliest Inhabitants: The Dynamics of the Jamaican Taíno* and the coeditor of *Rock Art of the Caribbean*. Her first children's book is *Boianani: A Taíno Girl's First Adventure*. Atkinson Swaby is currently founder and managing director at Plum Valley Publishing and founder and camp director at Kulcha Konnection Camp.

Amanda Byer is a lawyer whose interests include the role of the environment (encompassing the historic environment) in the sustainable development of small island developing states and innovative approaches to heritage protection that link landscape theory with spatial justice. She has worked as an environmental legal consultant and drafted environmental and heritage legislation for Caribbean countries. Amanda completed her PhD in cultural heritage law at Leiden University in 2020. Within Leiden's Nexus 1492 project, she examined the development of Commonwealth Caribbean heritage law and conducted a legal geographical analysis of these laws, with emphasis on the Lesser Antilles. Amanda is currently a postdoctoral researcher at University College Dublin Sutherland School of Law.

Roger Colten is the senior collections manager for the Anthropology Division at the Peabody Museum of Natural History at Yale University. He has worked in several museums managing anthropology collections for almost 30 years and has participated in archaeological research projects in California, Germany, Israel, Italy, Malta, Michigan, and Nevada. His research focuses on human adaptation to coastal environments using faunal remains as a primary source of data. While his most recent projects focus on the Caribbean, he has also analyzed collections from British Columbia, California, and France.

L. Antonio Curet is a curator of the National Museum of the American Indian. His research focuses on cultural and social change in the ancient Caribbean, but he has participated also in archaeological projects in Arizona; Puerto Rico; and Veracruz, Mexico. He has directed several projects including excavations at La Gallera, Ceiba, Puerto Rico, and the Archaeological Project of the Valley of Maunabo. Since 1995 he has been conducting excavations at the Ceremonial Center of Tibes, Ponce, Puerto Rico, and since 2013 has been codirecting a regional project in the Valley of Añasco in western Puerto Rico. Curet is the author of *Caribbean Paleodemography: Population, Culture History, and Sociopolitical Processes in Ancient Puerto Rico* and coeditor of numerous books, such as *Islands at the Crossroads: Migration, Seafaring, and Interaction in the Caribbean* and *Beyond the Blockade: New Currents in Cuban Archaeology*. He is also the is the editor of the Caribbean Archaeology and Ethnohistory series of the University of Alabama Press.

Mariana C. Françozo is associate professor in museum studies in the Faculty of Archaeology, Leiden University. Her research focuses on the collection and circulation of indigenous artifacts and indigenous knowledge from South America and the Caribbean to Europe. She is the author of *De Olinda a Holanda: O gabinete de curiosidades de Nassau* and of articles on early modern kunstkammers as well as on present-day indigenous heritage in museums. Currently, Françozo is principal investigator of the European Research Council Starting Grant Project BRASILIAE, Indigenous Knowledge in the Making of Science: Historia Naturalis Brasiliae (1648).

Alexander Geurds is associate professor at the School of Archaeology, University of Oxford, and associate professor in the Faculty of Archaeology, Leiden University. He is also an associate professor adjunct at the University of Colorado (Boulder). He has carried out archaeological fieldwork and researched museum collections and archives throughout Latin America. His broader research interests focus on monumental sculpture, technology and practice in prehistory, archaeological ethics, the contemporary conditions of archaeological fieldwork, and the history of archaeology. He is coeditor of *Creating Authenticity: Authentication Process in Ethnographic Museums* and *The Routledge Handbook of Archaeology and Globalization*.

Elena Guarch Rodríguez (January 1, 1965, to September 19, 2020), was the director of the Departamento Centro Oriental de Arqueología de Holguín, Ministry of Science and Technology, Cuba. She directed and participated in archaeological research in various parts of Cuba. Her expertise spanned the archaeology of Cuba and the Caribbean, philology, public archaeology, and museology. Her last projects included directing rock art research in the province of Holguín and managing the archaeological caves in the Cristóbal Colón Park, Cuba.

Jonathan A. Hanna is curator at the Grenada National Museum in St. George's. He holds a PhD in anthropology from Pennsylvania State University, and his research focuses mainly on geoarchaeology and ancient human behavioral ecology in Grenada and the Eastern Caribbean.

Corinne L. Hofman is professor of Caribbean Archaeology in the Faculty of Archaeology, Leiden University in the Netherlands, and senior researcher at the Royal Netherlands Institute of Southeast Asian and Caribbean Studies (KITLV). She has conducted fieldwork in many of the Caribbean islands over the past 30 years. Her research and publications are highly multidisciplinary, and major themes of interest center on mobility and exchange, colonial encounters, intercultural dynamics, settlement archaeology, artifact analyses, and provenance studies. Her projects are designed to contribute to the historical awareness, preservation, and valorization of indigenous heritage. From 2013 to 2019 she was the coprincipal investigator of the European Research Council–Synergy NEXUS 1492 project. She is the author of many articles and book chapters and has coedited several volumes on Caribbean archaeology. Her most recent books are *Managing Our Past into the Future: Archaeological Heritage Management in the United States, The Caribbean before Columbus*, and *Material Encounters and Indigenous Transformations in the Early Colonial Americas*.

Menno L. P. Hoogland is an associate professor in the Faculty of Archaeology at Leiden University and senior researcher at the Royal Netherlands Institute of Southeast Asian and Caribbean Studies (KITLV). He is an expert in archaeothanatology and Caribbean archaeology. He has conducted fieldwork in many of the Caribbean islands. Hoogland's research focuses on settlement organization and the funerary practices of precolonial and early colonial Amerindian societies in the Caribbean and the application of taphonomical methods for the reconstruction of funerary behavior. He was principal investigator of the Dutch Research Counci (NWO) project Houses for the Living and the Dead (2005–2008) and senior researcher in the European Research Council–Synergy project Nexus 1492 (2013–2019). He is the coauthor of many articles and book chapters on Caribbean archaeology and editor of the forthcoming *Bioarchaeology of the Caribbean*.

Vernon James Knight is professor emeritus of anthropology and curator emeritus of American archaeology at the University of Alabama. Among his publications are *Mound Excavations at Moundville: Architecture, Elites, and Social Order* and *Iconographic Method in New World Prehistory*.

José R. Oliver is a reader in Latin American Archaeology at the Institute of Archaeology, University College London. He has directed numerous archaeological projects in Puerto Rico, Dominican Republic, and the Virgin Islands as well as in the southeastern and midwestern United States. Since 2013 he has directed archaeological fieldwork in the lower and middle Orinoco in Venezuela and the Colombian Orinoco (Atures Rapids area), Department of Vichada. In the Caribbean he is better known for his work in Caguana and the Karst region of Utuado. He has investigated all periods of human occupation, from Paleo-Amerindian (El Jobo in Pedregal, W. Venezuela) and Archaic (María La Cruz Cave, Puerto Rico) to the early contact periods in Macorix Abajo (Dominican Republic) and the Sabana del Rio Dagua (Vichada, Colombia). His Caribbean publications include *Caciques and Cemí Idols: The Web Spun by Taíno Rulers between Hispaniola and Puerto Rico*, *El Caribe Precolombino: Fray Ramón Pané y el universo taíno*, and *Caguana: Legado histórico*.

Joanna Ostapkowicz is research associate in Caribbean archaeology at the School of Archaeology, University of Oxford. Her research focuses on bringing a wide span of analytical techniques to better understand the chronological range, materials, and provenience of Caribbean artifacts in museum collections. Of particular interest are the histories of collecting Caribbean artifacts, from the earliest voyages and European *kunstkammern* to recent reinterpretations of precolumbian imagery for a wide variety of purposes, including indigenous and nationalist movements as well as the forger's "art." She has been the principal investigator on several international, multidisciplinary research projects that focus on Caribbean material culture and bridge the arts and sciences, including Pre-Hispanic Caribbean Sculptural Arts in Wood; Black Pitch, Carved Histories: Prehistoric Wood Sculpture from Trinidad's Pitch Lake; and SIBA: Stone Interchanges in the Bahama Archipelago. Her current project, jagWARS: Jaguars, Raptors, and the Patterns of War, explores fourteenth- to eighteenth-century northeastern South American indigenous sculptural arts.

Peter E. Siegel is professor and chair of anthropology at Montclair State University, Montclair, New Jersey. He is a New World archaeologist with research interests in historical ecology, ethnoarchaeology, spatial analysis, and cosmological and political organization. He has conducted projects throughout eastern North America, much of the West Indies, lowland South America, and eastern Bolivia. He is the editor of *Ancient Borinquen: Archaeology and Ethnohistory of Native Puerto Rico*.

John G. Swogger is an archaeologist and illustrator who specializes in the use of graphic narratives and comics for communicating archaeological research, outreach, and education. He publishes archaeological comics about field excavation and laboratory science, archaeological ethics, and museum repatriations to indigenous communities, the importance and significance of national and global cultural heritage, and the wider relationship between communities and local pasts. He was the project illustrator for the Çatalhöyük Research Project and now he works on field projects in the Caribbean and the United Kingdom.

Roberto Valcárcel Rojas is professor at the Instituto Tecnológico de Santo Domingo (INTEC), Dominican Republic. His research interests include the indigenous societies in the Caribbean and their legacy, the study of museum collections, ethnic and cultural interaction, archaeometallurgy, and archaeology and history of early colonial times in the Americas. He is the author of several books and articles about Cuban and Caribbean precolonial and colonial archaeology, including *Archaeology of Early Colonial Interaction at El Chorro de Maíta, Cuba*. He coedited *De la desaparición a la permanencia: Indígenas e indios en la reinvención del Caribe*.

Donna Yates is an associate professor in criminal law and criminology at Maastricht University. An archaeologist by training, Yates is a founding member of the Trafficking Culture Research Consortium, which seeks to use criminological tools to study the global illicit trafficking in cultural goods.

Index